CONCEPTS OF KNOWLEDGE : EAST AND WEST

Papers from a Seminar
held from 4 January to 10 January, 1995
at the Ramakrishna Mission Institute of Culture

THE RAMAKRISHNA MISSION INSTITUTE OF CULTURE

Gol Park, Kolkata 700 029

Published by
Swami Sarvabhutananda, Secretary
The Ramakrishna Mission Institute of Culture
Kolkata-700 029, India

First Published in March 2000 : 500
3rd reprint : June 2007 : 1000
Total Print : 2500

Price in India : Rupees Eighty only

ISBN 81-87332-01-8

Printed in India
Computer typeset at the Ramakrishna Mission Institute of Culture
Photo-offset at Rama Art Press
6/30, Dum Dum Road
Kolkata 700 030

PUBLISHER'S NOTE

How do we know? This seemingly simple question has aroused the interest of numerous philosophers of East and West from ancient times down to the present, and innumerable answers have been given.

Because of the wide interest in this vital question, and at the urging of Dr. J. L. Shaw of Victoria University, Wellington, New Zealand, an international seminar on Knowledge was organized by the Ramakrishna Mission Institute of Culture in Calcutta. It was hoped the seminar would help narrow the wide gap of misunderstanding on this subject between modern philosophers of East and West.

Thus, from the 4th to the 10th of January 1995, the seminar, titled 'Concepts of Knowledge : East and West', was held at that Institute. Thirteen scholars from overseas and ten from India participated. A number of notable scholars also attended as observers and took part in the discussions though they did not present papers.

Five all-day sessions were held in the Conference Room. After each paper was read, participants and observers discussed its contents. The present volume is a collection of twenty-one seminar papers. Two papers, one by Prof. Sylvan, the other by Prof. Lepore, who were unable to attend, have been included.

Prof. R. K. DasGupta in his paper, 'Swami Vivekananda's Concept of Knowledge', discussed Western epistemology (concepts of knowledge), comparing it with Swami Vivekananda's views. The editors decided that because of the paper's relevance to the subject of the seminar it would be a fitting introduction to this volume. Therefore, it has become the Foreword.

We record our heartfelt thanks to Susan Walters and Dr. J. L. Shaw for helping us with the editorial work.

The greatly Revered Swami Lokeswaranandaji, for many years Secretary of the Ramakrishna Mission Institute of Culture, passed away on 31 December 1998. He was responsible for planning and conducting this seminar. This volume is a memorial to his dedicated labour.

8 March 2000 — Swami Prabhananda

CONTENTS

Publisher's Note iii

Foreword : *Swami Vivekananda's Concept of Knowledge* vii
R. K. DasGupta

The Epistemological Point of View of Bhartṛhari 1
Ashok Aklujkar

Cultural Presuppositions as Determinants in Experience : A Comparison of Some Basic Indian and Western Concepts 20
Swami Atmarupananda

An Epistemological Study of Mysticism in Christianity and Hinduism 43
Swami Bhajanananda

Rāmānuja's Concept of Knowledge 66
Pandit Dinesh Chandra Bhattacharya Shastri

Some Remarks on the Definition of Knowledge 74
Sibajiban Bhattacharyya

The Use of the Word *Pramā* : Valid Cognition in Advaita Vedanta 83
Pandit Srimohan Bhattacharya

Theories of Error In Indian Philosophy or Five Types of *Khyāti* 93
Pandit Sukhamaya Bhattacharya

Valid Cognition (*Pramā*) and the Truth (*Satyatā*) of its Object 107
Pandit Visvabandhu Bhattacharya

The Concept of 'Realization' Re-examined 119
Margaret Chatterjee

Classical Yoga Philosophy and Some Issues in the Philosophy of Mind 132
Gerald James Larson

Epistemology from a Relativistic Point of View 152
Henri Lauener

Epistemology and Understanding of Language 171
Ernest Lepore

Confucian Knowledge : Commensurability and Alterity 201
John Makeham

Knowledge and Ignorance 212
J. N. Mohanty

Truth Vs. Workability Rehashed 223
Karl Potter

Knowledge, Truth, and Scepticism 234
Pranab Kumar Sen

Knowledge : Some Contemporary Problems and their Solutions from the Nyāya Perspective 244
J. L. Shaw

Madhyamaka on Naturalized Epistemology 262
Mark Siderits

What Limits to Thought, Inquiry and Philosophy ? 277
Richard Sylvan

The Action of the Subject towards the Outer World in Indian Realism 310
Toshihiro Wada

Patañjali's Classical Yoga: An Epistemological Emphasis 322
Ian Whicher

FOREWORD

Swami Vivekananda's Concept of Knowledge

It may not be possible to state *Swami Vivekananda's concept of knowledge* in terms of Western epistemology. Since the first use of the word 'epistemology' by J. F. Ferrier in his *Institutes of Metaphysics* (1854) all discussions on the theory of knowledge have dealt with knowledge in relation to metaphysics, logic and psychology. And such discussions have been very largely influenced by the epistemology of Kant. Actually the expression 'theory of knowledge' is an English equivalent of the German word *erkennistheorie* used by the German Kantian K. L. Reinhold in a German work on the subject published in 1789. Since then Western epistemology has been dominated by the Kantian view that the theory of knowledge must precede the theory of Being or Reality. Swami Vivekananda knew this and yet he never made that theory a major philosophical concern. In Indian philosophy knowledge is vital as it is the means of salvation and therefore its nature has to be understood. But the Indian mind is more concerned with ignorance which has to be dispelled and it was believed that when ignorance is dispelled knowledge will dawn upon a pure soul. Although there was a strong philosophical tradition concerned with questions of perception, inference, and testimony as instruments of knowledge, Vivekananda gave his mind to the moral side of the pursuit of knowledge as a means of *mokṣa* or release.

Still Vivekananda did have a theory of knowledge and in presenting it he firmly rejected the Kantian idea of reason as its only source. Kant says that the thing-in-itself is unknown and unknowable. Vivekananda affirms that Kant says this because he thinks reason is the only instrument of knowledge. While speaking on man's quest for the Absolute in his *Raja-Yoga* Vivekananda says : 'Kant has proved beyond all doubt that we cannot penetrate the tremendous dead wall called reason. But that is the very first idea upon which all Indian thought takes its stand, and dares to seek, and succeeds in finding, something higher than reason.' Swami Vivekananda's epistemology is based on this idea of a state of the mind which transcends reason.

In an address delivered in New York in 1896 Vivekananda says : '(religion) is beyond all reasoning and is not on the plane of intellect.' What then is the source of the highest knowledge? In his *Bhakti-Yoga* Vivekananda speaks of a state of the mind which is 'beyond the hazy and turbulent regions of reason.' In his address 'The Ideal of a Universal Religion' Vivekananda says : 'Logic becomes argument in a circle.... There must be some other instrument to take us beyond, and that instrument is called inspiration. So instinct, reason and inspiration are the three instruments of knowledge.'

Vivekananda does not reject reason as an instrument of the kind of knowledge we see in science, etc. But he says that reason cannot give us the highest knowledge which is not really an acquisition but a realization. Moreover as a believer in science and as a rationalist he says in the same address that 'one instrument is a development of the other and therefore does not contradict it. It is reason that develops into inspiration and therefore it does not contradict reason, but fulfils it.' This comprehensive theory of knowledge makes room for the operation of those faculties of the mind which give us our common knowledge and the highest achievements of science. Actually Vivekananda calls religion itself a science. In his essay, 'Sankhya and Vedanta' Vivekananda says that knowledge itself is *Vijñāna*, neither intuition, nor reason, nor instinct. The nearest expression for it is all-knowingness. This *Vijñāna* or all-knowingness is something that reason cannot give. For reason, he adds, is really stored up and classified perception, preserved by memory. We can never imagine or reason beyond sense-perception. The experience of Reality is not a sensory experience. It is something that transcends our life of the senses.

R. K. DasGupta

The Epistemological Point of View of Bhartṛhari

ASHOK AKLUJKAR

Professor of Sanskrit and related subjects, Department of Asian Studies, University of British Columbia, Vancouver, Canada. B.A. and M.A. degrees in Sanskrit and Pali from the University of Poona; Ph.D. in Sanskrit and Indian Studies, Harvard University, 1970. Head of the Department of Asian Studies, University of British Columbia, 1980-85. Research Interests: Pāṇinian grammatical tradition, Sanskrit non-religious philosophy, Sanskrit belles-lettres in general. Has published research mainly on Bhartṛhari, the Grammarian-philosopher. Has also published numerous articles and reviews in professional journals, and in 1992 published *Sanskrit : An Easy Introduction to an Enchanting Language*, in three volumes, along with 5 ninety-minute audio cassettes.

§1.1 There are several reasons why Bhartṛhari's Trikāṇḍī (respectively, 'B' and 'TK' in abbreviation) or *Vākyapadīya*[1] constitutes a very important watershed in the history of Indian philosophy. I have indicated them in some of my earlier papers (e.g., Aklujkar 1993:§§3.2-6) and stated them explicitly and somewhat extensively in the Introduction to my forthcoming publication *Excursions into Pre-Bhartṛhari Thought.* One of the reasons why the TK is a very significant landmark in the history of Indian philosophy—in fact, in the history of philosophy in general—is the epistemological viewpoint implicit in it. This viewpoint is, indeed, as I hope to demonstrate presently, quite unique.

§1.2 There are some relatively superficial and partial parallels to parts of B's viewpoint in the Sāṁkhya, Yoga and Mīmāṁsā traditions. For example, the accepted means of cognition[2] are *pratyakṣa, anumāna* and *śabda,*[3] and, correspondingly, the implicit kinds of cognition are *pratyakṣa, anumiti* and *śābda*[4] in the TK, as they are in the Yoga-sūtra and the Sāṁkhya-kārikā. The *buddhi,* roughly speaking, 'intellect-will' or 'mind,' is viewed as essentially consisting of linguistic units in both the TK and the Yoga-bhāṣya (YB in abbreviation).[5] Thought or epistemological concern in the form of *jñāna* is associated with (a) language or linguistic concern in the form of *śabda* and (b) reality or ontological concern in the form of *artha* in the Śabara-bhāṣya and the YB, as it is in the TK.[6] However, such similarities are more a sign of the age to which B's work belongs and do not cover the core of his epistemological theory or his original contribution.

§**1.3** Among the surviving texts on semantics in the tradition of Pāṇinian grammar, the TK is the earliest. It is also unique in that it has many statements of epistemological import, corresponding to which the later *artha-granthas* such as the *Vaiyākaraṇa-siddhānta-kārikā* by Bhaṭṭoji-dīkṣita, the *Vaiyākaraṇabhūṣaṇas* by Kauṇḍa-bhaṭṭa, the *Vyākaraṇa-siddhānta-sudhā-nidhi* by Pārvatīya Viśveśvara-suri, and the *Vaiyākaraṇa-siddhānta-mañjuṣās* by Nāgeśa have very few. In fact, as far as epistemology goes, except for the theses of sentence primacy and *sphoṭa* in verbal communication, the traditions of Kashmir Śaivism and Poetics *(alaṁkāra-śāstra, kāvya-śāstra)* may be said to have continued the line of B's epistemology more than the tradition of the Pāṇinīyas. It is not that the later Pāṇinīyas have rejected B's epistemology. They have simply not expressed much interest in restating, extending or modifying it. Being more interested in the grammatical or linguistic semantic (as distinct from the philosophical semantic) side of their topic, they have rarely gone beyond quoting relevant pronouncements of B.

§**2.1** The TK, as would be clear to anyone who reads all of its three books, was not *primarily* composed as a work in what we would call philosophy. As Kārikās 1.24-26 state, it pertains to eight topics which are primarily topics we would include in the theory of language or theory of grammar.[7] Both these theories could be called 'philosophy' in a secondary sense ('philosophy as identification of abstract underlying principles,' 'philosophy as a product of theorizing') in our time, but, as is implied by the overall context of this paper, such an extension of the term 'philosophy' is not what I have in mind. That the theories give the remaining philosophy proper a 'linguistic turn' and make B the earliest philosopher known to us who approaches problems of epistemology and ontology from a linguistic point of view is, from B's perspective, an incidental but, from our perspective a very significant achievement

(Aklujkar 1999, lecture 2). I have not read another work in Sanskrit philosophy, except the Yoga-sūtra, which achieves so much in so few words. For this reason, we should not expect to find in the TK statements that put epistemology or ontology at the forefront. These branches of philosophy, rather, appear as raising their heads within the frame of a linguistic-grammatical theory. Thus, most of the epistemological observations figure in as analogies or occur as asserted parallels, although, for the purpose of the present essay, I shall look upon them as if they are made with the intention of speaking specifically about epistemology.

§2.2 Even within the limits I have set for myself, some of you will immediately notice that my interpretation of B's philosophy differs significantly from that of Gaurinath Sastri, K.A. Subramania Iyer, Bishnupada Bhattacharya, Madeleine Biardeau and Raghunath Sharma—to name only some of the scholars who have published extensive expositions of B's thought utilizing the original Sanskrit texts. This has not been done just for the sake of carving a niche (or erecting a tomb) for myself. B is considerably earlier than Śaṅkara. Much misunderstanding of him has occurred at the hands of scholars who could not shake off, while thinking of B, what they read in or about Śaṅkara's works. Secondly, none of the scholars whom I have named above has put together or was in a position to put together, because of the earlier bad editing of B's text, all the pieces of evidence which should be taken into account to determine B's philosophy. I undertook this exercise in my unpublished 1970 Harvard University dissertation, *The Philosophy of Bhartṛhari's Trikāṇḍī.* There I have given all the evidence I could gather from his own words and from the words of his ancient commentators for every single view I have attributed to him. I have done my best to read B internally (that is, from within), comprehensively and consistently from a philosophical point of view only. I have also specified the few areas in which he and his ancient commentators may be suspected to differ.

As my objective here is the limited one of determining the general features of B's epistemological viewpoint and as my dissertation will probably be published in a revised form in the next few years, I have not given here the evidence that would support my determination of the general features through the supporting details. If the evidence I have gathered in the dissertation for establishing the details is deemed satisfactory, it follows that the general features I see in B's epistemological approach must also be there.

The present paper should also be read as complementing the following papers of mine: 'Prāmāṇya in the philosophy of the Grammarians' (1988), 'The number of pramāṇas according to Bhartṛhari' (1989) and 'Bhartṛhari's concept of the Veda' (1991).

§3.1 The first and most important general feature of B's epistemological—indeed, his entire philosophical—approach which we should note is that the approach is linguistic. While it is fair to say that this sort of characterization of his approach is essentially to be found beginning with Hemanta Kumar Ganguli's 1963 book, *Philosophy of Logical Reconstruction,* neither Ganguli nor his successors in the field such as Bimal Krishna Matilal, as far as I can recall, have explained why this approach should be considered linguistic and in what sense it is linguistic or what its extent as a linguistic approach is. This is what I intend to accomplish in the following.

§3.2 As already intimated in §1.2, we find B speaking of three categories: *śabda* (or *vāc*), *artha*, and *jñāna*. The first stands for language, the second for things or entities, and the third for cognitions. In other words, B is concerned with (what we would call) a theory of language, with ontology, and with epistemology—with language, reality and thought (note 6). We then find B trying to establish some general theses about language with appropriate argumentation. Once they are established, he simply asserts parallel or logically related conclusions in the sphere of epistemology; he does not try to establish the epistemological theses in their own right. Similarly, as §§4.3-4 below will indicate, B merely works out the implications of his theses regarding language for the problems of ontology; he does not discuss ontological problems separately or as independent of considerations of language. One can, therefore, conclude with justification that, in his view, the key to typically philosophical problems, to topics of ontological and epistemological interest, is to be found in reaching certain definite conclusions about language.

§3.3 This evidence furnished by silence, however, is only one piece among others. That B's approach to epistemology is essentially linguistic can be argued for also positively. Assigning centrality to language in our awareness of the world, acceptance of the thesis that our view of the world is through language—that we cannot conceive things independently of language, in pure abstraction, is an important feature of the linguistic approach. It is espoused in an absolutely unambiguous way in B's work. According to him, that which is never reflected in language, i.e., is never expressed by a linguistic expression, directly or indirectly, cannot be assumed to exist. An entity or a category of entities may possibly come into and remain in existence independently of language. But it cannot be cognized or determined as existent without language (Aklujkar 1970:§6.1).[8] Moreover, B does not stop just with the common assumption of Sanskrit philosophers that forms of cognitions can be judged only from the linguistic forms used to express them. He goes a step further and explicitly states that no cognition either takes place or is noticed without the involvement of linguistic units (see §5.1 below for a possible qualification).[9]

§3.4 As the third piece of evidence, we should note what I have pointed out in my 1988 article on *prāmāṇya,* namely that the common Indian division of cognitions into *pratyakṣa* 'perception,' *anumiti* 'inferential cognition,' and *śābda* 'testimonial cognition' is viewed by B as secondary and non-essential; it is not the case that language is present only in *śabda* and not in the others. In accordance with this, B's notion of *śabda* as a *pramāṇa*—*āgama* is his preferred term—is multilevel and is, at its deepest or highest level, very similar to that of conceptual scheme developed in the writings of Quine.[10]

§4.1 Having thus made a case that philosopher B's approach is essentially linguistic, I will now give a few details about how it affects his epistemology. These details will, in turn, bear out the centrality language enjoys in his thinking and thus constitute a fourth piece of evidence in favour of the characterization offered in §3.1.

While developing a theory of cognition, one is required to postulate at least three entities:

(a) sentience, pure consciousness, or life-principle *(cit, citi, caitanya),*

(b) a cognizor, determinate consciousness or intellect *(buddhi)*, serving as the agent of specific acts of cognizing, and

(c) a state, act, or event of cognizing, a particular cognition (*jñāna*).[11]

As can be seen from the following table, in what B accepts as existing, in the field of cognition, that is, in the ontology of his epistemology, so to speak, there is a correlation of these entities with the levels of language he accepts:

vaikharī 'language 1, speech'	
madhyamā 'language2'	=*jñāna* 'cognition'
paśyantī 'language3'	=*buddhi* 'mind, intellect'
paraṁ paśyantyāḥ rūpam	=*cit/citi/caitanya* 'sentience, consciousness'
sūkṣmā nityā atīndriyā vāc,	
vācaḥ uttamaṁ rūpam,	
śabda-tattva-brahman,	
'language-principle, language 4'.	

Not only is there a correlation, B identifies the three entities—*cit, buddhi,* and *jñāna,* respectively with language 4 *(parā paśyantī-rūpa)*, language3 *(paśyantī)*, and language2 *(madhyamā)*. This is not explicitly stated in his extant works. But there are numerous indications in his remarks to the effect that the situation must be as I have outlined.[12] His ancient commentators too give or presuppose the equations I have given.

The reasoning behind the identifications probably was this: If we find no reason to hold that the intellectual[13] counterparts of utterances, the totality of linguistic units, and the language-principle are different, respectively, from the cognitions, the intellect, and the principle which assumes the form of these two, then we must conclude that we have here not six entities, but only three. Otherwise, (a) there will be unnecessary postulates in the theory; the criterion of theoretical economy or simplicity *(lāghava)* will be sacrificed; and (b) we will also have subscribed to the naive realism that every name has a corresponding object—that six names must imply actual existence of six different entities.[14]

§4.2 B thus exhibits a distinctive linguistic approach to epistemology.

The approach may seem extreme. But it can also be viewed as showing the courage of following an insight to all its logical consequences. It is not an ideal language philosopher's approach. B was familiar, at least to a considerable extent, with an ideal language in the form of Pāṇini's metalanguage. But he viewed it too as inherently incapable of remaining unambiguous or free from philosophical problems. Nor is B's approach that of an ordinary language philosopher. He does deconstruct some ordinary Sanskrit expressions that had assumed philosophical significance such as *abhāva, samavāya* and *śakti.* But he does not accomplish this so much through an exploration of the usage of these words as through drawing attention to one or more general truths about language that he has established elsewhere. *In spirit,* therefore, his approach is closest to that of Quine and Chomsky—an approach depending primarily and directly upon determining the general nature of language, although its similarity with Quine's overall philosophical position is probably far greater than with Chomsky's.

§4.3 Now, to the second and last general feature of B's epistemology which I wish to point out. I think we are realizing increasingly that, although, as students of philosophy, we distinguish between ontology and epistemology, the two are not independent of each other in any philosopher's practice. A philosopher's ontological views are shaped by or revised in the light of his epistemological views, and *vice versa.* The truth of this observation is seen in an unparalleled way in B's philosophy at least as far as the Indian philosophical tradition goes.

We get one piece of evidence for the observation if we ask the question: What type of apparatus does B propose in order to explain the fact (or what is generally accepted as a fact) that we experience the world?

There is no discussion in the extant TK about the apparatus that must be presupposed in order to explain our knowledge or experience of the world. This apparatus, as mentioned above in §4.1, should be the *buddhi.* The *buddhi* or *buddhi-tattva* of B, as his commentators point out, is identical with *paśyantī,* the third level or aspect of language. It is not an evolute, either logical or chronological, from *prakṛti* as it is in the Sāṁkhya and Yoga systems.[15] Nor is it distinguished from *manas, ahaṁkāra,* etc. It is simply *citi* or *caitanya* in its aspect of holding the entire diversity of linguistic units (phonemes, words and sentences, i.e., *varṇas, padas* and *vākyas)* of which a person is aware. There is no physical or material distinction between *citi* and *buddhi.* Just a functional one or one on the level of realization of truth.

This is the view of B's *buddhi* as a static entity—when *buddhi* is at rest. But there is also a dynamic aspect to *buddhi.* In that aspect, it is a continuum of cognitions reflecting specific linguistic units (Aklujkar 1970:§§3.4-5)—cognitions here being sentences or functional equivalents of sentences.[16]

Why, how and in exactly which sense B reduces awareness of the external world to linguistic units is part of his ontological exploration. The conclusions he reaches as a result of that exploration have a bearing on his epistemology. The *buddhi* as consisting of linguistic units is a point where his epistemology ties in with his ontology.

§4.4 To explain briefly, B's reduction seems to have its roots in his investigation of linguistic meaning (*artha*). Through scattered but multisided argumentation, that goes much beyond Frege and those who have developed Frege's insight, B establishes that word meanings are not external things or physical objects.[17] He also points out that it would not do to think of word meanings as images of external things, as precepts. Nor would it be theoretically economical or justifiable to admit a secondary, linguistic, reality *(upacāra-sattā)*—something, I believe, corresponding to Putnam's internal realism. If not tied to the perceptible empirical reality, this reality would amount to an uncontrolled licence, a *carte blanche,* and lead to distinction without difference. Thus, ultimately the distinction between a meaning and its signifier must be only in the view we are accustomed to taking. We must be making an artificial distinction between the cognitions in which signifiers are apprehended and the cognitions in which meanings are reflected; *artha* must be a *vivarta* of *śabda* (Aklujkar 1970: §§5.15-17, 28).

§4.5 B seems to be saying that sense experience must precede conceptualization,[18] although it may not be possible to prove the primacy of sense experience. There is no statement in his writings which would allow us to conclude that denial of the independent existence of physical objects out there in the world was his final philosophical position. At a particular level in his thought, he unites the *generalized* existence of physical objects *(bhāva-sattā, mahā-sattā)* with the existence implicit in words or conceptualizations. But, except for a person in the state of spiritual liberation, physical objects are not said to cease to exist (Aklujkar 1970:§§6.6-8). The question of whether they are, *per se,* derivable, in the final analysis, from *śabda-tattva brahman,* the ultimate principle in B's philosophy, is left open.[19]

It suffices for B's purpose that (a) the *differentiation* of the physical world be viewed as coming from the *śabda-tattva brahman,* the language principle, and (b) the possibility of a person succeeding in wiping out the traces of the world be admitted.

B is aware of a stronger version according to which the physical objects themselves would be evolutes of the Ultimate, and the physical world would be a lower, dispensable reality—the Ultimate alone would be the final truth.[20] But he neither accepts that version as his only *philosophical* position nor does he deny the possibility of its being true.

Following his general tendency or strategy of going beyond specific conflicting positions to a non-conflicting common factor or meta-position—of achieving theoretical ascent wherever possible, B takes the minimum he needs to develop a coherent view of his own and declines to be further involved in possibilities that probably cannot, in his view, be proved or disproved logically—that become a matter of accepting this scripture or that scripture, with his personal preference going with the Veda as scripture.[21]

A philosopher wishing to determine whether the physical world consisting of distinct objects or our internal conceptual/linguistic world having a (generally corresponding) diversity should be accorded precedence may conclude that, from our perspective as subjects, the latter should be assigned a more fundamental status on the ground that if the latter did not exist the former would not exist *for us.* However, this does not amount to denying the existence of the former. In fact, it does not amount to anything more than holding that language is our window to the world (a thesis acceptable to B as pointed out earlier, but one which is really epistemological in nature, not ontological).

§4.6 In consonance with the preceding is B's concept of *avidyā,* the tying point between epistemology and ontology for many schools of Indian philosophy. His *avidyā* does not consist in seeing *sva-bhāva* or essence where it does not exist (the Nāgārjunian version) or in believing in the reality of the perceptible world (the Vijñāna-vādīya, Gauḍapādian or Śaṅkarite version). While it can possibly accommodate these understandings of *avidyā,* that is, while it does not necessarily conflict with them, its core consists in not being aware of the distortion that language introduces.

Śaṅkara's assertions (a) *avidyāvad-viṣayāṇyeva śāstrāṇi*[22] and (b) one does not acquire *vidyā*, one simply removes *avidyā*[23] have their parallels in B's pronouncement *śāstreṣu prakriyā-bhedair avidyaivopavarṇyate / anāgamavikalpā tu svayaṁ vidyopavartate* (TK 2.233), but B's reasons for making the pronouncement are significantly different.

B's *aviḍyā* consists in the inability of linguistic expressions to refer to things precisely or only as they are. Language is said to introduce distinctions where there are none and to obliterate distinctions where they exist.

The introduction of distinctions is two-dimensional. There is a dimension of space and there is a dimension of time: *mūrti-kriyā-vivartāv-avidyā-śakti-pravṛtti-mātram* (Vṛtti 1.1).

Further, since *avidyā* is a property, attribute or capacity of the language principle, it and its two basic dimensions (or its two modes of asserting itself) should be beginningless, just as the language-principle should be beginningless for a philosopher: *caitanyavat sthitā loke dik-kāla-parikalpanā / prakṛtiṁ prāṇināṁ tāṁ hi ko' nyathā sthāpayiṣyati* (TK 3.6.18).

Consequently, in B's view, there has never been a situation at the level of ordinary experience in which there was only pure perception, unattended by any conceptualization, of something in the world. The separation between sense experience in itself and conceptualization is either only theoretical (it is to be accepted as a theoretical necessity, as a kind of a priori) or can be entertained as a possibility only in the case of spiritually advanced beings, that is, only in the case of beings who are not like us—and only at the level of extraordinary experience.

There is no evidential or empirical wedge which would prove the primacy of sense experience.

§5.1 In the preceding, I have implicitly made a distinction between B as a philosopher (in our most prevalent contemporary Western sense of the term) and as a religious thinker. What that distinction suggests is that B, as a philosopher, need not be seen as needing the concept of *mokṣa* or, to use his expression in Vṛtti 1.5, of *brahmaṇaḥ prāptiḥ* for the other elements of his philosophy to stand.

Another implication of what I have said so far is that there are levels in B's ontology and they are related to his roles as a thinker. As a Grammarian or Vaiyākaraṇa, he accepts as existing everything that words can denote (even 'hare's horn' is deemed to exist from the Grammarian's perspective).[24] As a philosopher, he admits only the physical things and the language principle as truly existing. Everything else is seen as inseparable from either the things or the principle (time and space, as capacities of the latter, are inseparable from it; all other entities such as qualities, universals, etc. have no separate existence from substance). And as a religious thinker, he entertains the possibility that his philosophical ontic world could be superseded by one in which the language principle alone remains. The assumption then is that a person *can* reach a certain stage in which his mind *(= buddhi, paśyantī)* is divested of diversity and he 'becomes' the language principle.

§5.2 The distinction between B's roles as a Grammarian thinker and as a non-Grammarian thinker is conveyed by the remarks of his ancient commentators, particularly the remarks of Helā-rāja. The differentiation between a *śabda-pramāṇaka* ontology and a non-*śabda-pramāṇaka* (in effect, corresponding to our philosophical) ontology, which Helā-rāja makes,[25] has support in B's remarks.[26] That the non-*śabda-pramāṇaka* ontology is not explicitly characterized as philosophical or is not further divided into philosophical and religious is due to the absence of distinctive terminology for philosophy and religion in the Indian tradition.[27]

Post-script :

As the preceding text was read toward the end of the seminar, it then contained, at this point, the following additional observations pertaining to the earlier exchanges in the seminar :

(a) The discussions we have had so far in this seminar have done justice, as far as Indian philosophy is concerned, mainly to the Nyāya concept of knowledge and have almost entirely left untouched those branches of Indian philosophy which are not included in the traditional enumeration of six *āstika darśanas.*

(b) The paṇḍitic tradition of the last two or three hundred years has been caught in the grooves of certain texts. It needs to bring back into its discussions texts such as Maṇḍana-miśra's *Vibhrama-viveka* and B's TK. It also needs to learn to discuss texts with a sharper awareness of the historical development of ideas.

(c) There are anticipations in B to the effect (i) that a distinction between belief and knowledge is useful only as a convenient theoretical fiction, (ii) that a distinction between cognition, mental state, attitude or disposition, and feeling is also useful only as a fiction convenient in our philosophical deliberations and (iii) that the Vaiśeṣikas did not remain pure realists when they accepted qualities, movements, universals, particulars, inherence and absence, just as, as was pointed in Dr. Wada's paper, they compromised their realism when they accepted numbers beyond 'one/1'.

Notes and References

1 (a) The extant works of the Grammarian-philosopher Bhartṛhari, who may or may not be identical with the poet-philosopher Bhartṛhari, are : (i) *Trikāṇḍī or Vākyapadīya,* (ii) *Mahābhāṣya-ṭīkā or Tripādī,* published under the title *Mahābhāṣya-dīpikā.*

(b) The physical structure of the Trikāṇḍī, which word roughly means '3 books,' and the relationship of that structure with the available ancient commentaries is as follows :

Brahma-kāṇḍa or Āgama-samuccaya (kārikās+Vṛtti):
ṭīkā on kārikās as well as Vṛtti by Vṛṣabha
Vākya-kāṇḍa or Vākyapadīya proper (kārikās + Vṛtti): ṭīkā on kārikās only; said to be by Puṇya-rāja but more likely to be an abridgment of a ṭīkā by Helā-rāja, Pada-kāṇḍa or Prakīrṇaka (kārikās in 14 samuddeśas): ṭīkā by Helā-rāja

2 For an indication of why I do not employ here the word 'knowledge,' meaning 'valid cognition' or 'reliable awareness,' see the last remark in Aklujkar 1988:§2.7 and note 22 that goes with it.

3 (a) See Aklujkar 1988:§§2.1-2.

(b) The actual terms used may be different (e.g., *āgama* and *ānuśravika),* and they may have connotations revealing the special concerns of the systems. That their core contents agree is alone relevant here.

4 (a) The terms *anumiti* and *śābda* themselves may not occur in all the texts mentioned here.

(b) There is a sense in which all cognition would be *śābda* according to the TK philosophy. This is pointed out in §3.3 below and in Aklujkar 1988 and 1989.

5 (a) ... *śabdo' pi buddhisthaḥ* TK 1.47; ... *śabda-bheda-bhāvanā-(bījā) nugate buddhi-tattve yo'yaṁ śabdaḥ*... Vṛtti 1.47; ... *śabda-śakti-saṁsṛṣṭayā śabdānuviddhayā śabdātmikayā buddhyā* ...Vṛtti 1.123; ... *vāg-rūpāyāṁ buddhau* ... Vṛtti 1.133. Supporting indications are available in: Vṛtti 1.53, Vṛtti 1.130.

(b) In the case of the YB, the evidence for the view attributed to it here is in the form of implication of several statements, that is, indirect.

There is a movement away from *śabda* when the practitioner progresses from *savitarka* to *nirvitarka samādhi* (YB 1.42-43).

Similarly, there is a movement away from narrow intentional-referential activity, oriented toward specific individual objects, to increasingly wider or subtler categorial intending-referring in the substages of *savicāra samādhi.* The substages are expected to culminate in such a wide or subtle intending-referencing that, strictly speaking, it no longer remains intending-referencing—the act involved loses all specificity; it becomes *nirvicāra* (YB 1.44-45).

This is from the point of view of the object. From the point of view of the meditating subject, similarly, inward referring is expected to grow gradually less and less specific, ultimately ceasing to take cognizance even of meditational bliss *(ānanda)* and I-awareness *(asmitā)*—to become, as YB 1.17-18 puts it, *nirvastuka, artha-śūnya.*

These statements indicate that the starting point assumed by the YB for the journey from the ordinary states of consciousness to those of *samādhi* is a mind which has the means of intending and / or referring, namely internalized linguistic expressions.

(c) In the above, I am not suggesting that the notion of *buddhi* is identical in the TK and the YB. Unlike in the TK, there is evidence of acceptance of the Sāṁkhya notion of *buddhi* in YB 2.15, 2.20; 3.35.

(d) Those statements in both the works in which *buddhi* is used in the sense 'cognition, cognizing act or event,' as distinct from 'cognizing organ,' (e.g.,YB 3.17) are, of course, not intended in the present context.

6 (a) Śabara on Jaimini 1.1.5 has a long discussion bounded by the notions of *śabda, artha* and *jñāna/vijñāna.*

(b) *gaur iti śabdo, gaur ityartho, gaur iti jñānam ityavibhāgena vibhaktānām api grahaṇaṁ dṛṣṭam.*YB 1.42.

(c) Words indicative of the streams of thought in the TK, as well as of B's areas of thinking, are:

śabda/vāc 'linguistic expression (regardless of extent),' 'language'→language-and-grammar theory

artha 'thing, entity,' 'reality'→ontology.

jñāna 'cognition, mental state,' 'thought'→epistemology.

Cf. TK 3.1.103; 3.3.59; also, *etaddhi tat sarvaṁ yad uta jñānaṁ vāg arthaśceti* Vṛṣatha 1.122, p.181.

7 Eight topics or subjects as stated in TK 1.24-26 (this list of topics is primarily applicable to the kāṇḍa in which it appears, that is, to the first book):

anvākhyeya	*śabda*	*vākya* and *pada* 'sentence and its (ordinarily) meaning-bearing units'
pratipādaka	*śabda*	stems, roots, affixes (artificially meaning-bearing)
apoddhārapadārtha	*artha*	meaning in the stage of analysis
sthita-lakṣaṇa artha	*artha*	meaning in actual communication, meaning which does not need analysis to come into effect, typically sentence meaning and, at a certain level, word meaning.
kārya-kāraṇabhāva	*saṁbandha*	cause and effect relation between signifier and signatum.

yogya-bhāva/yogyatā	*saṁbandha*	compatibility relation between signifier and signatum.
pratyayāṅga (*pratyaya-*)	*saṁbandha*	relation responsible for cognition.
dharmāṅga	*saṁbandha*	relation responsible for (cognition and) merit.

8 (a) Especially clear is the evidence furnished by the remark: *sad api vāgvyavahāreṇānupagṛhītam artha-rūpam asatā tulyam.* Vṛtti 1.129

(b) The point made here has a bearing on B's notions of *vivarta* and *pariṇāma* and our understanding of them. § 4.4-6 will observe that B's notion of *vivarta* is different from the one commonly associated with post-Śaṅkara philosophers. Consequently, his notion of *pariṇāma* is also different. A detailed delineation of these notions, however, can be undertaken only in a separate publication.

9 (a) *na so'sti pratyayo loke yaḥ śabdānugamād ṛte/ anuviddham iva jñānaṁ sarvaṁ śabdena gṛhyate* TK 1.131. Variant readings for the last word are: *bhāsate, gamyate, vartate.*

(b) B's view given here does not imply that one must be aware of linguistic units *at the time of cognition.* He argues for his view by concentrating specifically on those cognition situations in which one is generally not aware of the role of language (Aklujkar 1970: §1.19-26).

10 B may further be understood as holding that, ultimately, there is no division between analytical truths such as '2 + 2 = 4' and synthetic truths such as 'Snow is white.' If we acquainted him with our notion of 'conceptual scheme', he would probably come up with a conceptual scheme that is inter-related and interdependent.

11 (a) It may be objected that some philosophers (e.g., the Buddhist philosophers) have not accepted the need to postulate all three entities. However, note that, in the case of entity (a), I am not saying that it must be a constant, stable, durable or eternal self. All I am saying is that a life force or fulfilment of the condition of being a living being is required. The Buddhists are not known to have rejected this (rather obviously needed) condition of ordinary experience. They have come close also to accepting the *buddhi* in their acceptance of a *vijñāna-saṁtāna, ālaya-vijñāna, etc.*

(b) Whether the Sanskrit terms used to designate the three entities are precisely the ones I have given here is not a major consideration. A terminology like *citta, caitta,* etc. will also do.

12 For example, *śabda-tattvam evedaṁ vāṅmanasākhyam avibhāgam* Vṛtti 1.86.

13 I am using the neologism 'intellectal' to avoid the connotations of 'mental' and 'intellectual,' but I do not hold that its introduction is absolutely necessary.

14 B indicates awareness of the arguments that are likely to be made to assert a real difference between the linguistic entities, on the one hand, and the epistemological entities, on the other, but he does not explicitly deal with them. Given the nature of the problem, the onus of proving that there is in fact a difference should be on those who

assert the difference. Their proofs or arguments, it seems, would boil down to a determination of whether cognition without symbols is possible and whether the symbols involved can be essentially different from the symbols that constitute language. B's view, as stated in § 3.3, is that cognition without linguistic symbols is not possible. He also holds that language is innate. The view that all so-called nonlinguistic symbols are ultimately based on linguistic symbols can also be attributed to him with great probability. Thus we can infer that he would prefer to take the position that cognition without symbols is not possible and that the symbols involved will not, in the final analysis, be nonlinguistic. In other words, we can interpret him as saying that a wider definition of language and an admission of all symbols as ultimately linguistic in nature together constitute a better theory than a theory which would take the (apparent) separation between linguistic and nonlinguistic symbols as a given not to be given up.

15 In Vṛtti 2.31, B states the Sāṁkhya-Yoga view after what seems to be a statement of the Nyāya-Vaiśeṣika view.

16 B advocates primacy of the sentence. He accepts the possibility of single-word and single-phoneme sentences (TK 2.40, 270-71).

17 The Sanskrit terms are: *buddhyartha* or *śabdārtha* 'sense, meaning'; *bāhyārtha* or *vastvartha* 'reference, referent, actual thing.'

18 I infer this from the direction reflected in B's remarks made in contexts other than those in which sense—experience or conceptualization *per se* is discussed, that is, from remarks made 'unawares,' as it were, in which his subconscious assumptions are likely to be revealed. One such remark is *sad api vāg-vyavahāreṇānupagṛhītam artha-rūpam asatā tulyam* (Vṛtti 1.129) quoted in note 8. The stance or assumption of its author is clearly that physical things exist first and then come into the purview of language, implying that, in general, sensing precedes concept formation [although he would still be free to hold that no particular time can be specified at which the intertwining of the physical world and language can be said to have begun; cf. the characterization of *avidyā,* which is primarily a language-based notion in B's thought (§4.6), as beginningless]. We can probably detect similar evidence in other statements of B, suggesting that in his view physical things and their experience through senses deserves priority in systematization.

19 I say this despite several current interpretations in which B is represented as deriving both the concepts and physical objects from *śabda-tattva brahman* or as declaring all diversity in the world to be an illusion or a lower-level truth superimposed on *śabda-tattva-brahman*. I do not agree with those modern interpreters of B who, by adopting a later version of the *'vivarta : pariṇāma'* distinction declare B to be a *pariṇāma-vādin* or a *vivarta-vādin*. As I will point out in a future article, the understanding of *vivarta* and *pariṇāma* in the early period of Indian philosophy, to which B belongs, was different.

20 Note the citations in the Vṛtti of TK 1. 124. The kārikā itself reads thus : *śabdasya pariṇāmo'yam ityāmnāyavido viduḥ / chandobhya eva prathamam etad viśvaṁ vyavartata* .

21 (a) See Aklujkar 1991 for B's concept of the Veda, according to which even the nāstika philosophies have their ultimate source in the Veda.

(b) The remark made here, obviously, has a bearing on the question of B's religion. I view him as a follower of Brahmanism or Vedism who was not anti-Buddhist and who was, most probably, not anti-Jaina either. I expect to be able to be more specific in a future publication.

22 The words quoted here are a part of a longer statement in Śaṅkara's bhāṣya introducing the Brahma-sūtra or Vedānta-sūtra 1.1.1. Cf. Upadeśa-sahasrī 1.1.40, summarized in Potter 1981:221.

23 (a) Since acquiring *vidyā* would mean acquiring liberation, Śaṅkara's statement in the Bṛhadāraṇyaka-bhāṣya 3.3, summarized in Potter 1981:195-96, to the effect that liberation, truly speaking, is not acquired—it is not a production, an attainment, or a modification or purification—implies that *vidyā*, 'liberating knowledge,' is, truly speaking, not acquired. Note also Upadeśa-sahasrī 2.17.22, summarized in Potter 1981:240, where *vidyā* is said to be revealed—not produced or obtained.

(b) It follows that, in the following statement in Potter 1981:6, the use of 'manifested' is appropriate, but the use of 'acquiring' could be misleading: 'Since bondage depends on ignorance, liberation is manifested upon the removal of ignorance by acquiring its opposite, namely knowledge *(vidyā)*'.

24 Compare Quine's procedure of beginning the investigation of what exists with the position 'everything.'

25 *śabda-pramāṇakānāṁ hi yacchabda āha tat paramārtha-rūpam.* Helā-rāja 3.1.11 p. 24.8-9. *śābde vyavahāre nirūpitasyaiva vastutvāt.* Helā-rāja 3.7.152 p. 351.1-8. *nāsmābhir darśana-vivekaḥ prārabdhaḥ.* Helā-rāja 3.9.58 p. 70.25-28.

26 *asamākhyeya-tattvānām arthānāṁ laukikairyathā / vyavahāre samākhyānaṁ tat prājño na vikalpayet* TK 2.142; *śabdapramāṇako lokaḥ sa śāstreṇānugamyate* TK 3.7.38; also TK 2.296-97 and Vṛtti thereto; *sarvatra hi prasiddhirevārtha-vyavasthā-kāraṇam. anavasthitaiva hi tarkāgamābhyāṁ bhinneṣu pravādeṣu vastu-gatā vyavasthā.* Vṛtti 1. 106.

27 (a) The intention behind the remarks made here is not to suggest that B's interest in what we would call religion or religious philosophy was not sincere. In his own perspective, the *mokṣa* or *brahma-prāpti* frame of his thought could, of course, have been meant seriously. The question of the relationship of the Ultimate or First Principle in his philosophy with the material world, however, is a philosophical question (one to be determined on the basis of logic and argumentation that does not rest on testimony, appeal to extraordinary experience of some kind, or depend on admitting an unverifiable possibility). The answer given to that question does have implications for religious thinking (e.g., for the notion of *mokṣa* to be accepted and for the method to be advocated for *mokṣa* attainment), but the answer itself is not decided at the level of religious thinking. The approving references to the *mokṣa* possibility that B may be seen as making or the *mokṣa*-supporting citations he gives from texts authoritative to him cannot,

therefore, be used as argument to establish that the religious ontology is B's final *philosophical* ontology as well and that, since in that ontology only his language principle remains, the physical world must actually be somehow derivable from it in his philosophy too.

(b) It also should not be said by way of objection that, if B's ontological thinking is restricted the way I have done, he would become a Dvaitin, whereas the tradition holds him to be an Advaitin. The 'Dvaitin: Advaitin' distinction pertains to the level of religious ontology. B would still remain an Advaitin at that level.

Bibliography and Abbreviations

(Publication details have not been given in the case of those Sanskrit texts which are available in many editions and in whose case access to a particular edition is not likely to make any difference. The publications of well-known and much published Western philosophers have also not been specified.)

Aklujkar, Ashok. 1970. *The Philosophy of Bhartṛhari's Trikāṇḍī.* Ph. D. dissertation, Harvard University. Unpublished.

—1988. *'Prāmāṇya* in the philosophy of the Grammarians.' *Studies in Indology: Professor Rasik Vihari Joshi Felicitation Volume,* pp.15-28. Eds. Kumar, Avanindra, et al. New Delhi: Shree Publishing House.

—1989. 'The number of *pramāṇas* according to Bhartṛhari.' *Wiener Zeitschrift für die Kunde Südasiens* 33:151-58.

—1991. 'Bhartṛhari's concept of the Veda.' *Panels of the VIIth World Sanskrit Conference.* Vol. IV-V. Ed. Bronkhorst, Johannes. pp. 1-18. Leiden: E.J. Brill.

—1993. 'An introduction to the study of Bhartṛhari.' *Asiatische Studien/Études Asiatiques* 47.1: 7-36.

—1999 (forthcoming). *Excursions into Pre-Bhartṛhari Thought.* Three lectures given at the Bhandarkar Oriental Research Institute, Pune. Expected to be published by the Institute.

B = Bhartṛhari. *Trikāṇḍī* or *Vākyapadīya.* I have reproduced the text of the kārikās and the Vṛtti from my critical edition under preparation. Those wishing to verify my references to the Vṛtti prior to the publication of my edition should consult the editions by K.A. Subramania Iyer: (a) *Vākyapadīya of Bhartṛhari with the Vṛtti and the Paddhati of Vṛṣabha-*

deva. Poona: Deccan College Postgraduate and Research Institute. 1966. Deccan College Monograph Series no. 32. (b) *The Vākyapadīya of Bhartṛhari, Kāṇḍa II with the Commentary of Puṇya-rāja and the Ancient Vṛtti.* Delhi, etc: Motilal Banarsidass, 1983. I have followed the enumeration of *kārikās* in: *Bhartṛhari's Vākyapadīya, Die Mūlakārikās nach den Handschriften herausgegeben und mit einem Pāda-Index versehen.* Rau, Wilhelm (ed.). Wiesbaden: Kommissionsverlag Franz Steiner GMBH, 1977. Abhandlungen für die Kunde des Morgenlandes XLII, 4. Hence the numbers in my edition and those in the editions by Subramania Iyer do not always match. However, they are not far removed from each other. For the third kāṇḍa of the TK, which has a commentary by Helā-rāja, see: (a) Vākyapadīya of Bhartṛhari with the *Commentary* of Helā-rāja. Kāṇḍa III, *Part I* [*samuddeśas* 1-7]. Subramania Iyer, K.A. (ed). Poona: Deccan College Postgraduate and Research Institute. 1963. Deccan College Monograph Series no. 21. (b) *Vākyapadīya of Bhartṛhari with the* Prakīrṇaka-prakāśa of Helā-rāja Kāṇḍa III, *Part II [samuddeśas 8-14].* Poona: Deccan College. 1973. [Continuation of Deccan College Monograph Series no. 21].

Ganguli, Hemanta Kumar. 1963. *The Philosophy of Logical Construction.* Calcutta: Sanskrit Pustak Bhandar.

Helā-rāja: see under B.

Potter, Karl H. 1981. (ed.) *Advaita Vedānta up to Śaṅkara and His Pupils.*

Delhi: MB. The Encyclopedia of Indian philosophies, vol. III.

TK = *Trikāṇḍī*: see B.

Vṛtti: see under B.

Vṛṣabha: see under B.

YB= *Yoga-bhāṣya*: see Vyāsa under Patañjali.

Cultural Presuppositions as Determinants in Experience : A Comparison of Some Basic Indian and Western Concepts

SWAMI ATMARUPANANDA

Swami Atmarupananda, a monk of the Ramakrishna Order, is in charge of Vivekananda Retreat, Ridgely, at Stone Ridge, New York, U.S.A. He is a member of the Snowmass Conference, an interreligious body organized to foster an interreligious perspective on the inner life.

The thesis: We inherit certain basic, unquestioned beliefs from our culture about the nature of ourselves and our world of experience, which in turn determine to a significant degree what and how we experience. This influences all levels of our experience, from the experience of self, time, and space, to our experience of bodily movement.

'Presupposition' here means an assumption, without thought of possible error, made prior to experience; that is, an unquestioned assumption about the nature of things 'through which' we experience. These presuppositions are not conscious and therefore not normally examined or chosen, and are therefore held 'without thought of possible error.'

A presupposition is a tendency to interpret experience in a certain manner. There are personal presuppositions, cultural presuppositions, and presuppositions common to humanity. Presuppositions common to humanity include, for example, the tendency to see the world as real, abiding, and satisfying. These latter presuppositions are extremely important, and most of Vedanta philosophy and practice are aimed at replacing these presuppositions with what Vedanta considers to be ideas based on truth, followed by the attainment of true perception, free of presuppositions. Because they are thoroughly discussed in Vedantic works, we won't discuss these common presuppositions here. As for cultural presuppositions and personal presuppositions, both are important in ordinary life and in spiritual life, but we are here limiting our interest to cultural presuppositions, about which it is possible to generalize.

Again, a presupposition is not an exotic concept. It just means a preconscious tendency to interpret experience in a certain manner. A cultural presupposition is a culturally determined tendency to interpret experience in a certain manner.

The basic thesis is not new. These days we speak in terms of the 'global village' and 'multiculturalism.' As a result of this new planetary awareness people are increasingly sensitive to the fact that 'different' does not mean 'wrong' or 'inferior.' But old ways of thinking do not die so easily. Practically every culture has had some form of the idea that its people are 'the chosen' and live at the centre of the universe. That still influences the thinking of people. (The sentence just used—'that still influences the thinking of people'—shows that this sense of cultural superiority is a presupposition, a cultural bias which influences thinking: that is, it is more than just one thought among many. It is a presupposition which acts as a determinant in experience.)

Therefore, the world has not become so cosmopolitan and sophisticated that a study and development of this thesis is unwarranted. There is not only room for further understanding of the subject, but a desperate need to understand it. When widely different cultures are brought into close and regular contact, the only three long-term methods of interaction seem to be confrontation, toleration, or understanding. Many countries—including those of the West and Middle East—have historically followed largely the course of confrontation. India followed mainly the course of toleration; in fact, one of the positive aspects of the caste system was that it allowed communities with widely differing customs and mores to live side by side without friction by defining roles and restricting social contact. However, of the three courses open to us—confrontation, toleration, and understanding—understanding is not only the safest but the most positive and creative course. As a step toward understanding, we need to examine presuppositions.[1]

Cultural presuppositions influence the process of knowing. It is in and through our presuppositions that we experience or 'know' the world around us as well as the inner world of self. In this way the subject of this paper is connected to the seminar topic—'Concepts of Knowledge.' By understanding our presuppositions, we understand more about why we experience things the way we do. The process of knowing is not just an objective process as conceived in naive realism. There are unseen influences on the process of knowing which influence the resulting knowledge as well. Presuppositions are one such significant influence, and need to be considered in any comprehensive theory of knowledge.

This does not mean that cross-cultural understanding is impossible: presuppositions do not encase us in a windowless cultural milieu. Rules of rational dialogue in science, philosophy, and other disciplines are designed to maximize understanding and minimize individual and cultural influences. Besides, all people share an underlying common humanity with much common experience. But it does mean that for full cross-cultural understanding, a conscious examination of presuppositions is necessary.

The subject is very large, and my expertise limited. So I have chosen to approach the subject in a restricted context. That context is the meeting of the modern Western mind with the Hindu tradition of Vedanta. This meeting brings into focus a contrast between Western and Hindu presuppositions, and thereby illustrates the existence and nature of cultural presuppositions, and thus of presuppositions in general.

It would be good to point out here that this paper is not purely theoretical, but rests on an experiential foundation. An attempt is made to explain that experience through a theoretical framework. This is a first attempt, and like all first attempts, it is not mature but provisional. The danger here is that, seeing imperfections in the theoretical framework, others are liable to throw out the whole thesis without seriously considering the experiential basis.

The central experiential foundation is twofold: (1) when comparing different cultures, culturally based differences are found in the sense of time, space, self, relationship, and other broad categories of experience; (2) on examination the nature of these differences is seen to be normally preconscious, resistant to change, and influential in experience. The first point is so obvious as to be beyond debate. The second is problematic only when we come to discuss the degree to which experience is influenced by these cultural differences.

One of my underlying hypotheses is that presuppositions as defined here are partly mythical in character. That is, the mythical foundations of a culture influence cultural presuppositions. Twentieth-century scholars like Carl Jung and Joseph Campbell have shown—I think convincingly—that myth underlies all cultures. Even secular humanism and Marxism, thus, are founded on their own myths about human nature, the nature of society, history, and so on. The mythical foundations of a society are not passive, imaginative 'stories' told for the entertainment and edification of the masses, but dynamic forces which mould the lives and experiences of a society's members.[2] Presuppositions, being mythical in nature, partake of this dynamism.

Let me here put a qualification on all that follows. India has been in close contact with the West for the past two hundred years. Right now in particular, India is undergoing tremendous social changes, with industrialization, the development of a market economy, the rise of a middle-class culture, the disappearance of caste-based occupations, the influx of Western ideas and images through the media, and so on. The West is similarly going through major changes with the widespread mixing of cultures and races and religions with their varying presuppositions, the radical changes in worldview that twentieth-century science has caused, the influence of New Age thought which emphasizes in its own way many Eastern ideas (often in a Christian context, and often applied in ways strange to their origin). It is as yet premature to say where these changes, East and West, are going to take us; all we can say is that everything at present is in question. Therefore, some of the following characterizations of Hindu and Western thought may seem too tightly compartmentalized. That is true. But for clarity's sake I have described the two cultures in terms of their traditional tendencies which, until very recently, were quite distinct. And even now I think these generalizations hold true as general cultural tendencies, as long as we remember that they are not absolutes and that they are being minimized.

I became interested in the subject a number of years ago. One factor that led to this interest was my observation of Westerners, myself included, taking up the Vedantic path. During two and a half decades I have seen many people take up the study and practice of Vedanta. Some have been much more successful than others. A number of elements factor into the degree of success, such as the individual's diligence and sincerity, purity of purpose, morality, mental stability, etc. But another factor is not normally recognized. That is, how thoroughly they have integrated the Vedantic worldview into their own worldview. Here I am not speaking of cultural observances, like eating only with the right hand or sitting on the floor in yoga posture to meditate: those external observances have little to do with success or failure as a Vedantin. I am speaking of deeper, unspoken philosophical and mythical influences that the person is rarely aware of: ideas of time and space, ideas of self and self-image, attitudes toward other people—in other words, cultural presuppositions.

Most aspiring Vedantins in the West—and I'm sure the same is true of aspiring Buddhists and aspiring Taoists in the West—try to tack a few broad Eastern generalities that they find attractive onto their unchanged Western mentality. These are often ideas such as, 'God alone is real,' 'Enlightenment solves all of life's problems,' 'Meditation is the supreme means to peace and inner fulfilment,' 'All is one.' But their whole personality is oriented toward a different direction, and so the ideas never go deep, they never take on transformative power. They are not integrated into the larger personality.

Some thinkers like Carl Jung would say that East is East and West is West: you can't fight the collective, ethnic unconscious which has formed you into who you are. I don't agree, at least not fully, because I've seen change individually, and we've all seen historical change and periods of great synthesis between two radically different cultures.

You do see people, however, who try to cut down the tree of Western culture which grows within their psyche and then transplant a Hindu cultural trunk onto the remaining stump, expecting it to grow there. It rarely if ever does. In all the cases I have seen, the person eventually has a reaction, or else he finally has to assimilate what he has learned from India into his own personality with its distinctive roots and trunk. So I will agree with Jung to a limited point. But I cannot agree that presuppositions are absolute or inherent in any sense, but are imbibed and to a large extent modifiable. Some are more changeable than others; and some cannot be changed without personal degeneration.

Presuppositions are also not self-contained 'things' which can be unplugged and replaced. It is perhaps more accurate to think of them as differently coloured waters—if you want to change one, you pour the desired coloured water into the old until the old is effectively dominated by the new; yet something of the old remains, giving a special tint to the new colour. Thus it is a matter of integration, not replacement. The coloured water analogy is defective, however, because, unlike coloured water, tendencies are dynamic and can selectively reassert themselves under certain conditions.

From where do the presuppositions of Western people come? Primarily from three sources: the Greco-Roman, the Judeo-Christian, and the indigenous, pre-Christian influences in Europe like the Celtic, the Gallic, the Teutonic, the Norse, etc.[3] In America there is also the rarely recognized influence of the Native Americans, or so-called American Indians, on the dominant culture.

Let us now plunge into the presuppositions themselves, examining their nature and how they affect the encounter between the Western mind and the Vedantic path. Because of time-limitations, I will have to limit myself to a few important presuppositions, but that will be enough to illustrate the basic point.

Presuppositions can be ordered according to their depth of influence, some having extensive influence over a person's perceptions, and others having less extensive influence, some being easier to manipulate or change, others being more difficult to affect. We will examine some of the deeper presuppositions.

First, time. All of our perceptions, thoughts, and actions take place in time, and so our concept of time obviously has a profound influence over us. We often hear about Western, linear time as opposed to Eastern, cyclical time. Linear time has an absolute beginning, a progressive development, and an absolute end. Cyclical time sees universe after universe arising, developing, decaying, and being destroyed, without beginning and without end. The difference is real and significant. It is not that we choose to have a linear concept of time from among a list of options. We grow up with a particular concept of time which we have unconsciously imbibed from our culture. It is just there, determining our mental and physical experience without our knowledge and without our conscious consent. Our life proceeds within this culturally defined sense of time, and we are quite unconscious of its nature unless it is brought to our attention.

Greco-Roman time is generally considered to have been cyclic, not linear, but that has had little or no influence over the present sense of time in Western civilization.[4] The Judeo-Christian linear concept of time, however, has had a profound influence. Judeo-Christian time was not always exclusively linear. Origen, the great Christian thinker of the second century, believed that this present universe is only one of a succession of universes, and such views were held by some Jewish thinkers also. But from an early time in Christian history, linear time — with its belief in an absolute beginning and absolute end and progress in-between—became the accepted view. Linear time became the accepted view in Judaism, as well. And certainly the account of creation in Genesis and the rest of Biblical revelation lends itself most easily to the idea of linear time.

In the Judeo-Christian tradition, God is seen as intimately involved with human history; and for the Christian in particular, history itself is seen as progressive, leading toward a final, glorious fulfilment, when the righteous shall get their grand reward. The ancient Jews sought to replace the complex mythology and ritual of their part of the world with the study of history, believing that God's action could be seen in the events of history. There was therefore no need to seek him, they thought, through elaborate myths and rituals.[5] Of course, neither the ancient Jews nor the later Christians and Muslims who grew out of the same tradition succeeded in totally eliminating mythology or even ritual, but they did minimize their elaboration, if not their influence.

Not only is modern Western religious thought founded on this idea of linear time, but so is Darwinian evolution and its relatives, so is the

Marxist view of dialectical materialism, so is the promise of technology on which most of the modern scientific endeavour has been based.[6] This shows the tremendous power of myth and thereby, I think, the power of presuppositions. Darwin and his successors see evolution as linear, starting at a beginning point, working through greater and greater manifestations of life, tending toward an unknown endpoint of greatest manifestation.[7] (We are not arguing here whether evolutionary theory is true or false, but trying to see what idea of time it is based upon.) Social evolutionists similarly see society evolving, with a gradual reduction of evil and increase of good. Marxists see human history as a linear process leading through various evolutionary stages until the fulfilment, wherein the state withers away, being no longer needed. Modern technology has driven the development of modern science largely through the promise of greater and greater control of the natural world, which in turn will provide greater and greater good for humanity (good being defined here largely as comfort and security).

This view of time is contrasted with the Hindu view, where time is cyclical.[8] In cyclical time there is no absolute beginning or absolute end. History is not tending toward a final, glorious end. Every creation is followed by destruction which is followed by creation. Summer is followed by winter which is followed by summer. The sun rises and sets only to rise and set again and again. Birth is followed by death, which is followed by birth. As Swami Vivekananda used to point out, evolution implies involution: you cannot get out of a machine that which was not first placed there in potential form. If there is evolution, there is involution. As for social evolution where evil is gradually conquered and only good remains, that is impossible according to the Hindu view. Good cannot exist without evil. If physical pain is removed, the potential for mental pain is increased.[9] There are periods of increase and periods of decrease, golden periods and dark ages; but there is an overall balance of good and evil through time.[10]

These differing views of time have profound effects on our inner and outer lives. They are not just philosophical ideas to play with. One who practises spiritual disciplines becomes aware of their dynamic power and influence. The power of these views is seen by the fact that, e. g.,

Judeo-Christian linear time, has influenced not just the devout but everyone: scientists, Marxists, and others. But before discussing these influences, let us look at two more presuppositions: our concepts of self and of space, because they are tied together with time in their effects.

Our concept of self is at least as important as our concept of time. All of our thoughts and actions take place in conjunction with our sense of who we are, which is to say, they are coloured by our sense of self. The Western concept of self is complex, and far from philosophically or psychologically consistent. There is no need here to examine the concept as seen by philosophers and psychologists, for we are more interested in the preconscious concept of self as it is actually found in people.

The Christian influence is strong. Under this influence, a person is considered to be created and therefore dependent, not self-existent. A person 'has' a soul—and it is commonly (not theologically) understood to be a 'has-a' relationship—but the nature of that soul is nowhere clearly developed and is therefore left hazy in conception.[11] It is commonly understood that a person is a complex psycho-physical being, with the soul not being distinguished from the mind. Every human creature is considered to be loved by God the Creator, but basically sinful and corrupt, the soul itself being tainted. The will is corrupt and therefore all actions are corrupt and incapable of leading us to blessedness in themselves. (That is why Jesus is essential to the economy of salvation.)

Just how deep and penetrating this influence is can be seen by looking through the eyes of one brought up outside of the tradition. Swami Prabhavananda of the Ramakrishna Order, the founder and long-time head of the Vedanta Society of Southern California who came originally from India, used to say that the biggest personality 'problem' (from a Vedantic perspective) he found among the many Western people he counselled over almost fifty years was guilt. He was not speaking of the natural, temporary guilt that is associated with committing a particular moral wrong, which is found in healthy people everywhere, but deep-seated guilt associated with one's sense of self-identity.

There is also a strong influence on the Western view of self from the Greco-Roman or Classical tradition which was reintroduced into Europe during the Renaissance. This is in many ways contrary to the Christian influence, but the two have somehow coexisted in the Western psyche since Renaissance times. Whereas Christianity put God at the centre of the universe, with humanity existing for the glorification of God, the Classical tradition was humanist, putting humanity at the centre. Man was the measure of all things. Man's power to know and to discover was glorified, the power of reason was almost deified. This view is largely at the root of Western self-confidence and passion for intellectual understanding. In conjunction with the indigenous traditions of Europe, it is also at the root of the Western tradition of adventure, conquest, and expansion.[12]

The Hindu view of self stands as quite a contrast. First of all, the Hindu view is that a person *is* a soul and *has* a body. As Swami Vivekananda would point out, the English saying has it that so-and-so 'gave up the ghost,' whereas a Hindu says, so-and-so 'gave up the body.' A real difference in attitude underlies the difference in language. Secondly, though Hindus experience guilt, deep-seated guilt associated with one's self-image is by and large not characteristic of Hindus, and is certainly not fostered by the Vedantic tradition. In all traditions of Hinduism, the soul is seen as spirit, intrinsically pure by nature, separate from the body and mind. Of course, the average Hindu does not *experience* the soul as such, but this idea has nonetheless affected the ordinary person's sense of self.

There are other related elements which need to be examined here. Albert Schweitzer made the famous statement that Christian saints are pictured with their eyes open, looking to the greater reality of the external world, whereas Eastern saints are pictured with their eyes closed, self-absorbed. The implication, of course, is that Christian saints are greater because they are unselfish, whereas Eastern saints are closed up within themselves in a selfish and solipsistic absorption. And here we are getting to one of the primary distinctions between Western presuppositions and Hindu presuppositions which is central to our concern here, and it is a distinction which draws together the views of time, space, and self.

In the Western view of linear time, fulfilment is always in the future, whether it is religious fulfilment or secular fulfilment. For the religious, fulfilment comes either after death—which for the living is always in the future—or at the time of the millennium when history is fulfilled. For the evolutionist, countless species including our own are being sacrificed for the gradual perfection of life. For the social evolutionist, we and billions before us are being sacrificed to a process which promises fulfilment some time in the future. History for the Marxist is leading toward the perfection of society when each will receive according to his or her need and will give according to his or her capacity, and work will be a means to self-actualization. Technology promises to lead us toward perfect control over nature where the evils and discomforts of life will be annihilated. Thus, Western man looks to the future for fulfilment. This is true of the individual as well. It doesn't take a statistical study or scientific survey to see that people in the West are always looking around the next corner for fulfilment.

If, however, our view of time is cyclical, and history for us is repetitive, then the process of time doesn't promise the same value. And where we don't see promise, we don't put expectation. This does not mean that Hindus do not seek temporal fulfilment. Certainly they do, like any other human beings. But that temporal fulfilment is seen more as something presently necessary for a good life, while the long term goal is to go beyond such needs. The Hindu tradition says: Time must have a stop. You can't imagine a thoroughgoing Westerner saying that. The Western response might be: If time stops, why, we'll be stuck right here, and what a tragedy that would be because things aren't finished yet!... or else: If time stops, then nothing is left!

This isn't to say that history has no interest to the Hindu. Hinduism would not have preserved its ancient traditions if that were true. It is important, but for different reasons, and is expressed in different ways due to the different sense of time. In the West we put our history in museums and textbooks where it can be studied objectively. In India history is preserved in everyday life through conservation of tradition. It is also preserved in mythical form through the Puranas. History is thus important to the Hindu also, but not in the same way as it is to the Westerner, and that difference arises because of the different view of time. If time is repetitive, then tradition is preserved—and therefore history is important—in order to accumulate wisdom, so that we don't need to repeat the past.

One aspect of India that almost all visitors notice is this different sense of time: so strong is it that even casual visitors notice it. I'm not talking about the Indian tendency to be late for everything nor about the frustrating slowness of Indian bureaucracy, but about a certain timeless quality that Westerners notice here. Swami Vivekananda used to say, 'You [meaning Western people] live in time; we live in eternity.' Even if the visitor to India is not articulate, they will at least say, things in India are so much more relaxed; and that, it would seem obvious, is directly related to the sense of time.

One of the ideas I'm getting at is, presuppositions change the nature of our experience itself. Differing views of time cause us to experience time differently, and thereby to experience events—all of which take place in time—differently. We don't just have a concept of time which is separable from our experience. Presuppositions are dynamic factors which give shape to our experience.

This brings up the topic of space. In the West people are looking to the future in time, and looking outside of themselves in space for fulfilment. Since the Renaissance, and particularly since the European Enlightenment, Western people have looked outside in space for adventure and conquest as well. Nowadays in the post-colonnial world, we look outside for business opportunities, ever seeking to expand into new markets.

Tied in with time and space is the concept of self. The Christian saints may be pictured with their eyes open, either looking toward the heavens or looking in love on fellow beings. That is wonderful. But implied in Schweitzer's statement is the belief that looking inside is selfish. This is a presupposition which is seriously challenged by Eastern thought. In spite of the Western glorification of the individual, which came largely through the Classical influence as it developed in the Renaissance and more particularly during the European Enlightenment,[13] the West looks with suspicion upon introspection. 'Self-absorption,' 'self-satisfaction,' 'self-preoccupation,' and other such terms have negative connotations to the Westerner. The European Renaissance and Enlightenment bred an aggressive individual, seeking conquest and adventure, not an inward-looking individual. Christianity, with its belief in the basic sinfulness of humanity and emphasis on humility, held the social fabric together, which would probably not have been possible had aggressive individualism not been so bridled. But on one point both Christianity and the individualism of the Enlightenment met: fulfilment is not to be found within the individual, and to look for it there is wrong.

A wise Hindu will also say that preoccupation with one's egocentric concerns is selfish and therefore harmful and immoral. But the Hindu yogi looks within, not to hide from life nor out of narcissism, but in order to find the ground of existence; and that, the yogi believes, unites him with all existence. Furthermore, since all of our perceptions are coloured by our self concept, we cannot see anything truly, according to the Hindu, until our self-experience is true. Unless I know who I am, all of my relationships with things and people, even with God, will be tinged with ignorance and therefore less than true and trustworthy.

Look into the future, look not into the self, look into external space. These are at the basis of Western civilization, not so much as conscious instructions but as presuppositions directing our lives, imbibed in thousands of ways through images and stories and behaviour training from early childhood on.

A Western follower of Hinduism is told to 'be here now,' but everything in his culture says, 'be there then.' So just tacking the statement 'be here now' onto his Western mind is not going to be effective.

Admittedly, I have a bias here toward the Hindu concepts of time and space and self. But I certainly admit that there are good things which have come from the Western viewpoint. Linear time adds motivation and justification for social and technological development. Turning away from the self probably leads to greater social involvement. Looking into external space leads to a greater spirit of adventure and consequently the development of a heroic temperament capable of accomplishment of deeds.

Twenty years ago when I first lived in India, as I would sweep the floor with an Indian broom I often used to wonder why, after thousands of years of using the same type of broom, no one had ever thought to put a handle on it so they wouldn't have to bend over double. A thousand and one such observations will come to a Westerner living in India. One also sees in India more people who seem prematurely self-satisfied than in the West.

At the same time, the price paid for the West's development has been great. That price is a continual, vague sense that things are not what they should be, a dissatisfaction with the present time and place, a continual waiting for something that will fix things.

Swami Vivekananda used to say that the West has developed the power to do; India has developed the power to suffer. These two powers are obviously related to the sense of time in each culture. The West sees perfection in time, and so is busy fixing and improving; India sees perfection outside of time and seeks to adapt to circumstances within time. Swami Vivekananda said further that the perfect humanity would come from the blending and harmonizing of these two powers: the power to do and the power to endure. Both, in other words, have their value.

A Westerner taking up the Hindu religious path must integrate a new self concept and a new time concept. It is not possible to glue the Hindu view of the pure, divine self, all conscious, all blissful, onto the Western concept of self. The latter must be radically altered. An aspirant has to learn to think that fulfilment is inside, not outside, that inside is a wonderful world of consciousness, that by going inside one is actually coming closer to real unity with other beings. I'm not arguing the truth of these ideas about the inner self, but I am saying that, if one takes up the Hindu path as being true and desirable, these things must follow.

So with time. An aspirant must learn to seek truth in the present, seeing every moment in infinite time as equal, giving up the Western preoccupation with the future. Those who have moved in this direction find a new sense of inner quiet developing, a sense of being centred, with their psychological centre of gravity inside, not outside as before. They begin to experience time as a subtle current which carries them forward, unfolding things and events almost of itself: all that is required in life is participation, not instigation. On the contrary, the Western image of time might be of a path down which you have to walk and where you must *make* events happen. Such psychological changes cannot come, as far as I've seen, without altering one's presuppositions. That takes time, and it usually takes conscious, deliberate effort, because presuppositions are not surface thoughts, but are preconscious and tied to values and emotions which makes them dynamic.

Concepts of physical space do not seem to be as crucial as time and self. Much more important is the concept of mental space. Often in Western thought, thought and matter have been contrasted, matter being that which extends in space, and thought being non-spatial. However, in Vedanta psychology, mind has its own realm of space, *chittakasha*, and thoughts exist in that space. Developing a sense of internal space is crucial. Most people, not just in the West, exist on the very surface of their senses. We are always looking outside. As the *Kaṭha Upaniṣad* says:

'The Self-Existent One in creating the outer senses wounded them; therefore one sees without and not the inner Self. Some wise one [however] saw the inner Self, having turned his eye inward, desirous of immortality.'[14]

To follow the Vedantic path one must develop a sense of inwardness, a sense of having an inner centre of gravity. For the practice of discrimination and detachment this is essential. When a stimulus comes from the outer world, if we exist on the surface of the senses, we respond automatically. As we develop a sense of inwardness, we find we have more time to examine the stimulus and choose an appropriate response. There is a sense of inner mental spaciousness which allows this freedom. I am not suggesting that Hindus have this naturally. It is a condition that comes with some meditative practice. Still, it shows how our experience changes as our presuppositions change. Or perhaps it would be better to say, it shows how new types of experience are made possible when our presuppositions are changed.

Swami Vivekananda used to point out that in Indian dance, movements are circular and smooth, whereas in Western dance, movements are more angular and abrupt. That he attributed to the difference in the time concept, cyclical as opposed to linear. That we can't prove, of course, but it is an interesting hypothesis. It is supported by the experience of some Western Hindu aspirants who find that a changed sense of time and a greater sense of inwardness have given them a sense of inner balance they didn't have before; and they even say that the nature of their movements changes, becoming less abrupt.

We discussed time, space, and self, not thoroughly by any means but enough to make the basic point intended. Let us now examine some other presuppositions, some which, though not as pervasive as our concepts of time, space, and self, are in some ways more difficult to change and, I would suggest, not desirable to be changed completely.

One such is a modern Western presupposition associated with democracy. Political theories about democratic government are not of interest here. What is of interest is the sense that all people are in some way equal in value and therefore deserving of respect and equal opportunity. This basic democratic premise goes very deep in the modern West. It is not a Judeo-Christian concept, though it finds definite support in that tradition, nor is it purely a Greco-Roman concept, though it does have roots in ancient Greece. It is largely a product of various influences active during the European Enlightenment and later.[15] As a child in India grows up assuming the truth of reincarnation, so a child in a country like the United States grows up assuming the truth of the democratic premise just enunciated. It is so natural a part of the thinking there, that to think any other way seems absurd and immoral, even though modern democracy has a very brief history and controls even now a limited part of the globe.

India is the largest democracy in the world, and in spite of the bad press India receives in the West, it is a successful democracy. Yet the presuppositions supporting an Indian's sense of democracy and those supporting an American's sense of democracy are quite different. (Because I am more familiar with it, I will for now speak of 'American democracy' rather than the more general 'Western democracy': though modern Western democracies share much in common, there are a few minor differences between the American and the European democratic presuppositions.)

Many Americans have a surprisingly immature sense of democracy in certain areas: the suspicion of all authority just because it is authority, the resentment of all government regulation, the feeling of the common man that 'I could do a better job than the President' whoever the current president might be, the lack of respect for the wisdom of seniority and age. But underneath all that is a solid conviction in the basic premise of democracy, which has found embodiment in certain forms of social behaviour. Those forms of behaviour in turn are expected of others. And this is an area where the American aspirant invariably comes into conflict sooner or later with the Indian Hindu tradition, because Hindu society is hierarchical. It is also not mobile and flexible like American society, and so there is not the same sense in India that a person who is poor today might be rich tomorrow, or that a person from a labour-class background might go to school in mid life and become a scholar or respected artist or whatever.

It is strange that such profound, pervasive, and ancient cultural presuppositions as space, time, and self are more easily changed than an idea about democracy. But that has been my observation. Not that ideas of time, space, and self are easy to change: it is very difficult and takes many years, but it can be done if a person becomes convinced that another way of viewing these aspects of experience is more valid and valuable. Why the one which is deeper, older, and more pervasive is easier to change, will have to wait for a moment, until we have examined two more presuppositions which are also very hard, and I would say not desirable, to change.

I must give a little historical background.

The freedom of intellect so prized in the West did not come easily. In fact it didn't just 'come.' It had to be won by a long battle with the Church. The tremendous enthusiasm for knowledge and experience and inquiry which started with the introduction of Classical thought in twelfth century Western Europe found at first a welcome within the Church. But that enthusiasm and the Church soon came into direct conflict. The story of the freeing of the Western mind from Church authority is a story of great conflict and sacrifice.

The freedom of conscience which is equally prized in the West also came through great conflict and sacrifice. That struggle began with the Reformation, when Luther put the individual conscience above Church authority.

Modern Western people stand on the shoulders of these two struggles. The Christian Church[16] itself stands on the shoulders of these struggles.

Just as the basic democratic premise has become part of the fibre of the Western personality, so has the belief in the sanctity of the individual conscience and the freedom of inquiry. If those are touched, the Western mind jumps with alarm. I have seen so many times an Indian unwittingly touching a Westerner there and receiving an explosive reaction, and not having the faintest idea what has happened. And to the Westerner what has happened is often so obvious that he can't imagine that explanation is needed: he has been violated. This has given some Hindus the belief that Westerners are completely unpredictable and subject to strange fits of moodiness and anger.

Belief in freedom of inquiry and sanctity of the individual conscience often makes it difficult for the Westerner to come to terms with the Hindu institution of the guru. This is an area where many Western aspirants go through great inner—and sometimes outer—struggles. Whereas an ethnic Hindu has an ingrained respect for the spiritual teacher and the belief that service to the teacher brings great benefit, the Western Hindu aspirant comes with quite different presuppositions: he often equates service with servitude, one of the most deplorable words to a modern Westerner, and he equates respect with kowtowing, obedience with abdication of personal judgement and conscience. Fortunate is the Westerner who is sensitive to spiritual greatness and who finds a guru whose greatness is so evident that appreciation of him comes spontaneously. Even then there are liable to be great struggles, but they can be overcome if the two qualifications just mentioned are met.

The democratic premise, the sanctity of the individual conscience, and freedom of inquiry: these are three presuppositions that are very deep in the Western personality, so deep that they are assumed to be self-evident and absolute and therefore unquestionable. And my feeling, based upon observation and experience, is that they are not to be eliminated. They need to be matured, made more conscious and therefore less a source of automatic emotional reactions, but not eliminated. So again the question arises, why should time, space, and self be changeable, when presuppositions concerning democracy etc., which are less pervasive (in their sphere of influence) and more recently acquired, are so resistant to change?

One possibility is that the advantages of a different self-concept and time-concept can be explained, and many Westerners see the advantages and therefore work toward effecting a change. But it is very difficult or impossible to convince a Westerner that their conscience is not sacred, or that freedom of inquiry is wrong, or that the democratic premise is unsound. These values are seen as advances over the values of authoritarian societies.[17] It may also be—from a Jungian standpoint—that the long struggle for freedom of conscience and inquiry and for democracy has left a memory in the collective unconscious which protects these principles which were so hard won.

My own hypothesis is that, wherever a presupposition is seen as a positive value, it cannot be changed without personal degradation, unless that associated sense of value is seen to be misplaced. The stronger the sense of value is, the less amenable to change is the presupposition. And in the case of the sanctity of the individual conscience, freedom of inquiry, and the democratic premise, I see no need to replace them for the sake of the Vedantic path. In fact, Swami Vivekananda had great appreciation for these very qualities in the Western character. Only they need to be matured so that they do not become the source of unconscious, aggressive reactions when casually threatened, and so that they are tempered by respect.

There are other presuppositions which are important in the life of a Westerner who aspires to follow the Vedantic path. But those that we have discussed illustrate the existence and nature of cultural presuppositions, and give an idea of the problems faced by the Western aspirant and also the possibility of a solution to the cultural conflict experienced within the aspirant.

Is this thesis just another example of radical postmodern perspectivism? No, I don't think so. I agree with postmodernism that experience does not result from a detached observer witnessing an objective reality; the experiencing subject is creatively involved with his experience. I also agree that any purely intellectual position can be countered by another intellectual position, thus relativising intellectual knowledge. And I agree that no cultural perspective is absolute, thus relativising cultural perspectives up to a point.[18] However, I am rescued from the 'absolute relativism' and terminal ambiguity of postmodernism by at least three principles of Vedanta: (1) The principle of dharma which is the moral order underlying the universe. Isn't this just another theory among countless other relative theories? I claim not, because if we truly attune ourselves to this moral order, we find our minds becoming clearer, our lives becoming uplifted in a way that we know to be superior to what was experienced in an immoral state. Thus dharma is experiential, not just a theory, and contained within that experience is the experiential—not theoretical—certainty of its rightness. (2) The *experience* of spiritual truth which is uncontradicted by relative intellectual truths. Such experience carries its own absolute certainty. As the traditional analogy is given, when you see the sun, you don't need to hold a candle to it to see if it exists. Furthermore, such experience comes only when we transcend the relative mind with its presuppositions, its hidden desires and motivations and imaginations. (3) The principle that there are many valid paths to—or views of—truth. Postmodern deconstructionism sees all standpoints as relative, contingent, and therefore in the final analysis equally invalid. Vedanta sees every viewpoint as having a partial view of *truth*, because it sees a universal, spiritual truth which can be experienced as the background of all ideas, and as the background of all experience. And this, too, is experiential, not theoretical.

In conclusion:

A presupposition or tendency to experience in a certain way is not just one thought among many other thoughts in the mind. It is a directing force, moulding experience. It doesn't do this in a gross way; for instance, by changing our presuppositions we don't suddenly see red as blue, nor does the world turn inside-out. But a presupposition does nonetheless have a definite impact on experience, subtle though it be.

Presuppositions are tied to values, and values are associated with emotions. Thus they affect our evaluation of experience, and affect the emotional impact of experience. Therefore our interpretation of experience is affected by presuppositions. Or, if you do not like to think in terms of an objective experience coloured by subjective interpretation, we could say that the nature of our experience itself is affected by presuppositions.

A presupposition can also open the possibility of experience which is absent in the absence of that presupposition, as in the experience of time described earlier. It is not that the presupposition of cyclical time makes time into a current which carries us forward, but it opens the possibility of that experience. And it is for this reason that Vedanta gives so much attention to *śravaṇa* and *manana.*[19]

By recognizing and understanding presuppositions, we understand an important element in the process of knowledge.

Notes and References

1 Let me add here that I am not suggesting an extreme cultural and moral relativism, where there is no standard of truth or goodness other than what 'feels good' to the individual person or culture. In keeping with my Vedantic background, I believe there is a moral order to the universe and also an absolute and universal truth which can be experienced. But also in keeping with Vedanta, I am convinced that there are many valid approaches to that truth, that even a crooked, roundabout path is still a path if it leads toward truth, and that even through folly an individual or culture can come to wisdom.

2 See Paulos Mar Gregorios, *A Light too Bright: The Enlightenment Today* (Albany: SUNY Press, 1992), pp. 158 and 166. Hereinafter, *A Light too Bright*.

3 See *A Light too Bright*, p. 71.

4 During the European Renaissance there was for a while a revival among intellectuals of the Classical idea of cyclical time, but this was temporary and superficial in its effect.

5 See Karen Armstrong, *A History of God* (New York: Ballantine Books, 1993), p. 43.

6 Paulos Mar Gregorios argues very effectively in *A Light too Bright* that technology has not been a by-product of the search for pure scientific knowledge inspired by a simple love of truth; rather desire for technological development has largely been the driving force behind scientific research.

7 The author is aware that most evolutionists (Teilhard de Chardin being an exception) do not see any teleological process at work in evolution. Whereas mainline Christians believe that the consummation of world history has already been decided, evolutionists do not see a known end toward which evolution is working. Still, evolutionists do see the process as having an absolute beginning point and as progressive.

8 Admittedly, not all schools of ancient Hindu philosophy view time as cyclical, but then, how much practical influence have the Cārvākas and the Naiyāyikas had on Hindu life and worldview? The Hindu worldview has largely been formed through the Upaniṣads, Itihāsas and Purāṇas, where time is definitely cyclical.

9 The relativity of good and evil, pleasure and pain, is a different subject, but is here tied to the Western concept of time.

10 The Hindu seeks to rise above relative good *and* evil, but does so through moral action because that alone leads to transcendence, not immorality.

11 Judaism and Christianity spent their greatest energies developing the idea of God, whereas Hinduism spent its greatest energies developing the idea of the soul. Perusal of such works as the article on 'Soul' in the Roman Catholic *Sacramentum Mundi: An Encyclopedia of Theology* [ed. Karl Rahner (Bangalore: Theological Publications in India, 1978), vol. VI] bears this statement out.

12 See *A Light too Bright*, pp. 53 ff. Christianity also played a part in this tradition of conquest and expansion by its belief that conversion of the pagans was a duty. And

it contributed to Western self-confidence through its conviction that it alone among religions was true.

13 The Reformation also contributed by its valuing of the individual conscience over institutional (i.e. Roman Church) authority, though it couldn't be said to have 'glorified' the individual.

14 *Kaṭha Upaniṣad*, II.vi.1.

15 The influence of the Native American traditions should also be mentioned, since it is important but almost completely ignored even in America where modern democracy had its first full practical application. For discussions on this, see two books by Jack Weatherford: *Indian Givers* (New York: Fawcett Columbine, 1988), pp. 117-50, and *Native Roots* (New York: Fawcett Columbine, 1991), *passim*.

16 I use 'Church' in the singular here, not to imply that I am speaking of a particular denomination of Christianity, but because the different denominations can be seen as parts of a larger phenomenon, which is Christianity.

17 That seems to be the nature of freedom in any field: once it is attained, it is rarely given up willingly. Where it *is* given up willingly, it is normally the giving up of a lower freedom to facilitate attainment of a higher freedom, as when one takes employment under the owners and executives of a commercial enterprise in order to become financially free, or when one joins a monastic order and submits to its rules and authority structure for spiritual freedom.

18 See footnote 1.

19 That is, 'hearing' and 'reflecting' on Vedantic truth.

An Epistemological Study of Mysticism in Christianity and Hinduism

SWAMI BHAJANANANDA

Swami Bhajanananda was the editor of *Prabuddha Bharata*, the Ramakrishna Mission's English journal, for eight years. He is currently an Assistant Secretary of the Ramakrishna Math and Ramakrishna Mission, Belur Math.

The main purpose of this paper is to compare the epistemological theories of mystical experience in Christianity and Hinduism.

There are a number of excellent treatises on Christian mysticism.[1] There are also a few books on comparative mysticism.[2] Fewer still are books on Hindu mysticism. However, in most of these books mystical experience has been studied from the ontological standpoint. In the ontological approach the main question is, what is the content or goal of mystical experience? By contrast, in the epistemological approach the main question is, how the experience takes place; the primary interest is in the mental processes involved in mystical experience. To the best of my knowledge a comparative study of the epistemological theories of the mental processes involved in mystical experience in different religions has not been attempted so far.

In the works of the great mystics we come across wonderful descriptions of the vision of God and other mystical experiences but hardly any mention of the mental processes which produce these experiences. It is the commentators, theologians and philosophers who work out the epistemological theories regarding these experiences. Apart from explaining how mystical experiences take place, they have also to explain why all people do not get such experiences. If God is all-pervading, why is it that we don't see Him ?

Another related problem which epistemology has to solve is the bewildering diversity of spiritual experience. It is very often held that although religions of the world show great diversity in their outer expressions, such as creeds and rituals, they reveal transcendental unity. That is to say, the transcendental experiences of mystics in different religions are basically the same. On this point Swami Vivekananda, who was himself one of the greatest mystics, has stated: 'Mystics in every religion speak the same tongue and teach the same truth.'[3] The German scholar Rudolph Otto writes, '...it is often claimed that mysticism is the same in all ages and in all places, that timeless and independent of history, it has always been identical. East and West and other differences vanish here. Whether the flower of mysticism bloom in India or in China, in Persia or on the Rhine, its fruit is one.'[4]

However, it is well known that the experiences of mystics of different religions, even of the same religion, show irreducible differences. The mystical experiences of St. Teresa and Mīrābāī, of St. John of the Cross and Tukārām, of Śaṅkara and Eckhart are not the same. According to some scholars[5] these differences are due to the influence of the cultures of the mystics. The present paper attempts to show that there are also basic differences in the epistemological pre-suppositions regarding mystical experience in Christianity and Hinduism.

Mysticism in Relation to Forms of Knowledge

Before discussing the nature of mystical experience, it is necessary to place it in the right perspective in Western thought and Indian thought.

In Western thought we are here concerned only with those views which accept the validity and cognitive import of religious experience. (There are other views such as Logical Positivism, Marxism and certain forms of realism which deny this.) These views fall into two groups. According to the first group, the apprehension of the Divine is the result of inference from, or interpretation of, religious experience. They accept the validity of religious experience but deny that it can be understood as wholly immediate and self-evident, as it needs analysis and critical interpretation.

The second group takes religious experience to be an immediate and self-authenticating encounter with the Divine. However, there are two kinds of immediacy: revelational and mystical. Revelational immediacy pertains to the peculiar character of the human mind to apprehend God in the form of an insight or certitude. This is usually regarded as a higher form of faith, but is also known as 'religious *a priori*'. The German Protestant theologian Schleirmacher was one of the first to propound this kind of religious experience. Later on Emil Brunner and several other Protestant theologians spoke of the 'divine-human encounter', and Martin Buber spoke of religious experience as an 'I-Thou' relationship.

The other type of immediacy known as mystical immediacy refers to the direct experience of God obtained by transcending the senses through contemplation. This is what is called mysticism. Its validity is accepted by Roman Catholic and Eastern Churches.

The dominant and living system of philosophy in Hinduism is the Vedanta which is divided into several schools. All these schools accept at least three main *pramāṇas* or valid means of knowledge, viz. perception (*pratyakṣa*), inference (*anumāna*), and verbal testimony (*śabda*). Of these, perception alone is regarded as a direct (*aparokṣa*) means; the other two means give rise only to indirect or mediate (*parokṣa*) knowledge.[6] However, all these three 'means' of knowledge refer only to empirical knowledge.[7] Mystical knowledge is different from these. Mystical knowledge of the ultimate Reality is not considered a 'means of knowledge' but its supreme end.[8] The relation between the above three 'means' (*pramāṇa*) of knowledge and mystical experience of the ultimate Reality has not been properly clarified by Vedanta teachers. A noted authority, Prof. T. M. P. Mahadevan, says, 'The knowledge of the self that is said to liberate the soul from bondage is direct knowledge which is like perceptual knowledge. Only, even perceptual knowledge is not so immediate as self-knowledge. In sense-perception there is the intervention of a sense-organ between subject and object.'[9]

Types of Mystical Experience

The word 'mystic' is said to be derived from the Greek *mystikos* which means 'of the mysteries', which in its turn is derived from the Greek word *mystos*, 'keeping silence' (akin to Sanskrit *mouna*). William

James in his celebrated work *Varieties of Religious Experience* has given the 'four marks' of the mystic state: ineffability, noetic quality, transiency, and passivity. According to Evelyn Underhill, the chief characteristics of mysticism are: practicality, transcendence, love, and a sense of oneness.

We may, however, define mysticism as the transcendent, life-transforming experience of the ultimate Reality. The word 'transcendent' in the definition distinguishes mysticism from ordinary empirical experiences; the word 'life-transforming' refers to its pragmatic import; and 'ultimate Reality' distinguishes mysticism from clairvoyance and other extra-sensory or psychic phenomena.

Three types of mysticism are usually recognized: Nature mysticism, God mysticism, and Soul mysticism. Christian mysticism has always been God mysticism. All three types are found in Hinduism. Perhaps the earliest type was nature mysticism, as shown by many hymns in the Ṛg-Veda. But this was soon completely superseded by the Soul mysticism of the Upaniṣads and God mysticism of Bhakti schools.

Mysticism is also divided into two main pathways: the path of love and divine Grace, and the path of knowledge and self effort, which are known respectively as *Bhakti-mārga* and *Jñāna-mārga* in Hinduism. Though called *mārga* or path, they are based on quite different ontological pre-suppositions regarding the nature of God and human destiny. Hinduism is the only religion in which these two paths have been recognized as two independent highways and have co-existed as such from time immemorial. Christian mysticism has developed mostly along the path of love and grace, though some elements of the path of knowledge have been integrated into it by mystics like Meister Eckhart and Ruysbrock.

Basic Doctrinal Differences

In spite of the similarities between the mystical experiences of Christian and Hindu Saints, Christian theologians have always insisted on the uniqueness of Christian spiritual experience because of the uniqueness of the Christian revelation and Incarnation. There are indeed basic doctrinal differences between the two religions.

The first difference is regarding the nature of man. In Christian theology human personality is regarded as dichotomous, consisting of only the body and the mind, the mind itself being called soul and spirit. And, according to the Pauline doctrine of Original Sin, the sin of Adam, transmitted to all humanity, has tainted the human soul so much so that man is incapable of saving himself.

All schools of Hindu philosophy hold that human personality is trichotomous, consisting of body, mind and spirit which is known as the Ātman or self. Evil tendencies, which are derived from one's own actions in previous life, taint only the mind. The real self or Ātman is ever pure and untainted by evil.

A second doctrinal difference refers to the soul's relationship with God. In the whole Judeo-Christian tradition, God is regarded as the 'wholly Other'; He is the self-existent creator whereas all other beings (including human souls) are created things. Mystical experience may bring God and the soul closer together but they can never become one because of the difference in their nature. On the contrary, in Hinduism all schools of Vedanta hold that God is the Supreme Self and that the individual selves, which are self-existent and of the same nature as God, are only reflections or parts of Him. Mystical experience is only the realization of this integral relationship between God and souls. It may also be noted here that in Hinduism whereas some sects accept God as the impersonal Absolute, other sects accept Him as personal and even anthropomorphic.

A third doctrinal difference is regarding the salvific value of mystical experience. St. Paul held that ordinary religious practices such as sacrifice and penance were incapable of wiping off the stain of Original Sin. Divine grace, won by Christ through his self-immolation on the cross, alone could remove that stain. This grace, known as 'Sanctifying Grace' (*gratia gratum faciens*), is communicated to man through baptism and other sacraments. A soul that is thus freed from Original Sin will attain salvation (that is, go to God's presence in heaven) after death. This makes mystical experience unnecessary for salvation.[10]

By contrast, in Hinduism mystical experience of the ultimate Reality is considered to be a *sine qua non* for salvation (known as *mukti* or *mokṣa*, Liberation).[11]

In the *Bhagavad-Gītā* the Lord speaks of mystic experience and liberation brought about by divine Grace.[12] But it may be stated that the doctrine of grace did not develop much in Hinduism.

Another doctrinal difference between Christian and Hindu mystical traditions is regarding the content of mystical experience. In the Judeo-Christian tradition it is a widely accepted belief that the real *Essence* of God can never be seen by any living person. In the Old Testament God tells Moses, 'Thou canst not see My Face, for man shall not see Me and live.'[13] To see God's Essence, to see Him as He really is, to see Him face to face (*facie ad faciem*) is possible only in heaven after death. Some Catholic theologians hold that there are two exceptions to this rule, Moses and St. Paul who were granted a vision of the real Essence of God, the *lumen gloriae* or 'Beatific Vision'.[14] All the others, even the greatest mystics, could get only a distant or indirect vision of God. Theologians of Greek Orthodox church also hold that God's Essence *(ouisia)* can never be perceived, and according to them, what mystics see through visions is only the *Energeia* (*enereia)* of God.

By contrast, from very ancient times Hindu sages and philosophers have held that God's actual Essence can be directly experienced. In *Bhakti* schools God is regarded as having not only personal attributes but also a transcendent anthropomorphic form which is real and can be directly perceived. In the *Gītā* it is repeatedly asserted that through *Bhakti* it is possible to know and perceive the true essence of God and attain oneness with it.[15] Even Advaita Vedantins, who deny that the impersonal Absolute known as Brahman can be made the object of knowledge, assert that the attainment of the total identity of the individual Self with Brahman is possible in this very life.

The Mystic Path in the Roman Catholic Tradition

There are two main mystical traditions in Christianity: the Western or Roman Catholic and the Eastern, chiefly Greek Orthodox. We shall study the former first.

Catholic mysticism is centred on prayer. 'Prayer', as used in mystical life, is a blanket term which covers a variety of mental exercises expressing the soul's dependence on and quest for God. It is often called 'Mental prayer' to distinguish it from worldly prayers. In the Middle Ages prayer was regarded as consisting of three stages: *meditatio, oratio,* and *contemplatio.*[16]

Reflection on scriptural passages was what *meditatio* or meditation meant (Christian meditation may be said to correspond to *śravaṇa* and *manana* in Hinduism). By *oratio* was meant intense emotional prayer, nowadays called Affective Prayer. (This may be said to correspond to Hindu *prārthanā*). These two disciplines[17] when sincerely practised were found to lead to an intimate knowledge, *gnosis,* of God which was what *contemplatio* or contemplation really meant. Unlike Meditation (also known as 'Discursive Prayer') and Affective Prayer which are within the reach of man's self-effort, Contemplation is a passive state of stillness and silence in which God infuses love and divine knowledge into the soul. This infused contemplation may be said to correspond to Hindu *samādhi.* As in the case of *samādhi,* mystical contemplation also has different stages or degrees, although the terms used to denote these stages are often metaphorical and vague.[18] Contemplation is the real field of mystical experience.

The conceptualization of mystical experience in Christianity went on for centuries. Among the influences that shaped this process the most important was that of Neoplatonism propounded by the 3rd century Greek mystic and philosopher Plotinus. Two fairly distinct phases are discernible in the development of mysticism in the West. During the first phase which extended from the third to the tenth century, Image mysticism prevailed; during the second phase, which extended from the tenth to the seventeenth century, mysticism became more and more Christo-centric.

Image mysticism had its origin in the Biblical creation myth that God created man in His Image. This ancient Jewish idea combined with the Neoplatonic concept of the immanence of God gave rise to the belief that the soul in its pristine nature contained the Image of God, and that owing to the stain of sin this image cannot be seen. Through purificatio[n] and contemplation the Image of God within can be recovered. Some o[f] the early mystics identified this Image with the Word, the Logos, who incarnated itself on earth as Jesus Christ. Others like Gregory the Great identified it with the 'Unencompassed Light' (*incircumscriptum lumen*) of God.[19]

This more impersonal and intellectual Image mysticism gave way to an intensely emotional and personal 'bridal mysticism' in the tenth century. The person who brought about this paradigm shift in mystical life was St. Bernard, the celebrated abbot of the Cistercian monastery at Clairvaux in France. He made the image of the crucified Christ the object of contemplation. He looked upon Christ as the Bridegroom and the human soul as the bride. However, Bernard took the precaution of identifying Christ with the Word of Logos and the human soul with the collective soul of the Church. This precaution was ignored in the subsequent centuries, and most Western mystics after the tenth century made the humanity of Jesus the object of their love and quest.

Cataphatic and Apophatic Path-ways

Almost running parallel to the distinction between Image mysticism and Christo-centric mysticism was another important distinction between two approaches to knowledge of God; the path of affirmation and the path of negation, known respectively as *via positiva* and *via negativa* and also as cataphatic and apophatic pathways. In the cataphatic path the mystic sees the fullness of God everywhere. The best example is St. Francis of Assisi who saw the glory of God in all beings—in the sun, in animals and plants. For such a mystic all created things serve as a rung in the ladder of ascent to God. In the *via negativa* or apophatic pathway all created things are rejected as insufficient or impermanent and even all thoughts and images are negated in order to realize the transcendent glory and fullness of God.

Like the idea of the Image, apophatic mysticism also had its origin in Neoplatonism. It entered the Western Church through the writings of a fifth century Syrian monk known to scholars as Pseudo-dionysius. Though the work was translated into Latin in the ninth century, its influence became widespread only in the twelfth century. St. Thomas Aquinas gave apophatism an epistemological foundation. Blessed John Ruysbrock,

Meister Eckhart and St. John of the Cross were some of the great mystics of the Middle Ages who were influenced by the Dionysian apophatism.

The apophatic principle is frequently conveyed through the Biblical story of Moses going up Mount Sinai to receive the Ten Commandments. At the heights he was lost in a cloud, and it was through the cloud that Moses saw God face to face. In the same way, the mystics say, God can be realized only through a Cloud of Unknowing—a state of mind in which it is free from all forms of cognition, thinking, imagination, conceptualization, etc. As far as worldly objects and knowledge are concerned, it is a state of total ignorance. It is described as 'darkness' only in comparison with the 'super-luminous light of God'. To quote a passage from Dionysius's famous work which was cited throughout the Middle Ages as the *locus classicus* for the method of contemplation :

> In the earnest practice of mystic contemplation, you have to leave the senses and the activities of the intellect and all things in this world of nothingness or in that world of Being, and with your understanding laid to rest you should strain as much as you can towards union with Him whom neither being nor understanding can contain. For by the unceasing and absolute renunciation of yourself and all things... you shall be led upwards to the ray of that Divine Darkness which transcends all existence.[20]

Dionysian apophatism reached its culmination in Meister Eckhart who spoke of the 'desert of the godhead' and in St. John of the Cross who wrote about the 'Dark Night of the Soul'. Although apophatic (*via negativa*) mysticism dominated spiritual life in the West, cataphatic (*via positiva*) mysticism was also quite popular especially with women saints.

Types of Spiritual Experience

The Roman Catholic Church has produced a large number of saints many of whom have left vivid descriptions of their spiritual experiences. Not all these experiences, however, can be called 'mystical'. According to St. Thomas Aquinas, the most authoritative Roman Catholic theologian after St. Augustine, God can communicate spiritual truth to man in three ways : (a) by a 'corporeal vision' of something real together with an intellectual light to judge it; (b) by an 'imaginary vision' in which mental images are either produced or rearranged in the imagination, along with an intellectual light to judge its meaning (These 'visions' and 'locutions' are difficult to distinguish from false imaginations produced either by one's own brain or by the devil.); (c) by an 'intellectual vision' of pure, unfalsifiable truth without any phantasmata; known as *lumen sapientiae,* this is the knowledge which angels have (and also Adam had before the Fall) and is not in itself liable to error. This true knowledge is infused during contemplation devoid of all conceptualization. It was this apophatic experience of divine truth that St. Thomas regarded as true mysticism.[21]

However, even this intellectual vision (*lumen sapientiae*) is far lower than the direct experience of the Essence of God which takes place in heaven when God is seen as He really is without any medium.This vision known as *lumen gloriae* or '*Beatific Vision*' is possible only after death for the blessed. This is the ultimate end of human life which Christ has won for mankind through his self-sacrifice. St. Thomas, however, held that this Beatific Vision of glory was granted to Moses and also perhaps to St. Paul while they were still on earth.[22]

Since our main approach to mysticism in this paper is epistemological, we now pass on to a brief study of the epistemological presuppositions of Roman Catholic mysticism. The foundation of the epistemology of Catholic mysticism was laid by St. Thomas Aquinas. Later writers did little to add to this, and what great mystics like St. John of the Cross did was to build the superstructure of their experiences upon this foundation.

Thomistic Epistemology of Mysticism

The epistemology of St. Thomas Aquinas was derived from Aristotelean psychology. From this psychology he took two main ideas: (a) all knowledge is the result of an impression made on the mind; (b) the intellect has two dimensions : a passive one and an active one. The central idea of the scholastic theory of cognition is that, just as our senses perceive objects by means of an impression on the sense-organ, which impression is not itself perceived but is the 'medium by which' we perceive the objects, so also our intellect knows by means of impressions which are the 'medium by which' it knows ideas.

Thus there are two kinds of impressions or *species impressae.* Sense impressions are called *species sensibilis impressae*; the resulting conscious precept is known as *species expressae.* Intellectual knowledge stems from the phantasms (mental images of objects) out of which the 'active intellect' disengages the universal nature which, as *species intelligibilis impressae*, inform the 'passive intellect' and there become concepts known as *species expressae* or *verbum mentis.*

(i) *Ordinary human knowledge* : Ordinary people can know God only indirectly. In his major work *Summa Theologica* St. Thomas explains how this happens. In man's present state the only *species impressae* that he receives are conveyed to the mind through the senses; they are but attributes of material objects 'abstracted' (that is, considered apart) from the objects. Hence by means of these impressions the mind (a) directly knows abstract qualities which exist individually in material objects. Further, (b) our intellect knows the individual things themselves indirectly by their qualities and (c) it can arrive at some kind of knowledge of non-material things by reasoning from its abstract ideas. Thus it cannot know God directly, but can demonstrate His existence and His nature from creatures by abstraction and negation.

But the intellectual ideas thus formed in the mind are not really understood by the mind unless it represents them by the imagination; it 'turns to images' (*phantasmata*) so that it may behold the universal in the particular, wherein alone it has real existence. We can represent to ourselves spiritual truths and spiritual substances (God, angels and souls) only by *phantasmata* (images) which we know to be inadequate, yet in which we behold something more than the *phantasma.*

(ii) *Angelic Knowledge* : An angel or a disembodied soul is an intelligence independent of bodily organs; it understands spiritual things as they are, without 'turning to *phantasmata*'. Since it has no bodily sense-organs, it cannot get impressions by the senses. Therefore its impressions (*species impressae*) must be 'infused' in some way natural to it, but unknown to us. These species will not be abstractions from matter, but purely non-material. Furthermore, such pure intellects instead of knowing the universal in the particular, know the particular in the universal in one glance; they do not argue from fact to fact, from premiss to conclusion, but in one act know the conclusion and the premisses in it. Thus the angelic cognition resembles the intuitive perceptions of sense rather than the analytic and synthetic process of reason. Its knowledge is direct, immediate, intuitive, in comparison with the abstracting and reasoning mind of ordinary people. In this way it is possible for angels to know God intuitively instead of by reasoning.

(iii) *Mystic knowledge* : The main thesis of St. Thomas Aquinas is that it is this angelic knowledge of God that is attained in apophatic contemplation by the infusion of pure intellectual species. When the soul is freed from all desires and images, God infuses knowledge in Himself through pure intellectual species into the soul, resulting in *lumen sapientiae* or 'intellectual vision'. This angelic intuition is utter 'darkness' to the intellect itself but it inflames the will with intense love. This pure contemplation was termed 'Dark Night of Spirit' by St. John of the Cross. The mystic or prophet can understand and communicate the truth which he has thus received only by 'turning to *phantasmata*'.

St. Thomas held that Adam in his state of innocence (before the fall) could see God in this angelic fashion by pure species. In other words, pure apophatic contemplation restores to man the state of Adam before his fall. The only difference is, Adam's infused knowledge was 'from the irradiation of divine Wisdom', whereas we get it by divine Grace ('sanctifying grace') infused at baptism. (It is regarded as one of the seven 'gifts of the Holy Ghost'). This view of higher mystical experience had earlier been propounded by St. Bernard and Richard of St. Victor; but St. Thomas gave it a proper epistemological foundation.

St. Thomas also held that God may infuse images also along with intellectual species; then an 'imaginary vision' described earlier results. This is the realm of prophecy. Images and words, however, can express pure truth only in an inadequate and symbolic way, and spiritual images often get mixed with worldly images and concepts. Hence such visions and locutions are liable to error except in so far as the 'intellectual light' helps the prophet to understand them.

Finally, according to St. Thomas, all mystic experiences, including the highest *lumen sapientiae*, fall far short of the 'Beatific Vision' of God in heaven which is possible only after death. In this vision God is seen 'as He is' by means of Himself, He Himself being united immediately to the human intellect so that He is both the thing seen and the 'means by which' it is seen. This divine impression is called *lumen gloriae*. Thus the blessed 'participate' in their measure in the act in which God knows Himself without medium, and are united to Him as Act (God is *actus purus*, 'pure Act') without losing their own individuality; they are transformed into God without ceasing to be themselves. This participation in divine Glory is the ultimate goal of all mankind.[23] Catholic theology holds that Jesus Christ's salvific work will be completed only when all human beings are elevated to this state and thereby the Divine *Pleroma*, (fullness) is restored.

Mysticism in the Greek Orthodox Tradition[24]

Apart from the differences in dogma, the Greek Orthodox Church differs from the Roman Catholic Church in the greater emphasis it lays on mystical and ascetic life. Whereas in the Catholic Church spiritual life is mostly liturgical, in the Eastern Churches individual prayer and contemplation constitute the main part. In Eastern Churches mystical experience is considered to be the natural culmination of Christian spiritual life. They possess a rich mystical literature in the form of the collection of the teachings of contemplatives and ascetics who lived as hermits in the desert regions of Egypt, Sinai, and Syria. Orthodox mystical theology was developed mainly by three theologians who lived in Cappadocia in the 4th century : St. Basil, his friend St. Gregory of Nazianzus (also known as Gregory the Theologian) and St. Gregory of Nyssa (who was Basil's brother).

One of the important points in the theology of the Cappadocian Fathers is the clear distinction they made between God's Essence (*ouisia*) and Energies (*energeia*). According to St. Basil, man cannot know even the real substance of the physical world; we can perceive only the properties of matter, not matter itself. Still less can we see of the actual Essence of God; what we can perceive is only the Energies of God.[25]

In mystical contemplation these divine energies become manifested as the 'uncreated Light'. This Light is identified with the light that appeared on Mount Tabor during Christ's Transfiguration.[26] The vision of this uncreated light is the goal of contemplation known as *theoria*.

For the attainment of the uncreated Light a distinctive spiritual technique known as Hesychasm was developed by the Desert Fathers in the 4th and 5th centuries in the desert regions of the Middle East[27] by combining (a) austerities, (b) apophatic prayer without images and (c) repetition of the Jesus Prayer which may be regarded as a kind of Greek Mantra. To this was added in the 11th century a certain body posture and breath control. All these, however, represent only the first stage of *hesychasm* known as 'praxis'.

As this prayer deepens, it becomes *theoria* or contemplation and the seeker sees the uncreated Light. Greek saints have given vivid descriptions of this interior mystic Light such as, 'far surpassing in brilliance the whole light of the heavens' 'a truly divine fire, uncreated and invisible, eternal and immaterial, perfectly steadfast and infinite, inextinguishable and immortal, incomprehensible, beyond all created being.'[28] The vision of the uncreated Light is one of the most distinguishing features of Greek mysticism.

However, it is not the last stage of contemplation. Beyond that lies the union (*henosis*) of the soul with God and the resulting divinization (*theosis*) of the whole personality. Surprisingly, this union takes place not in light but in darkness. Gregory of Nyssa who developed this idea of union in darkness compares it to Moses entering the cloud.[29] Gregory's apophatic mysticism was carried further by Simeon the New Theologian in the 11th century and by Gregory Palamas in the 14th century, but it never assumed the extreme form found in the Catholic mystics such as Eckhart and St. John of the Cross.

Mystic union is not the union of substances but of energies. It results in *theosis* or deification of the whole personality. This is the ultimate goal of human life on earth. The idea of deification is far more common in Greek mysticism than in Catholic mysticism. Thus, Purification, *theoria* and *theosis* constitute the three stages of the Greek mystical path known as *Hesychasm*. These stages do not exactly correspond to the three stages of contemplation in Catholicism, namely, Purgation, Illumination and Union.

How does mystical experience take place? We have seen that in Roman Catholicism, mystical experience is understood in terms of certain mental processes. But in Greek mysticism mystical experience is regarded as the function of certain faculties. Just as physical eyes are needed to perceive external objects, so also an inner spiritual sense is needed to perceive the energies of God.[30] This spiritual sense, regarded as the 'eye of the soul', is the *nous*. Unfortunately, the word '*nous*' is used in different senses in the teachings of Greek mystics. We may, however, take it to mean the intuitive faculty. It is different from reason and is said to be located in the heart. Owing to Original Sin, the *nous* remains stained or clouded. When it is purified by divine grace during contemplation, it becomes fit to receive the reflection of Divine Light. The *nous* then becomes as clear as a mirror. Describing this process, St. Gregory of Nyssa says :

> Just as those who look at the sun in a mirror (even though they cannot gaze at the sky itself) see the sun in the shining of the mirror no less than those who look at the solar disc itself; so too if you have been dazzled by the light (of God), in so far as you recover the grace of the image deposited in you at the beginning, you possess what you seek within you.[31]

Image mysticism (that man carries the image of God in his soul) which we encountered in the Catholic tradition finds clear expression in the Greek tradition all through its history.

Basic Epistemological Differences

Some of the major doctrinal differences between Christianity and Hinduism were mentioned at the beginning of this paper. Here we would like to mention two main epistemological differences between the mystical traditions of the two religions.

(1) The apophatic (*via negativa*) and cataphatic (*via positiva*) paths of Christian mysticism have their counterparts in the *neti, neti* ('not this,

not this') paths of Vedanta. But there are basic differences between them. In Christian theology God is a personal Being endowed with many divine attributes, only his essential nature cannot be perceived by ordinary mortals. What Christian apophatism does is to deny the ability of discursive thinking and the rational mind to perceive the real transcendent nature of God. In other words, Christian apophatism is mainly epistemological.

In Hinduism, according to the Advaita school of Vedanta, the ultimate Reality known as Brahman is *nirguṇa*, the impersonal Absolute devoid of all attributes. And what the apophatic process of *neti, neti*[32] does is to negate all qualities attributed to Brahman owing to ignorance. In other words, Vedantic apophatism is mainly ontological.

Furthermore, Vedantic apophatism, which originated in the Upaniṣads, belongs to *Jñāna mārga,* the Path of knowledge followed by Advaitins. The Bhakti schools of Vedanta follow only the cataphatic, *iti, iti,*[33] approach. In *Bhakti-mārga* images, concepts and visualization are freely employed either as pointers to the transcendent Reality or as agents for the transformation of consciousness. But in Christian mysticism the apophatic technique is applied in the path of love itself. This is what gives to Christian mysticism its uniqueness.

There is, however, another pair of concepts, *Asamprajñāta Yoga* and *Samprajñāta-Yoga* in Patañjali's *Yoga-Sūtras,* which bear a striking resemblance to the apophatic and cataphatic paths of Christian mysticism. A comparative study of *Asamprajñāta Yoga* and Christian apophatism, although these are based on different presuppositions, may lead to some new understanding of mysticism.

(2) The second difference is with regard to cognition. The basic assumption in Thomistic epistemology based on Aristotelean psychology is that knowledge comes from outside, that is to say, the basic cognitive act is a movement from the outer world to the inner world. First comes an impulse from outside in the form of a *species impressae*, which changes into *species expressae* within. This applies to God vision also. God is seen only when He impresses Himself upon the soul in a direct or indirect manner.

The basic assumption in Hindu psychology is that the source of all knowledge is within, in the Ātman, and the basic cognitive act is a movement from the inner to the outer. God vision is the culmination of an intentional act originating in the human soul, although divine grace may facilitate this process by removing the ignorance covering the soul.

Two Means to Mystic Experience in Hinduism

We have seen that in the Greek Orthodox tradition mystic vision is regarded as the function of a spiritual sense or a faculty of the soul, whereas the Catholic tradition explains it in terms of certain mental processes. A similar difference in approach may be seen in Hindu mysticism also.

In the Vedas we find the awakening or purification of a higher faculty mentioned as the means to mystic experience. In the earlier parts of the Vedas this higher spiritual faculty or intuition is named *dhī* and *medhā*. The famous *Gāyatrī Mantra* is a prayer for the awakening of the *dhī*. In the Upaniṣads that higher faculty is often referred to as *buddhi*. The *Kaṭha Upaniṣad* states, 'This Ātman is seen through a subtle, one-pointed Buddhi'; the *Muṇḍaka* says, '(The luminous inner Self) is seen when the mind is purified and knowledge becomes clear.'[34]

In the *Gītā* also we find this idea of a higher faculty. In the eleventh chapter Kṛṣṇa tells Arjuna that he would give him a 'divine eye' to see the transcendental 'Cosmic Form' and the Divine Mystery.

In later Hinduism this 'faculty psychology' gave way to a more dynamic psychology, and the mental processes involved in perception were formulated in the form of theories of perception. Though these theories mostly refer to empirical experience, a study of these theories is necessary to understand the epistemology of Hindu mysticism.

Theories of Perception in Hinduism

Epistemology underwent a high degree of development in India, and almost every school of Hindu philosophy has its own theory of perception. These different theories may, however, be brought under three main groups.

Before discussing these theories it is necessary to note the important role that the Ātman or Self plays in perception. A unique characteristic of Hindu thought, shared by all schools of Hindu philosophy, is the recognition of the true Self or Ātman as the ultimate source of consciousness and an autonomous entity distinct from the mind. Each theory of perception has a different concept of the Self.

(i) *Sense contact theory* developed by Nyāya-Vaiśeṣika and Prabhākara-Mīmāṃsā schools. This theory states that the chief cause of perception is the contact of the sense organs with their objects.[35] According to the Vaiśeṣika school, Ātman is one of the nine ultimate substances, and knowledge exists in it as a *guṇa* or attribute. The contact of the sense-organ with the mind makes the Ātman manifest the knowledge. The actual cognitive process is an intentional movement from the Ātman to the mind to the senses to the object.

(ii) *Vṛtti or mental modification theories.* These theories hold that the chief cause of perception is the modification (*vṛtti*) that the mind undergoes when it comes into contact with an object (through the sense-organs). And according to this view, the Ātman (also known as *Puruṣa*) is of the nature of pure consciousness (*cit*); in fact, it is the only source of consciousness, everything else being unconscious (*jaḍa*). The view has three versions.

The first version is that of Sāṁkhya-Yoga. According to this view, the mind (known as *citta*) goes out through the sense-organs and takes the form of the object; upon the modification of the mind (called *vṛtti*) thus produced, the light of *Puruṣa* falls revealing the nature of the object.[36]

The second version is that of Advaita Vedānta. It accepts the first version but adds that the mind (*antaḥkaraṇa*) does not merely go out and take the form of the object; its primary function is to remove the ignorance (*ajñāna*) covering the object. According to Advaita, everything is Brahman, and the appearance of subject and object as different entities is due to ignorance. *Antaḥkaraṇa* overcomes this ignorance and establishes the unity of consciousness underlying the subject and the object. This Advaitic view itself has three interpretations which cannot be discussed in a brief survey such as this one.[37]

Quite a different version is provided by Rāmānuja and Madhva.

According to them, the Ātman directly perceives objects. The *antaḥkaraṇa* only serves to classify and identify the objects. Rāmānuja holds that the Ātman has two kinds of knowledge : *svarūpa-jñāna* by which it knows itself, and *dharma-bhūta-jñāna* which reveals objects. This view occupies a position in between the Nyāya-Vaiśeṣika theory and the Sāṁkhya-Yoga theory.

(iii) *Recognition* (*pratyabhijñā*) *theory*. This theory was propounded by Kashmir Śaivism and some schools of Tantra. It holds that all knowledge is a recognition or recollection of something known earlier. When we see a known person after several years we say, 'This is that person'. Furthermore, according to this school, consciousness has not only the power (known as *prakāśa*) to reveal objects but also the power (known as *vimarśa*) to reveal itself. This view is linked to the ontological view that mind and matter are only different states of vibration of consciousness. The dynamic aspect of consciousness is called *Śakti* and the static aspect, *Śiva*. The evolution of the universe takes place in the form of a series of emanations of the ultimate Reality which is of the nature of Pure Consciousness. The individual self is only an aspect of the ultimate Reality in a dormant form. The whole system of thought has some resemblance to the Neoplatonism of the Greek pagan philosopher Plotinus.

Epistemological Bases of Hindu Mysticism

The theories of perception mentioned here are applicable only to experiences of the empirical world. How then can supersensuous, direct experience of God or ultimate Reality be obtained? Surprisingly, not much information is available in the various texts and commentaries of Hindu spiritual teachers. Whatever is available may be briefly stated as follows.

(1) The Nyāya-Vaiśeṣika school accepts the possibility of supernormal experience known as *Yogi-pratyakṣa* but does not explain the mental processes involved in it.

(2) According to Patañjali's Yoga, all experiences from those of external objects to the highest knowledge known as *Viveka-khyāti*

(knowledge of the distinction between *Prakṛti* and *Puruṣa*) take place only through *vṛttis.* When the mind is sufficiently purified a superior kind of awareness rises in it known as *ṛtambhara-prajñā* which reveals supersensuous truths. The resulting transcendental state of mind is known as *samprajñāta-yoga.* Patañjali, however, holds that the final liberation takes place only in an apophatic state devoid of all *vṛttis,* (hence of all experience) known as *asamprajñāta yoga.*

(3) Advaitins, as we have seen, accept the theory of *vṛttis* but according to them, the function of *vṛttis* is only to remove the *ajñāna* or ignorance covering objects. Since Brahman is infinite, the *ajñāna* covering it (known as *kāraṇa-ajñāna* or *mūla-ajñāna*) can be removed only by a *vṛtti* which can take an infinite dimension; it is known as *akhaṇḍākāra-vṛtti.* When *ajñāna* is removed, Brahman reveals Itself. How this takes place is a matter of controversy, although all are agreed upon purification of mind as a precondition. According to the Vārtika and Vivaraṇa schools, knowledge of Brahman arises in a purified mind by the mere hearing of the sacred statements of the Upaniṣads about the unity of *Jīva* and Brahman. (How exactly sound symbols produce this superior knowledge is not properly explained.) According to the Bhāmatī school, knowledge of Brahman arises by the combined effect of hearing sacred texts, reflection, and a higher type of contemplation known as *nididhyāsana.*

(4) The Bhakti schools frequently speak of visions of the anthropomorphic forms of the Supreme Deity but do not explain clearly the mental processes which produce such experiences. It is, however, usually assumed that such experiences are produced by higher refined *vṛttis* in the mind which are roused by Divine Grace.

Rāmānuja accepts the validity of *Yogi-pratyakṣa,* the direct intuition of Yogis. But his own explanation of God experience is different. According to him, higher spiritual experience takes place by the expansion of the *dharmabhūta-jñāna* inherent in the Ātman. The expansion is facilitated by purification and Divine Grace.

(5) It is only in the system of religious philosophy known as the Tantras that we find an elaborate treatment of the psychology of mystical experience. The Tantras provide an entirely different psychological-epistemological paradigm which is so complex that it cannot be dealt

with here. We would, however, like to mention that it is the only system which attempts to provide a cogent explanation of the way sound symbols affect the mind and give rise to higher spiritual experiences.

Since Hindu mysticism is a vast subject, and is also more widely known, our treatment of it here is brief. Our main attempt in this paper has been to focus attention on Christian mysticism and compare it with the mystical traditions of Hinduism. In these days of dialogue it is hoped this kind of study at a deeper level of religious life will help to foster greater inter-religious understanding.

Notes and References

1. The most widely known of these is Evelyn Underhill's *Mysticism,* an interpretation and syncretic work. A more authentic presentation is Dom Cuthbert Butler's *Western Mysticism.* Some of the other books are translations from French or Spanish. Among these mention should be made of P. Pourrat's *Christian Spirituality* in three volumes, A. Poulain's *Graces of Interior Prayer,* Pere Garrigou-Lagrange's *Christian Perfection and Contemplation,* L. Saudreau's *The life of Union with God,* J. Marechal's *Studies in the Psychology of the Mystics* and L. de Besse's, *The Science of Prayer.*

2. Rudolph Otto's somewhat prejudiced work, *Mysticism East and West* and Jacques de Marquett's *Introduction to Comparative Mysticism* may be mentioned here.

3. *The Complete Works of Swami Vivekananda* (Calcutta : Advaita Ashrama, 1973), Vol. 6, p. 81.

4. Rudolph Otto, *Mysticism East and West* (New York : Collier Books, 1962), p. 13.

5. See, W. T. Stace, *Mysticism and Philosophy.*

6. This is only partly true, for, according to the Vārtika and Vivaraṇa schools of Advaita Vedanta, certain Upaniṣadic statements such as 'That thou art' can produce direct intuitive knowledge.

7. See, *Vedānta-Paribhāṣā,* 8, first line.

8. cf. Swami Satprakashananda, *Methods of Knowledge* (Calcutta: Advaita Ashrama, 1974), p.18. Śaṅkara also says in his commentary on Brahma-sūtra 1.1.2, 'Because it ends in direct experience' (*Anubhava-avasānatvāt*).

9. ibid., p. 15.

10. All Christian theologians are agreed on the view that mystical experience of God is not a direct means to salvation and can at best serve only as an indirect means, as an aid to the attainment of greater holiness, faith etc. Most Protestant theologians find no use for mystical experience. Among Catholic theologians there were, until the Second Vatican Council, two groups. One group held that mystical contemplation was possible for all; it should be the natural culmination of Sanctifying Grace. The other group held that mystical contemplation was meant only for certain rare souls who are endowed with the extraordinary grace known as *gratia gratis data.* On this issue see Pere A. Poulain S. J., *The Graces of Interior Prayer* (St. Louis : B. Herder Book Co., 1957), pp. lxvii ff.

11. cf. *ṛte jñānāt na muktiḥ.*

12. *Gītā,* 11.8; 12.7; 9.31; 18.66.

13. Exodus xxxiii.20.

14. For a discussion on this see Dom Cuthbert Butler, *Western Mysticism* (London: Arrow Books, 1960), pp.50-4.

15. *Gītā,* 11.54; 18.55.

16. For a brief account of these three stages from the historical standpoint see, Paul Philippe in *Mental Prayer and Modern Life* (New York: P. J. Kennedy and Sons, 1950).

17. According to some authors, after Affective Prayer, and before Passive Contemplation begins, there is an intermediate stage known by different names such as

'Prayer of Simplicity', 'Prayer of Faith', 'Prayer of the Heart' and 'Acquired Contemplation'. See, *Graces of Interior Prayer,* op.cit.pp.8 ff.

18. St. Teresa, for instance, speaks of four stages of contemplation: Prayer of Quiet, Prayer of Union (Betrothal), Ecstatic Union and Deifying Union (or Spiritual Marriage).

19. For a detailed discussion of Image Mysticism see Louis Dupre, 'Mysticism' in *The Encyclopaedia of Religion*, Ed. Mircea Eliade (New York : Mac Millan, 1987). It may be seen that the idea of the image of God in the soul, shorn of the mythical trappings, comes close to the Vedantic concept of the Ātman.

20. *Mystical Theology* I, trs. C. E. Rolt (London : Spek, 1977), pp. 191-92 (slightly modified).

21. *Summa Theologica,* II. ii. qucl xxi.

22. St. Paul himself has stated, 'For now we see through a glass, darkly; but then face to face : now I know in part; but then shall I know even as also I am known.' (I Corinthians 13 : 12). On this point see Dom Cuthbert Butler, *op. cit,* pp. 52-5; 148 ff.

23. The above account of St. Thomas's epistemology is based chiefly on Dom J. Chapman's article on 'Mysticism' in *Hasting's Encyclopaedia of Religion and Ethics* I Edn. Some Catholic authors have questioned the validity of this interpretation.

24. The Russian Orthodox tradition is also almost the same as this one.

25. See, Vladimir Lossky, *The Vision of God* (New York : St. Vladimir's Seminary Press, 1983), pp.77-8.

26. Matthew. 17.

27. Hesychasm is derived from the Greek *hesychia* which means 'tranquility' and corresponds to *quies* in Latin. The collection of the teachings of the Greek orthodox saints and ascetics from the 4th to the 14th century, known as *Philokalia* has been made popular in recent years by the Russian classic *The Way of a Pilgrim.*

28. *Vladimir Lossky,* op. cit., pp. 74, 145.

29. ibid., This idea of darkness following light has its parallel in the *Īśāvāsya Upaniṣad* in which the seeker prays to the Sun to withdraw its dazzling rays.

30. This idea of a 'spiritual sense-organ' was originally propounded by the great theologian and mystic Origen, who was later condemned as a heretic. St. Thomas Aquinas rejected this idea.

31. Vladimir Lossky, op. cit., p. 86.

32. The full formula is : *na idaṁ brahma iti* ('That this is not Brahman'). The first particle *na* and the last particle *iti* when combined give rise to *neti.*

33. *iti* is the last particle in the formula *idaṁ brahma iti* ('That this is Brahman').

34. *Kaṭha Upaniṣad* 3.12; *Muṇḍaka Upaniṣad* 3.1.8.

35. *Indriyārtha-sannikarṣa-janyaṁ jñānaṁ pratyakṣam* (*Tarkasaṁgraha* 4.31)

36. One of the oldest and most authoritative works on Sāṁkhya is Īśvara Kṛṣṇa's *Sāṁkhya-Kārikā.* This book gives only a cryptic definition of perception. Nor does Patañjali's *Yoga-sūtra* give anything better. It is Vyāsa's Commentary on *Yoga-sūtra* 1.7 that gives a clear account of how perception takes place.

37. The three interpretations are: *abhedābhivyakti, ciduparāga,* and *āvaraṇabhṅga.* For a lucid account of these three views, see D. M. Datta, *The Six Ways of Knowing* (Calcutta : University of Calcutta, 1972).

Rāmānuja's Concept of Knowledge

PANDIT DINESH CHANDRA BHATTACHARYA SHASTRI

Pandit Dinesh Chandra Bhattacharya Shastri, Tarkatirtha, Vedantatirtha, is Professor of Higher Studies and Research, Ramakrishna Mission Institute of Culture, Calcutta; Acharya, Probationers' Training Centre, Ramakrishna Math, Belur, W. B.; formerly U.G.C. Professor, Calcutta University; lecturer, Jadavpur and Calcutta Universities; Extra-mural lecturer, College of (Post Graduate) Medicine, Calcutta University; Adhyapaka, Institute of Higher Sanskrit learning and Research, Asiatic Society; Shastra-Chudamani Scholar, Govt. of India (1989-90); Rabindra Memorial Prize, W. B. Govt., 1974; Hanuman Prize, Sahitya Anusandhan Samsthan, Varanasi, 1976. Author of 12 books, 7 of which have been published by the West Bengal Government.

All the realistic schools of Indian philosophy reasonably define knowledge as revelation of some object—*Arthaprakāśo jñānam.* Rāmānuja also considers our ordinary knowledge as illumination of some object to a knowing soul, '*Svasattaiva svāśrayaṁ prati kasyacit viṣayasya prakāśanaṁ hi saṁvedanam.*'[1] Accordingly Rāmānuja defines *pramā* or valid cognition as such revelation of objects which leads to the usage of things as they actually are, '*Yathāvasthita-vastuvyavahārānuguṇaṁ jñānaṁ pramā.*'[2] He states again that *jñāna* or cognition is an attribute of the soul whose essential nature also is *svaprakāśa cit* or *jñāna*. Cognition (or jñāna) revealing objects are also *svaprakāśajñāna* in the sense that while revealing objects they are also revealed to its locus—the soul, without the help of any other knowledge such as *anuvyavasāya,* as the Tārkika holds.[3]

Śrīnivāsa, the author of the *Yatīndramata-dīpikā* clarifies this statement saying 'Attributive knowledge is a *svaprakāśa insentient* substance revealing some object.' Like light *prabhāvat* is both a substance (*dravya*) and an attribute (*guṇa*). It is also defined as— '*Arthaprakāśo buddhiḥ.*'[4] Cognition is the revelation of some object.

Thus we see that according to Rāmānuja knowledge is of two kinds, (1) *Dharmībhūtajñāna* or substantive knowledge which is the essential nature of both *jīva* and *Īśvara.* While *Īśvara* is *bibhu-cit*—all-pervading consciousness, *jīva* is *aṇu-cit* (atomic consciousness). But the knowledge of *jīva* pervades the whole body like the light of a lamp (*pradīpa-prabhābat*). *Īśvara* and *jīva* both are *svaprakāśa* because they are *cid-rūpa*—of the nature of consciousness.

(2) The other kind of knowledge is *dharmabhūtajñāna* or attributive knowledge which belongs to both *Īśvara* and *jīva. Īśvara* is omniscient by his all-pervading *dharmabhūta jñāna,* while *jīva* is not so, because its *dharmabhūtajñāna* becomes limited and contracted by its *karma.* Liberated souls possess omniscience like the Godhead, through their all-pervading nature of the attributive knowledge.

This knowledge or *dharmabhūtajñāna* is also *svaprakāśa* in the sense that at the time of revealing its object the knowledge is also revealed to its locus—the soul, without the help of any other cognition. It does not require any other cognition like *anuvyavasāya* as is held by the Tārkikas.

Not only is cognition thus self-revealing, but all other attributes like pleasure, pain, etc. are also revealed to the soul whenever they originate, because those attributes are but different modes or forms of cognition ('*dhī viśeṣāḥ prakīrtitāḥ*').[5]

This cognition or *dharmabhūtajñāna* is actually the subject matter of our discussion, since this is really Rāmānuja's concept of knowledge proper, which reveals objects. Rāmānuja defines *dharmabhūtajñāna* as *svayaṁprakāśacetana-dravyatve sati viṣayitvam.*[6] Being *viṣayī* it reveals some object. But in the case of Ātman, though it is *svaprakāśa,* being *cidrūpa* or *jñāna* which is illumination itself, it is the meaning of the word '*aham*'. It does not reveal any object as cognition does. Rāmānuja presents a peculiar inference—'*Ātman* is *svaprakāśa*' because it is *jñāna,* just like *dharmabhūtajñāna.*[7] Thus it is evident that according to Rāmānuja *dharmibhūtajñāna* (soul) is *svayaṁ-prakāśa* because it is *cidrūpa* (illumination itself), and *dharmabhūtajñāna* is *svayaṁprakāśa* because it is revealed to its locus-soul only by its existence and not by any other knowledge. Rāmānuja's concept of indeterminate and determinate perception is also very peculiar. The first perception of one member of a class is indeterminate because it does not produce *anugatipratyaya* or the class concept, while the perception of a second member of the class and the subsequent perception are determinate since they produce the idea that there are other such individuals and thus produce the class concept.

With regard to the origination of validity in a cognition, Rāmānuja supports the view of *svatastva* or spontaneousness like the Mīmāṁsakas. A cognition acquires its validity from the general causes of Knowledge and not by any other merit or *guṇa* as is held by the Tārkikas. The validity of the cognition is also apprehended *svataḥ*[8] spontaneously by the soul, provided there be no knowledge of *doṣa*—any vitiating factor. Doubt about the validity of a cognition originates if there be any knowledge of defect (*doṣa*) like darkness, distance, etc.

Knowledge is both a substance and attribute just like the light of a lamp (*prabhābat*). *Buddhi* or cognition attains various forms or modes like pleasure, pain, desire, hatred, and volition through different adjuncts.[9]

It has already been stated that *pramā* is defined as that knowledge which leads to (is favourable to) the usage of things as they actually are (*yathāvasthitavastuvyavahārānuguṇaṁ jñānaṁ pramā*). If so, *smṛti* or recollection is also *pramā*. But since recollection or *smṛti* requires *saṁskāra* (knowledge-residue) which is produced by a *pūrvānubhava* or previous knowledge, *smṛti* is included in that previous perception or *anubhava*.

Pramā is of three kinds : (1) *Pratyakṣa,* (2) *Anumiti,* and (3) *Śabda-bodha,* i.e., perception, inference, and verbal knowledge.

Pratyakṣa, of course, requires sense-object contacts in most cases, which are either *saṁyoga* (conjunction) or *saṁjuktāśrayanam* (inherence in what is conjoined), etc.

Rāmānujites define inference as the logicians do. Valid cognition of a particular *vyāpaka*, or pervader through the knowledge of the thing pervaded (*vyāpya*), is inference. Pervasion (cohesion) or *vyāpti* has been defined as *'nirupādhikatayā niyatasambandho vyāptiḥ'*, i.e., invariable relation without having any *upadhi* or adjunct is *vyāpti.* If a person infers the existence of smoke through the existence of fire, then the cohesion (*vyāpti*) is vitiated by an adjunct, viz., conjunction of wet fuel (*ādrendhana-saṁyoga*). If the black colour of a particular son of 'Mitra'—a mother, is inferred because of the black colour of her other sons, then the *vyāpti* in this inference is vitiated by the adjunct of *śāka-pākajatva*, i.e., being born after her eating too many vegetables. In this way adjuncts are to be examined to see that the *vyāpti* is not vitiated by any such adjunct.

To define *vyāpya,* they rightly assert that '*nirupādhika-sambandhavat vyāpyam iti siddham*'—that one is the *vyāpya* or the pervaded which has relationship without any *upādhi* or adjunct. Thus, different kinds of *upādhis* or vitiating adjuncts have been mentioned by them. The *liṅga* or the *sādhana* known as possessing two forms (*rūpa*) of having *vyāpti* and *pakṣadharmatā*, i.e., having cohesion of the probandum (*sādhya*) and its abiding in the *pakṣa*, i.e., subject of the inference, are the causes of an inference. But a valid *hetu* or probans should have all the five *rūpas* or characteristics of *pakṣa-sattva, sapakṣa-sattva, vipakṣavyāvṛtti, avādhita-viṣyatva* and *asatpratipakṣitatva,* meaning respectively (1) abiding of the probans in the subject, (2) ascertained abiding of the probans in the *sapakṣa* where the probandum is ascertained to be existing, (3) not abiding in the place where the probandum (*sādhya*) is known to be non-existing, (4) whose probandum cannot be negated in the *pakṣa*, (5) and that which has no opposing counter-proposition. These are the five necessary characteristics of a valid probans or *saddhetu.* In the case of *parārthānumāna*, the logicians favour five premises or *pañcāvayava* called 1) *pratijñā,* 2) *hetu,* 3) *udāharaṇa,* 4) *upanaya,* 5) *nigamana.* But the Rāmānujites hold that the number cannot be fixed (*niyata)* in every case. There may be three or even two in the case of meritorious persons. *Vyāpti* and *pakṣadharmatā* which are the main factors for an inference may be captured from even two premises of the *udāharaṇa* and the *upanaya,*[10] which involve *vyāptijñāna* and *pakṣa-dharmatājñāna*, necessary for an inference.

Rāmānuja admits five kinds of *hetvābhāsa* or false probans, almost the same as held by the logicians.

Since *upamiti* and *arthāpatti* (analogy and postulation) have been included in inference, let us discuss *śabdabodha* or verbal knowledge according to Rāmānuja. That knowledge is *śabdabodha* or verbal knowledge which is produced by some words not uttered by any *anāpta* (ignorant, deceitful person or liar). The knowledge produced by the Vedic texts is also covered by this definition, since those words are not uttered by any person, being *apauruṣeya* or impersonal. But the works and words composed by ordinary persons which are evidently *pauruṣeya* also produce verbal knowledge if attended with the other conditions of verbal knowledge viz., *ākāṅkṣā, yogyatā* and *sannidhi*—expectancy, fitness, and proximity.

Without having any novelty in these points, Rāmānuja emphasizes the point that all sentences must mean things attributed and different by nature. '*Sarvaṁ vākyajātaṁ saviśeṣaviṣayakaṁ bheda-viṣayakañca*'.[11]

Thus, we find that Rāmānuja has exhibited some originality in his interpretation of the *Upaniṣadic* texts and the Brahma-sūtras by holding two kinds of knowledge—substantive and attributive—*dharmībhūta* and *dharma-bhūta*, both all-pervading and eternal by nature, though limited in the *jīvas* through their karma. Though *buddhi* (or *jñāna*) means *artha-prakāśa*—revelation of some object to some knowing soul,[12] knowledge is eternal in the case of God and liberated souls. But it is not manifest in the *jīvas* in bondage—'*baddhānāṁ tirohitameva.*' That some knowledge is produced and destroyed, is due to the fact that it is either manifested or veiled.

Rāmānuja, though a strong advocate of *sat-khyāti-vāda* in his theory of error which means that the object revealed in an error is not false, but true to some extent, he seems to be also in favour of *anyathā-khyāti* or otherwise-apprehension when he states—'*khyātyantara-vādināñca sudūramapi gatvānyathāvabhāsa eva avaśya-māśrayaṇīyaḥ.*' All other theorists have to admit something as appearing otherwise, however far they may go in arguing in favour of their theories. But he strongly supports his *sat-khyāti* with the help of the *pañcīkaraṇa* process of the Vedas asserting that all things contain everything in greater or less proportion. That some cognition is said to be *bhrama* or error is due to *vyavahāra-bādha,* i.e., contradiction in usage, and not due to the falsity of the object.[13] There is silver *(rajata)* also in the shell *(śukti)* in a very small proportion. When he knows the shell to be predominant there, his error is sublated. Rāmānuja cites some significant verses composed by himself in favour of his theory of *sat-khyāti*, as *yathārthaṁ sarvavijñānamiti vēdavidāṁ matam.*[14] Rāmānuja is somewhat akin to the Jainas and Buddhists by holding pleasure, pain, desire, etc., to be different modes or states of knowledge or *dhī*.

Dream-objects according to Advaitins are totally false, being temporarily created by the *jīva* (*sahi kartā*). But Rāmānuja and other Vaiṣṇava philosophers interpret the text as, *Īśvara eva kartā*—God-head is the creator of the dream-objects of such a temporary unstable character, according to the *adṛṣṭa* of the *jīvas*. So dream-objects are not false, but realities of a different nature.

Knowledge is both a substance and an attribute like the flame of the lamp (*prabhāvat*).

It is also very striking to note that according to Rāmānuja, *Bhakti* and *Prapatti*—devotion and complete surrender, which are the means of the final realization and liberation, are also modes of knowledge.[15] Supreme Knowledge or *Brahmajñāna* is the same as *Brahmopāsanā* or *Brahma-bhakti.* It is through devotion or meditation that the mediate knowledge of Brahman produced by the Vedic texts is transformed into immediate perception which brings the final liberation after death.

APPENDIX

The Upaniṣadic and Śaṅkarite Concept of Knowledge as Basic Pure Consciousness

Like the materialists, scientists and realists, the Upaniṣads also hold ordinary knowledge, or *Vṛttijñāna* as always a relationship between some object and subject, *jñeya* and *jñātā*. The Upaniṣads and Advaita Vedanta dive deeper into the problem and hold that the basic principle of revelation or illumination called *cit, bodha,* or *prakāśa* underlies and reveals the three known poles of knowledge, viz., the knower (*jñātā*), the knowledge (*jñāna*) and the known (*jñeya*). How do we know that there are those three poles of knowledge? Because, we feel that knowledge has and must have some subject and object, and because common logic also supports the feeling. Then we must admit that I exist, or my feeling exists. But, what is the testimony or evidence of my existence except that feeling of I-ness, or I-hood? We could not have felt or known anything if there were no basic principle of illumination or revelation—*prakāśa* or *bodha*.

The materialist scientists like Pavlov may contend that the feeling of I-ness, or any other feeling is only a function of the material brain, and so does not involve, or presuppose any basic principle of consciousness. This consçiousness can be stopped, and produced again by medicines. But, still the question remains : How do you know that your brain exists, and that there are many other such brains? Because they are revealed as such to your consciousness, which is the basic principle of illumination. This basic principle of illumination or *prakāśa* does not require any proof or testimony because it is the bedrock on which proofs and testimonies have been established. What are testimonies or *pramāṇas* but some means or ways by which some reality or truth may be brought into our consciousness, which is self-established (*svataḥsiddha*), and which is the Supreme Ultimate Light itself (*sva-prakāśa*).

This basic Reality has been asserted in the Upaniṣads : *sākṣādaparokṣād brahma*—Brahman is direct perception itself, the Eternal Pure Consciousness is the essence of perception.

Śaṅkara also states that one who enquires about the proof or testimony of *bodha* or consciousness which establishes and proves all the *pramāṇas*, certainly desires to burn fire by the fuel (*tattvopadeśa*). Āçārya Sureśvara, a follower of Śaṅkara, also states : While perception and all other *pramāṇas* are established based on the Self as consciousness, what *pramāṇa* can possibly prove the Self (*sambandhavārttik*)? No *pramāṇa* or testimony can do that, Śaṅkara states elsewhere, *Na hi ātmā pramāṇa-praśnamarhati*—Ātman is the ultimate light or revealer—which does not require any *pramāṇa* or testimony to prove it. If you do not agree, then you are the Ātman, the Self as Consciousness, since assertion, denial, query and solution—all involve, imply, presuppose, Consciousness.

Whether this Eternal Pure Consciousness is the only Reality without a second, is a different issue.

Advaitins uphold this view of non-dualism with sound reasons of their own while Sāṁkhyāites and Pātañjalāites differ and to them matter or *prakṛti* as well as Eternal Consciousness is a fundamental Reality.

References

1. *Śrī Bhāṣya*, 90 (Nirnayasagar Ed.)
2. *Yatīndramatadīpikā*, 3 (Anandashram Ed.)
3. *Śrī Bhāṣya*, 90 op.cit.
4. *Yatīndramatadīpikā*, 56 op.cit.
5. ibid., 49, 98 (Anandashram Ed.)
6. *Śrī Bhāsya*, 56 op.cit.
7. *Ātmā svaprakāśaḥ jñānatvāt dharmabhūtajñānavat.* (*Śrī Bhāṣya*, 73)
8. *Sarvaṁjñānaṁ svata eva pramāṇaṁ svaprakāśañca.* (*Śrī Bhāṣya*, 57)
9. *Yatīndramatadīpikā*, 58 op.cit.
10. ibid., 21
11. ibid., 33
12. '*Sva-sattaiva sāśrayaṁ prati kasyacit viṣayasya prakāśanaṁ hi samvedanam*', (*Śrī Bhāṣya*, 90, Nirnayasagar Ed.)
13. *Vyavahāra bādhādeva bhramatvaṁ na tu viṣaya satyatvābat, Śrī Bhāṣya* 12 (Nirnayasagar Ed.)
14. *Śrī Bhāṣya*, 382, op.cit.
15. *Yatīndramatadīpikā*, 61, op.cit.

Some Remarks on the Definition of Knowledge

SIBAJIBAN BHATTACHARYYA

Prof. Sibajiban Bhattacharyya, a National Fellow of the Indian Council of Philosophical Research, New Delhi, has taught philosophy for more than 45 years in Universities and Institutions in India and abroad; has published more than 80 papers in Journals, Anthologies, Encyclopaedias (Indian and foreign); has published 5 books and edited 6 books (some in collaboration with others).

Introduction

The Sanskrit term *jñāna,* though philologically cognate with the English *knowledge* through the Greek *gnosis*[1] has a very different meaning in Indian philosophy in general and Navya-Nyāya in particular. The sense in which it is used is at once wider and narrower than the sense in which 'knowledge' is used in Western philosophy.

It is wider because *jñāna* is used to denote not merely true but also false cognitions, doubt, belief, assumption, and also the usual perception, introspection; it denotes non-propositional states like sensing.

It is narrower because *jñāna* is used only in the episodic sense, while 'knowledge' is used in Western philosophy in both dispositional and episodic senses.

True *jñāna* is called '*pramā*'. As 'knowledge' is by definition true, I shall compare and contrast only *pramā* with knowledge.

Let us examine cases of inference where the conclusion is *pramā*, but the probans defective (*kūṭa-liṅgaka-anumiti*). Two types of cases are usually distinguished. (i) The hill has dust, dust is pervaded by fire (wherever there is dust, there is fire); the hill has dust pervaded by fire. Hence the hill has fire. (ii) The hill has kitchenhood (i.e., is a kitchen), kitchenhood is pervaded by fire (in every kitchen, there is fire); the hill has kitchenhood pervaded by fire. Hence, the hill has fire. These two cases are different, for in (i) the probans (dust) is really on the hill; only the pervasion 'wherever there is dust, there is fire' is wrong; hence the consideration 'the hill has dust pervaded by fire' is also wrong. Yet the conclusion is true accidentally, by fluke. In (ii) the probans 'kitchenhood' is not really located in the hill, does not belong to the hill; but the pervasion is correct, 'in every kitchen there is fire'. So the consideration which is a synthesis of the cognition of the presence of the probans in the locus of the inference and the cognition of pervasion—in this case, 'the hill has kitchenhood pervaded by fire'—is wrong. Yet the conclusion happens to be true; its cognition is *pramā*.

This point needs further discussion.

The first example may be put in the traditional Western form thus :

IW (1) All dusty things are fiery.
(2) The hill is a dusty thing.
(3) The hill is fiery.

This is a formally valid syllogism, although (1) is false, and (2) irrelevant for the conclusion. This formally valid inference is thus different from such an unconnected pair of sentences :

IU (4) 2+2 = 4.
(5) Hence grass is green.

For IU is not a formally valid inference, mediate or immediate. In the Navya-Nyāya form of inference for oneself the inference IW may be put thus :

IN (6) Dust is pervaded by fire.
(7) The hill has dust.
(8) The hill has dust pervaded by fire.
(9) Hence the hill has fire.

As (6) is false (7) is not only false, but irrelevant for the conclusion. The conclusion is true, but not justified by the premises; the conclusion, for all we know might have been false. There might have been a lake on the hill, and no fire. The fact that it is true is just an accident.

It may be argued that the conclusion is made true by (8) piecemeal; for in this cognition, i.e., consideration (*parāmarśa*), some of the objects cognized are fire and hill. This makes the conclusion true. So the conclusion is not true by accident, by fluke, but is made true by (8).

This argument is totally wrong. For although the object 'fire' is cognized in (8), yet *pervasion by fire* is cognized as a qualifier of the *dust*, and not of the hill. So cognition (8) is false. It cannot be argued that simply because fire is an object of cognition, therefore the conclusion where fire is a qualifier of the hill, is made true by (8). As a matter of fact, according to Nyāya, this case is peculiar and worthy of special note, as a true conclusion is a consequence of false cognitions.

A question may be asked here : If the cognition of the conclusion is true, i.e., is a *pramā*, it must be due to a *pramāṇa*, for no cognition can be generated without a cause, especially, an instrumental cause. So what is the *pramāṇa* of the *pramā* which the conclusion is? The reply to this question is that the *pramāṇa* here is *anumāna* (inference). (Note that the inference is formally valid according to traditional Western logic.)

Then the question may be asked : how can the *anumāna* be a *pramāṇa* in this case, as it is defective ? ('*Kūṭa*' means 'defective' in the phrase '*kūṭa-liṅgaka-anumiti*'.) The answer to this question requires a close examination of the Nyāya concepts of *pramā*, *pramāṇa*, and *doṣa* (defect). First, we note that Nyāya defines both *pramā* and *apramā* without referring to *pramāṇa* or *doṣa*. As a matter of fact, the concept of *pramāṇa* is defined in terms of the concepts of *pramā* and instrumental cause. Secondly, the Nyāya philosophers hold the theory that if there is *apramā*, then there must be a *doṣa* (defect) in the *pramāṇa* which causally produces the *apramā*. But the counter-implication that if there is a *doṣa* in the *pramāṇa*, then it produces *apramā* is not accepted। The present case (IN) proves the invalidity of the counter-implication.

There is another type of case which also proves the invalidity of the counter-implication. In cognizing a connected objective situation as meant by a sentence, it is necessary, as an auxiliary causal factor, to believe that the words occurring in the sentence mean these objects, (*śakti-dhīḥ sahakāriṇī*). Yet the Nyāya theory is that even if this belief that the words mean these objects be false, the cognition of the whole sentence may be true. According to Gadādhara, this is what happens when one understands the meaning of a sentence in a regional language. According to Gadādhara only words in Sanskrit have the semantic power to mean an object; no words in any regional language have that power. Yet sentences in regional languages produce *pramā*. What is necessary is that we should cognize the correct objects which are connected correctly to be meant by the sentence, even though we falsely believe that the words *mean* those objects. This false belief leads to *pramā* in this case. Thus Nyāya philosophers do not accept the counter-implication that if there is a *doṣa* in a *pramāṇa*, then an *apramā* results.

This may be corroborated by the text of *Bhāṣāpariccheda*, 141, which is '*doṣa* causes *apramā*, and *guṇa* causes *pramā*'. Explaining this in *Siddhāntamuktāvalī*, Viśvanātha says, '*Doṣa* is a cause of *apramā*, *guṇa* is a cause of *pramā*.' Now, according to Nyāya, we can infer the cause from the effect, for the cause is the pervader and the effect is the pervaded. We can infer the presence of the pervader from the presence of the pervaded. In the definition of cause, cause pervades the effect. 'Because *niyatatva* is an adjective of *pūrva-vṛtti*, the object existing immediately prior to the effect will be the pervader of the effect. That which is not a pervader of the effect can never be a cause of the effect. *Pervader* here means that which is invariably present immediately before the effect, i.e., that which will not be absent then, is the pervader of the effect.'[2] So one can infer the cause from the effect but not conversely.

It may be argued here that in Vātsyāyana's *Bhāṣya* on Gautama's *Nyāya-Sūtra* 3 kinds of inference are admitted. *Pūrvavat anumāna* is one of them. *Pūrvavat* inference is inference of effect from its cause. So we may infer the effect from the cause, hence it is the effect which is the pervader and the cause is the pervaded. But Vātsyāyana gives a second interpretation of the term '*pūrvavat*' according to which two objects which had been previously cognized to be in the relation of pervasion produce a *pūrvavat* type of inference from the perception of the pervaded to the presence of the pervader. Phaṇibhūṣaṇa says that Vātsyāyana accepts this second interpretation.[3] In later Nyāya, all causal inferences are from the effect to the cause, as in the familiar example of inferring the presence of fire (cause) from the presence of smoke (effect). So the pervaded is the probans, and the pervader is the probandum.

In the present case, too, *doṣa* (a cause) is the pervader and *apramā* (the effect) is the pervaded. So we can infer from *apramā* the presence of *doṣa*, but not *conversely*, from the presence of *doṣa* (a cause) to *apramā* (the effect).

If *doṣa* is present, the resulting cognition may yet be *pramā* even in the case of perception. For example, a person suffering from jaundice may yet perceive truly that this is a conch-shell. The jaundice will be a *doṣa* only for perception of colour of the conch-shell. But which *doṣa* produces which kind of *apramā* is to be determined by back-calculation. If the colour is wrongly cognized as yellow, then jaundice, yellow light or some other cause has to be postulated.

It may be argued here that *guṇa* in the case of inference is a true *parāmarśa*. Only a true *parāmarśa* can produce an *anumiti* which is *pramā*. But if a *parāmarśa* is not correct the *guṇa* is absent; from the absence of the pervader we can infer the absence of the pervaded. So from a *parāmarśa* which is not true, we may infer that the *anumiti* is *apramā*.

In reply to this objection, we may point out that if *anumiti* is *apramā*, then there must be a *doṣa* which is not a mere absence of *guṇa*.[4]

We now come back to the case of inference (*anumāna*). In the definition of *anumāna,* in which the causal factors which produce the cognition of the conclusion are listed, no mention is made of the truth of the causal beliefs. In '*karaṇaṁ vyāptidhīrbhavet*' the term *vyāptidhīḥ* does not mean true belief, only belief.

Now, although it appears that knowledge and *pramā* are different concepts, it may be shown that even knowledge in some cases need not involve justification. This may be proved as follows.

Definition of Knowledge

This definition is generally stated thus :

DK1 *Kxp* = Df *Bxp* & *p* & *Exp*

where '*Exp*' is to be given different interpretations to suit different versions of this definition; for example, '*Exp*' may mean '*x* is justified in believing that p' or 'p is evident to *x*'; thus Ayer's and Chisholm's definitions are both accommodated. I shall try to show that the differences between knowledge and true belief in expressions with iterated '*K*' cannot be made, *if* we assume (i) the KK-thesis, and (ii) obviously valid rules of inference (with the usual propositional logic as the basis).

The KK-thesis is often stated thus :

(KK) $Kxp \rightarrow KxKxp$

The rules of inference which I assume are

R1 $\quad Kx\,(P \,\&\, Q) \rightarrow Kx\,(P)$

R2 $\quad Kx\,(P \,\&\, Q) \rightarrow Kx\,(Q)$.

Then the following theorem is easily proved.

THEOREM 1 $KxKxp \equiv Kx\,(Bxp \,\&\, p)$

Proof 1.	$KxKxp$	
2.	$Kx\,(Bxp \,\&\, p \,\&\, \mathrm{Exp})$	1, DK1
3.	$Kx\,(Bxp \,\&\, p)$	2, R1
4.	$KxKxp \rightarrow Kx\,(Bxp \,\&\, p)$	1-3, CP
5.	$Kx\,(Bxp \,\&\, p)$	
6.	Kxp	5, R2
7.	$Kxp \rightarrow KxKxp$	(kk)
8.	$KxMxp$	6, 7, M, P
9.	$Kx\,(Bxp \,\&\, p) \rightarrow KxKxp$	5-8, CP
10.	$KxKxp \equiv Kx\,(\mathrm{Bxp} \,\&\, \mathrm{p})$	4, 9, *Conj*

If knowledge is something more than mere true belief, then I should be able to know when I have knowledge and when I have mere true belief. Theorem 1 suggests, however, that no one is able to make that discrimination in his own case.

Theorem 1 shows the condition of *x*'s knowing that *x* knows that *p* *is* exactly the same as the conditions of his knowing that *x* believes truly that *p*. Now it may be argued that this is really not a serious charge against DK1.

That consequence is supposed to be an embarrassment to those who accept the classical definition of knowledge. But I intend to defend the classical definition. First I shall show the limitations of the theorem. It is crucial to the truth of the theorem that the verbs be expressed in the present tense : I know *now* that I know *now* that *p,* if and only if, I know *now* that I *now* believe truly that *p.* If we were to mix present and past tenses, the proof of the theorem would fail. You cannot *prove this* : I know *now* that I *knew p,* if and only if, I know now that I *believed* truly that *p*. In order to prove that, you would have to assume the KK-thesis with mixed tenses. The KK-thesis would have to be read thus : If I know now that *p*, then I know now that I *knew p*. That is more like an assertion of Plato's theory of recollection, which few people would accept.

So nothing in Theorem 1 says that I cannot distinguish cases where I *knew* that *p* from cases where I merely *believed truly* that *p*. I can make the distinction between my past cognitive states.[5]

This defence of DK1 however, involves difficulties. It is not clear what sense can be given to 'I *knew* that *p*'. There is a perfect sense of 'I came to learn that *p*', but what can be the sense of 'I *knew* that *p* (in the past)' ? Moreover, Theorem 1 uses all the verbs in the present tense, but it does not follow that the present tense should mean an action going on at the present moment. 'I know that I know that *p*' does not mean the same thing as 'I know *now* that I know *now* that *p*', for knowing is not an event in the present, in the past, or future. If, however, Falk's contention that there is a radical difference between 'I know *now* that *p*' and 'I *knew* that *p*' is true, then it is not clear how we can say that in future 'I can look back on them and detect a difference in retrospect'. Thereby I would have detected only a difference between 'I knew that *p*' and 'I believed truly that *p*', and not that between 'I know that *p*' and 'I believe truly that *p*'. Thus Theorem 1 shows that justification of true belief need not be the same as knowledge at higher levels.

So there are two alternatives here : either the KK-thesis or the classical definition of knowledge has to be rejected to avoid Theorem 1. Nyāya does *both*, by modifying the KK-thesis, and using 'knowledge' in the sense of true belief. The modified KK-thesis of Nyāya is that every cognition—knowledge, belief, doubt, assumption—can be known directly by a higher order act of introspection if one so desires. This introspective knowledge is infallible. Secondly, identifying true belief with knowledge, Nyāya stipulates that in knowing that one knows the subject infers that a true belief, which is as a matter of fact true, is true by acting successfully on it. It is of course, not necessary to have true belief to know (infer) that the belief is true. Thus, according to Nyāya philosophers, correspondence of what is believed with reality is the nature of truth; successful activity is the test of truth.

This Nyāya theory may be challenged on various grounds. It may be pointed out that the concepts of correspondence with reality and successful activity resulting from the belief are logically unconnected. It is quite possible that belief in what is false may cause successful activity. For example, if one mistakes the lustre of a gem for the gem itself, and then proceeds to pick up the gem, one succeeds in this, for the gem is quite near the lustre of the gem.

Nyāya philosophers point out the inadequacy of this objection. If a belief produces successful activity as a rule, and not by fluke, then it has to be true. When one mistakes the lustre of a gem for the gem, and proceeds to pick it up, he first realizes that his belief was wrong; and this realization is followed by the veridical perception of the gem, which leads one to successful activity. The situation may be more complex, if the gem itself is hidden in a bush or in a hole; one can pick up the gem only when one has located it. This veridical perception of where the gem is leads to successful activity; not the earlier non-veridical perception of the lustre as the gem.

Successful activity is self-intimating; whether I get the object I seek or not is self-evident; it does not need to be known by a different act of knowing.

In Western epistemology, a similar example is cited to criticize the classical definition of knowledge as justified true belief. Chisholm argues that when one perceives a white thing (which is really a dog) as a sheep and says 'there is a sheep there', and if there is by a chance a sheep there, the belief will be true and justified, but one cannot be said to know it.

Now this criticism is really beside the point. There may be a real sheep there, but the perceptual knowledge is not 'there is a sheep there', but 'this thing (which I see) is a sheep' and that is not true. If one goes over to the place where the thing is, one may find a sheep nearby, but one also realizes that the perception was non-veridical by finding out that a dog was mistaken for a sheep.

References

1. 'Know "... L & GK gno SKr jna"' CDO.
2. Navya-Nyāye Anumiti, by Savita Misra, 10.
3. Nyāyadarśana, Vol. 1, 173.
4. Siddhāntamuktāvali
5. Arthur Falk, 'Comments', *Rabindra Bharati Journal of Philosophy*, Vol.2, 1987, pp. 15ff.

The Use of the Word *Pramā* : Valid Cognition in Advaita Vedanta

PANDIT SRIMOHAN BHATTACHARYA

Pandit Srimohan Bhattacharya, Tarka-Vedantatirtha, presently, Adhyapaka, Ramakrishna Mission Institute of Culture, Calcutta; Principal, Professor, or Adhyapaka of Indian Philosophy at various institutions, including: Sanskrit College, Contai; Sanskrit Vidyapith, Murshidabad; Berhampur Jubilee Sanskrit Mahavidyalaya, Murshidabad; all in West Bengal. Silchar Government Tol, Assam; Jagatpur Ashram, Chittagong, undivided Bengal. Part-time Lecturer: Calcutta University; Rabindra Bharati University; Asiatic Society; Visiting Professor, Jadavpur University—all in Calcutta.

Author of a number of scholarly books, including: Translation of *Vedānta Paribhāṣā* by Dharmarāja, into Bengali, with a commentary in Sanskrit titled *Arthabodhinī*; translation of *Sarvadarśana Saṁgraha* by Mādhavācārya, with commentary; *Kārya-Kāraṇbhāvarabasyam*, original composition in Sanskrit; *Bhāratīya Darśana Koṣa*—Dictionary of Indian Philosophical Terms, in Bengali; Commentary on the *Śaṅkarabhāṣya* of *Brahmasūtras*, with elaborate Introduction and copious explanatory notes; *Nyāya-Kusumāñjali*, with Bengali translation.

I would like to say a few words before I deal with *pramā* (valid cognition) in Advaita Vedanta. In different books of Advaita Vedanta we come across passages which appear to be inconsistent. As a result, readers get confused and raise objections which cannot be refuted. But if we introduce the principle of different levels of spiritual competency in our discussion, then there is no scope for contradiction in Advaita Vedanta. In order to illustrate this concept I have divided my discussion into three levels.

First level

At this level only Brahman as pure consciousness (*jñānasvarūpa*) is the transcendent reality (*paramārtha*). This consciousness has no form. There is no distinction between the knower and the known. This is the hightest level. Expressions such as '*cit*' ('consciousness'), '*citiśakti*' ('the power of consciousness'), '*jñāna*' ('cognition'), '*anubhūti*' ('apprehension'), '*saṁvit*' ('supreme knowledge'), etc., refer to the same transcendent reality. This self-revealing unconditioned consciousness (*svarūpa-pratiṣṭha-kūṭastha-caitanya*) is also known as truth, consciousness and infinity (*satyaṃ jñānamanantam*).

In the Vedic literature it is called 'Brahman' or 'Ātman'. Since it is not revealed by anything else, it is called '*jñāna*' ('Consciousness'). Hence it is different from matter or inanimate (*jaḍa*) objects. It cannot be included in any of the categories such as substance, quality, etc., of the Vaiśeṣika philosophy. Since it is self-revealed (*svayaṁ-siddha*), it cannot be an object of cognition. It is not an object which can be used, although it is the basis or the foundation for the use of any empirical object of the world. The external or the unchanging nature of this reality has been mentioned in the *Pañcadaśī*. Time can be divided into past, present and future, but this self-revealing Consciousness has no past, present, or future. It remains the same without any beginning or end.

The words '*pramā*' ('valid') and '*apramā*' ('invalid') are used to signify respectively the truth (*yathārthatā*) or falsity (*ayathārthatā*) of a cognition. Since the ultimate Reality is timeless, contentless, and consciousness-as-such, it cannot be said to be valid or invalid.

Second level

At the second level Brahman is conceived as 'I' due to beginningless ignorance (*avidyā*) which is an imposed property (*upādhi*). It is due to this imposition that one appears as two, the infinite appears as finite, and the ever-free appears to be bound by consciousness and unconsciousness. But this 'I' belongs to a higher level. For this reason even if this 'I' had cognition of itself and of the world, it would have had the realization that all these are appearances. It would realize that all cognitions other than the cognition of Brahman were invalid (*apramā*). Since the cognition of the 'I' or the cognition of the world occurs when it is known to be false, it is called '*āhārya-jñāna*' ('adventitious cognition').

The person who belongs to this level is our guru or ācārya (spiritual preceptor), and he is free from bondage while he is alive. Since he knows the real nature of both sides and the difference between the Self and that which is different from the Self, he is to be placed at the second level. The difference between the third level and the second level is comparable to the difference between the person who is under delusion (*bhrānta*) and the person who is aware of the delusion (*bhrāntijña*). The person who belongs to the second level is a follower of the theory that creation depends upon apprehension (*dṛṣṭi-sṛṣṭivādī*). According to the followers of this view an object is created as soon as it is cognized.

There is no uncognized existence of anything other than Brahman. For this reason the cognition of an object does not require certain causal conditions such as *pramāṇa* (the chief instrumental cause of a valid cognition) or *vyāpāra* (an operation which is due to the chief instrumental cause). A cognition which has this type of object is a mode of ignorance (*avidyāvṛtti*), and it cannot be regarded as valid (*pramā*). In fact, it cannot be called '*jñāna*' in the strict sense of this term. As illusory objects do not have uncognized existence, so the empirical objects do not have uncognized existence. Hence an empirical object such as a pot does not have uncognized existence. Since both the types of objects do not have uncognized existence, there is no reason to consider one of them illusory (*prātibhāsika*) and the other empirical (*vyāvahārika*). On the contrary, all of them should be considered as illusory, and their cognitions which are modes of ignorance should be considered as invalid (*apramā*). According to this view no object is public. Hence it cannot be claimed that we observe the same object. This is due to the fact that whatever a person observes is a product of his ignorance at that time and it will exist as long as he observes it.

Third level

At this level two types of cognition, namely, consciousness-as-such (*svarūpajñāna*) and cognition as mode (*vṛttijñāna*) have been recognized. Moreover, cognition as mode has been divided into two types, valid (*pramā*) and invalid (*apramā*), and the objects of cognition have been divided into three types, transcendent (*pāramārthika*), empirical (*vyāvahārika*), and illusory (*prātibhāsika*). That which can never be denied (or contradicted) is a transcendent object. Since Brahman cannot be denied, it comes under this category. That which cannot be denied at the empirical level is an empirical object. Objects such as a pot come under this category. That which cannot be denied when it appears, but can be denied at the empirical level, is an illusory object. In a snake-rope illusion, the snake is an illusory object. Hence it comes under this category.

At the second level objects are divided into two types, transcendent and illusory. But at the third level objects are divided into three types. The followers of the third level have accepted three types of existence. In another way also objects can be divided into three types, (1)self-revealing (*svataḥ siddha*), (2) revealed by the witness consciousness (*sākṣisiddha*), and (3) revealed by the instruments of valid cognition (*pramāṇa siddha*).

Only Brahman which is unqualified (*nirguṇa*) is self-revealing. It is due to the revelation of Brahman that the world is revealed to us. Hence Brahman comes under the first type.

Ignorance (*avidyā*), a mode of ignorance (*avidyāvṛtti*), mind or internal organ (*antaḥkaraṇa*), and mode of mind or internal organ (*antaḥkaranavṛtti*) are revealed by the witness consciousness. Hence they come under the second type. The consciousness differentiated by ignorance or a mode of ignorance is called '*sākṣī*' ('witness'). The objects which cannot remain unknown or which are not covered by ignorance are revealed by the witness (*sākṣisiddha*).

Objects such as a pot, a cloth etc., are revealed through the instruments of valid cognition such as perception, etc. Hence they come under the third type.

According to the Nyāya philosophy the knowledge of an object depends upon the instruments of valid cognition (*mānādhīnā meyasiddhiḥ*). In this context the word '*meya*' ('knowable') refers to every object as the property '*meyatva*' ('knowability') is a property of everything (*kevalānvayī*). Hence the revelation of any object requires the instruments of valid cognition. But according to the Vedanta it cannot be said that the revelation of every object depends upon the instruments of valid cognition. This is due to the fact that only the cognition of the knowable (*prameya*), which is an object of a mental mode that is due to an instrumental cause, is dependent upon the instruments of valid cognition. But the witness-consciousness (*sākṣicaitanya*) which is not an object of knowledge (*aprameya*) and the objects which are revealed by the witness (*sakṣisiddha*) are not revealed by any instruments of valid cognition.

Jñāna (Cognition or Consciousness)

In our scriptures as well as in common usage we come across expressions such as '*jñānāgni*' ('cognition-fire'), '*jñānāloka*' ('cognition-light'), etc. In such expressions the word '*jñāna*' is used to signify its power of revelation or destruction. Among its different uses the consciousness-in-itself (*ātmasvarūpa caitanya*) is referred to by the word '*jñāna*'. Since consciousness-as-such signifies revelation (*prakāśa*) or that which reveals (*prakāśaka*), the word '*jñāna*' is used to refer to this consciousness. In Vedanta literature this consciousness is also called '*svarūpajñāna*' ('consciousness-as-such').

On the contrary, the word '*jñāna*' is used to refer to a mode of the mind (*antaḥkaraṇavṛtti*) which takes the form of an object. Since this mode of the mind destroys the veil of ignorance which covers the object, the word '*jñāna*' is used to refer to this mode of the mind. This type of *jñāna* (cognition) is of something (*saviṣayaka*) and non-eternal (*anitya*). Even God's cognition in the form of a mode of nescience (*māyā-vṛtti*) is of some object and non-eternal.

According to Vedanta any transformation (*pariṇāma*) of ignorance (*avidyā*) or the mind (*antaḥkaraṇa*) which has the form of an object is called '*vṛtti*' ('mode'). If a *vṛtti* (mode) is opposed to ignorance (*ajñāna*), then it is called '*jñāna*' ('cognition'). It is to be noted that each and every mode of the mind cannot be called '*jñāna*'. In the scriptures, desires, fears, etc., are regarded as mental modes, but they are not cognitions. Hence a mode of the mind is called '*jñāna*' if it has the form of an object and it is due to instruments of valid cognition. The result of this mode is the destruction of the veil of ignorance. As light is opposed to darkness, so this type of mental mode is opposed to ignorance (*ajñāna*). For this reason this type of mental mode is called '*jñāna*'.

But illusory or invalid cognitions are not called '*jñāna*' ('cognition'), but '*jñānābhāsa*' ('seeming-cognition'). They are due to some defects, dispositions, etc. An illusory cognition is a mode of ignorance (*avidyāvṛtti*), not a mode of the mind (*antaḥkaraṇavṛtti*). In the case of the illusory perception of silver in a piece of mother-of-pearl, the perception of silver is a mode of ignorance (*avidyāvṛtti*). Since this perception is not opposed to ignorance (or does not destroy the veil of ignorance), it cannot be called '*jñāna*'. But there is some similarity with a mental mode. As a mental mode that is a cognition (*jñāna*) is a cause of mental disposition (*saṁskāra*), this mode of ignorance (*avidyāvṛtti*) is a cause of mental disposition. For this reason it looks like a cognition (*jñāna*). As a pseudo-probans in an inference is not considered as a probans, so this mode of ignorance which looks like a cognition is not considered a cognition (*jñāna*). It is called '*jñānābhāsa*' ('seeming-cognition').

In this context it is to be noted that the person who belongs to the third level is a follower of the theory that apprehension depends upon creation (*sṛṣṭi-dṛṣṭivādī*). According to this theory an individual (*jīva*) apprehends the world which is created by God. First, God has created the world and then we perceive the world. Since there is a prior-posterior relation between the creation and its apprehension, we have to accept the existence of uncognized objects prior to their cognitions by individuals. This view accepts the empirical existence of objects such as a pot, etc.

But the view of the second level is contrary to this view. According to the followers of the second level the world is due to the ignorance of the individuals. An individual is a creator of his / her world. Since perceivable objects do not have uncognized existence, they are illusory in nature.

Pramā (Valid cognition)

The word '*pramā*' consists of the prefix '*pra*' and the root '*mā*'. The word '*pra*' means '*prakṛṣṭa*' or '*yathārtha*' ('things as they are'), and the word '*mā*' means '*jñāna*' ('cognition'). So *pramā* means 'cognition of things as they are'. If we take this meaning of the word '*pramā*' ('valid cognition'), then we have to accept true memory-cognition as *pramā* (valid) and the previous apprehension which is its *kāraṇa* (the chief instrumental cause) as an additional *pramāṇa* (instrument of valid cognition). In order to avoid this consequence the Nyāya philosophers have interpreted the word '*jñāna*' as 'apprehensive cognition' (*anubhavātmaka jñāna*). Hence a true memory-cognition is not considered as valid (*pramā*) and its chief instrumental cause (*kāraṇa*) is not treated as an instrument of valid cognition (*pramāṇa*). The Nyāya philosophers have defined 'truth' ('*prakarṣa*') or ('*yathārthatva*') as 'correspondence'. Thus from the Nyāya definition it follows that if the cognition *A* has *F* is true, then the entity *A* has *F*. But the Mīmāṁsā philosophers do not define 'truth' in the way the Nyāya philosophers do. From their definition it follows that if the cognition *A* has *F* is true, then it will never be contradicted and its object has not been cognized before.

But Vedanta philosophers differ from both Nyāya and Mīmāṁsā philosophers. They define 'truth' ('*prakarṣa*') as 'the property of having an object which has not been revealed before' ('*ajñātārthaviṣayakatva*'). According to them everything other than Brahman is imposed upon the non-dual Brahman. Since reality can never be characterized by any property, any cognition of the form *A* has *F* cannot be true. Hence the Nyāya concept of truth is not applicable to the cognition of Brahman.

The Mīmāṁsā definition of 'truth' ('*prakarṣa*') is also not acceptable to the followers of Vedanta. The followers of the Bhaṭṭa Mīmāṁsā have introduced the property of having an object which has not been cognized before (*anadhigata-viṣayakatva*) in their definition of 'truth' so that the memory-cognitions are excluded from being valid (*pramā*). Moreover, they have introduced the property of having an object which will never be contradicted (*abādhita-viṣayakatva*) in their definition of 'truth' so that the illusory cognitions are excluded from being valid. But according to Vedanta both memory (*smṛti*) and delusion (*bhrama*) are modes of ignorance (*avidyāvṛtti*). Hence they do not have cognitionhood (*jñānatva*).

From this it follows that the question of applying validity to memory and illusion does not arise in Vedanta philosophy.

Secondly, illusion and memory cannot be considered valid as their objects do not have *ajñātasattā* (uncognized existence). Here the word '*ajñāta*' does not mean 'that which has not been cognized'. In other words, it does not mean that which has absence of cognition, as there is no absence of cognition in Vedanta philosophy.

According to the followers of Vedanta the word '*jñāna*' refers to either *svarūpa-jñāna* (consciousness-as-such) or *vṛttijñāna* (cognitive mental mode). Since consciousness-as-such is eternal, there cannot be any absence of it. Again, there cannot be absence of the cognitive mental state, because the cognition of the negatum (*pratiyogī*) is a causal condition (*kāraṇa*) for the cognition of an absence. If there is cognition of the negatum (*pratiyogī*) or the locus of the absence (*anuyogī*), we cannot say that there is absence of cognition.

The word '*ajñāna*' refers to an entity, which is different from an absence (*abhāva*). The word '*ajñāta*' ('uncognized') refers to an object which is covered by ignorance. A mode of mind which is due to an instrumental cause and which has the form of an object is called '*jñāna*' ('cognition'). This type of mental mode is also called '*pramā*' ('valid'). It destroys the veil of ignorance which covers the object and reveals the object by its own reflection of consciousness (*cidābhāsa*). This is what the cognitionhood (*jñānatva*) or the validity (*pramātva*) of a mental mode is. Whatever is a cognition is valid. The followers of the Prabhākara Mīmāṁsā have also claimed that every cognition is valid. In this respect the conclusion of the Vedanta resembles that of the Prābhākara Mīmāṁsā.

Now an objection may be raised in the following way :

> According to Vedānta the objects of illusion do not have uncognized existence. For example, the snake which is cognized in place of a rope does not exist as uncognized. Similarly, an empirical cognition, which is called valid cannot be about an object which is uncognized. This is due to the fact that 'uncognized' means 'being covered by ignorance'. An empirical object such as a pot cannot be said to be covered by ignorance. If an object can be covered, then it has the ability to reveal itself. For example, the all-pervasive self-revealing Consciousness. It can be covered as it has always the possibility of revealing itself. But empirical objects, such as a pot, etc., by their very nature lack revelation as they do not have

consciousness. Hence they cannot be covered by ignorance. From this objection it follows that only pure consciousness is the locus and the object of ignorance. Since empirical objects cannot be covered by ignorance, how can their cognitions be said to be valid ? It is doubtful whether they can be called 'cognitions'.

As an answer to this objection it has been said that when it is claimed that 'the cognition of a pot is valid', what is meant is that the consciousness which is manifested in the mental mode which has the form of a pot is limited by it. The property of being uncognized (*ajñātatva*) which is applicable to pure Consciousness has been projected on an empirical object such as a pot. The cognition of Brahman is the only cognition and it is valid. This is due to the fact that it is about something which is uncognized. Hence all other cognitions cease to be valid. Since pure Consciousness is the object of ignorance, the instruments of valid cognition such as perception, etc., are about this Consciousness which is covered by ignorance.

Glossary

Technical terms of the Vedanta (in order of appearance in the text)	English Translation
adhyāsa	imposition
pramā	valid cognition
jñāna-svarūpa	pure consciousness or consciousness-as-such
jñāna	(1) cognition, (2) consciousness
cit	consciousness
anubhūti	apprehension
Saṁvit	supreme knowledge
paramārtha	transcendent
svayaṁ-siddha	self-revealed
apramā	invalid cognition
yathārthatā	truth
ayathārthatā	falsity
upādhi	imposed property
avidyā	ignorance

prātibhāsika	illusory
vyāvahārika	empirical
avidyāvṛtti	mode of ignorance
ajñāta	uncognized or covered by ignorance
pramāṇa	chief instrumental cause of a valid cognition
vyāpāra	operation
jñānābhāsa	seeming-cognition
vṛttijñāna	cognition as a mode
sākṣin	witness or witness consciousness
sākṣi-siddha	revealed by the witness consciousness
svataḥ-siddha	self-revealing
pramāṇa-siddha	revealed by the instruments of valid cognition
antaḥ-karaṇa	internal organ or mind
antaḥkaraṇavṛtti	mode of the mind
māyā	nescience or cosmic illusion
caitanya	Consciousness or pure Consciousness
meya	knowledge
meyatva	knowability
pariṇāma	transformation
jīva	individual
saṁskāra	disposition or mental disposition
prakarṣa	truth
anadhigata	not being cognized before
abādhita	not being contradicted
pratiyogin	(1) the negatum (2) the second term of a relation
anuyogin	(1) the locus of an absence (2) the first term of a relation
cidābhāsa	reflection of consciousness*

* Translation and Glossary by J. L. Shaw

Theories of Error in Indian Philosophy or Five Types of *Khyāti*

PANDIT SUKHAMAYA BHATTACHARYA

Pandit Sukhamaya Bhattacharya, Reader in Philosophy at Visva-Bharati University for much of his career, is now retired. Has written many books and papers, including *Mahābhārater Caritābalī* ('Characters of the Mahabharata'), *Mīmāṁsā Darśana, Vaiśeṣika Darśana.*

The primary meaning of the word '*khyāti*' is 'renown' or 'cognition.' In Sanskrit literature this word is used in either of the senses, but in Bengali literature it is used in the sense of 'renown' only. Both Gautama in his *Nyāya-sūtra* and Uddyotakara in his commentary on the *Nyāya-sūtra* have used the word '*khyāti*' in the sense of 'cognition'. Similarly, Gadadhara Bhattacharya in his commentary on *Anumitidīdhiti* has said that '*khyāti*' means 'cognition' (***khyātirjñānam***). Patañjali, the author of *Yoga-sūtra*, has used the word '*khyāti*' in the sense of 'true cognition'. But in the context of the discussion of illusion the word '*khyāti*' means 'erroneous cognition'.

Sometimes a word is used to refer to its proper subset only. For example, the word 'Pārtha' is used to refer to Arjuna only, although Arjuna's mother Pṛthā had three sons. In this respect it is similar to the use of the word '*paṅkaja*'. (The word '*paṅkaja*', literally means 'that which grows in mud', but it is used to refer to the lotus.)

Indian philosophers have critically discussed the nature of erroneous cognition and have proposed different theories of it. In an erroneous cognition, the fact *a* being *F* is cognized as *a* being not *F*. In different systems of Indian philosophy we come across different views on this topic. Five theories have been mentioned in the following verse :

ātmakhyātirasatkhyātirakhyātiḥ khyātiranyathā
tathānirvacanakhyātirityetat khyātipañcakam.

In other words, there are five types of *khyāti*, namely, (1) *ātmakhyāti,* (2) *asatkhyāti,* (3) *akhyāti,* (4) *anyathākhyāti,* and (5) *anirvacanīya khyāti.*

[Jayanta Bhaṭṭa, the author of *Nyāyamañjarī,* has not accepted *anirvacanīya khyāti.* According to him there are only four types of theories of erroneous cognition, (1) *viparītakhyāti,* (2) *asatkhyāti,* (3) *ātmakhyāti,* and (4) *akhyāti.*]

Now let us discuss the above five types of theories of error:

(A) **Ātmakhyāti** :

According to the *Vijñānavādī* Buddhists (a type of idealist) in every error there is an imposition of an object, which is of the nature of cognition, on an imaginary external object. According to them our soul is of the nature of cognition. Hence it is known internally. A cognition and its object are not different. An imagined external object is also of the nature of cognition. The perception of a snake in a rope or the perception of silver in mother-of-pearl is in fact nothing but a cognition. Hence error is another form of a cognition.

The upholders of this view have not denied the fact that some of our experiences of external objects are correct and some of them are incorrect. In order to give an account of this phenomenon they have accepted the imposition of cognition on imagined external objects. According to them an imagined snake or a piece of silver is unreal (*asat*) if it is considered as different from a cognition. In an erroneous cognition, a rope is cognized as a snake or mother-of-pearl is cognized as silver. It is due to error that a rope-cognition is revealed as a snake or a mother-of-pearl-cognition is revealed as silver. It is to be noted that in an erroneous cognition, a rope is not cognized as a moving snake. What is cognized is a stationary snake. This type of error is an error of cognition. For this reason the *Vijñānavādī* Buddhists are called '*ātmakhyātivādins*'.

We come across several arguments against this theory of error in the philosophical systems of the Nyāya, Vaiśeṣika, Mīmāṁsā and Vedanta. Some of them may be stated in the following way :

It is a universally apprehended fact that an external object (such as a stone) is not a cognition. It is necessarily different from a cognition. Since nothing prevents this cognition, it cannot be rejected. Vyāsadeva in the *Vedānta-sūtra* has claimed that perceptual experience of the waking life is not the same as dream-experience. After having established this fact he has demonstrated fallacies in the inferences of the followers of the Vijñānavāda. In the *Vyāsabhāṣya* of the *Pātañjala-sūtra* also it has been claimed that the perception of externalhood or largeness of an object, such as a pot or a cloth, cannot be a property of cognition. For this reason a large object cannot be said to be a cognition. Moreover, we apprehend largeness when our visual sense-organ is in contact with the object. If objects are momentary, it is impossible to perceive the largeness of objects. This is due to the fact that the objects cease to exist when we perceive their largeness. For this reason the thesis of the Buddhists that everything is momentary cannot be established.

According to the followers of the Vijñānavāda the snake which is of the nature of cognition is imposed on the external rope in an illusory cognition. Similarly, the silver which is of the nature of cognition is imposed on the external mother-of-pearl in an illusory cognition. According to them both the rope and the mother-of-pearl are nothing but cognitions. Now the question is : If one cognition is taken as another without having any relationship of the external world, then how can we explain the externality of an erroneous cognition? If there is no external object having the property externality, then how can it appear as external in an erroneous cognition? In order to explain the appearance of externality we must accept external objects. But the followers of the Vijñānavāda do not subscribe to this thesis.

If an imaginary external object is unreal and is the locus of an illusory object such as a snake, which is of the nature of cognition, then there cannot be any error. This is due to the fact that there is no similarity between a real and an unreal object. If it is said that there can be an error even if there is no similarity, then we can ask whether a rope is cognized as a human being or a cow in an erroneous cognition. According to them a human being or a cow is also of the nature of cognition. But a rope is never cognized as a human being or a cow.

As an answer to the above objection the supporters of the Vijñānavāda might say that it is the very nature of a cognition that it appears as another cognition. If it were so, then it would lead to an infinite regress. This is due to the fact that the nature of a cognition, say *a*, is of the nature of another cognition, say *b*. But the nature of the latter is still of the nature of another cognition, say *c*, and so on.

The Jaina philosophers are the upholders of seven forms of judgements. They have accepted two types of cognition, viz, *pratyakṣa* (direct) and *parokṣa* (indirect), which are not being contradicted. Their view is similar to that of Vijñānavāda.

(B) Asatkhyāti :

According to the Śūnyavādī Buddhists and a section of the atheists everything in this world is unreal. In an erroneous cognition an unreal object is imposed on another unreal object. Since all the elements are unreal, this view is called '*asatkhyāti*'. The followers of this view accept the erroneous cognition of objects such as the sky-flower, the son of a barren woman, etc.

According to Madhvācārya, a Vedanta philosopher, the locus of error is real, but the object imposed upon it is unreal. Hence in an erroneous perception of silver the mother-of-pearl is real, but the silver is unreal. Since Madhvācārya has accepted the imposition of the unreal upon the real, he is called '*Saduparakta asatkhyātivādī*'. Thus his view is not the same as '*asatkhyātivāda*'.

According to the Cārvākas (a type of materialist) also, everything is not unreal but objects or persons such as God which are not amenable to the senses, are unreal. Since the Cārvāka philosophers have accepted the erroneous cognition of unreal objects, their view is also called '*asatkhyātivāda*'.

Some of the followers of the *āstika* (believer) school also have accepted the cognition of unreal objects. They claim that we cognize unreal objects when we understand the meaning of expressions such as 'sky-flower'. References to this type of view can be found in the Yoga school as well as in Kumārila Bhaṭṭa. Ālaṅkārikas (literary critics) have also accepted the cognition of unreal objects. According to them also we cognize unreal objects when we understand the meaning of expressions such as 'sky-flower'.

The followers of the Nyāya-Vaiśeṣika do not accept the cognition of an unreal (*asat*) object when the meaning of a sentence or an expression is understood. Understanding the meaning of the expression 'a yellow conch-shell' does not involve the cognition of an unreal object. But it is a debatable issue whether Jagadīśa, a Navya-Nyāya philosopher, would accept an unreal relation when the meaning of the sentence 'There is no yellow conch-shell' is understood.

In his *Sāṁkhya-sūtra* Kapila has not accepted *asatkhyāti.* He has refuted *anyathākhyāti.* His view is called '*sadasatkhyātī*'.

The view of the *Śūnyavādī* Mādhyamika Buddhists is called '*asatkhyātivāda*'. According to some Mādhyamika Buddhists such as Nāgārjuna everything is not unreal. According to them *śūnya* is (a) not real, (b) not unreal, (c) not both real and unreal, and (d) not different from both real and unreal. Mādhavācārya in his *Sarvadarśana-saṁgraha* has claimed that according to the followers of the *Śūnyavāda,* reality, which is *śūnya,* is free from all four alternatives. Both the existence and the non-existence of an object are unreal. The existence of an object is imaginary. It is called '*sāṁvṛta sattā*'. The word '*saṁvṛta*' means 'imaginary'. Hence the view of the Mādhyamika philosophers such as Nāgārjuna cannot be identified with *asatkhyātivāda.* Śāntideva also in his *Bodhicaryāvatāra* has made a similar claim.

Since the followers of this type of Śūnyavāda have accepted two types of truth, they are closer to the Advaitavāda in some respects. But they have not accepted any eternal object as the ultimate locus of error. For this reason their view cannot be said to be '*anirvacanakhyātī*'. Ācarya Śaṅkara in his commentary on the *Brahma-sūtra* has refuted both *kṣaṇikavāda* (the theory of momentariness) and *śūnyavāda* (the theory of emptiness). In spite of his refutation of *śūnyavāda,* he has been considered as a Buddhist in disguise by some commentators.

According to Śaṅkarācārya, Brahman is a real entity. It is neither free from all the four alternatives of the *śūnyavāda*, nor is it a momentary entity. Brahman is the eternal truth. Hence it does not come under the false cognition of the Mādhyamika philosophers. From the above discussion it follows that the Buddhist philosophers such as Nāgārjuna are not followers of *asatkhyātivāda.*

(C) Akhyāti :

Guru Prabhākara, a follower of the Pūrva-Mīmāṁsā, is the propounder of the theory of *akhyāti.* He does not accept illusory cognition. In fact, there is no error. According to him every cognition is true. The term '*akhyāti*' means 'absence of error'.

A person may take a rope to be a snake or mother-of-pearl to be silver. But this is not one unitary cognition. It consists of two cognitions. In the case of the snake-rope illusion, there is a cognition of the rope as this. Subsequently, due to the similarity between a snake and a rope, the memory-cognition of a snake, which has been observed in the past, takes place. Similar is the case with respect to any other perceptual erroneous cognition. In such cases, first we have perception, and then memory-cognition. In other words, two types of cognition take place and both of them are true. There is no one unitary qualificative cognition; instead there are two cognitions, perceptual and memory; there is no need to accept erroneous cognition.

Now an objection has been raised against this view. It may be asked why there is fear in the case of snake-rope example and effort to acquire the silver in the case of silver-mother-of-pearl example if there is no erroneous cognition. In other words, if there is no one unitary qualificative cognition, then it is difficult to explain the psychological attitudes or the behaviour associated with erroneous cognitions.

In reply, it is said that the cause of psychological attitudes such as fear, or certain types of behaviour such as effort, is not one unitary qualificative cognition. According to the followers of this view the cause is the absence of the cognition of difference between the two items or entities. In the case of our snake-rope example, we do not cognize the difference between the rope which is in front of us and the snake which has been perceived in the past. Similarly, in the case of silver-mother-of-pearl example, we do not cognize the difference between the mother-of-pearl which is in front of us and the previously perceived silver. Śālikanātha, a disciple of Prabhākara, has explained this theory in his book *Prakaraṇa-Pañjikā.*

According to Rāmānuja, a propounder of Viśiṣṭādvaitavāda (the theory of qualified non-dualism), every cognition is true. The cognition of the snake in a rope or the cognition of silver in mother-of-pearl cannot be said to be erroneous. This is due to the fact that a rope is similar to a snake and mother-of-pearl is similar to silver. Since a person fails to cognize all the parts or properties of the rope or the mother-of-pearl, he/she might have certain psychological attitudes such as fear towards one or desire to acquire the other. After having observed some of the specific properties of the rope or the mother-of-pearl, the previous cognitions are nullified.

Bodhāyanamuni, a propounder of qualified non-dualism, is a commentator on the *Brahma-sūtra*. If he is innovator of the theory of *akhyāti*, then the view of Guru Prabhākara cannot be said to be an original thesis. However, we come across original arguments in the theory of Prabhākara. Moreover, there are certain differences in their views. Prabhākara is not a follower of qualified non-dualism. Furthermore, he has not claimed that an element of snake is present in a rope or an element of silver is present in a mother-of-pearl. He is a dualist, and has accepted the multiplicity of individual souls and their agenthood.

Ācārya Śaṅkara, a propounder of non-dualism, and his followers have refuted the *akhyātivāda* of Prabhākara and the qualified non-dualism of Rāmānuja. Thus they have paved the way for the establishment of the theory of imposition (*adhyāsa*). Advaitavāda (the theory of non-dualism) cannot be established without the theory of imposition (*adhyāsa*).

Some of the major arguments against *akhyātivāda* may be stated in the following way :

After having observed the mother-of-pearl we have the cognition *This is silver*. This cognition cannot be said to be two separate cognitions such that one of them is perceptual and the other is memory. Unless we have one unitary qualificative cognition, there is no desire or effort to acquire it. This is due to the fact that qualificative cognition gives rise to a desire (*icchā*) and the latter generates a mental effort (*pravṛtti*). If there is desire to acquire the silver, then the postulation of the absence of cognition of the difference between the mother-of-pearl and the silver is useless. Since there is a difference between mother-of-pearl and silver, there would be cognition of the difference. If there is something which prevents this cognition, then it is to be considered as a defect (*doṣa*). If there is a defect of this sort, then it is to be considered the cause of the erroneous cognition, *This is silver.*

Moreover, if there were two cognitions, there would have been mental perception of these cognitions. Since there is no mental perception of these two cognitions, an erroneous cognition cannot be said to be two separate cognitions. In our example, we do not have the mental perception of 'I have perceived this object with my visual sense-organ' or of 'Thereafter I remember the silver'. Hence this theory goes against empirical facts.

(D) Anyathākhyāti:

Another name for '*anyathākhyāti*' is '*viparītakhyāti*'. The Nyāya Vaiśeṣika schools of philosophy have accepted *anyathākhyāti.* Jayanta Bhaṭṭa, the author of *Nyāyamañjarī,* and Gaṅgeśa Upādhyāya, a Navya-Nyāya philosopher, have established the theory of *anyathākhyāti.*

According to the Nyāya philosophers, in the case of an erroneous perception of silver in mother-of-pearl, both the silver and the mother-of-pearl are real. The mother-of-pearl is in front of the perceiver, but the silver is elsewhere. The silver which is elsewhere appears in the locus of the mother-of-pearl. Hence, the mother-of-pearl, without appearing as the mother-of-pearl, appears as something else. In this case it appears as silver. For this reason the theory is called '*anyathākhyāti*' ('appeared in a different way').

The perception of silver in mother-of-pearl is a type of extraordinary perception. With respect to shininess there is similarity between mother-of-pearl and silver. The cognition of shininess gives rise to the memory-cognition of silver. This cognition is a causal condition of the perceptual cognition of silver. The relation of this type of perception is extraordinary. It is called '*jñānalakṣaṇa sannikarṣa*' ('cognition as relation').

It is not possible to perceive the elsewhere or the elsewhen object by means of ordinary relations such as contact, inherence, etc. Since there is no material cause of silver, an unreal silver also cannot be produced. According to the Advaitavāda, ignorance is the material cause of this type of silver. But according to the Nyāya philosophers ignorance does not belong to the type of object to which silver belongs. An object of a different type cannot be a material cause. For example, an earthen jar cannot be made out of gold. Moreover, the Nyāya philosophers claim that there is no evidence in favour of the Advaita conception of ignorance.

In the philosophy of Patañjali also we come across a type of modification of the mind (*citta-vṛtti*) called '*viparyaya*'. Hence he is also in favour of the theory of *anyathākhyāti*. In his *yoga-vārtika* Vijñānabhikṣu has also developed this view. In *Ślokavārtika*, Bhaṭṭa Kumārila has also accepted this theory. Moreover, it is also close to common sense.

Since *akhyātivāda* has ignored the very conception of error, it does not have much appeal to other philosophers. But several schools of Indian philosophy and a large number of Indian philosophers have accepted *anyathākhyātivāda*.

The gist of the theory of *anyathākhyāti* is that one object appears as another (or is cognized as another). When we cognize a snake in a rope, our visual sense-organs are related to the rope and there is some defect (*doṣa*). It is due to this defect that the previously observed real snake is cognized in the rope. Hence the cognition of the elsewhere snake in the rope is *anyathākhyāti*. According to this view the cognition of the rope qualified by snakeness is true, but the cognition of the snake in the locus, which is a rope, is erroneous.

This view has also been criticized. It is claimed that if the previously observed snake is perceived in the locus, which is in front of the perceiver, due to some defect in the visual sense-organ or in the objective conditions such as darkness, then the place where the snake has been observed would also be cognized. If that were so, there would not be any error.

According to the Navya-Nyāya philosophers, in the case of snake-rope illusion, first we cognize the rope as *this*. But due to some defect in our sense-organs or in the objective conditions the rope is not cognized as qualified by ropeness. The cognition of the rope as *this*, which is generic in nature, generates the expectancy for a more specific cognition. This is due to the fact that a generic cognition is a cause of a specific cognition. Since there is a similarity in shape between the rope and a snake, the cognition of this similarity energizes the disposition (*saṁskāra*) of a snake or gives rise to the memory-cognition of a snake. The memory-cognition of a snake becomes the relation and gives rise to the perceptual cognition of a snake which has been observed in the past. This type of extraordinary relation is *jñānalakṣaṇa sannikarṣa*.

According to some other Nyāya philosophers there is no need to introduce the memory-cognition and the extraordinary relation in order to explain an erroneous perception. The disposition which is energized is erroneously perceived as a property of the object which is in front of the perceiver. Since there is a similarity between the rope and a snake, the disposition of a snake can be energized. Thereafter the object in front of the perceiver appears as qualified by snakeness. This is how the erroneous cognition of 'This is a snake' occurs.

There are certain other types of erroneous cognitions where there is no scope for *jñānalakṣaṇa sannikarṣa*.

Let us consider a necklace made of gold and a piece of fashion jewellery which looks like gold but is not made of gold. If both necklaces are side by side, one may take both of them to be made of gold. Similarly, in the case of twin brothers one may be mistaken for another due to similarity between them. This type of error is not very uncommon. Hence ***anyathākhyāti*** is a cognition of the form '*a* is *F*' when *a* does not have *F* but *F* is elsewhere or elsewhen.

(E) Anirvacanīya *khyāti* :

Ācārya Śaṅkara has propounded the Advaitavāda (the theory of non-dualism) by establishing Brahman as the ultimate locus of cosmic illusion. The Advaitavāda cannot be substantiated without establishing imposition (*adhyāsa*). Everything is imposed upon Brahman. There are three types of existence, namely, empirical, illusory, and transcendent. It is impossible to survive if we do not accept empirical existence. We have to admit differences among objects even if everything is Brahman from the point of view of transcendent existence. All our empirical activities will cease to exist if we think 'I am Brahman, you are Brahman, and all the animate and inanimate objects of the world are Brahman.' Hence we cannot deny the empirical existence of things as long as we have not realized Brahman.

It is a common fact that we sometimes perceive one thing as another. But those who have known Brahman cognize everything as Brahman. This is due to the fact that everything *is* Brahman. The transcendent existence of each and everything lies in Brahman. This is embedded in the very meaning of the term '*Advaita*'. According to this theory, transcendent object is one and it is Brahman. Our cognition of multiplicity will continue so long as we have not realized Brahman. The cognition of multiplicity is due to ignorance (*ajñāna*) which has no beginning.

Expressions such as '*adhyāsa*', '*āropa*', '*viparyaya*', '*viparyāsa*', etc., signify error (or illusion), and are synonymous. Error can be classified into five types:

(a) The erroneous cognition of silver in mother-of-pearl is not beginningless. It is due to some defect.

(b) Sentences like 'I am a human being', 'I am happy', 'I am unhappy', etc., express erroneous cognitions of identity. This type of erroneous cognition is due to beginningless ignorance.

(c) Ignorance about Brahman or the imposition of ignorance on Brahman is also beginningless.

(d) Expressions like 'My body', 'My house', etc., represent relational imposition (*saṁsargādhyāsa*). Here the illusion is with respect to the relation which holds between a property and its possessor.

(e) Imposition of a divine spirit on a stone or a lump of clay is also an erroneous cognition. For example, the imposition of Lord Viṣṇu on a *śālagrām* (a special type of stone). We know that the stone is not Viṣṇu, but still we impose Him on this stone.

Now the question is : What is the nature of ignorance which makes us visualize the world as different from Brahman?

Ignorance cannot be said to be real (*sat*). Nor can it be said to be unreal (*asat*). But it can be dispelled by knowledge (*jñāna*). Ignorance is not absence of knowledge. It is a positive entity. It consists of three principles, the principle of intelligence (*sattva*), the principle of activity (*rajaḥ*), and the principle of inertia (*tamaḥ*). *Sattva* has the ability to generate mental effort (*pravṛtti*), *rajaḥ* the ability to generate suffering (*duḥkha*), and *tamaḥ* the ability to generate attachment (*moha*). The fact that ignorance cannot be described as real (*sat*) or unreal (*asat*) is not its demerit; it is to be considered as its merit (*bhūṣaṇaṁ na tu dūṣaṇam*).

Ignorance is not something which cannot be substantiated. Everyone is aware of ignorance when he/she says 'I am ignorant of it.' It is very difficult for an individual to be free from ignorance. Ignorance has two types of power, concealment and projection. Mother-of-pearl does not have silverness, but it is covered by the *concealment* power of ignorance, and the silver which is cognized is created by the *projection* power of ignorance. Later on it is realized that the object is not silver, but mother-of-pearl. This realization (or cognition) reveals the illusory nature (*mithyātva*) of the silver and the true nature of the locus which is mother-of-pearl. This is how everything is imposed upon Brahman. The realization of this truth is liberation (*mukti*), which is of the nature of Brahman.

As the silver is imposed upon mother-of-pearl, so mother-of-pearl is imposed upon Brahman which is of the nature of consciousness. Hence, ultimately, the locus of the silver which is indescribable (*anirvacanīya*) is the consciousness qualified by the mother-of-pearl. Here the word '*anirvacanīya*' ('indescribable') means '*mithyā*' ('false'). If something is *anirvacanīya* (or *mithyā*), then it cannot be determined either as real (*sat*) or as unreal (*asat*). If the silver imposed upon the consciousness qualified by the mother-of-pearl were real (*sat*), then the cognition of the silver would not have been contradicted by the true cognition of the mother-of-pearl. If the silver were unreal (*asat*) like the sky-flower, then it would not have been cognized. Again the silver cannot be said to be both real and unreal, because an object cannot have opposed properties at the same time.

From our above discussion it follows that the Sautrāntika, Vaibhāṣika, and Vijñānavāda philosophers have accepted *ātmakhyāti*, the Śūnyavāda philosophers *asatkhyāti*, the Prābhākara Mīmāṁsā philosophers *akhyāti*, and the followers of the Nyāya, Vaiśeṣika, Yoga, and Bhaṭṭa Kumārila have accepted *anyathākhyāti*. But these four theories are opposed to the conclusion of the Advaita Vedanta. By propounding the theory of *anirvacanīya-khyāti* Ācārya Śaṅkara has revealed the mysterious nature of the embodied soul and the world in its totality.

It may be noted that everyone does not cognize the same object in the same locus in an erroneous cognition. Someone may cognize a snake in a rope, but someone else may cognize a stick in a rope. This is due to the fact that the ignorance of different individuals takes different forms. This difference has been explained in terms of the different energized dispositions of individuals.

Now an objection may be raised in the following way : If we accept the consciousness qualified by a rope as the locus of the snake, stick, etc., then it is possible for an individual to cognize all of them at the same time in an erroneous cognition. But no one cognizes all of them at the same time. This is due to the fact that different dispositions are energized at different times. A snake is imposed on the rope when the disposition of the previously experienced snake is energized. Similarly, a stick is imposed on the rope when the disposition of the previously experienced stick is energized. In this context it is to be noted that there is no rule that the previously experienced snake or stick has to be a genuine snake or stick. It may not be a genuine snake or stick. According to the Advaita Vedanta one of the auxiliary causes of imposition is a disposition which is due to the cognition of the same type of objects.

The real significance of the discussion of erroneous cognition in the Advaitavāda is the establishment of the thesis that it is due to ignorance that the world in its totality is imposed upon Brahman. One of the auxiliary causes of this imposition is the disposition which is due to the cognition of the world which has no beginning. This theory is called '*sṛṣṭi-dṛṣṭivāda*' ('the theory that apprehension depends on creation'). Hence, according to this view, the cognition of objects depends on objects which were created prior to the cognition.

As regards the relation between the world and its cognitions there is another theory as well in the Advaita Vedanta. As dream-objects depend upon the dream for their existence, so the world depends upon our cognition for its existence. This theory is called '*dṛṣṭi-sṛṣṭivāda*' ('the theory that creation depends upon apprehension'). According to this view, the world which is imposed upon Brahman is dependent on our cognition or apprehension.

The gist of what Ācārya Śaṅkara has said in his discussion of *anirvacanīya khyāti* is that an embodied soul (*jīva*) is not different from Brahman. The difference is apparent, not real. It is due to ignorance that the *jīva* appears to be different from Brahman. But, in fact, *jīva is* Brahman. Ignorance has no beginning, but it has an end. It can be dispelled by the knowledge of reality. Hence by removing ignorance the identity between *jīva* and Brahman can be realized.*

* Translation by J. L. Shaw

Valid Cognition (*Pramā*) and the Truth (*Satyatā*) of its Object

PANDIT VISVABANDHU BHATTACHARYA

Pandit Visvabandhu Bhattacharya Shastri, Tarkatirtha, Nyaya Shastri, Nyayacharya, Bihar Sanskrit Association, Vedantatirtha; Adhyapaka: Balananda Sanskrit College, Prachya Siksha Sadan, Ramakrishna Veda Vidyalaya; Lecturer: Government Sanskrit Colleges, Nabadwip and Calcutta; Visiting Professor, Centre of Advanced Study in Philosophy, Visva Bharati; Reader, Visva Bharati, Jadavpur University; Senior Research Fellow, Indian Council of Philosophical Research; Visiting Fellow, Department of Philosophy, Jadavpur University; Visiting Professor, Dept. of Indology, Ramakrishna Mission Institute of Culture.

Select Bibliography of Professional Works : *Prāmāṇyavādaḥ of Harirāma Tarkavāgīśa*, with a Commentary in Sanskrit, *Prabhā*; Bengali works : *Abhāvīya Pratiyogitā, Samavāya Lakṣaṇa Vicāra, Akhyātivāda, Bhāratīya Darśane Duḥkha, Vyakti Vācaka Pada vā Proper Name, Anuvyavasāya, Pramār Lakṣaṇa, Jñāna Saṁvedana, Nyāyamate Katipaya Pada O Tadvācya, Svarūpa Sambandha, Pramāṇa;* In Sanskrit : *Indriyanānātva-Vimarśaḥ, Pratibadhya-Pratibandhaka Bhāva, Śabdabodha*. The above Bengali and Sanskrit articles were published in various journals, beginning in 1954.

At present working on the whole of the *Anumānakhaṇḍa* of Gaṅgeśa's *Tattvacintāmaṇi*, hoping 'this will generate new creative philosophical activity in the country.'

If a cognition does not deviate from its object, then it is called '*pramā*' ('valid cognition'). If an object *a* has the property *F* and is at a particular place or time, then respectively the cognition that *a* has *F* or is at that place or time, does not deviate from the object. In other words, if an object *a* has the property *F* then its cognition that *a* has *F* is called '*pramā*'. Hence the validity (*pramātva*) and the invalidity (*apramātva*) of a cognition will depend respectively upon the truth (*satyatā*) or the falsity (*mithyātva*) of the object of cognition. But it has been claimed by some contemporary philosophers that even if the object of cognition is true the doubt-free cognition (*niścaya*) of it cannot be said to be '*pramā*' ('valid cognition').

In this paper I would like to discuss some of the counterexamples (put forward against the justified true belief conception of knowledge) from the Nyāya point of view.

It is to be noted that in some counterexamples the objects of cognition are not true. In some other counterexamples the cognitions are true due to the truth of their objects, but their validity (*pramātva*) cannot be determined. For this reason, perhaps, they are not considered as valid. But, in fact, they are also valid cognitions. Since there is doubt about the validity of these cognitions, there is no certainty in them. For this reason some philosophers might not call them '*pramā*'. In some other counterexamples, the cognitions are true (*yathārtha*) or valid (*pramā*) due to the truth of their objects, and there is no difficulty in determining their validity. Hence one should not object to the use of the word '*pramā*' in such cases. I shall explain my points in the context of the following counterexamples.

First counterexample

Jadu and Madhu have both applied for the same job. The employer told Jadu that Madhu would get the job. From the utterance of the employer Jadu got the doubt-free (*niścaya*) cognition (a) that he (the person) who will get the job is Madhu. Jadu has also noticed (b) that Madhu has ten rupees. From this evidence Jadu got the doubt-free cognition (c) that he (the person) who will get the job has ten rupees. In fact, Jadu got the job and he also had ten rupees. Now it has been claimed that even if the object of (c) is true the cognition of it cannot be said to be *pramā*.

In this counterexample, the pronouns 'he' (the person) and 'who' have occurred. In other words, there is a relative pronoun 'who' and a demonstrative pronoun 'he'. It would be difficult to explain my view on this topic without explaining the meanings of these words. Hence let us say a few words about the referents of these expressions.

Expressions such as 'that', 'he/she', 'who', etc. are pronouns and are capable of indicating many different objects or persons. But each and every use of a pronoun, demonstrative or relative, cannot be said to indicate every object. A particular use of a relative or demonstrative pronoun refers to that object which is intended by the person who uses it. A speaker also uses it to refer to the object which is the referent of another word in the same sentence or a previous sentence. For example, Rāma is sitting in that room, please tell him to come here.

In this sentence the word 'him' refers to the person who is referred to by the word 'Rāma'. Now let us consider a sentence which contains what Frege would call a 'subjective clause'. For example : He (the person) whom I saw before has come. In this sentence the pronoun 'he' refers to the person who is referred to by the pronoun 'whom'.

Now let us discuss the above example in the light of the rules for the use of the demonstrative and the relative pronouns. In the example above, the person *Madhu* has been referred to in the sentence 'Madhu would get the job'. Again, Jadu's doubt-free cognitions that the person who will get the job is Madhu and that Madhu has ten rupees are about Madhu. Therefore when Jadu utters the sentence 'He (the person) who will get the job has ten rupees', he refers to Madhu by the word 'he', not to himself. If 'Madhu' is the referent of the word 'he' in this sentence, then the relative pronoun 'who' refers to the same person. Hence the object of Jadu's cognition is that Madhu will get the job. But later on Jadu himself got the job, not Madhu. Therefore, the cognition of Jadu is erroneous. Since the object of his cognition lacks truth, his cognition cannot be valid (*pramā*).

If a sentence contains pronouns such as 'that which' or 'he/she who' without having reference to anything prior to its use, then the predicate of the referent of the relative pronoun (who or which) is to be considered as being pervaded by the predicate of the referent of the demonstrative pronoun (that or he/she). (In other words, the former predicate is the pervaded and the latter is the pervader.) For example : That which has smoke has fire.

In this case *smoke* is the predicate of the referent of the relative pronoun 'which' and *fire* is the predicate of the demonstrative pronoun 'That'. Hence this sentence gives rise to the cognition that smoke is pervaded by fire. In other words, there is a cognition of whatever has smoke has fire. The sentence 'That which has a horn is an animal' is to be explained in the same way. Here also the predicates are related by the pervader-pervaded relation. The sentence generates the cognition of whatever has a horn has animality, which is the pervader of a horn.

If we do not admit that the predicate of the referent of the demonstrative pronoun has the property of being the pervader of the predicate of the referent of the relative pronoun, then the sentence 'That which has fire has smoke' would be as true as the sentence 'That which has smoke has fire' is true. Similarly, 'That which is an animal has a horn' would be true as 'That which has a horn is an animal' is true. But no one admits the truth of 'That which has fire has smoke' or 'That which is an animal has a horn'.

Let us consider the sentence 'He (the person) who will get the job has ten rupees'. If this sentence simply states that the property of having ten rupees is the pervader of the property of having the job, then its cognition cannot be said to be invalid. This is due to the fact that both Jadu and Madhu had ten rupees, but only one of them got the job. So the property of having ten rupees is the pervader of the property of having the job.

Now it may be said that the sentence 'He (the person) who will get the job has ten rupees' is to be taken in isolation from the previous sentences in the above counterexample. 'He (the person) who will get the job has ten rupees' is an inference. This is due to the fact that the previous sentences have simply presented the probans (*hetu*) and the probandum (*sādhya*) of this inference. The rule that the referent of a demonstrative or relative pronoun is a previously mentioned object is applicable to a verbal cognition only. Hence it is not applicable to an inference. Therefore, the word 'He' or 'who' in this sentence will not give rise to the cognition of Madhu. This is how the previous objection that the cognition expressed by this sentence is erroneous can be rejected. Now the question is: what is the probans or the probandum of this inference? In other words, what is being established by what? This can be answered in the following way :

(1) From the probans having a job we infer the probandum having ten rupees, or

(2) From the probans having ten rupees we infer the probandum having a job.

But neither of them is tenable. The first alternative is not acceptable because there are people who have jobs but do not have ten rupees. Similarly, the second alternative is not acceptable. This is due to the fact that there are people who have ten rupees in their pockets but do not have any job.

In order to avoid this objection it may be said that the inference is represented by the sentence 'He (the person) who will get the job, between Jadu and Madhu, has ten rupees', not by the sentence 'He (the person) who will get the job has ten rupees'. One of them will get the job, but both of them have ten rupees. Hence we can infer having ten rupees from having the job.

But this inference also is not acceptable. In this case the probans is having the job. Jadu cognizes this property in Madhu because the employer told him that Madhu would get the job. Since Madhu did not get the job, the conclusion of this inference is derived from an erroneous cognition. Since there would be doubt about the validity of this cognition, it cannot be said to be valid.

Second counterexample

Having seen Madhu driving a car Jadu has a doubt-free cognition that he (Madhu) owns a car. From this cognition he infers :

Either Madhu owns a car or Rama is in Delhi. Later on, it has been found that Madhu does not own a car, but Rama happens to be in Delhi. The fact that Rama was in Delhi was not known to Jadu. Although the object of Jadu's inferential cognition that Madhu owns a car or Rama is in Delhi is true, the cognition itself cannot be said to be valid (*pramā*).

I think this is a case of disjunctive inference. If one of the alternatives of a disjunction is established, then the disjunction is established. Hence a disjunction can be inferred from any one of its disjuncts. For example,

(1) 'There is a pot or a piece of cloth' can be inferred from

(2) 'There is a pot.'

If the latter is true, then the former is true. Similarly, (1) can be inferred from

(3) 'There is a piece of cloth.'

Again, if a conjunction is true, then a disjunction is also true. Hence if (4) 'There is a pot and a piece of cloth' is true, so (1) is true. In this counterexample, Jadu has inferred the disjunctive conclusion from his previous doubt-free cognition that Madhu owns a car. But, later on, it has been found that Madhu does not own a car. The probans (*hetu*) of the inference is the disjunct that Madhu owns a car. Since this disjunct is false, the conclusion is derived from a defective causal condition. If a conclusion is inferred from a defective probans, then sometimes it is true (*yathārtha*) or valid (*pramā*) and sometimes it is false (*ayathārtha*) or invalid (*apramā*). Since the conclusion of this inference is derived from a defective probans, there will be doubt about the validity of its conclusion. Similar is the case with the following inference :

There are animals in this forest, because there are horses with horns in this forest.

In this case the probans is horses with horns. Since the probans has no exemplification (*aprasiddha*), there will be cognition of invalidity (*aprāmāṇya-jñāna*) in this inference.

In our above counterexample also, there will be cognition of invalidity. This is due to the fact that the conclusion has been inferred from the probans which has not been established (*asiddha*). If there is a cognition of invalidity in a doubt-free cognition, then it becomes very weak. Hence a cognition which is related to a cognition of invalidity cannot produce the consequences which can be produced by a cognition which is not related to it. This type of cognition cannot prevent the cognitions which can be prevented by a doubt-free or certain cognition. A cognition that is related to a cognition of invalidity does not have the status of certainty. For this reason some philosophers are not willing to call it 'doubt-free valid cognition'. Hence the conclusion that Madhu owns a car or Rāma is in Delhi cannot be a doubt-free valid cognition as it is related to a cognition of invalidity.

In fact, according to our view, if one of the disjuncts is unexemplified (*aprasiddha*), then the entire disjunction becomes unexemplified (*aprasiddha*). For example, a hare with a horn or a horse. Since a hare with a horn is unexemplified, the entire disjunction is unexemplified.

Third counterexample

It has been claimed that there is no false cognition in this counterexample.

Suppose a person driving through the countryside saw several barns and got a doubt-free cognition (*niścaya*) of these barns. In fact, there are both real barns and barn facades. In spite of having truth in the object of cognition, the cognition itself has not been claimed to be valid (*pramā*).

Since there is no false cognition in this counterexample, the doubt-free cognition of the person must be about the real barns. If it were so, then this cognition would have the status of a valid cognition to the person in question. Hence the observer would take it as valid. But those who know that there are barn facades will have doubt about the validity of his cognition. Since there are barn facades, they think that he might have taken a barn facade to be a real barn. Then his cognition might not be claimed to be valid. But there should not be this type of objection.

If the observer has taken a barn facade to be real barn, then his cognition cannot be valid. This is due to the fact that it is about something which is false.

If the observer has taken both a real barn and a barn facade to be real barns, then his cognition would be partly valid and partly invalid. This is similar to the situation when there is a piece of silver and a piece of shell in front of an observer. If the observer claims both of them to be silver, then his cognition is valid with respect to silver but invalid with respect to shell. Hence, in our above counterexample, the cognition is valid with respect to the real barn but invalid with respect to the barn facade.

Fourth counterexample

Suppose Jadu sees a round object that looks red to him. On the basis of this observation he has the doubt-free cognition that this round object is red. In fact, the round object is red. But Jadu does not know that the object is illuminated by red lights and it would look red to him even if it were not red. In this case the object of cognition has truth (*satyatā*) in it, but the cognition is not claimed to be valid. With respect to this example, I think the cognition of Jadu is true, although the round object is illuminated by red lights. Since the object is red, the cognition should be considered as valid. The cognition has revealed the object in the way it in fact is.

Now it may be said that the round object would look red even if it were white. This is due to the fact that it has been illuminated by red lights. Since there is possibility of error, the cognition in question cannot be claimed to be valid.

In reply, we can say that if a true (*yathārtha*) cognition cannot be said to be valid due to the fact that there is possibility of error, then it would be almost impossible to have valid cognition (*pramājñāna*). Let us consider an inferential cognition. Suppose I am asleep while it rained. After having seen the streets being wet I inferred that it rained. Everyone would consider this cognition as valid. But here also there is possibility of error. The same street would be wet if it were washed. If we apply the previous argument then in this case also the true inferential cognition of rain cannot be said to be valid. Consider another example. A yellow piece of cloth has been seen to be yellow in day light. This is a valid cognition. But if the observer were jaundiced, then he/she would have seen a white piece of cloth to be yellow. Hence by applying the same argument one may claim that the cognition of the observer cannot be said to be valid. But the followers of the Nyāya would not claim that a doubt-free cognition which has revealed a true object cannot be said to be valid. In our above counterexample, if the round object is red, then its doubt-free cognition must be valid. But if the round object is white and it looks red due to red lights in it, then the cognition that it is red must be erroneous.

Fifth counterexample

Suppose both Jadu and Madhu work in the same office and Jadu has always found Madhu to be a reliable and trustworthy person. Madhu has told Jadu that he owns a car. When he made this utterance he was in a state of hypnosis. In fact, Madhu does not have any car, but he won a car in a lottery after entering the state of hypnosis, and it remained unknown to both Jadu and Madhu. From the utterance of Madhu, Jadu got the cognition that someone in my office owns a car. But this cognition cannot be claimed to be valid.

In this context it is to be noted that when Madhu uttered the sentence 'I own a car', his use of the word 'car' does not refer to the car which he has won in a lottery. This is due to the fact that he does not know that he won a car when he made this utterance. One does not use a sentence to convey an unknown thing to someone else, so the intended referent of the word 'car' in this sentence cannot be the car which he has won in a lottery. It refers to a car which he has cognized before. Since Madhu does not own this car, the cognition generated by his utterance is erroneous. Hence invalidity will be cognized in all other subsequent cognitions which are due to this erroneous cognition. Therefore, none of them can be said to be valid.

Now it may be said that the word 'car' in the sentence 'I own a car' does not refer to any specific car. It refers to any car. The cognition generated by this sentence does not have any specific car as its object. Since the cognition is about a car which Madhu owns, it should be considered valid.

It can be asked whether Jadu knows that Madhu was in a hypnotic state when he uttered the sentence 'I own a car'. If he does not know, then he would cognize the car which is related to Madhu by the ownership relation, although the word 'car' would generate the cognition of cars in general. This is due to the fact that there is semantic competency between Madhu and the car he owns, so his cognition would be valid. But if Jadu knows that Madhu is in a hypnotic state, then Madhu's utterance would not generate any cognition. This is due to the fact that the utterance of an abnormal person is not to be taken seriously. It is to be ignored.

Sixth counterexample

Suppose Jadu saw Madhu stealing a book from the library and reported this incident to the library. After having heard this report,

Madhu's mother visited the library and averred that Madhu was not in the library on that day as he was thousands of miles away. She also said that Madhu's twin brother who looks like Madhu was in the library. His name is Rama, so Rama, not Madhu, has stolen the book. But Jadu does not know anything about this report of Madhu's mother. Later on it has been found that Madhu's mother was insane when she made this statement. In fact, Madhu has no twin brother and it is Madhu who has stolen the book from the library. In this counterexample, it is claimed that the previous doubt-free cognition of Jadu is not valid.

With respect to this counterexample, I think Jadu has seen Madhu stealing a book from the library. Hence the cognition of Jadu is free from doubt and it is certain. Since it is true and completely free from doubt, there is no reason to consider it as invalid.

It may be said that although Jadu did not know the report of Madhu's mother, those who have known the report would doubt the validity of Jadu's cognition, so his cognition cannot be claimed to be valid. In reply, we can say that others might doubt the validity of Jadu's cognition so long as they do not know that Madhu's mother was insane and told a lie. But when they would come to know that she was insane and told a lie, they might not doubt the validity of his cognition. If we accept the view that a valid cognition loses its validity if there is a doubt about its validity, then every valid cognition would lose its validity as we could doubt its validity. This is due to the fact that there is always the possibility of telling a lie which will lead us to doubt the validity of a cognition.

Now let us discuss whether those who are not aware of the false report of Madhu's mother would consider the cognition of Jadu to be valid or invalid. Since they do not have any reason to consider it as invalid, they would consider it as valid. But those who are aware of the report of Madhu's mother might not consider it as valid. As a result, the same cognition would be considered valid by someone and invalid by someone else. Hence there would be a problem in determining who is right and who is wrong.

It may be said that if a cognition is valid, then no one will have a cognition which is opposed to it. In other words, no one will have a contrary or contradictory cognition. In our above counterexample, since there are cognitions which are opposed to the doubt-free cognition of Jadu, his cognition cannot be said to be valid. If we accept this view, then no cognition would be valid.

It may be asked if a valid cognition is unchangeable and if it will never be destroyed by an opposite cognition.

This claim also cannot be justified. This is due to the fact that a valid cognition can be destroyed by an illusory cognition which is opposed to it. If an opposite illusory cognition occurs after the occurrence of a valid cognition, then the latter would be destroyed by the former. As a result, no cognition will be called 'valid'.

It may be said that after the occurrence of a valid cognition there will not occur a contrary or contradictory illusory cognition in the same individual. If a cognition is self-evident (*svataḥ siddha*), then after its occurrence no other contrary or contradictory cognition would occur. Hence a self-evident cognition will be valid. For example, 2+2 = 4. If a person cognizes 2+2=4, then he/she would not cognize 2+2=5 or 2+2=3. For this reason the cognition of 2+2=4 is valid.

This view also is not acceptable. We may accept 2+2=4 as self-evident, but we can never accept its cognition as self-evident. This is due to the fact that children are being taught from their childhood that 2+2=4. This type of practice from childhood leaves an impression (*saṁskāra*) which is so strong that one remembers 4 as soon as '2+2' is uttered.

On this point the supporters of this view might claim that although the cognition of a self-evident truth is not itself self-evident, it can stop the occurrence of an opposite illusory cognition if it is cognized repeatedly. Hence a cognition of this type is to be considered as valid.

In reply it may be said that even if a person has a valid cognition of 2+2=4, which is due to repeated practice, he/she might suffer from dementia. As a result, he/she might cognize 2+2=5 or 2+2=3. If it were so, then the previously held valid cognition would no longer be considered valid. For this reason the above interpretation of validity is not tenable.

Notes

1. The author uses the word '*pramā*' which is usually translated as 'valid cognition'. But in some contexts it may be translated as 'knowledge'. This is due to the fact that sometimes a justification condition is included in it.

2. Here the author uses the word '*satyatā*'. It is a property of an object. If a cognition of the form *a* has *f* is true, then the object *a* has the property *satyatā*. Since *a* is a truth-maker or makes the cognition true and *satyatā* is its property, the word '*satyatā*' may be translated as 'truth'. If the cognition is false, then *a* does not have the property *f*. Hence it lacks *satyatā*. In other words, it has the property *mithyātva* (falsity).

3. In the first two counterexamples the author is discussing the Gettier problem from the Nyāya point of view.

4. Here the author uses the word '*yat*' which includes relative pronouns such as 'who' and 'which'.

5. Here the author uses the word '*tat*' which includes not only demonstrative pronouns such as 'this' or 'that' but also personal pronouns such as 'he' or 'she'.

6. An inference, according to the Nyāya, involves three terms, viz, *sādhya* (probandum), *pakṣa* (the locus of inference) and *hetu* (probans). The term '*sādhya*' refers to what is to be inferred. The term '*pakṣa*' refers to the locus where there is some doubt about the presence of the *sādhya*. The term '*hetu*' refers to the reason or the mark by means of which the *sādhya* is inferred in the *pakṣa*.

7. In other words, Jadu will have doubt about the conclusion when he comes to know that Madhu does not own a car.

8. In the remaining counterexamples the author is discussing the post-Gettier counterexamples from the Nyāya point of view.*

---

* Translation and Notes by J. L. Shaw

The Concept of 'Realization' Re-examined

MARGARET CHATTERJEE

Prof. Margaret Chatterjee, teacher of philosophy, Westminster College, Oxford, taught philosophy in Delhi University from 1956 to 1990, with stints at Visva-Bharati, Drew University in Madison, New Jersey, USA, and the Indian Institute of Advanced Study, Simla, during this period. Has lectured and taken part in philosophical conferences in many countries, and is a frequent lecturer on Gandhian thought in the U. K. and the USA. A Visiting Fellow at Wolfson College, Oxford in 1991, and at the University of Calgary, Canada. In 1994 was Lady Davis Visiting Professor at the Hebrew University of Jerusalem.

Formerly President of the International Society of Metaphysics, has published widely in learned journals on philosophy and religion. Publications include : *Our Knowledge of Other Selves, The Existentialist Outlook, The Religious Spectrum, The Concept of Spirituality,* and *Gandhi and His Jewish Friends.* Editor of *Contemporary Indian Philosophy* for Allen and Unwin, and of *The Philosophy of Nikunja Vihari Banerjee* for the Indian Council for Philosophical Research and Munshiram Manoharlal.

In the modern era, epistemologists have by and large assumed that to cognize involves : (a) objectivity (b) distinctness from the affective and the volitional. Even where subjective conditions of a theoretical kind (cf. Kantian conceptual frameworks or theoretical constructs as found in the sciences) are deemed indispensable to knowledge they are deemed such in virtue of their being presuppositions of objectivity. The two considerations are interconnected in that feeling and willing are taken to detract from objectivity or, the stronger case, are irrelevant to it. It is not difficult to see how such a view of cognition detaches epistemology from ontology, to say nothing of detaching it from aesthetics or ethics. That scientific knowledge requires a bracketing out of the personal equation may almost seem a commonplace even though personal records of scientists concerning their work in process would suggest that discovery is by no means cut loose from its matrix, which in turn accommodates much that is not strictly cognitive. Even to say this makes clear the view that epistemology customarily sets its sights on the end term of cognitive processes rather than on those processes themselves. Such a line of thinking runs through the whole project of demarcating psychology from epistemology which eventually led to the capture of the cognitive enquiry by linguistic analysis, something which, to my mind, amounted to a virtual departure from the analysis of cognition *per se*. Of course there is a sense in which analysis of cognition is self-defeating, for to question what it is to know leads to an infinite regress. No matter how many grounds or warrants be trotted out there is an inbuilt gap between these and the intuitive insight that provides the terminus *ad quem*. Even those who make much of the contrast between belief and knowledge might concede this.

But what if there be a mode of cognition which is not hamstrung by our two initial considerations, one in which objectivity is not the be-all-and-end-all and in which feeling and willing are intimately bound up with knowing? Indeed there seems to be not one such mode of cognition but several such. Traditional demarcations between branches of philosophy should not hold us up at this point. We do in fact speak of knowing what we ought to do even though there may be situations where it takes much time and thought to determine it. We similarly speak of knowing one activity to be more worthy than another (cf. helping someone in distress *vis a vis* an act of self-indulgence). Even if such judgements may not be free of cultural filters this does not invalidate the use of the term 'know' with reference to them. Polanyi in his book *Personal Knowledge* provides a host of examples of situations in which it would be Pickwickian to deny that human beings were knowing in some sense or other. One qualm about such cases can be stilled. In such examples the possibility of being mistaken is not ruled out. On the contrary what comes into play is a process of self-correction at which most people of standard endowments* are quite adept. In fact our ability to comport ourselves in situations of great variety brings into play knowledge of a fine-grained kind whether this be recognized by philosophers or not.

Let us take a different sort of example. X says to you, 'You know

* I here borrow a phrase often used by H. H. Price in his classroom lectures on perception.

you are always welcome whenever you care to come round.' While in English it would be natural to use the word *know,* the same meaning could be conveyed in Bengali without using it. Such is the genius of each language. My point is that although we are no doubt referring to knowledge it would be pedantic and perhaps artificial to speak of cognition *simpliciter* in this case. How would one set about unpacking the sentence? No doubt the speaker and the addressee find themselves in a situation which in turn is part of a shared life-world. Without this (say, to someone distributing pamphlets or selling washing powder) the occasion for saying anything of the kind would not arise. The addressee does not make a telescoped induction on the basis of previous experience in order to understand or verify what is said. The point of reference is really the shared life-world of the two friends which 'makes sense of' the locution. Let us make the case a little more elaborate. Objectively speaking there might be ground for doubting the welcome if one so wills. X does not stop what he or she is doing when Y arrives—the food has to be cooked or proofs corrected to catch the post, the phone call continued or whatever. It is the shared world with all its multitude of significations that gives Y confidence in his or her present and future welcome. So the apparent discourtesy of X's continuing with whatever he or she was doing when Y arrived is in fact *not* taken as a ground for doubting the welcome. It may quite possibly provide evidence of the strength of the relationship and so X may say 'You don't mind if I finish this, do you?' I would sum the situation up by saying that Y's understanding of the original sentence, 'You know you are always welcome whenever you care to come round', is based on the *relationship* which both have jointly built and in which the notion of grounds is somehow alien or at least *de trop.*

II

In the foregoing I have not done more than prepare the ground for an approach which would extend the range of applicability of the word *cognition* beyond its usual usages in epistemology and, in particular, free it from any necessary connection with theories about the conditions of objectivity. The use made by certain Indian philosophers at the turn of the century of the terms *realization* and *self-realization* is worth looking into in this connection, it seems to me. Discussion of these terms has, as far as I can make out, been accommodated for the most part in discourses about religion, more especially mysticism, or—a more minimal treatment—under 'intuition'. On investigation, however, the idea, although not the terms, trails a longer lineage. This includes the conception of *adhikāra* or eligibility to know, carrying as this does the implications of the relevant instruction and discipline, and the accompanying caveat that the cultivation of certain powers requires the curbing of others. This latter point, *inter alia,* seems to be based on common sense. For example, the preoccupations of the householder preclude *tapasyā* of a meditative kind.

The words *realization* and self-realization were frequently used in the nineteenth century, especially in Bengal, and, as far as I am able to judge, entered philosophical discourse through British idealism without directly tapping the original German source from which this in turn was derived. At about the same time the word *spirit* came into circulation, likewise losing its diverse moorings in Western thought, including both its Greek and German roots.* It was perhaps not surprising that those in search of a term which would denote a unitive mode of awareness in which duality would be overcome should find in *realization* a term which could serve their purpose.

However there are considerable differences between the thinkers who used the word, to say nothing of the diverse associations trailed by it in ideational contexts outside India. In fact, to turn the searchlight of inquiry on some of these thinkers is above all to reveal the extent of the incompatibility between, say, Hegel and Śaṅkara, something which is masked in the valiant efforts of neo-Vedantic philosophers to speak of non-dual experience in terms which English-knowing readers with some knowledge of philosophy in the West would find intelligible. What they wished to press home was the concept of *higher* knowledge, something which in the nature of things was not susceptible of theorization but only of experience. But at this point a significant modality appeared. In lieu of

* Some of these are set out in my *The Concept of Spirituality*, Allied Publishers, 1989.

the more traditional teaching (traceable in the main to Patañjali), that the development of some faculties depended on the restraint of others, the notion of integral experience appeared. Those who spoke of this did not all mean the same thing by it, but the idea that all human faculties could be drawn upon can be found especially in Sri Aurobindo and Radhakrishnan. In the latter's case there also appears an interpretation of Tagore's thought with which Tagore himself may not have been fully in agreement. There was herein most surely a synoptic motive. But I believe there was something more—an Indian alternative to *paideia* and to *bildung*, a rethought, modern *Saṁskṛti.* I would even say the spelling out of realization in Indian terms encapsulated *anubhāva yoga*, and *darśana* (in its root meaning). That the Indian perspective in this respect was believed to be quite distinctive is writ large in Swami Vivekananda, Sri Aurobindo and Radhakrishnan.

It may not be an exaggeration to say that, for all these thinkers what realization was for the individual, *freedom* would be for India on a national scale. The image of awakening for both the individual and the nation is invoked by both Sri Aurobindo and Tagore. Philosophical reflection and *jātīya bhāva* often converged. Another motif in realization discourse, and in Swami Vivekananda especially, was opposition to the strategies of the missionaries, a *Kulturkampf* that had been in process especially in Bengal since the time of Raja Rammohun Roy. Its main focus was sustained opposition to doctrine and dogma. The need of the hour—to Swami Vivekananda and his successors—was not belief but practice, not creeds but *sevā.** There is clearly an affinity in the various treatments of realization as higher knowledge, ranging from integral experience to the goal of the unitive, from idealism seen as ethical rather than speculative, to a synoptic understanding which as Brajendranath Seal insisted (using the word *synthetic*) was seen as typically Indian. In any case, for all the Germanic lineage of the word 'realization' Indian thinkers were by and large not concerned

* I take this to be distinguishable from the *augmentation* of cognitive faculties through theurgic (*alaukika*) means. And yet the association of special cognitive capacity with *powers* (usually of an esoteric kind) has been a feature of many cultures. The association of scientific knowledge with *power* is after all a kind of secularized form of this.

with *geist*, or alienation, or the Kantian distinction between the possible, the actual, and the necessary. If the Absolute were to be brought down to earth, that is, made accessible, it could not be in Hegelian fashion through the State, for the State apparatus was not as yet in Indian hands. Self-realization was a feasible target for a self-respecting individual, and not without relation to the coming of that dawn into which the country would eventually awaken.

III

It may not be generally known that in the early part of this century Martin Buber, whose concept of I and Thou later brought him into prominence in the English-speaking world, had been deeply attracted to realization as a philosophical idea.* Buber's pre-dialogical thinking, that is, in the first decade of this century, centred on the concept of *Erlebnis* or lived experience, a term which came into philosophical currency through Dilthey's distinction between *Naturwissenschaften* and *Geisteswissen-schaften* and the associated distinction between *Erfahrung* and *Erlebnis.* What was at stake was not only the contrast between the natural sciences and the human sciences but also the experience of things as against the interiority of lived experience. The notion of lived experience no doubt owed much to Kant's treatment of inner sense. Very unKantian overtones appeared, however, when Buber rethought *Erlebnis* in the light of his doctoral work on Nicholas of Cusa and Jacob Boehme. Buber held that a mystic had a special type of *Erlebnis* in which he could achieve unity with the *Urelebnis* of the world spirit.

At the same time fundamental questions about the methodology of psychology were in the air. All this was fully discussed at a club called the Neue Gemeinschaft at the University of Berlin while Buber was a student there. How could subjective minds interact socially? This was

* The following may be of interest in this connection. Franz Rosenzweing, a close friend of Buber, wrote to his former teacher Friedrich Meinecke, Cognition (*Erkennen*) no longer appears to me an end in itself. It has turned into service, a service to human beings. Rosenzweing to Friedrich Meinecke, 30 August 1920, cited in Nahum N. Glatzer, *Franz Rosenzweing*: *His life and thought*, 2nd Rev. Ed., New York, Schocken, 1972.

the question posed by Simmel, Buber's teacher. In the meantime Dilthey, his other teacher, posed philosophical questions about life, something which was not to be conflated with *Geist*. Buber's own search for unitive experience at this stage drew him away from the individuation presupposed by the concept of social interaction. He polarized cognizing man (*der Erkennende*) to experiencing man (*der Enlebende*). And yet on reflection the notion of the 'lived through' is hardly adequate to express either the mystical experience or the relation between one person and another. A similar difficulty may attend the concept of *anubhava* which of course has a different cultural setting. What ensued after Buber is part of the story of continental thought in this century. While some found in *Existenz* an alternative to both *Geist* and *Leben*, Buber moved from mysticism* to dialogue or what he called '*die Ontologie des Zwischenmenschlochen*'. What years later he described as 'the narrow ridge, where I and Thou meet' could not be fitted into the rarefied atmosphere of 'realization'.

His early work entitled *Daniel,*** however, still repays study for it provides the most deeply thought-out attempt by a scholar outside Indian traditions to do justice to the concept of realization, and to this we now turn. *Daniel* was published in Leipzing in 1913 and manifested the many influences working in Buber's mind during the first decade of the century. He was familiar with a certain amount of 'Oriental' thought, especially Taoism, but it is more likely that his own way of envisaging *realization* was derived from Western sources. Those who spoke of the human sciences, Dilthey in particular, detected an element of empathetic awareness therein which provided the condition for the possibility of 'entering into' human

---

* In so doing he distanced himself, for example, from Rudolf Steiner's *Geistesforschung* and the question that gives the title one of his books '*Wie erlangt man Erkenntnisse hoeherer Welten*?' Steiner had a considerable influence on a close friend of Buber's, Hugo Bergman, who did not rule out the existence of upper worlds (hence his interest in Sri Aurobindo). Buber's answer to this is contained in his rhetorical question 'What concern of ours, if they exist, are the upper worlds?' (*The Origin and Meaning of Hasidism* 181).

** *Daniel*: *Dialogues on Realization,* McGraw-Hill Book Company, New York, Toronto 1965.

phenomena. This was a notion of *verstehen* very different from the Kantian one. In a religious, rather than social context, Kierkegaard spoke of the need to 'appropriate' the truth, to make it one's own rather than treat it objectively. This involved *living* in a certain way rather than being intellectually persuaded through argument or informed through perception.

This reference to life rather than thought chimes in with the Hasidic belief in the need to actualize the divine through daily life, something made possible through an intensifying of religious experience which yet steers clear of pantheism. The influence of Nietzsche on German philosophers at this time can also be recalled. This took various forms. The most common, and the one discernible in the young Buber, was an anti-intellectualism which drew on confidence in powers other than the intellect within man, powers which work in the direction of unities, of dynamism, rather than in the service of categories and distinctions. That herein lies a certain romantic effusiveness must be admitted. But let us turn to the work itself.

It consists of five dialogues in which Daniel and his friends (each dialogue being Socratic in form, friends succeeding each other in dialogue) close in on the meaning of reality given that, as Daniel says in the first dialogue, 'We cannot ascend into the spaceless.'[1] In the second dialogue he speaks of a two-fold relation of man to his experience—classifying, and realizing or making real. Realization, he explains, means heightened existence, heightened knowledge. (Dilthey had spoken of the philosopher's task as that of heightened awareness.) In this heightened existence, power is drawn from the depths and collected and moved to action and renewed in work.[2] In Buber's view 'the power to become unified and to enter into reality'[3] is in everyone. But it is not actualized in all. He mentions the 'hero and the wise men', 'the poet and the prophet', as 'unifying men'.[4] What is happening in today's world, Buber goes on to say, is the replacing of 'realizing men' by 'producers', 'those who work without being, who give what they do not possess, who triumph where they have not fought : the pet children of appearance'.[5] This sounds very much like the concept of objectivity seen as embodied in the consumer society. What Buber decries is *manipulation*, 'the dams of theories, of programs, of parties', each of which, when thought through, is manipulative in some manner or other.

The third dialogue stresses that realization is the kingdom of holy insecurity[6] for 'All creation stands on the edge of being; all creation is risk'.[7] The fourth dialogue speaks of tension and incompleteness in drama and poetry and the polarity within man that 'wills unity'. The fifth dialogue centres on the most difficult moment of the work. By unity Buber does not mean identity, for unity is won in the midst of polarity and tension. It is probably Kant whom he strives with in the following : 'Human life cannot escape the conditioned. But the unconditioned stands ineffaceably inscribed in the heart of the world.'[8] The focus is on death and life. The call is to 'take upon yourself the tension of life and death and live through the life and death of the world as your life and your death'.[9] The concluding symbol of the book is the sea,[10] a fitting metaphor for a unity which surrounds, which is ever-moving, which invites, and yet, to so many, spells fear. It is a symbol used by Sri Ramakrishna Paramahamsa for a somewhat different purpose, namely, to point up the need for a total self-giving, a willingness to lose all in order to gain all. The folk element which is so strong in Sri Ramakrishna is by no means absent in Buber. In the latter's case it is derived from the legends of the Ba'al / Shem Tov. Both men, that is to say, are sensitive to the wisdom of the people, a wisdom which shows itself in story rather than in discourse. If a work such as *Daniel* occasions disquiet among the scholarly this is because its form is not the form of argument. It preserves the quality of confession but, *qua* dialogue, uses the dramatic form. The leap in thought required of the reader involves the willingness to grant the interrelatedness of ontology, aesthetics and ethics, and to allow that there is cognitive import in such interrelatedness. To rule out such an enterprise is to rule out a great deal of both Indian and Western thought, to say nothing of Chinese and Japanese thought. In any case I take it that Indian scholars should not find it difficult to agree that there are contexts in which living in a certain way is a condition of knowing and that knowing in turn manifests itself in certain characteristic ways of acting.

IV

The purpose of the foregoing has been to examine realization as a mode of cognition rather than simply a mode of experience. In the Indian treatments we found that the reference to realization often accompanied the discourse of spirit and the spiritual, and an appeal to *anubhava*. Whereas the first two of these terms, realization and spirit, seem to have a post-Hegelian flavour, the third term has a longer lineage. Neo-Vedantic thinkers found nothing strange in making cognitive claims for realization under the umbrella of 'higher' knowledge. The language of 'degrees of knowledge' was sometimes involved, unsuited though it was for referring to the *pāramārthika* since the latter had invariably been regarded as different in *kind* and not only in degree by classical Vedantins. In Indian philosophical circles at the turn of the century this was not the only incompatibility which surfaced. The pedigree of the word *Geist*, correlated though it was to Nature as its counterpart was to be discerned at work in *history* seen as the operation of a rational principle. No such association has ever been attributed to the Brahman-Atman equation, nor can it.

To go back a bit, some clarification may be needed of my distinction between cognition and experience at the beginning of the last paragraph. By non-cognitive experiences I have in mind what Patañjali calls 'perturbations' and some German idealists called 'agitations' or 'affections'. What Kant regarded as *Schwaermeri* belongs in this category. Of *another* type are the *transitions* between *noeses* spoken of by Husserl as non-cognitive. As for realization, the difficulty in specifying what the putative cognition was *of* was dealt with by putting it in a unique basket of its own wherein the distinction between subject and object would be inappropriate. It was precisely this aspect of it that justified the extended term *self-realization*. The diverse motivations that lay behind such thinking are not hard to divine. They include, for example, an affirmation of the superiority of *ātmavidyā* to other sorts of *vidyā*, a shift from textual to experiential warrant (vouchsafed to specially qualified persons) and this is not all. The political agenda, if I may call it that, could not easily be accommodated in the programme, or at least in the programme as I am venturing to see it, within the context of *kulturkritik*. For realization to be both individual and national, the *pāramārthika* had to be related to the *vyāvahārika* in a way which, on reflectior, cut at the root of the distinction. And yet an attempt to relate the two is surely made by the most adventurous of neo-Hindu thinkers, not only as a necessity recognized by nationalist consciousness, but in no small measure thanks to a Comtian undercurrent especially in Bengali intellectual life which looked to the *future* rather than the past, that is, which looked to the possibility of progress. Bankim Chandra Chatterjee's joint advocacy of *anuśīlana* and *svadeśaprīti* set the tone. Moreover a generation grew up in Bengal which had read Tom Paine's *Age of Reason* in Bengali translation. Perhaps only in Bengal could the term *śakti* also be invoked as Bankim does in order to elicit a dynamism of powers no less vigorously promoted by Swami Vivekananda.

Those who spoke of realization were trying to bring the *turīya* down to earth. Swami Vivekananda's ability to identify with the poor made the whole exercise credible by turning it upside down, that is, seeing God in the eyes of the poor. Realizing for him took on its root meaning of 'making actual', insight actualizing itself in service. In this way he was able to discover an ethical imperative in an insight which of itself was bootless unless translated into action. Or, put in another way, the 'achieved' cognitive import of 'realization' *indicated* embodiment in the world of action. Cognition *simpliciter* is neatly put in its place.

In going along this path Vivekananda encounters Buber in the latter's response to 'the other'. But for Buber this necessarily meant a turning away from the mystical. Vivekananda's insights antedate Buber's by about a decade and a half. But it is worth noting that while both thinkers grant that the concept of realization amounted to a cognitive category of a privileged kind, Vivekananda makes it fully compatible with social consciousness, indeed with conscience, these being the very factors the need for which drives Buber away from it. The achievement of each is considerable. Vivekananda's neo-Vedanta regenerated the notion of realization by transferring it from the realm of *vita contemplativa* to *vita activa*. And Buber saw that the making actually involved in *Verwirklichung* was in practice not an individual task so much as one which drew upon the relations between 'man and man'. Interestingly enough there are passages like the following written by Buber which match in fervour both Bankim's and Vivekananda's thought : Power of the storming spirit to stir up the conflagration, security of the constructing soul to hold itself in the purifying fire : these are the forces which guide a people to rejuvenated life.[11]

At all events in the treatment of realization by some modern Indian thinkers we find a chiming in of insight with a Western thinker where we might least expect it. In each case we find both drawing on heritage and a surmounting of it. Furthermore in each there is a refusal to divorce the cognitive from the world of human relations, and this without turning to the manipulative contexts focussed on by pragmatism.

I find the comparison of interest, in fact, precisely because the thinkers I have touched on refused to confine cognition to epistemology but saw that the highest aspirations to knowledge must have radical bearing on human relations and be firmly rooted in them. Only thus can illumination illuminate the world.[12]

Notes and References

1. Daniel, 50
2. *ibid.*, 69
3. *ibid.*, 72
4. *ibid.*
5. *ibid.*, 73
6. *ibid.*, 95
7. *ibid.*, 98
8. *ibid.*, 143
9. *ibid.*, 144
10. Cf. The monograph written in 1917 by Franz Rosenzweing in which the author finds in Thalatta (the sea) the proper symbol for unity, since the earth inherently has boundaries. Also relevant is the desire of members of the Patmos circle at this time to break away from historicism, not to say that the being and becoming which the sea *is* can effectively counter what the historicist wants to say.
11. This is the insight which drew him to the *Halutz* (pioneer settler) movement. In 1919 he said: 'The true locus of realization is community and true community is that in which the divine becomes realized among men' (Oration delivered in memory of Gustav Landauer), and in 1923, 'that to "realize God" is to help the world to become divine reality (*gottwirklich*)'. (Introduction to *Reden ueber das Judentum*, p. xviii.)
12. *Die juedische Bewegung*, I, 216ff.

Classical Yoga Philosophy and Some Issues in the Philosophy of Mind

GERALD JAMES LARSON

Prof. Gerald James Larson, Director of the Indian Studies Program, Indiana University, U. S. A.; formerly Professor of the History of Religions, University of California, Santa Barbara; editor and author of numerous books and articles on Indian religion and philosophy, including, *Samkhya: A Dualist Tradition in Indian Philosophy* (co-edited with Ram Shankar Bhattacharya), *Interpreting Across Boundaries* (co-edited with Eliot Deutsch), and most recently, *India's Agony over Religion.*

Introduction

In the present paper[1] I propose to address some important issues in the area of the Western philosophy of mind and to show how these issues are dealt with in the classical Yoga philosophy (or the classical Sāṁkhya-yoga philosophy) of India. Specifically, I shall be discussing the 'mind-body' problem (or the 'mind-brain' problem) and current explanatory approaches in terms of various formulations of dualism (substance-dualism, epiphenomenalist-dualism, elemental-property-dualism and interactionist-property-dualism) and in terms of other formulations such as reductive materialism or identity-theory, functionalism, non-reductive materialism and eliminative materialism.[2] I shall not explicitly deal with so-called 'mentalist' conceptions of the mind-body problem—for example, the thought of Berkeley, other 'idealist' formulations or the so-called 'neutral monists,' et al.—for two reasons, first, since such conceptions are for the most part considered not to be plausible in current discussions within philosophy of mind, and second, since there are few if any interesting comparisons to be drawn with classical Yoga philosophy.

The various formulations of dualism, functionalism and materialism, however, are very much at issue in current discussions within philosophy of mind and bear interesting and somewhat unexpected affinities with classical Yoga philosophy. The manner in which physical states differ or are the same as mental states, the manner in which physical states relate or are 'identical' with mental states, the manner in which physical states cause, run parallel with, systematically interact with, or are simply the equivalent of mental states, the manner in which physical states and mental states relate to the problems of 'consciousness' and 'self-consciousness,' and the manner in which one or another traditional notion of the 'person'—what is sometimes called the traditional 'folk psychology' of the 'person' can be retained are some of the more important issues that come up for discussion among these various formulations of the 'mind-body' problem in the area of Western philosophy of mind; and I want to argue that classical Yoga philosophy (a) analyses these basic issues in an interestingly different manner, and (b) that the classical Yoga formulation may well provide some helpful new directions for research and reflection regarding these important issues.

Dualism versus materialism

Put very simply, the basic difference between dualist claims and materialist claims has to do with whether mental states can plausibly be reduced or at least reinterpreted in terms of physical states. The dualist wishes to maintain that finally it is implausible to argue that such capacities as the creative use of language, the processes of logic and reasoning, the intrinsic qualities of sensations, feelings and emotions, and the semantic significance of beliefs, desires and other intentional states can ever be adequately explained or accounted for solely by way of the neurophysiology and neurochemistry of brain-states as described in terms of chemical and electrical interactions and-or 'firings' of impulses across the 'synapses' of countless thousands and millions of neurones, dendrites and axons throughout the specialized structures of the emergent, organic brain. The materialist maintains, to the contrary, that the growing body of research in biological science, cognitive science, physics, chemistry, biochemistry, cybernetics and computer science, holds out the promise that in fact a purely materialist account is not only possible, but indeed, quite likely. As Paul Churchland has put it : '...the important point about the standard evolutionary story is that the human species and all of its features are the wholly physical outcome of a purely physical process.'[3]

Apart from this basic and fundamental difference, of course, there are a variety of positions that have been formulated by way of explaining or analysing the dualist or the materialist claim, or put somewhat differently, there are various kinds of dualism and various kinds of materialism, as well as the position of functionalism, that have been and are currently being argued; and, as indicated at the outset, I want to offer a brief analytic survey of some of the more important of these positions by way of providing an overview of the possible positions regarding the 'mind-body' or 'mind-brain' problem in current discussions within the philosophy of mind.

Substance dualism

That the realm of the mind or the realm of ideas is fundamentally distinct from the realm of material stuff or the realm of the body is as old in Western philosophical traditions as Pythagoras and Plato, but the *locus classicus* for the discussion of dualism in modern Western philosophy is, of course, the substance dualism of Descartes. Says Descartes in his Sixth Meditation :

> ...because, on the one hand, I have a clear and distinct idea of myself in so far as I am only a thinking and unextended thing, and because, on the other hand I have a distinct idea of the body in so far as it is only an extended thing but which does not think, it is certain that I, that is to say my mind, by which I am what I am, is entirely and truly distinct from my body, and may exist without it.[4]

A somewhat fuller statement of Descartes's own method and his basic deductions are nicely set forth in his 'Letter from the Author to the Translator of the Principles of Philosophy, to serve as a Preface,' as follows :

> ...by considering that he who decides to doubt everything cannot nevertheless doubt that he exists while he doubts, and that what reasons thus, in not being able to doubt itself and doubting nevertheless all the rest, is not what we call our body, but what we call our soul or thought, I have taken the being or the existence of this

> thought for the first principle, from which I very clearly deduced the following truths, namely, that there is a God who is the author of all that is in the world, and who, being the source of all truth, has not created our understanding of such a nature as to be deceived in the judgements it forms of the things of which it has a very clear and distinct perception. Those are all the principles of which I make use concerning immaterial or metaphysical things, from which I deduce very clearly the principles of corporeal or physical things, namely, that there are bodies extended in length, breadth and depth, which have diverse shapes and move in various ways. Such are, in brief, all the principles from which I deduce the truth of all other things.[5]

Quite apart from the philosophical difficulty of how to account for causal interactions between unextended thought and the extension of body, which Descartes struggled to explain with his 'animal spirits' and the pineal gland, his characterization of the physical in terms of extension in space is, of course, fundamentally flawed and simplistic. Matter or the body is now understood, not simply in terms of simple mechanics and spatial extension, but in the broader terms of mass, energy, the point-instants of electrons and electro-magnetism, atomic and subatomic particles, quantum mechanics, probability theory, and so forth. The old Cartesian substance dualism, in other words, is implausible both philosophically and scientifically.

Epiphenomenalist dualism

In an effort to solve the problem of interaction between unextended mental states and physical brain-states, a second sort of dualism has been proposed, based not upon notions of separate substances (thought and extension) but rather, on the notion of emergent properties. That is to say, mental states are different from physical states, but rather than representing two substantive realms, the realm of the mental is simply a set of emergent properties that come into being at certain higher levels of organic evolution. This, of course, is the position of epiphenomenalism and has been argued by Thomas Huxley and other Darwinians.[6] According to what I am calling epiphenomenalist dualism, the realm of mental states is a realm that is different and finally irreducible to physical states, and it is for this reason that epiphenomenalism is a dualist position. The mental is a realm that has emerged as a result of the long process of evolution. Moreover, while it is the case that physical states can act causally on mental states, and indeed, that mental states first emerged as a new realm out of or from older physical states, it is not the case that mental states can act causally on physical states. In other words, there is no interaction between mental states and physical states. Mental states are simply epiphenomenal emergents out of older physical states, and any apparent causal action on physical states is fundamentally illusory. Causal action is only in one direction, namely, from the physical to the epiphenomenal mental. This is, to say the least, an odd account of the relation and interaction between mind and body or mind and brain, but it is one somewhat plausible, if unlikely, way of preserving dualism without buying into a full substance dualism.

Interactionist property dualism

A somewhat more commonsensical or popular interpretation of dualism is what John C. Eccles and Karl R. Popper have called their 'strong dualist hypothesis,' involving a full interactionism between mind and body, and even more than that, a dominant role for 'self-conscious mind' that controls attention, provides overall integration or a unitary sense of identity, actively modifies physical brain events and performs ongoing scanning functions with respect to the well-being of the organism.[7] Like epiphenomenalist dualism, this version of dualism interprets the realm of 'self-conscious mind' as an emergent property or development in the long process of evolution. Self-conscious mind, therefore, is very much a product of physical, organic evolution, but once it emerges it becomes a dominant force with respect to the survival of the human organism. Hence, self-conscious mind exerts what Eccles and Popper call a powerful 'downward causation.'[8] Self-conscious mind has no extension in space, but it does have temporal duration. Eccles and Popper speak of Worlds 1, 2, and 3, World 1 being the realm of physical, brain states (with spatial extension and temporal duration), World 2 being the realm of subjective, mental states (with only temporal duration), and World 3 being the derivative, cultural world of artifacts (books, art works, scientific theories, literatures, and so forth, with spatial and temporal duration), all three of which Worlds regularly interact to support the uniqueness of specifically human existence. Worlds 2 and 3 are irreducible to World 1 and indeed are essential for the survival of world 1. Interestingly, Eccles and Popper come very close to a kind of substance dualism, although Popper maintains a basically agnostic position regarding a possible separate survival of the mental World 2 apart from World 1. Eccles, on the other hand, is more inclined to a traditional view of World 2 as involving a kind of immortal soul able to survive separation from the body by reason of a divine providence. The great weakness in the 'strong dualist hypothesis,' of course, is that it finally fails to explain much of anything in terms of the relation between mind and body. To be sure, it is able to present each side of the dualist claim with great sophistication and subtlety. Especially noteworthy is John C. Eccles's remarkable command of brain neurophysiology and neurochemistry. On the other side, Popper brings to bear the full force of the various philosophical arguments against reducing mental states to physical states. In the final analysis, however, they simply assert that mind and body are totally irreducible to one another and that the final explanation of the relations and interactions must remain something of a mystery. This is all well and good, but it is finally only prolegomenon. That is, it only brings us to the threshold of the problem of mind and body but cannot seriously be considered a reasoned treatment or explanation of the problem.

Elemental property dualism

Yet another interpretation of dualism that takes seriously the irreducibility of mental states to physical states while also maintaining a strong interactionism between mind and body, but at the same time seeks to offer a plausible explanation of the relation between mind and body is what has been called 'panpsychism' or what can also be called 'elemental property dualism.' Inasmuch as mental properties and physical properties are irreducible to one another, it must be the case that both sorts of properties are intrinsically or inherently part of what is from the beginning. In other words, reality has a 'mental' side in terms of elemental properties as well as a 'physical' side. Sometimes these two sides are expressed in terms of the 'inside' and the 'outside' of events or entities, or sometimes these two sides are characterized as fundamental 'attributes' of nature or the world. Leibnitz's 'monadology' is one important articulation of panpsychism. Spinoza's 'thought' and 'extension' as attributes of 'Nature' or 'God' is another. A more contemporary version of the same type of position is the process philosophy of a Whitehead or a Hartshorne. The problem with panpsychism or elemental property dualism is that it comes close to begging the basic question. In terms of very simple forms of life or simple objects, if one wishes to use the terms 'mental' and 'physical,' quite obviously the terms cannot mean the same as they mean with more advanced forms of life. One has to posit something like 'pre-mental' and 'pre-physical' tendencies that will later emerge or show themselves as mature mental states and complex physical states. But however one wishes to characterize the earlier stages of 'mental' and 'physical' processes or tendencies, one still has the problem of accounting for the transition to mature mental states or complex physical states. Moreover, the problem of the relation between mature mental states and complex physical states still remains to be addressed by the panpsychist or elemental property dualist.

Eliminative dualism

There is one other version of dualism that should also be mentioned, but as Paul Churchland has pointed out, it has never been seriously argued, at least in Western philosophy. Churchland suggests that there is a possible dualist position :

> ....that to my knowledge has never been cited before, but it is real just the same. Specifically, the P-theory (that is, the notion of mental states or the 'Person-theory') might prove to be replaceable by some more general theory...but to be irreducible to that more general theory. The ontology of the P-theory would thus be eliminated in favour of the ontology of the more general theory that displaced it. We might call this possibility 'eliminative dualism'![9]

According to eliminative dualism, in other words, the usual characterizations of so-called 'folk psychology' in terms of a 'self-conscious mind' or 'person' having certain sensations or feelings or having such propositional or intentional states as hoping that p, or believing that p, or desiring that p, and so forth, are fundamentally mistaken and require reformulation in terms of a dualist framework that goes beyond conventional 'folk psychology.' Churchland offers the following wry comment about this possible position of 'eliminative dualism' :

> It is perhaps not surprising that this possibility has gone unremarked, since the preservation of the common-sense ontology of the mind has always been part of the dualists' sales-pitch.[10]

I shall be suggesting in the sequel that although Churchland is quite right that the position of eliminative dualism 'has gone unremarked' in the history of Western philosophy, it is not the case that it has gone unremarked in the wider history of philosophy. I want to suggest, in other words, that the position of eliminative dualism has been argued in Indian philosophy, and specifically within the classical Yoga philosophy of Patañjali.

Before turning to classical Yoga philosophy, however, let me first complete my summary overview of commonly held positions regarding the mind-body problem by looking at reductive materialism or identity theory, functionalism, non-reductive materialism and eliminative materialism.

Reductive materialism or identity theory

This position is close to the various property dualisms already discussed (epiphenomenalism, interactionist property dualism and elemental property dualism) with the crucial difference, however, that the reductive materialist argues that there is simply no need to posit any sort of special status for mental states. Mental states simply are physical states, and when neuroscience reaches a mature stage of sophistication, the so-called 'mental states,' including sensations, feelings, and the various intentional or propositional attitudes, will all be shown to be numerically identical with specific brain-events or neurological events within the central nervous system. Just as we now know that our experience of 'light' is simply another way of talking about sequences of electromagnetic waves and our experience of 'warmth' is simply another way of talking about high average levels of molecular kinetic energy, so eventually in a mature neuroscience our mental states will have a precise intertheoretical reduction to physical states or processes within the central nervous system. Such a position of reductive materialism has been maintained by such theorists as H. Feigl, J.J.C. Smart, et al.[11] 'Mind-' or 'mentalistic'-talk will be completely reduced to 'brain-process' talk. Mind, thought, ideas, sensations, and so forth, will be reduced to some sort of material stuff, energy, or force. The reductive materialist or identity theorist position is, of course, an attractive position inasmuch as it purports to accomplish two important philosophical tasks, that is, (a) it simplifies the task of explanation of the mind-body problem to a single level of neuroscientific discourse in contrast to the much more complicated dualist frameworks; and (b) it preserves all of traditional 'folk psychology' by providing a full and complete intertheoretical reduction. The problem with the position, however, is that both claims have become suspect even among materialists themselves. Regarding the first claim of economy or simplification of explanation, it is becoming increasingly evident in empirical research that the functioning of the brain or the central nervous system is much more complex than earlier theoretical work suggested. To claim to be able to offer a simple neuroscientific explanation of mental states in terms of numerical identity is coming to be recognized as naive as well as implausible, certainly in terms of a 'hard' correlation of a 'type-type' characterization (between the mental and the physical) and even suspect in terms of the much 'softer' 'token-token' account.[12] Similarly, regarding the second claim of a complete intertheoretical reduction of 'folk psychology,' it is becoming increasingly clear that such a direct one-to-one reduction is not only highly unlikely because of the magnitude of the task but, more to the point, because such a reduction is unworkable in principle.

Functionalism and non-reductive materialism

Functionalism and what can be called non-reductive materialism are perhaps best discussed together. The positions are logically distinct, but they coalesce to the extent that they both clearly reject reductive materialism or identity-theory. Moreover, most functionalists are also, in fact, non-reductive materialists.

The position of functionalism is most commonly linked with the work of Hilary Putnam—*cf.*, for example, his well-known essay, 'The Nature of Mental States,' anthologized in D. M. Rosenthal's *The Nature of Mind*—and has been nicely summarized in the following characterization of Paul Churchland :

> ...psychological states are functional states in the sense that for any being to have a psychology (to be subject of psychological states) is for it to instance or embody a certain functional organization among its sensory inputs, internal states and motor outputs. Talk of psychological states is therefore ontologically neutral...since descriptions at that level are innocent of any commitments as to the nature or constitution of whatever it is that instantiates the relevant functional organization.... Accordingly, psychological descriptions are not reducible to descriptions concerning any of the various substances that might instantiate them. They are descriptions at a level of abstraction from such matters.
>
> Thus emerges the essential point of difference with the identity theory: it is the reducibility of psychological descriptions that is denied by Putnam. And the reason for the denial is the multiplicity of different substrata that can instantiate those descriptions.[13]

Mental states as functional states operate at a higher level of abstraction. To reduce them to purely physical descriptions would be to undercut a proper understanding of their higher order functioning. Moreover, functional psychological states can exist in various kinds of physical embodiment, including, for example, embodiment in computers. In other words, there is no one-to-one correlation between functional psychological states and ontological physical states, and thus it is inappropriate, almost a kind of category mistake, to expect a complete reduction of the former to the latter. There is no need to maintain psycho-physical identities and, hence, no need to expect or even want intertheoretical reduction. Another way of putting the functionalist position is to say that psychology is still both possible and desirable as an independent academic discipline. Because the functionalist position does not commit itself to a particular ontological description regarding mental states, it is compatible with either a materialist or dualist, or even an idealist, position, even though most functionalists are, in fact, also materialists or physicalists—for example, Putnam himself is a materialist, arguing that the actual instantiation of functional states is a matter of empirical research, the evidence for which (at least currently) is largely materialist.

What I am calling non-reductive materialism is represented by such figures as Donald Davidson and John Searle. Davidson argues for a position known as 'anomalous monism,' a materialist position which combines (a) the notion that mental states and physical states interact, (b) the notion that causality is law-like or 'nomological' among physical states, but that (c) mental states cannot be captured by the law-like principles of causality, that is, that they are somehow also 'anomalous.' Priest has characterized Davidson's position as follows :

> The two central tenets of Davidson's anomalous monism are the materialist view that every mental event is identical with some physical event, and the view (usually denied by materialists) that there are no psycho-physical laws. It remains an open possibility on Davidson's theory that every event is mental under some description, but he holds it certain that, if some event is mental, then it is also physical. The fact that there exist no psycho-physical laws—that no mental events may be subsumed under deterministic scientific generalizations—entails that mental events cannot be explained in purely physical terms. For example, no law about physical events enables any prediction about a mental event.[14]
>
> A materialism which will have room for freedom is possible.[15]

Searle's non-reductive materialism sets forth a distinction between 'macro-level' descriptions (for physical, neuronal processes), arguing that the macro-level and micro-level are both causally real.

> Both of them (that is, mental and physical) are causally real, and the higher level causal features are both caused by and realized in the structure of the lower level elements.
>
> To summarize : in my view, the mind and the body interact, but they are not

two different things, since mental phenomena are just features of the brain. One way to characterize this position is to see it as an assertion of both physicalism and mentalism. Suppose we define 'naive physicalism' to be the view that all that exists in the world are physical particles with their properties and relations.... And let us define 'naive mentalism' to be the view that mental phenomena really exist. There really are mental states; some of them are conscious; many have intentionality; they all have subjectivity; and many of them function causally in determining physical events in the world. The thesis of this first chapter can now be stated quite simply. Naive mentalism and naive physicalism are perfectly consistent with each other. Indeed, as far as we can know anything about how the world works, they are not only consistent, they are both true.[16]

The problem, one might well suggest, about all of these views, namely, Putnam's functionalism, Davidson's anomalous monism and Searle's macro-level-cum-micro-level analysis is that although they avoid the difficulties of reductive materialism or identity-theory, they really do not go very far in accounting for the mental beyond simply asserting that the mental cannot be reduced to the physical. And of course, in this sense they are hardly more plausible than the dualism of an Eccles or a Popper.

Eliminative materialism

Finally, mention must also be made of what Eccles and Popper have called 'radical materialism' or 'promissory materialism,' and what I am calling, following Paul Churchland, 'eliminative materialism.'[17] Unlike reductive materialism, functionalism, and non-reductive materialism, eliminative materialism does not accept the notion that mental states as conventionally understood in terms of traditional or modern 'folk psychology' is in any sense a corrigible interpretation of personal or mental life. In other words, our traditional understanding of the 'person,' or the 'self-conscious mind' as 'having' certain sensations or being the subject of intentional attitudes such as believing that p, or desiring that p, is fundamentally mistaken and flat out wrong or false. Traditional person-theory or 'folk psychology' fails to give an adequate account of reasoning; is inadequate in understanding learning theory; is vague and superficial in its account of perception; is murky and unsatisfactory in understanding the dynamics of emotion; and is nearly useless in understanding the nature or causes of mental illness.[18] It is a seriously incorrect view of the human condition, and far from being corrigible in terms of intertheoretical reduction (*à la* reductive materialism) or functionalist interaction (*à la* functionalism), it needs to be dismissed or eliminated in any attempt to set forth a cogent interpretation of the relation between mind and body or mind and brain—hence, the expression 'eliminative' materialism. Eccles and Popper refer to eliminative materialism as 'radical materialism' because it expels 'person-talk' from the lexicon of plausible accounts of mental states, and they also refer to it as 'promissory materialism' inasmuch as what new discourse will take the place of 'person-talk' is at present only a distant promise of what will emerge from a mature neuroscience.[19] Here again it is fair to say that the major problem with the position of eliminative materialism is that it also is finally only prolegomenon. That is to say, it is little more than a vague hope that eventually a mature neuroscience will give us the kind of discourse that will prove to be an adequate substitute for the 'folk psychology' that we are told must be eliminated. Furthermore, if 'folk psychology' is to be eliminated as simply wrong or false, the eliminative materialist bears the not insignificant burden of providing a new theory of meaning or semantics that is not itself caught up in the 'folk psychology' that has supposedly been expelled or eliminated from the explanatory corpus. There is very little evidence at the present time in current philosophy of mind that much progress is being made in devising the required new theories of meaning.

Classical Yoga Philosophy

I have briefly analysed a variety of interpretations of the mind-body problem in recent work in the philosophy of mind, five on the dualist side (substance dualism, epiphenomenal dualism, interactionist property dualism, elemental property dualism and eliminative dualism), and four largely on the materialist side (reductive materialism, functionalism, non-reductive materialism and eliminative materialism). There are, of course, some other possible interpretations—one thinks, for example, of the so-called Humean 'bundle' theory or one or another kind of 'mentalist' or 'neutral monist' view mentioned at the outset of this paper—but perhaps a sufficient number of interpretations have been analysed to provide a useful catalogue of the basic issues being addressed in most current discussions within the Western philosophy of mind.

Since so much of comparative philosophy has had a predilection for comparing traditions of Indian philosophizing with various formulations of Western idealism or 'mentalism'—witness the endless titles along the lines of Śaṅkara and Bradley, and so forth—one might anticipate that classical Yoga philosophy would come out on the dualist side of things and especially the strong dualist side tending towards 'idealism' or 'mentalism.' I want to suggest, to the contrary, a rather different perspective.[20] It is, of course, true that classical Yoga philosophy is a thorough-going dualism, but it is not at all a conventional Western mind-body or thought-extension dualism, nor is it tending in the direction of any of the Western idealisms or 'mentalisms.' In terms of dualism, classical Yoga philosophy appears to represent, as mentioned earlier and perhaps somewhat surprisingly, that formulation of dualism that, according to Churchland, '...has gone unremarked...' in Western philosophy of mind, namely, 'eliminative dualism.' Furthermore, and perhaps even more surprising, classical Yoga's eliminative dualism is built upon what Western philosophy of mind would characterize as 'eliminative materialism.' That is to say, classical Yoga philosophy is at one and the same time **both** an eliminative dualism **and** an eliminative materialism. In terms of Western philosophy of mind, in other words, classical Yoga philosophy represents a radically unconventional dualism and an even more radical physicalism.[21]

Let me offer some comments, first, about classical Yoga philosophy as an eliminative materialism. One way of putting the Yoga position is to say simply that there is nothing like a mind-body problem to be solved. The notion of *citta* (or *prakṛti*) can be translated either as 'mind-stuff' or 'brain-stuff,' and *citta* is constituted by the three constituent processes (*triguṇa*) of intelligible ordering (*sattva*), spontaneous activity or material energy (*rajas*) and determinate formulating or objectivation (*tamas*).

From an objective perspective, Yoga describes the tripartite process as a continuing flow of primal material energy that is capable of spontaneous activity, rational ordering and determinate formulation or objectivation. From a subjective perspective, Yoga describes the tripartite process as a continuing flow of experience that is capable of prereflective desiring, reflective discerning and continuing awareness of an opaque, enveloping world. For Yoga philosophy there is no polarity or bifurcation of subjective and objective within the tripartite process, no ontological distinction between 'mind' and 'matter' or 'thought' and 'extension.' The subjective flow of experience is simply another way of describing the objective primal material energy that unfolds in a continuing tripartite process of spontaneous activity, rational ordering and determinate formulation. The tripartite process of *citta* is, in other words, a sort of philosophical Klein bottle or Mobius strip in which the usual distinctions of subjective-objective, mind-body, thought-extension, private-public simply do not apply. One might think, then, that the classical Yoga philosophy is a kind of panpsychism with mental and physical states built into the very structure of reality but this would be a misreading, I think, of the Yoga position. Yoga philosophy, rather, is reducing the psychic or mental to the physical. In other words, its ontological intent with respect to *citta* is radically materialist. As E. H. Johnston has commented: 'Early Indian thought ...drew no clear line of demarcation between the material, mental and psychical phenomena of the individual....All classes of phenomena are looked on alike as having a material basis, the difference resting on the degree of subtlety attributed to the basis.'[22] The term 'panpsychic' can be used perhaps, but only if construed in a radically materialist sense.

But 'panpsychism' or 'mentalism' as well as 'materialism' in any traditional or ordinary Western sense are really misnomers, for the very notion of ordinary mental states of the transactions of 'mind' or notions of 'self' or 'person' are radically criticized in Yoga philosophy as are crude notions of 'materialism' in terms of unextended physical bits or particles that somehow eventually become the complex structures of reality as we experience them. Classical Yoga philosophy rejects an atomistic materialism that moves from the simple to the complex, and it also rejects conventional 'person' theory or 'self' theory. It argues, rather, for a kind of 'downward causation' model of a material *citta* (*triguṇa*) that eventually becomes this phenomenal, empirical world in which we find ourselves as 'persons' who are frustrated and suffering. Our simplistic notions of a material world in our ordinary experience together with our simplistic notions of selfhood are profoundly 'afflicted', distorted and flat out wrong or false. Disciplined meditation or, in other words, Yoga praxis will eventually reveal that our ordinary notions of 'mental states' and 'physical states' are profoundly mistaken. Our 'mind-stuff' and or 'brain-stuff' is distorted by reason of five basic 'afflictions' (*kleśa*-s) that are both genetically and culturally transmitted through the human species as well as other organic species, namely, ordinary intentional beliefs (*avidyā*), conventional or ordinary egoity (*asmitā*), desires (*rāga*), dislikes (*dveṣa*) and our clinging to conventional life (*abhiniveśa*). Moreover, the basic processes of the *citta* or mind-stuff or brain-stuff, namely, the so-called *citta-vṛtti*-s are hopelessly clogged with misconceptions. The five basic processes are (1) ordinary knowing in terms of perception, inference and reliable authority (*pramāṇa*), (2) positively incorrect notions (*viparyaya*) both genetic and cultural, (3) verbal constructs or linguisticality (*vikalpa*), (4) deep sleep and other forms of unconsciousness (*nidrā*), and (5) the storing and retrieval of memory (*smṛti*) in present life as well as previous life-trajectories. Classical Yoga philosophy, thus, takes an exceedingly pessimistic view of our ordinary understanding of ourselves or our world. What Churchland has called the conventional 'P-theory' ('person'-theory) or our usual interpretation of our mental states, as well as our usual interpretations of our external world are fundamentally flawed and cannot be salvaged in any reductive, intertheoretical interpretation. Our conventional understandings must simply be dispelled or eliminated from the explanatory corpus—hence, classical Yoga philosophy as a radical eliminative materialism. The Yoga view, it might be noted here, does not necessarily conflict with modern scientific notions of evolution, but classical Yoga philosophy would argue, I think, that the explanations currently given for evolution are rather naive both philosophically and scientifically.

In any case, let me quickly move on to the other dimension of Yoga philosophy, namely, its eliminative dualism. By interpreting 'mind-body' or 'mind-brain' in terms of *citta* ('mind-stuff' or 'brain-stuff'), one might well conclude that classical Yoga philosophy, finally, is a closed, eliminative materialism. Again, however, classical Yoga philosophy takes us in a surprising direction. To be sure, there is indeed a closed system of interactive, eliminative materialism, but Yoga praxis also reveals the presence of a non-intentional consciousness (*puruṣa, citi-śakti, cit-śakti*), totally distinct or separate from *citta*, running parallel with *citta* at every level and in every modality, but not interacting with *citta* other than being simply present. Again one might be tempted to think about this Yoga conceptualization as perhaps a theory of non-interactive parallelism *à la* panpsychism (a Leibnitzian or Spinozistic or even a Whiteheadian view) or *à la* a non-interactive, emergent epiphenomenalism, but again I would be inclined to argue that this would be a misreading of the Yoga view. Panpsychism or epiphenomenalism are both views struggling to incorporate some sort of notion of intentionality or propositional attitudes into our understanding of the physical world and the body. For Yoga philosophy, however, intentionality, the propositional attitudes, the 'private life of the mind,' sensations, feelings, and so forth, are all encompassed within the closed causal system of the eliminative materialism of the *citta*. Pure, contentless consciouness (*puruṣa* or *citi-śakti*) is radically distinct from intentional awareness of all kinds and from any content whatsoever (*a-samprajñāta-samādhi*). Only its presence can be intuited by the *citta* (*buddhi*) as not being an intentional awareness (*viveka-khyāti*). In other words, the classical Yoga dualism is as radically eliminative in its formulation as the classical Yoga materialism is eliminative in its formulation. Moreover, the radical eliminative dualism does not finally issue in some sort of murky, cosmic Selfhood. It is posed, rather, as the radical universality of the singular, not any-**thing** but, rather, that **singular presence** which allows all things to be.

Much more could be said about the eliminative materialism and eliminative dualism of classical Yoga philosophy, but I hope that enough has been said to suggest that the contemporary Western philosophy of mind could be well served by attending to one of the oldest experimental, empirically based research programs known to the human species, the classical Yoga of ancient India.

Notes and References

1. A first draft of this paper was given at the East-West Philosophers' Conference of the Society for Asian and Comparative philosophy held at Massey University in Palmerston North, New Zealand, in August 1994. The current, revised draft owes a great deal to the helpful critique of the earlier draft by Professor Roy Perrett of the Department of Philosophy, Massey University. Professor Perrett was also Convener of the summer conference, and I would like to express my thanks to him both for arranging the conference as well as for providing a number of helpful critical comments to this paper.

2. In terms of identifying and naming the various dualist and materialist positions, I have found the following discussions helpful : (1) Karl R. Popper's analysis and criticism of radical materialism, panpsychism, epiphenomenalism and identity theory in Karl R. Popper and John C. Eccles, *The Self and Its Brain* (London: Routledge and Kegan Paul, 1977), especially pp. 51-99; (2) John C. Eccles's discussion of radical materialism, panpsychism, epiphenomenalism, identity theory and dualist interactionism in Sir John Eccles and Daniel N. Robinson, *The Wonder of Being Human* (Boston: Shambhala Publications, 1985), pp. 25-45 and see especially p. 34: 'Diagrammatic Representation of Brain-Mind Theories'; and (3) Paul Churchland's discussion of substance dualism, simple dualism, property dualism (epiphenomenalist, interactionist, and elemental), reductive materialism, functionalism, and eliminative materialism in Paul Churchland, *Scientific Realism and the Plasticity of Mind* (Cambridge: Cambridge University Press, 1979), pp. 107-16, and Paul Churchland, *Matter and Consciousness : A Contemporary Introduction to the Philosophy of Mind*, Revised Edition (Cambridge, Mass. : MIT Press, 1988), pp. 6-49. Other important works that have been consulted for this paper are the following (in alphabetical order by author) : Daniel C. Dennett, *Consciousness Explained* (Boston: Little, Brown and Co., 1991); Henri Ey, *Consciousness: A Phenomenological Study of Being Conscious and Becoming Conscious,* trans. John H. Flodstrom (Bloomington: Indiana University Press, 1978); Richard L. Gregory, ed., *The Oxford Companion to the Mind* (Oxford: Oxford University Press, 1987); William G. Lycan, ed., *Mind and Cognition: A Reader* (Oxford: Basil Blackwell, 1990); Stephen Priest, *Theories of the Mind* (Boston: Houghton Mifflin Co., 1991); Hilary Putnam, 'The Nature of Mental States' in D. M. Rosenthal, ed., *The Nature of Mind* (Oxford: Oxford University Press, 1991), pp. 197-203; Richard Rorty, *Objectivity, Relativism and Truth,* Philosophical Papers, Volume 1 and especially the essay, 'Non-reductive Physicalism' (Cambridge: Cambridge University Press,1991), pp. 113-25; David M. Rosenthal, ed., *The Nature of Mind* (Oxford University Press, 1991); John Searle, *Minds, Brains and Science* (Cambridge, Mass.: Harvard University Press, 1984); and Anthony Smith, *The Mind* (Harmondsworth, England: Penguin Books, 1984).

3. Paul Churchland, *Matter and Consciousness: A Contemporary Introduction tc the Philosophy of Mind,* Revised Edition, p.21.

4. Rene Descartes, *Meditations on the first Philosophy in which the Existence of God and the real Distinction between the Soul and the body of man are re-demonstrated,* (trans., F. E. Sutcliffe) (London: Penguin Books, 1968), p.156.

5. Rene Descartes, 'Letter from the author to the Translator of the *Principles of Philosophy,* to serve as a Preface,' trans., F. E. Sutcliffe (London: Penguin Books, 1968), pp. 179-80.

6. For an excellent discussion of epiphenomenalism, see Karl R. Popper and John C. Eccles, *The Self and Its Brain : An Argument for Interactionism,* pp. 72-5.

7. *Ibid.,* especially pp. 373-76, but also see the entire book, *passim,* which argues at great length for the 'strong dualist hypothesis.'

8. *Ibid.,* pp. 14-21.

9. Paul Churchland, *Scientific Realism and the Plasticity of Mind,* p. 108.

10. *Ibid.*

11. For an excellent anthology which nicely brings together many of the most important articles regarding the various interpretations of materialism, see David M. Rosenthal, ed., *The Nature of Mind,* especially the articles in the part III, entitled 'Mind and Body,' pp. 161-288.

12. For a useful, brief discussion of the 'type-type' versus 'token-token' accounts, see Stephen.Priest, *Theories of Mind,* pp. 113-14.

13. Paul Churchland, *Scientific Realism and the Plasticity of mind,* p. 111.

14. Stephen Priest, *Theories of Mind,* p. 117.

15. *Ibid.,* p. 115.

16. John Searle, *Minds, Brains and Science,* pp. 26-7.

17. Paul Churchland, *Matter and Consciousness,* pp. 43-9, and Paul Churchland, *Scientific Realism and the Plasticity of Mind,* pp. 114-16.

18. Paul Churchland, *Scientific Realism and the Plasticity of Mind,* p. 114.

19. Eccles and Popper, *The Self and its Brain,* pp. 96-8.

20. I have developed my interpretation of Sāṁkhya and Yoga in four earlier publications, and I refer the reader to them as follows: Gerald James Larson, 'An eccentric ghost in the machine,' *Philosophy : East and West,* Volume XXXIII, No.3 (July 1983) : pp.219-33; Larson, 'Is South Asian Yoga "Philosophy," "Religion," Both or Neither,' *The Notion of Religion in Comparative Research,* Selected Proceedings of the XVth Congress of the International Association for the History of Religions, ed. Ugo Bianchi, Storia delle religioni 8 (Rome: LERMA di BRETSCHNEIDER, 1994) : pp.261-70; Larson, Krishna Chandra Bhattacharya and the Plurality of *Puruṣas (puruṣa-bahutva)* in Sāṁkhya, *Journal of the Indian Council of Philosophical Research,* Volume X, No. 1 (September-December 1992): 93-104; and Larson and Ram Shankar Bhattacharya, eds., *Sāṁkhya : A Dualist Tradition in Indian Philosophy,* Encyclopedia of Indian Philosophies, Volume IV, ed. Karl H. Potter (Princeton : Princeton University Press, 1987), especially pp. 73-83.

21. For the Sanskrit text of the *Yogasūtra,* the *Yogasūtrabhāṣya* of Vyāsa, and the Tattvavaiśāradī of Vācaspatimiśra, I have used *Pātañjala-Yogadarśanam,* ed. Ram

Shankar Bhattacharya (Varanasi : Bharatiya Vidya Prakashan, 1963). For the Sanskrit text and translation of Vijñānabhikṣu's *Yogavārttika*, I have used *Yogavārttika of Vijñānabhikṣu*, 4 vols., ed. and trans. T. S. Rukmani (Delhi: Munshiram Manoharlal, 1981-89). For translations of the *Yogasūtra*, Vyāsa, and Vācaspati, I have consulted *The Yoga-System of Patañjali*, trans. J. H. Woods, Harvard Oriental Series 17 (Cambridge, Mass.: Harvard University Press, 1914), and *The Yoga Philosophy of Patañjali*, trans. H. Aranya (into Bengali) and trans. P. N. Mukerji (into English) (Albany: SUNY Press, 1983). Also of great value for understanding the original texts of Yoga is Pandit Usharbudh Arya, ed. and trans., *Yoga-Sūtras of Patañjali with the Exposition of Vyāsa: A Translation and Commentary*, Volume I—Samādhi-pada (Honesdale, Pennsylvania : The Himalayan International Institute, 1986).

22. E. H. Johnston, *Early Sāṁkhya* (London : Royal Asiatic Society, 1937), p. 38.

Epistemology from a Relativistic Point of View

HENRI LAUENER

Prof. Henri Lauener, University of Bern, Switzerland, Institute for Philosophy; Ph. D. Sorbonne (dissertation on Hegel's Philosophy); Guest Lecturer at many universities, including, Helsinki, St. Gallen, Lausanne, California (San Diego), Geneva, Innsbruck; from 1974-77, President of Philosophischen Gesellschaft, Bern; 1977-84, President of Swiss Association for Logic and Scientific Theory; involved in a number of colloquiums in Biel, Switzerland, and active member in many Philosophy organizations and congresses. Has published over 58 articles in scholarly journals on a variety of subjects, including linguistics, logic, science, Quine, Putnam, D. K. Lewis, Hume and Kant; 8 papers in preparation for publication.

My relativistic version of transcendental philosophy has its roots in my firm conviction that any aspiration to total or absolute knowledge remains illusory. The term 'transcendental', which is not to be confused with 'transcendent', characterizes a philosophical enterprise chiefly concerned with the intellectual and practical tools we must employ in order to acquire reliable knowledge. Turning my attention to the normative tasks of the philosopher, I advocate a form of relativism opposed not only to naturalism but also to so-called cultural relativism. Norms are human creations conventionally adopted for structuring the reality sectors we impose on the outer world; scientific activity does not consist in mirroring an independently existing or objectively given structure of the world. In accord with the view generally taken for granted in natural sciences, I likewise reject Subjective Idealism insisting that knowledge—with the exception of certain human sciences—is about physical objects (in a broad sense), not about ideas or sense data. Since empirical control plays a decisive role as a safeguard against foolish speculations I do not yield to the cheap slogan 'anything goes' maintaining that, as a matter of fact, some theories work better than others.

In contrast to Kant's, my view on transcendentalism is antifoundationalist. Relativism recognizes the necessity of specific conditions which make the achievement of knowledge possible but it does not concede that, among these, there must be certain necessary sentences—synthetic judgements *a priori*—which have to be considered as absolutely true. One trivial condition for elaborating theories is that we use a language. A linguistic system is constituted by a set of syntactic, semantic and pragmatic rules which fix the correct use for the expressions in a context. Thus knowledge becomes relative to the linguistic instruments we have selected for a specific purpose and consequently any hope for establishing an absolute and complete theory of the world vanishes. Relativity goes all the way up to the standards of acceptability which—though not depending on private opinion—are susceptible of constant improvement in the process of building more and more sophisticated theories. As we cannot construct something from nothing our cognitive activities never start from a zero situation. When we engage in a rule-governed practice we rely upon certain presuppositions which are neither unshakeable nor purely arbitrary. Among other things we must agree on the choice of appropriate theories and instruments in order to attain a given aim. By calling such agreements, reached after careful deliberation, 'conventions', I detach from the word the connotation of arbitrariness it often carries in English. Certain choices are equally legitimate with regard to their empirical consequences so that the decision will have to be taken on grounds of convenience. There are, for instance, conceptually different but empirically equivalent accounts of physical geometry in order to represent observed metric relations.

In the absence of a fact of the matter distinguishing a system as the true one we have no other resource ultimately than to resort to a convention.[1] When convening on the employment of certain logical, mathematical or linguistic systems we create a relative *a priori* with corresponding analytic truths. These, however, will only count as analytical as long as we stick to that conceptual framework, for conventions can be withdrawn and replaced by more suitable ones if they cease to fulfil the purposes for which they had been devised. Norms quite generally are deemed more or less adequate with respect to our interests and they can accordingly undergo revisions when these change.

Therefore, scientific rationality must also be concerned with rules which make axiological debate and consensus in goal assessment possible. The usually mentioned methodological values as, e.g., consistency, coherence, simplicity, generality, explanatory power, testability, etc., will have to be analysed, defined, weighed against each other and eventually adopted for pragmatic reasons. In turn, the different methods activated in science—the mathematical, postulational, model-theoretic, statistical, hypothetico-deductive, genetic, evolutionary and other procedures—need careful scrutiny in order to be evaluated with respect to their respective merits or defects.

The fact that there is no Archimedian point of view in philosophy—'God's perspective' as Hilary Putnam labels it—involves our inability to talk about the universe as a whole, i.e., the totality of things that exist. Phrases like 'all languages', 'all objects' etc., make sense only relative to a criterion of identity for the entities referred to. As we have no universal standards for individuating things of any kind whatever, we cannot adopt the position of the extreme holist who requires us to quantify over all existing objects. The difficulty becomes especially obvious when we are discussing very general claims concerning 'the world'. What exactly do we mean when pondering whether a Cartesian demon could deceive us systematically or whether—according to Putnam's version—we could be brains in a vat? Since sentences expressing such questions are not formulated in a linguistic system with clearly stated semantical rules, but in pretheoretic informal discourse, I doubt that we can give a conclusive answer—let alone a proof. Lacking a workable theory on demons we have no other choice than to reject sceptical arguments of such a vague and general character as unsuitable for philosophical discussion. As the word 'brain', on the other hand, gains a precise meaning only within a context where we are using physiology, we may safely dismiss the claim that we are brains in a vat since vats and diabolic scientists have no place in such a theory. This, however, does not amount to a philosophical 'proof of the reality of the external world' because an absolute proof of the sort attempted by the philosopher cannot be stated in the language of a scientific theory. Indeed, what do we mean by 'reality'? What is the referent of the singular term 'the world' which is supposed to figure in the ontology of the total theory? What precisely is the contrast intended by a separation of 'the real' from the 'non-real'? Here the empiricist, who wants to express his belief in a world existing independently of his mind, encounters a serious obstacle.

The problem resides in the fact that we are unable to speak about reality as such or Kant's 'things-in-themselves' without using some language and thus imposing a structure we have ourselves devised on 'the world'. Each attempt of this kind fatally results in a self-defeating enterprise. However, an empirically-minded philosopher will not resign himself to give way to a form of linguistic idealism. In spite of the fact that 'reality as such' remains unattainable he must insist that we talk about physical objects but only about those of a specific reality sector whose structure is determined by the forms of the linguistic system we have settled on. In other words, empirical facts have to take the shape impressed on them by the use of a language. My concession to realism is limited to the minimal claim that there must be an outer world which we have not created by our will. Yet, at the same time, I frankly admit that we have no logical demonstration or empirical evidence for it; such a general presupposition formulated in an ordinary prescientific language does not express more than my deep intuitive conviction that what I perceive is not merely imagined but caused by material processes originating in 'the world'. Though not being able, for want of a Theory about the Universe—even cosmology deals only with very large reality sectors—to present a proof, I still can give practical reasons for believing in its existence. Without its presupposition our scientific activities would not make sense and all our endeavours would be in vain. Facing the utter absurdity of any other assumption with regard to human life, we do not have the choice: if we want to progress by devising successful theories we must remain confident that they do not rest on mere fancy. Let me finally remark that the adoption of such a *postulate*, expressed in an unregimented and therefore semantically unstable language, is not vacuous with regard to epistemology as some have suspected, for it guarantees that we are quantifying over physical objects, not mental entities, when doing natural science and thus reveals our intent to remain within the scientific tradition.

Though I make a minimal concession to realism my brand of relativism is decidedly opposed to Metaphysical Realism as the absolute position has been labelled. There still are philosophers who claim that 'the world' is neutrally presented to us through perception with a ready-made structure, individuated objects and their properties dividing them into natural kinds. They believe that the objects are given independently of any conceptual shaping and that an ideal and complete theory would provide us with the totality of all truths about it. Such a view presupposes that we have a direct access to physical objects and that our linguistic representations are faithful copies of them. As mentioned earlier the trouble is that we have no empirically tested theory about 'the world' and that, therefore, we remain incapable of stating a clear truth condition with regard to such claims. Indeed, how could the defender of a picture theory of language establish the existence of an objective correspondence between the structure of 'the given' and the structure of our representational system? If, on the other hand, we consider the statement as belonging to science, we should reject it as false since psychology does not favour the view that human perception functions like a camera; the Gestalt psychologists of the early century, J.J.Gibson in *The Senses Considered As Perceptual Systems*[2] and many others, have stressed the active part of the perceiving organism in perceptual processes. To the neopositivistic and Quinean view of a universal observation language with its fixed stock of observation sentences I object with Dudley Shapere that the latter transcend pure perception insofar as they are fashioned not only by the conceptual structure of the language in which the theory under scrutiny is framed but also by the structural organization of the perceptual and measurement theories we are using : Since all (internally) real objects must be observable in a more or less indirect way, vision as such cannot be fundamental for observation nor can visibility be decisive with regard to ontology as long as we use such instruments as accoustic microscopes and other sophisticated devices.

Experimentation does not boil down to mere observation; insofar as what is observable depends upon current knowledge the extension of the predicate 'observable' will be conditioned by the techniques we have developed for stating how the diverse theoretical entities of a particular domain behave, what they can do, etc. Conceptual networks generate taxonomy by imposing certain equivalence classes on that specific field of application. Theoretical terms which occur in observation reports stem from the relevant theory and therefore the structure of its observation and measurement language must be shaped accordingly in order to connect quantity with an empirical indicator system or measuring instrument.

Against Metaphysical Realism I argue that, knowledge being a public affair, we must regard using a language as a necessary condition for achieving it and for communicating the results. According to my view, however, employing a linguistic system requires us to relativize truth to this system since it is only through it that the expressions acquire their meaning—most importantly a determinate extension. I have repeatedly criticized Quine's extreme holism which tends to blur useful distinctions. If we want to avoid the mixing of different levels of discourse we should not affirm that the totality of science is needed for determining the signification of all the expressions, for the semantic network is constituted only by the specific theories with which we operate in a particular context. A properly conceived universe of discourse cannot consist in everything we talk about but must be restricted to the object over which we quantify in an intended domain. If we use Tarski's definition—not merely the convention T which is his criterion for material adequacy—we have no other choice than to concede that truth is an internal matter to be decided only with regard to the ontology postulated in a context. I consider Quine's holophrastic treatment of observation sentences as the Achilles' heel of his naturalistic system because it compels him to introduce a primitive notion of truth which rests on the behavioristic criterion of assent or dissent prompted in the presence of appropriate stimuli and has nothing to do with Tarski's definition. I contend that such sentences do not belong to the proper language of the theory and consequently that they are of no avail when it comes to testing it. If Quine is ready to acknowledge that we have to know the meaning, i.e., the extension and intension, of the terms of a language in order to understand it and that theoretical terms gain their meaning through their integration into some corpus of laws, he cannot maintain that only structure matters with respect to the external truth of a theory and thus discard referential questions as entirely irrelevant. Such a radical view on ontological relativity must threaten his doctrine of physical realism since it commits him to accept as equally true any ontologically different theory that fits the observation sentences. Being unable to grasp what the naturalist could mean when he declares our overall scientific theory to be true (pending further information), I prefer to resort to my method of relativizing to contexts, which avoids application of the truth predicate to whole theories. In this way truth ascriptions are limited to certain sentences and they can be performed only with respect to a language with fixed semantic relations. Thus truth relativized to a conceptual framework becomes a strictly internal notion exempt of any realistic connotations.

The form of relativism I am advocating amounts to an imposition view in a Kantian sense. Since we inevitably impress the structure of our linguistic tools on 'the world' when we describe it, we cannot know what it is independently of our ways of speaking about it. Therefore acquiring knowledge is not a passive process of mirroring neutrally given facts but a creative activity shaping facts with the help of linguistic forms. When using a language (with incorporated systems of logic or mathematics), we imprint a certain organization or arrangement of elements on the reality sector we are constructing. Accordingly the individuals of different sorts required in the domain for making sentences true can only exist relative to the theory employed. Thus galaxies, quagalaxies for instance exist exclusively in a context where we are using an astronomical or a cosmological theory whose empirical laws determine the intension of the theoretical terms. Contrary to Goodman I do not say that we 'make' physical objects; I rather insist that the answer to the question whether or not certain kinds of physical objects exist in a particular reality sector also depends on 'the world', i.e. on the evidence we can produce within that reality sector in order to ascertain the truth of the corresponding existential assertions.

Empirical control often requires very sophisticated methods. Looking at a picture taken in a cloud chamber and just seeing dark shapes is not sufficient for warranting the presence of a particle. For a correct interpretation of the photograph, familiarity with measuring techniques, with the working of instruments and with other experimental matters is needed. How do theoretical entities become experimental objects? The required evidence mainly rests on the possibility of measuring certain of their effects by interacting with them. We use an appropriate observation theory for the purpose of associating theoretical quantities with observable so-called raw data and thus realize the transition from an empirical event to a theoretically described state. Since such a relation holds by virtue of pertinent physical laws the testing strategy will eventually consist in rectifying possible distortions without falling prey to a vicious circle. Measuring instruments must reflect the nomological interconnections by which the concept is tied to others that are in turn reliably linked to an empirical indicator system. In this way the theory defines the pure states the instrument is supposed to record and at the same time it determines the facts regarded as basic in the given context. As far as I am informed, physicists have not yet been able to manipulate neutral bosoms; according to my view, we are not in a position to affirm their existence as long as this incapacity lasts and we will have to correct the theory in the case it should prove insurmountable. Let me remark that the features mentioned in this paragraph corroborate the claim that there are neither theory-independent facts nor transtheoretical referential relations: reference, truth and factuality are internal matters to be settled within a context.

Granted that our modes of conceptual organization are not found in the world but built into the reality sectors we have created by employing a system of representations, we must also concede that the use of the verb 'exist' has to be restricted to the values of the variables posited in the domain of the context and that, therefore, we are not in a position to formulate *absolute* existence claims. Considered from this perspective it becomes trivial to affirm that galaxies exist only relative to a theory whose vocabulary comprises the predicate 'galaxy'. Keeping aware of the distinction between objects and linguistic expressions we may calculate the age of galaxies within astronomy whereas in the context of the history of science we may find out at what time the term has been introduced in the terminology of an astronomical theory. Thus we obtain two statements about clearly distinct matters which should not be confused as in the argument that galaxies have existed long before the word 'galaxy'.

According to my contextual view on semantics, sentences like 'Stars have existed before they were called stars'[3] are to be banished as meaningless because they involve a conflation of two statements belonging to different contexts and thus conceal an equivocation in the use of 'exist'. Such mistakes clearly illustrate the overall importance of distinguishing between object-language and meta-language, the latter permitting us to speak about expressions of the former. Since the extension of a predicate is determined by the interpretation of the linguistic system to which it belongs we must use astronomy with its empirical laws in order to turn certain things detectable in 'the world' into galaxies; this, however, does not mean that we create them materially, but only *qua* objects satisfying that specific description. As a consequence it is not possible to mark out essential properties which would characterize an individual or a natural kind in an absolute manner. Contrary to what an Aristotelian Realist may believe, the world is not presented to us readily sorted out into unalterable categories which are supposed to exist irrespective of the way we speak about it. The necessary and sufficient condition for something to be, say, gold remains relative to the conceptual scheme used to express the laws of the theory. Before appropriate scientific theories were developed 'nominal essences' in Locke's sense had to do the job while in actual chemistry the atomic number may serve as a criterion.

Relativism stresses the fact that without an appropriate linguistic apparatus for individuating objects we would be unable to (re)identify individuals in a systematic way. As the logical laws of identity do not tell us how to proceed in practice we must elaborate criteria which will vary according to the nature of the different sorts of objects we want to identify. Philosophers have wondered whether a bronze statue is one thing or two things—a figure and a piece of bronze. Again, put in such a manner suggesting an absolute answer, the question strikes me as unintelligible. Kripke has argued that there must be two entities since the piece of bronze but not the figure could take the form of a sphere. As I do not consider modal properties as an adequate means for identifying individuals I do not find his argument convincing. According to his possible-words-semantics which presupposes an essentialist metaphysics, questions like 'Does the property of being this figure and the property of being this piece of bronze essentially apply to things in the world?' do make sense. The relativist, however, shuns them as raising pseudo-problems which do not arise when we acknowledge that the answer will depend on the particular aim pursued. In the context of metallurgy, for instance, we will choose a chemical criterion whereas in the context of the history of arts both form and material will be taken as decisive, provided we want to count several figures cast in the same mould as different instances of one artistic creation. Viewed from a relativistic perspective, we have one object in each context with 'a=this piece of bronze' being true in the first and 'b=this figure' in the other and no problem since individuals figuring in the domain of different contexts cannot be identical. Only in the very unlikely case that, one day, we should have elaborated a combined theory for metals and art works would we be in a position to affirm the truth of 'a=b'.

In spite of my deep conviction that whatever we say about 'the world' is informed by the representational means we employ for determining reality sectors, I wish to distance myself from extreme positions such as Goodman's irrealism. The mere use of words does not guarantee the existence of corresponding objects. I emphatically insist that in the case of synthetic statements we have to ascertain, in each domain assumed by the multiple context, the existence of objects satisfying the truth conditions which do not depend merely on language but also on what is actually found in the respective reality sectors. In this respect, relativistic transcendentalism is decidedly on the side of the empirical sciences. Theoretical entities can be considered as existing only under the condition that we have actually devised a procedure which renders them empirically accessible.

I have already briefly mentioned my opposition to extreme holism postulating a unique body of total (scientific) knowledge. According to my restricted version of holism the semantic network is woven by the logical, mathematical and empirical theories with which we operate in a particular context and whose laws implicitly define or fix the intension of the terms introduced in them. When dealing with reference and truth, on the other hand, we have to direct our attention to questions concerning interpretation. Here Quine, who couples naturalism with extreme holism, is confronted with a serious problem, namely the fact that the actual use of (total) language does not determine a unique interpretation. The formal structure of a theory is multiplicitly interpretable and does not by itself determine a specific domain of application. The designation of a preferred model is pragmatically motivated by the intent to extract some substantive content from the formalism. While this seems to be fatal for the Metaphysical Realist, Quine draws the conclusion that reference is indeterminate and ontology irrelevant to the truth of the overall theory. For me the news does not come unexpectedly since I have never believed that referential relations could be detected in nature by empirical investigations. However, as I am convinced that we do not understand a language without being informed about the objects its terms refer to, I doubt that a theory of meaning which ignores referential matters and establishes truth-values of whole sentences on a merely behavioristic account will do the job. Given the fact that no privileged model can be deduced from the formal theory, the only possible alternative is to admit that we have to interpret our linguistic systems by our own lights. According to my normative conception of semantics, we do so indeed by accepting rules which prescribe the correct use of expressions in a context and thus also fix the referential relations. A systematic interpretation requires us to adopt, among others, a rule which makes metalinguistic sentences of the form :

'*a*' refers to *a*

'*F*' refers to individuals that are *F*

analytically true thereby excluding that the proper name 'Hume' refers to Kant or that the predicate 'house' refers to trees. We need not assume a causal link between a singular term and its referent or between a general term and the objects to which it applies in order to obtain a convenient relation; it suffices to follow the rules once we have adopted the convention. In the case of proper names whose semantic function is limited to picking out exactly one individual, all we need is a form of baptism or tagging through which we assign an object to the term while in the case of predicates we must agree on a criterion taken from the working theory for deciding whether or not certain (*n*-tuples of) objects belong to their extension. I submit that the procedure is the same for all kinds of individuals be they natural or artifical or whatever.

Looking at reference not as a physical but as an abstract relation which has its origin in intentional acts performed by language users, I am in agreement with Quine who affirms that there is no (physical) fact of the matter. Lacking an objectively designated model we have no other choice than to concede the relativity of reference and consequently accept the relations established by the rules in a context as the intended ones. Considered from a transcendental point of view, this is the only adequate method for rendering (internal) truth ascriptions possible. By proceeding in this way I do not, however, reveal a property common to all referential relations; as I do not believe in the feasibility of essentialist definitions I stay content with a theory which only explains how we fix the extension of the predicate 'refer' in each context. And for accomplishing this purpose we need not enter into Putnam's (slightly scholastic) question of how we know that 'denote' denotes denoting!

The adherents of the redundancy theory affirm that truth is not a property attached to statements but merely a device for semantic assent. According to them, we may, instead of saying that a sentence is true, just assert it. Judged from a strictly semantic perspective this cannot be correct because we are performing distinct speech acts when speaking about objects taken from the domain of the object language and when we are speaking about linguistic expressions which exclusively belong to the domain of the meta-language. I suspect that such a view is due to a unilateral relying on Tarski's convention T to the detriment of his proper definition based on the notion of satisfaction. I have already voiced misgivings about Quine's account of external truth depriving reference of any significant role. His imperturbable willingness to save physical realism has driven him to a dubious holophrastic treatment of observation sentences involving a radical departure from Tarski. In opposition to such views I accord a fundamental importance to truth conceived as purely internal, i.e., as relative to a context. Remaining stubbornly convinced that it is impossible to rate an existential statement true without ascertaining the existence of an object satisfying the corresponding open sentence, I reject any claim to the effect that matters of truth may be settled irrespective of ontology. As the universe of discourse changes with each context we have to admit a plurality of separated ontologies some of which may be lumped together if the situation requires a common treatment of their objects and if we are capable of proceeding to the necessary conceptual adjustments. Thus shunning the vision of a global body of science inspired by the neo-positivistic ideal of unity of science, I countenance a form of ontological relativity which does not drive us into the 'debacle', avowed by Quine since the publication of 'Whither Physical Objects', namely the admission that ontology does not matter with regard to the truth of our overall theory.

Since the universes of distinct contexts are populated with different kinds of objects—physical, psychological, mathematical, fictitious and other entities—truth is not exclusively concerned with the relation of linguistic expressions to 'the world'. In the case of abstract objects as, for instance, natural numbers, the question whether the predicate 'square root of 4' applies to 2 and -2 depends merely on the choice of an appropriate arithmetic theory from whose axioms we can logically deduce the sentence '$\sqrt{4} = \pm 2$' and thus ascertain its truth without regard to any empirical matters. If, on the other hand, we are dealing with a theory of natural science mere deducibility from its empirical laws does not suffice to warrant the truth of a synthetic statement; we need empirical evidence from the reality sector under discussion and in case that such were not available we should have doubts concerning the reliability (not the truth!) of the theory. If we remain durably unable to spot the referent of a singular term or to present an instance of a general term, sentences like 'Vulcan is a planet', or 'Phlogiston is a fluid active in processes of combustion', will have to be rejected as false.

As one should expect, Tarski's definition is largely neutral with regard to epistemological positions with the exception perhaps of Metaphysical Realism which is discarded because of the relativization to a language. Some philosophers have objected that it does not define 'true in *L*' for variable *L* and that, therefore, it is not a properly philosophical explication of the concept of truth. Since I am not concerned with the essential properties of 'Truth' (with a capital T) I do not care; for the purposes of my system a definition which allows us to fix the extension of the predicate in a context is amply sufficient. It fits perfectly well my central request to internalize the notion of truth by relativizing it—a move which must seem inescapable if one rejects as unintelligible the claim that 'the world' consists of language, independent objects, and facts, and that the latter make sentences true. I surmise that Tarski himself did not believe in the possibility of comparing linguistic expressions with an unconceptualized 'reality' and, therefore, would have approved my method of internalizing truth. Thanks to it we can shy away from the spectre of external truth and turn our attention to a more tractable business: the question of how to justify the acceptance of theories.

The definition does not tell us by itself how to proceed in order to ascertain the truth of sentences in practice. One notorious difficulty resides in the fact that universal generalizations—sentences of the form '*(x) (Fx→ Gx)*'—are not conclusively verifiable and that existential generalizations—sentences of the form '*(Ex) (Fx. Gx)*'—are not falsifiable while sentences with combined quantifiers are neither. As a consequence, we cannot reach final decisions with regard to theories as a whole containing laws and existential claims. Evaluating them is a comparative affair which guides our preference to theories with better empirical adequacy, superior capacity of solving problems—or other qualities depending on similar considerations. Appropriate qualifications will therefore touch on pragmatic matters like applicability, usefulness, reliability, acceptability, etc. As explanations and predictive success are always relative to human aims they cannot warrant, with each successive theory, convergence to any kind of absolute truth content (provided we are able to make sense of such a vague notion). This is a sufficient reason for not applying the predicate 'true' to theories. Since all we can do is to subject them to severe and variegated tests the proper label to attach to them, as long as they pass the tests, is 'confirmed' which cannot be synonymous with 'true', for truth is to be considered as a timeless property while qualifications like 'well confirmed' or 'justified under optimal epistemic conditions' may change in time. When a theory ceases to function successfully—when it fails, for instance, to make true predictions with regard to newly investigated cases—we should not reject it as false but simply consider it as inapt to cover such cases. By using an appropriate meta-scientific terminology we make clear that our judgements rest on pragmatic standards themselves subject to improvement in the course of progressing science. As presumably all our theories will eventually be superseded, the Scientific Realist is ironically driven to the conclusion that all science is false—thus revealing the self-defeating character of this doctrine.

I have emphasized that according to my contextual view on semantics the meaning of a theoretical term is determined by the network of laws in which it appears—referential matters, in particular, being settled by the interpretation we provide in order to attribute a domain of application to the theory and referents to the terms. As an unavoidable consequence problems having to do with incommensurability arise. Since semantic and empirical content are no longer preserved and changes in the taxonomic categories prerequisite for scientific descriptions have intruded, theory transitions cannot arrive as a cumulative process. Through such (holistic) redistributions successive theories acquire diverging semantic structures and are not, therefore, translatable into each other. As they do not, strictly regarded, solve exactly the same problems or cover exactly the same ground they must be considered as incommensurable with regard to their topic and to their conceptual scheme. The oxygen theory of burning, for instance, did not really apply to the same phenomena as the phlogiston theory; since moreover it does not seem possible to express what one says in the language of the other we are not facing a simple case of revising hypotheses within an evolving theory but indeed a change concerning the whole conceptual framework. If one concedes that the nomic relation determining the empirical content of theoretical terms can only be grasped after the domain of application has been specified one will also have to admit that one of two theories with different semantic structures cannot be logically subsumed under the other. This is the reason why I have always refused to accept the widespread view that Newtonian mechanics represent a limiting case of relativistic mechanics or quantum theory. The latter impose constraints on the legitimate form of equations which are not satisfied by classical physics. Fundamental constants as, e.g., the velocity of light, *c* or the Planck constant, $h/2\pi$ (pi) are empirically established values beyond which the theory becomes inapplicable. I insist that for this reason Newton's theory remains conceptually unrelated to the others and that, therefore, it cannot be logically derived from them. We are rather confronted with a genuine case of incommensurability.

If we regard semantic rules as publicly shared norms of representation, on which we agree by convention in order to confer meaning on the expressions, we have to admit that reality is not simply given to us, ready-made and independently of language, but that the reality sectors created by the use of a conceptual scheme are structurally conditioned by the latter. As a consequence, sentences expressing facts must also depend on the adopted rules which make an assessment of their truth value possible by empirical evidence. Since norms are not found in nature but are invented by us for the purpose of coming to grips with all sorts of natural phenomena we cannot justify our choice by appeal to an alleged structure essentially inherent in 'the world'. We must rather resort to pragmatic reasons concerning the successful operations we can perform with their help. As there is no hope of distinguishing a particular representational system as the objectively true one—only observational reports expressed within such a framework are to be qualified as true or false—we have an additional ground for repudiating the notion of external truth. Language does not correspond to 'the world' or mirror 'bare' facts; it is rather a precondition for the very possibility of formulating facts about a reality sector we have constituted by its use. In this sense observational data are always informed by the operating theory and the reasons for preferring, say, Einstein's way of using theoretical terms like 'gravitation', 'mass', 'energy', etc. are pragmatic; for they rest on considerations regarding the practical superiority of the relativity theory in explaining certain experimental results.

If a theory is reckoned among the empirical sciences we must test its conceptual capacity by applying it to observational materials. We have to ascertain that the objects and the events required for making its observation sentences true have actually occurred and that they are adequately represented by the distinctive linguistic means. When examining whether an object of a certain kind exists we need a precise meaning for the verb and a criterion for judging the factual truth of the existence claim. If, following Quine, we take 'exist' to mean 'to be the value of a bound variable' we have to provide empirical evidence of the required sort for ascertaining the existence of the object in the domain of the reality sector under investigation. So, for instance, a report of the form 'The spot on the picture is the trace of an electron' will attest the general claim that electrons exist.

Putnam has argued that in the successive theories only what he calls stereotype of the term 'electron' had been revised while its extension stayed constant. This is a bold affirmation due to his peculiar conception of meaning. According to mine, however, we need to make sure that J.J. Thomson was really measuring the mass of the same entity which R.A. Millikan, H. A. Lorentz, E. Rutherford, N. Bohr and others have been talking about. Answering such questions requires information concerning the instrumental devices (relying on the causal properties of electrons) which were used in order to produce the desired effects. This shows that observation by far exceeds the data meeting the eye and that at the level of sophisticated science high power accelerators make it possible to affirm the existence of all sorts of particles not directly accessible to ordinary perception. It also reminds us of the fact that the meaning of expressions occurring in observation sentences is theory-dependent and that accordingly the truth of the latter remains relative to the selected linguistic system. In science where measuring techniques play an integral role—systems change when they are measured—the criteria for deciding whether they are actually true or not may take a highly complex form and become subject to controversy. Occasionally, accepted observational findings will have to be reconsidered, for instance, when the practical situation requires a redescription, or more accurate measuring results, or some other improvement.

If the reader accepts the foregoing he will admit that observation is not such a simple and straightforward a subject as its informal and unqualified treatment by Quine and others might suggest. As we do not actually rely on a common stock of unalterable observation sentences we should give way to the insight that the extension of the theory-laden term 'observable fact' differs with varying contexts. It encompasses only those objects, classes of objects and processes for which confirming evidence expressed in the language of the theory at work, can be produced.

I conclude that the standards according to which we accept or reject theories have nothing to do with their putative truth content. They do not, however, rest on mere opinion or subjective preference as certain fashionable forms of relativism as 'deconstructionism' for instance would have it. Epistemology remains with us as a serious business in spite of the fact that our standards of acceptability reflect human values and interests and that, like these, they undergo historical changes. Insofar as the success of a scientific theory is chiefly judged on account of the true predictions we obtain through its application and thus depends on the amount of accurate and repeatable observations enhancing its confirmation, 'successful' should not be taken as a semantic but as a pragmatic term. Therefore equating external truth with success—as certain pragmatists propose to do—is dangerously misleading and only furthers confusion. Relativized transcendentalism, as a kind of *methodological* realism in contrast to doctrinal realism, is in harmony with Putnam's conviction that rationality as a normative concept can be neither naturalized nor formalized and that consequently the vision of a unique and complete theory of the world matching the totality of facts is a delusive fantasy. As, however, I do not believe that evaluative discourse is reducible to descriptive discourse I do not adhere to his view according to which value judgements can have a truth-value, considering it to be a residue of naturalism. Sciences like anthropology, psychology, physiology and others take human beings as the passive *objects* of their investigations whereas epistemology deals with them as the active *subjects* who create these very scientific theories. Such a fundamental difference in perspective should deter us from looking at philosophy as a mere prolongation of science at a more general level.*

Notes and References

1. In his recent book *The Completeness of Scientific Theories* (Dordrecht/Boston/London, 1994), Martin Carrier has advanced convincing arguments illustrated by probative case studies which show why geometry remains conventional in important respects and how to avoid circularity or infinite regress when testing scientific theories. (Cf. Part B, Chapter IV)

2. Boston, MA, 1966

3. Cf. Israel Scheffler, 'The wonderful worlds of Goodman', *Syntheses* 1980, pp. 201-09.

* I thank Howard G, Callaway, Alex Burri, Michael Frauchiger and Avrum Stroll for useful criticisms and for stylistic improvements of earlier drafts.

Epistemology and Understanding of Language*

ERNEST LEPORE

Prof. Ernest Lepore, Associate Director, Rutgers Cognitive Science Centre, Rutgers University, New Burnswick, New Jersey, USA. Visiting Professor at a number of Universities, including, University of California, Berkeley; Washington University, St. Louis, Missouri; University of Venice; Helsinki University. Member of American Philosophical Association, and Society for Philosophy and Psychology in the USA, and The Society for Ibero-American Philosophers.

Has published 7 books dealing with a wide range of subjects related to Philosophy, including, semantics, holism, Donald Davidson, and language (some in collaboration with other scholars), and had 4 books in progress in 1996. Has published 55 articles in Italian, English, Finnish and Russian (and had 15 articles forthcoming in 1996), many in collaboration with Jerry Fodor and a few with other scholars.

Guest Lecturer at many places, including, Universities of California, Notre Dame, Butler, Florida State, Minnesota, South Carolina, Montclair State, Trenton State, Oklahoma, and philosophical associations in America; and many Universities and conferences in Europe, including those in Italy, Poland, Finland, France and Germany. Organizer and co-director of conferences and seminars in America and abroad, including 4 international conferences for SOPHIA in Mexico, Argentine, Brazil and Spain.

According to Davidson, natural languages are 'systematic in the sense that the interpreter can, on the basis of learning finitely many words and composition rules, come to understand novel sentences; and there is no clear upper limit to the number of utterances that can be interpreted'.[1] Davidson thinks—as does ALMOST everyone—that only a recursive theory with a finite basis can provide an adequate model of the

* Earlier drafts of this paper were read at Washington University and the Universities of Bologna, Graz, Helsinki, Lublin, and Rome. I'd like to thank the members of the Philosophy department at each university for their comments. I'd like to thank also Johannes Brandl, Lou Goble, Donald Davidson and especially Jerry Fodor and Kirk Ludwig for their comments and criticisms on various drafts.

interpreter's ability in this respect. But Davidson has always stopped short of saying that the speakers KNOW such a theory; rather, such a theory 'explicitly states something knowledge of which WOULD suffice for interpreting utterances of speakers of the language to which it applies' ('Reply to Foster,' my emphasis, p. 171); or, he asks 'What COULD we know that would enable us [to interpret another's words] ... [This] is not the same as the question what DO we know that enables us to interpret the words of others. For there may easily be something we could know and don't, knowledge of which would suffice for interpreting, while on the other hand it is not altogether obvious that there is anything we actually know which plays an essential role in interpretation.' ('Radical Interpretation', my emphasis, p. 125). And more recently, he writes, 'All that we should require of a theory of truth for a speaker is that it be such that IF an interpreter had explicit propositional knowledge of the theory, he WOULD know the truth conditions of utterances of the speaker' and, in the same paper, 'A theory of truth for a speaker is a theory of meaning in ... that explicit knowledge of the theory WOULD suffice for understanding the utterances of that speaker' ('The Structure and Content of Truth', my emphasis, p. 312). Talk of the interpreter (or speaker) using such a theory is, for Davidson, a shorthand way of saying that the interpreter makes use of a competence that is correctly described by the theorist's theory [Davidson 1976, p. 172].

Davidson is not alone. Semanticists in general are uncomfortable, if not downright skeptical, about attributing semantic knowledge, particularly knowledge of a semantic THEORY, to ordinary speakers [Quine 1970, Thomason 1974, Hacking 1975, Dummett 1975, Devitt. 1981, Evans 1981, Schiffer 1987, Wright 1987 and numerous others]. Dummett, for example, likens language comprehension more to a skill like cycling than to having the sort of propositional knowledge that underlies the predictions and explanations effected by physicists or chemists. He denies there is ANYTHING we know in virtue of which we understand our language.[2]

Those who do not feel the pinch usually adopt a two-pronged defence: they rebut skeptics with an array of distinctions (and hedges), contending that the skeptics' confusions arise because they ignore such distinctions [Lepore 1982; Higgonbotham 1983, 1987; George 1989]; at the same time, they argue that attributing such knowledge still provides the best available working (empirical) hypothesis we have to account for language comprehension [Partee 1975, 1979; Larson and Segal, forthcoming]. However, substantial challenges are on the table.

Skeptical arguments abound about the relevance of semantics in explicating language comprehension [Chomsky 1986; Fodor 1975, 1987; Hornstein 1984; Stich 1983; Schiffer 1987; Soames 1985]. More acutely, there are accounts of language comprehension that EXCLUDE metalinguistic (semantic) knowledge, and therefore, knowledge of semantic THEORY [Harman 1975; Fodor 1984, 1989; Schiffer 1987]. Unless these alternative accounts can be shown deficient, Davidson's reservation may be the sensible and prudent response. Yet a not inappropriate worry, one that persistently nags at some philosophers, me, for instance, is this: if semantic theories for natural languages merely MODEL linguistic comprehension, what can we learn from their construction? In an effort to assuage middle-aged fears about the worth of one's life's labour, I will here advance considerations to support the thesis that the semantic theories Davidson defends specify not only adequate MODELS of language understanding, but KNOWLEDGE by virtue of which speakers understand their language.

The paper will be structured as follows: Fodor and Schiffer will be the heavies. In Section 1, I will briefly discuss the nature of language comprehension and Fodor's and Schiffer's nonsemantic accounts of it, parrying obvious initial worries one might have about their accounts. In Sections 2-4, I will trace Fodor's long-standing disregard for semantics for natural languages far back to his early fling with structural semantics. To this end, in Section 2, I will quickly review the controversy between truth conditional and structural semantics. In Section 3, I will refute one attempt to deflate the significance of (truth-conditional) semantics. This defence will NOT, however, establish that speakers actually KNOW truth conditions, explicitly or tacitly or in any other way; nor, I might add, do standard Chomskian-style arguments [Higgonbotham 1983, 1987; George 1989]. This is because, unless Fodor's and Schiffer's alternative accounts of linguistic comprehension are shown deficient, semantic knowledge is inconsequential. This is reviewed in Section 4. So, in Section 5, I shift gears and argue that speakers must have METALINGUISTIC propositional knowledge about their language in order to understand it. In Section 6, I will argue that this metalinguistic knowledge is SEMANTIC. In this way I hope not only to turn Davidson's counterfactuals into factuals, but also to vindicate those who hold that language comprehension is best explicated by appeal to semantic knowledge.

One last qualification before we get started. I want to emphasize the difference between 'you don't need to know an EXPLICIT theory in order to understand L' and 'you don't need to know a theory to understand L, explicit or otherwise.' The latter is the stronger thesis and it's what's at issue in this paper, though I think it's the first that Davidson may be hiding behind in many of the passages I cited.

Section 1: Adequacy Conditions

Suppose Maria utters to Massimo the Italian words 'Sta nevicando'. Suppose further that Massimo understands Italian. In normal circumstances, Massimo would come to believe that Maria SAID that it's snowing. Barring behaviourists, all parties to this debate— pro and con—agree that minimally language comprehension consists in having the capacity to make specific direct/indirect quotation transitions of just this sort.

> A theory of understanding for a language L would explain how one could have an auditory perception of the utterance of a novel sentence of L and know what was said in the utterance of that sentence [Schiffer 1987, p. 113].
>
> I assume that language perception is constituted by nondemonstrative inferences from representations of certain effects of the speaker's behaviour (sounds that he produces, marks that he makes) to representations of certain of his intentional states, [in particular] a canonical representation of what the speaker said [Fodor 1984, pp. 5-6].

What's at issue is whether semantic knowledge underwrites these transitions. Fodor and Schiffer deny that knowledge or any other kind of epistemic/doxastic/psychological relationship toward internal cognitive states is required in order to account for language comprehension.

> ...Davidson evidently does NOT—and certainly SHOULD NOT—hold that ... understanding [a language] L requires knowing [a correct meaning theory for L] ... [W]hether or not knowledge of the kind alluded to in [the correct meaning theory] would, if one had it, suffice for understanding a language, it seems very clear that no actual speaker has such propositional knowledge [Schiffer 1987, emphasis in the original, p. 116].

In answer to the question, what semantic knowledge must someone have in order to understand a natural language, Fodor's response is NONE.

> What really matters is this: For any perceptually analysable linguistic token there is a canonical description (DT) such that for some mental state there is a canonical description (DM) such that 'DTs cause DMs' is true and counterfactual supporting [Fodor 1989, p. 8].

In Fodor's view, linguistic understanding consists in being a template for a causal network between the perceived linguistic sounds and shapes, and the subsequent internal mental states.

> The translation algorithm [from English into Mentalese] might well consist of operations that deliver Mentalese expressions under syntactic descriptions as output given English expressions under syntactic descriptions as input with NO SEMANTICS coming in anywhere except, of course, that if it's a good translation, then semantic properties will be preserved [Fodor 1990, my emphasis, pp. 187-88].

Schiffer writes that 'a theory that explains one's ability to go from auditory perceptions of utterances of sentences to knowledge of what propositional speech acts were performed in them... would not be a PHILOSOPHICAL theory' [Schiffer 1987, emphasis in original, p. 269]. He concurs with Fodor that no internally represented semantics is required for the use of a public language even if the language has a semantics. This is supposed to be the lesson of Schiffer's Harvey counter-example [Schiffer 1987, pp. 192-207]. Harvey can understand indefinitely many utterances of novel English sentences. This understanding consists in his ability to translate English sentences into his *lingua mentis*.

> Harvey thinks in Mentalese...and his language processing uses not an internally represented [meaning theory] of English but rather an internally represented TRANSLATION MANUAL from English to Mentalese.... Such a theory assigns no semantic values to the expressions of either language and in no sense determines a grammar (i.e., a meaning theory) for either language [Schiffer 1987, emphasis in the original, p.192f].

Schiffer here writes only about whether there need be an internally represented compositional semantics. The issue whether there need be ANY sort of epistemic relationship between a speaker and this semantics can't even arise if there is no need at all for postulating a semantic theory in the first place.

If either Schiffer or Fodor is right, then the semanticist's is not, as Fodor likes to say, the only game in town. But how could either be right? Isn't it just plain obvious that speakers of Italian, for example, do in fact know a range of semantic facts, including (1)-(3)?

1. 'Sta nevicando' means that it's snowing.
2. 'Sta nevicando' is true iff it's snowing.
3. 'nevicando' refers to snow.

Fodor and Schiffer can both agree that (1)-(3) and their ilk are truths about Italian expressions; they can also agree that every Italian speaker knows such truths. But these details aren't at issue in THIS debate. What is, is whether such knowledge is REQUIRED for understanding Italian. According to Fodor and Schiffer, it is not.

In Fodor's account, truths like (1)-(3) have a sort of second rate status; if known at all, they are known derivatively. (1)-(2), for example, are true because the THOUGHT that it's snowing is true iff it's snowing and speakers of Italian use 'Sta nevicando' to express this thought. If I know that (1) or that (2), it's only because I know first the truth or meaning conditions of my own thoughts and secondly I know that my words can be used to express this thought. From this it does NOT follow that I need invoke knowledge that (1) or that (2) in order to understand 'Sta nevicando'. This is partly what Fodor means when he writes that he is 'Gricean in spirit though certainly not in detail' [Fodor 1975:103-04; see, also, 1987:50].

According to Grice, what a speaker means by an expression is (logically) prior to what that expression means in a public language; and speaker meaning is itself reducible to psychological factors. Fodor and Schiffer are Gricean to the extent that they both hold that the semantic properties natural language expressions have, they inherit from (the language of) thought, Mentalese.[3] Natural language expressions do not, to use Haugland's term, have original intentionality [Haugland 1981]; they have derived intentionality. So, according to Fodor and Schiffer, any semantic knowledge we may have about our own natural language is derivative and therefore inconsequential; it plays no role in linguistic competence.[4]

Still, one might wonder whether Fodor and Schiffer aren't merely postponing the inevitable. After all, it's an empirical hypothesis whether speakers think in their own natural language. Suppose, as Harman believes, English speakers do think 'in English'. Then wouldn't it follow that understanding a natural language requires knowledge of the semantics for English expressions? It doesn't. Even if one could convince either Fodor or Schiffer to concede that one's *lingua mentis* is one's own public language [see Fodor 1975, p. 79ff; Schiffer 1987, p. 187], understanding would still involve only the capacity to make direct/indirect quotation transitions, regardless of which language we think in. As Harman puts it, '[w]ords are used to communicate thoughts that would ordinarily be thought in those or similar words' [Harman 1975, p. 271]. So, if we think 'in English', then this means that when someone who understands English hears an individual A utter 'It's snowing', she will, to speak with the vulgar, put into her belief-box the English sentence 'A said that it's snowing.' Where exactly were any assumptions about the semantic properties of A's words invoked, much less knowledge about these properties?

We don't understand thoughts; we merely have or entertain them. We don't say: he's thinking that it's raining but doesn't understand this thought. What we could mean by this is simply that he isn't clear in his conception of rain or some such thing. So, there is nothing we need KNOW in order to understand our thoughts. I certainly needn't know that my thought [Maria said that it's snowing] is true iff Maria said that it's snowing in order to UNDERSTAND this thought. It's not clear what this means; and even to the extent that it is intelligible it's not clear that it doesn't stick us with an obvious infinite regress.

Anticipating later discussion, let me note now that for Fodor the interesting questions about semantic properties are metaphysical and their answers won't involve semantic KNOWLEDGE. We needn't know any metaphysical theory about the nature of semantic properties in order to understand Italian, nor in order to think; if we did, we'd all be in trouble.

The basic challenge is now on the table:

i. Understanding a natural language involves nothing more than having a (perceptual) capacity to hook up the natural language expressions with symbols of (the language of) thought. This is partly what Fodor means when he calls himself a Gricean.

ii. This skill—partly acquired both before and after birth—is not constituted by propositional metalinguistic (semantic) knowledge.

iii. Natural language expressions lack original intentionality; they have derived intentionality.

iv. But if natural language expressions lack original intentionality, wherein lies original intentionality? Original intentionality lies with the contents of thoughts. If you're Fodor, this means with Mentalese symbols.

There's lots to fuss about here. Though Davidson, Fodor, and Schiffer are all physicalists, Fodor and (may be) Schiffer believe that physicalists must tell some story about how the semantic and the psychological are to be explicated in physicalistic (or topic neutral terms), whereas Davidson has offered an argument that there is no (philosophically) interesting explication about this confrontation [Davidson 1970]. This means for Davidson there is no (philosophically) interesting answer to (iv). Also, as already noted, both Fodor and Schiffer are committed to the view that thought is (logically) prior to public language. Davidson, however, ARGUES that there could not be thought without public language, and vice versa. To this extent, though Davidson doesn't embrace the terminology, he denies that public language lacks 'original intentionality'.

In short, I could write a paper detailing why Davidson rejects (iii) and (iv). However, perhaps unwisely, I don't think (iii) and (iv) matter much to the debate whether linguistic comprehension requires semantic knowledge. So, instead of trying to deconstruct Fodor's and Schiffer's arguments for (iii) and (iv) here, I will aim only to refute (i) and (ii). Before I set out to do this, though, I'd like to say more than a few words about how Fodor's and Schiffer's challenges illuminate anew both what most philosophers argued was a misguided research program (section 2) and what I've argued elsewhere is a desperate defence of this program (Section 3).

Section 2: Structural Semantics—A Misguided Research Program

In the 1960's and early 1970's, Fodor (along with Katz and Postal) was a proud peacocking structural semanticist (hereafter SS-ist). SS-ists countenance properties and relations like synonymy, meaningfulness, anomaly, logical entailment and equivalence, redundancy and ambiguity as a good initial conception of the range of semantics. Shunning details, SS-ists proceed by translating (or mapping) natural language expressions into (sequences or a set of) expressions of another language. There is no uniformity among SS theorists about the nature of this language or about how these translations or mappings are to be effected, but for my purposes I beg no interesting questions by restricting attention to Katz and Fodor's SS account [1963], where the language translated (or mapped) into is 'Semantic Markerese'. The culmination of the various mapping rules and other apparatus within the Katz/Fodor framework results in theorems like (4):

4. 'Sta nevicando' in Italian translates (or is mapped into) the language of Semantic Markerese as S.

Mappings like (4) are constrained, and this is the *raison d'etre* for them as well as for semantic markers, such that synonymous expressions of a language L translate into the same (sequence or set of) expressions of Semantic Markerese, ambiguous expressions of L translate into different expressions of Semantic Markerese, anomalous expressions of L translate into no expression of Semantic Markerese at all and so on.

Once the rest of the philosophical community surmised what SS was about, its practitioners became whipping posts for dissenting semanticists, who couldn't get into print fast enough to explain to Fodor and Katz what semantics was all about and how confused they were about it. Davidson [1967, 1973], Lewis [1972], Cresswell [1978], Partee [1975], among others, each argued that SS theories do not articulate relations between expressions and the world, that they do not provide an account of the conditions under which such sentences are true, and therefore, these theories are not really semantic. The critics charged that the phenomena SS concerns itself with represent only a small portion of the full domain semantics must deal with ultimately and, SS, they argued, cannot in principle accommodate this full domain. As David Lewis put it:

> ... we can know the Markerese translation of an English sentence without knowing the first thing about the meaning of the English sentence; namely, the conditions under which it would be true. Semantics with no truth conditions is no semantics [1972:169-170].

Critics, like Davidson, protested that even if a SS for Italian assigned an interpretation to every Italian sentence it would not specify WHAT ANY EXPRESSION OF ITALIAN MEANS. On the Davidsonian conception, an adequate semantic theory for L must not only ascribe meanings to expressions of L, it must also ascribe them IN A WAY THAT ENABLES SOMEONE WHO KNOWS THE THEORY TO UNDERSTAND THESE EXPRESSIONS. SS fails on this account because in the overall picture of SS there are three languages: the natural language, the language of Semantic Markers, and the translating (or mapping) language, which may be Semantic Markerese, the natural language, or some other language [Davidson 1973: 129]. Since SS proceeds by correlating the first two languages using the third, it is possible to understand its mappings, for example, (4), knowing only the translating (or mapping) language, in this case English, and not the other two. We can know that (4), perhaps on the basis of what Katz and Fodor tell us, without knowing what either 'Sta nevicando' or the Semantic Markerese sentence S means.

If someone understands Semantic Markerese, he no doubt can utilize (4) to understand the Italian sentence; but this is because he brings to bear two things he knows that (4) does not state, namely, that Semantic Markerese is a language he understands and the particular information he has in virtue of which he understands S. This latter knowledge is doing most of the work here—not the SS theory. And it is this information Davidson wants an adequate semantics to characterize.

Section 3: The Hopelessness of Semantics

Is Davidson asking too much of a semantic theory? Extreme sceptics 'argue' that any effort to satisfy Davidson's aim for semantics is bound, in principle, to fail. Chierchia and McConnell-Ginet write:

> What a Tarski-style definition of truth does is to associate sentences with a description of the conditions under which they are true in a certain metalanguage. It thereby seems to shift the issue of meaning from the object language to the metalanguage without really telling us what meaning is [1990, p.82].

Peter Seuren somewhat earlier wrote:

> It has often been stated that, essentially, meanings cannot be described in language. Sometimes they can be demonstrated by ostensive definition, but any description in terms of a language, natural or artificial, is bound to have its own meaning in turn, a description of which will again have its own meaning, etc. If this is true, we can only set up sets of synonymous expressions [1969, p. 219].

And Moritz Schlick much earlier once wrote:

> Philosophy is that activity through which the meaning of statements is revealed or determined.... Bestowing meaning upon statements cannot be done in turn by statements.... The final giving of meaning always takes place ... through DEEDS [1930, my emphasis, pp. 56-7].

The charge apparently is that a semantics for a natural language L must at least PROVIDE the meaning for each sentence of L. However, since any theory must be stated in some language, the meanings of sentences of L must be provided by means of expressions of the theory's language and therefore any semantic theory at best translates a natural language onto the language of the semantic theory. So, even a sentence like (1), according to Seuren, at best provides a translation for mapping

Italian onto English by describing the meaning of the Italian sentence in English.

I disagree. Neither (1) nor (2) describes or makes reference to meanings. In both sentences only an Italian sentence is mentioned and snow is possibly referenced. Nor does (1) or (2) articulate any RELATIONSHIP between expressions in the way that (4) does. It is true that words are used in articulating (1) and (2), but in this sense a semantics is no different from physics. Is there some special defect because we must use words when we do semantics that does not infect non-linguistic theories? Why else should any philosopher think that if we specify for every Italian sentence IN ENGLISH a sentence of the form:

S means that p

we are BOUND to fail to specify knowledge sufficient for understanding Italian?

The uninitiated and uncompromising frequently say something like knowing that (1) or knowing that (2) cannot suffice for understanding the Italian sentence since we must know what 'it is snowing' means before we can UTILIZE this knowledge. This is surely INcorrect since it's merely contingent that we articulate this fact about Italian in English. We could articulate it in French, German, Dutch or even Italian itself in much the same way that we can specify temperature employing any acceptable temperature scale. Whether I specify the temperature as 32 degrees Fahrenheit or 0 degrees Centigrade haven't I communicated the same information in some sense? Of course, we try to articulate a semantic theory for Italian in a language every relevant party understands since, as is true for temperature, were we to choose a language not understood by everyone concerned we risk failing to communicate knowledge we think suffices for understanding Italian.[5]

Someone still might argue that since we must use language in order to articulate semantic knowledge doesn't this show that we never succeed in fully characterizing even what is sufficient for understanding since whatever success we achieve always is parasitic on understanding the language of the theory? If this is sceptics' concern, it is misplaced. Davidson's aim is to specify information sufficient for understanding some particular language. Someone who lacks concepts, for example, someone who lacks the concept of quotation, or meaning (or truth), or snow, cannot grasp or understand sentences (1) [or (2)], but this individual is not one to whom our exercise is directed. Should he lack these (or related) concepts he cannot understand Italian, at least not 'Sta nevicando'.[6] 'What as philosophers we can do... is ask how a competent interpreter (ONE WITH ADEQUATE CONCEPTUAL RESOURCES AND A LANGUAGE OF HIS OWN) can come to understand the speaker of an alien tongue' ['Three Varieties of Knowledge', my emphasis, p. 157].

We might undertake to explain what concepts are; in virtue of the fact that a concept of snow, for example, is about snow and not about grass; what having these concepts consists in. These may be legitimate concerns, some psychological, some apparently metaphysical. But the semantic task never was to determine what it is to have (knowledge of) the concept of truth or snow. Nor was it to determine in virtue of what a concept has its semantic properties. Yet there may be good reason to view these projects as part of a larger conception of a theory of content [a la Dretske 1981; Fodor 1987, among others]. But, and this is a big 'but', it is no part of semantics for natural language that we provide accounts of concept constitution or acquisition.

Section 4: Fodor's Revenge

Shortly after the assault on SS by practically the entire philosophical community, Fodor dropped out of the semantic scene and dove whole hog into philosophy of mind. Most philosophers thought, certainly I did, that Fodor had changed his mind about SS, that he no longer found it profitable to pursue semantics by studying mapping relations and the various constraints on them into Semantic Markerese. End of story. Closed case. When hell freezes over!

In 1975, in a passage expressing the same concerns of Chierchia/McConnell-Ginet, Seuren, and Schlick, Fodor wrote that he saw little difference, if any, between specifying meaning by translation and specifying meaning in terms of truth-conditions:

> This will hold for absolutely any semantic theory whatsoever so long as it is formulated in a symbolic system, and of course, there is no alternative to so formulating one's

> theory. We're all in Sweeney's boat; we've all Gotta use words when we talk. Since words are not, as it were, selfilluminating like globes on a Christmas tree, there is no way in which a semantic theory can guarantee that a given individual will find its formulas intelligible.... So the sense in which we can 'know the Markerese translation of an English sentence without knowing ... the conditions under which it would be true' is pretty uninteresting [Fodor 1975:120-21].

In a critical response, I and Barry Loewer argued that either Fodor misunderstood the objection reconstructed earlier to SS or he misunderstood the nature of truth-conditional semantics [Lepore & Loewer 1981]. We took Fodor to be misconstruing Davidson as saying that one must understand the language in which the canonical representation is expressed before one can utilize the semantic theory to determine what the represented sentences mean—and this is a problem not just an SS, but any, semanticist must face. This certainly is correct and I made this point myself in section 3. But Davidson's point is not this obvious one. Instead,. he is arguing that someone who understands a translation and knows it to be true need not understand the sentence of the translated language. No one denies we cannot understand (5) unless we understand English.

5. 'Sta nevicando' in Italian translates 'It is snowing' in English.

Similarly, no one denies that we cannot understand sentences (1) or (2) unless we understand English. But knowledge that (1) or that (2), unlike knowledge that (5), requires no competence with English. Simply note that whereas (1), (2) and (5) are all grammatical, (6) is not:

6. 'Sta nevicando' in Italian means that it is snowing IN ENGLISH.

One need know no more English to know that (1) or that (2) than Galileo knew for us truthfully to say of him that he said that the earth moves.

None of this shows any more (or any less) than that a semantics that specifies truth-conditions for sentences of a language may serve to characterize (at least partially) the knowledge sufficient for understanding a language, while a semantics that specifies translation from one language into another cannot. The conjectural inference from knowledge of truth-conditions (partly) SUFFICES to understand a language to knowledge of truth-conditions (partly) CONSTITUTES this understanding may seem natural, indeed, even good science, but Fodor, for one, balks.

It came as a great surprise to me when I realized that Fodor's early commitment to SS is of a piece with his current scepticism about semantics for natural languages. Indeed, Fodor hasn't changed his mind much since his early commitment to SS.

It is true that he repudiated much of the original Semantic Markerese program; he has even marshalled experimental data against it. For example, SS requires commitment to an analytic/synthetic distinction that Fodor now despairs of [Fodor and Lepore 1992]. It also requires commitment to certain views about conceptual decomposition that Fodor clearly rejects [see Fodor, Fodor and Garrett 1975; Fodor, Garrett, Walker, and Parkes 1980]. But there is a way of seeing commitment to SS as a denial of the cogency of semantics for natural languages, at least qua theory of understanding.

As I mentioned earlier in passing, for Fodor, the really interesting question about semantic properties is metaphysical: what bestows intentional (i.e., contentful) states on a cognitive system?[7] Semantic theories, whether of the SS or the truth-conditional variety, are of no use here. The semantic properties of mentalese 'expressions', for example, their truth and satisfaction conditions, are explicated not by devising semantic theories a la Davidson for Semantic Markerese, but rather by developing a viable naturalist story about the nature of content. Since natural languages are, according to Fodor, mere shadows of real intentionality, the real action takes place at the level of the mind, in fact, at the level of the symbols of the mind. But explicating the semantic properties of thoughts, according to Fodor, is a metaphysical enterprise. Metaphysical questions have metaphysical answers; not semantic ones, not epistemic ones, not psychological ones. According to Fodor, Davidson's emphasis on semantics for natural languages sweeps all the interesting philosophical questions under the rug.

How is this supposed to show that Fodor really hasn't repented his SS ways? Davidson's truth-conditional account is NO BETTER than the original SS translation suggestion not because they both use language, but BECAUSE both leave unanswered the interesting question : In virtue of what is the concept SNOW, for example, about snow (and not about grass)? As I've already emphasized, philosophers qua semanticists need not answer this question, nor should they be expected to. Fodor concurs. His conclusion is that truth-conditional semantics for natural languages is boring. But worse than boring is Fodor's charge that truth-conditional, as well as any other sort of, semantics is useless. This is his real challenge.

Fodor as well as Schiffer and Harman are challenging Davidson (and any other semanticist) to supply a purpose for the semantic endeavour. The rest of this paper is devoted to taking up this challenge. In what remains, I want to establish (a)-(c):

a. Understanding a natural language requires metalinguistic propositional knowledge.

My argument will be predicated on the proposition that speakers have REASONS for acquiring beliefs about what another says upon hearing his utterances. However, even if Fodor and Schiffer concede—fat chance!—after seeing my argument that metalinguistic propositional knowledge is required for understanding, they would still need to be convinced that this knowledge isn't constituted by a fully developed SS instead of a truth-conditional theory. Therefore, I will end my discussion by establishing (b) and advancing some considerations that incline me to conclude that (c):

b. The correct semantics for natural languages is NOT translational.

c. The correct semantics for natural languages is truth-conditional.

Section 5: Understanding and Justification[8]

Recall that Massimo came to believe that Maria said that it's snowing on the basis of his hearing Maria (assertively) utter 'Sta nevicando'. A natural question about Massimo is, What is his reason for (acquiring) this belief? Since it is consistent with Fodor's and Schiffer's cognitivism that Massimo has no beliefs ABOUT the causal connection between what he hears and what he believes is said; nor ABOUT any other relation between them, it is equally CONSISTENT with their positions, so I claim, that Massimo has no reason for his new belief. After all, according to

Fodor and Schiffer, Massimo understands Maria's utterance of 'Sta nevicando' IF HE IS CAUSED by this utterance to believe that Maria said that it is snowing. This, though, is consistent with Massimo not BELIEVING that [he believes Maria said that it is snowing BECAUSE he believes that she uttered to him 'Sta nevicando' in Italian].[9]

That is a bit quick and perhaps unfair to Fodor and Schiffer. Since, according to them, it suffices to understand a language that one instantiate a particular causal nexus involving perceived linguistic sounds and shapes and appropriate nonlinguistic beliefs, there is a temptation to say that Massimo's reason for his belief that Maria said that it snowed is that, by virtue of being an Italian speaker, Massimo's hearing Maria utter 'Sta nevicando' CAUSED him to believe that she said that it snowed. However, though reasons may be causes, it does not follow that every cause, even every cognitive cause, is a reason.

In some rather innocuous sense of the word 'reason', (e.g., 'cause') because of the causal connection between this perception and this belief, Massimo has some reason for holding this belief (in much the same way that the reason the vase is in pieces is because someone knocked it over). If no one knocked the vase over, it would not be broken. And, likewise, if Massimo had not heard Maria utter 'Sta nevicando', he would not have come to believe that she said that it's snowing. But this causal fact (and the counterfactuals it supports) alone do not provide Massimo with a reason for his belief. Our knowing that he perceived the sounds he did and that these sounds caused him to have this belief no more supply a reason for Massimo than were we to discover that he is subject to this peculiar psychological quirk: whack him upside the head, he believes it is snowing. Even if there were a nomological connection between whacks and the ensuing beliefs, this alone does not warrant the connection. So, distinguishing speakers from non-speakers in terms of causal connections alone, even when these causal connections comprehend patterned internal mental states, obscures from where the reasons we ordinarily expect derive. Or, so it seems.

In conversation (unfortunately, not in print), both Fodor and Schiffer submit that linguistic comprehension carries such warrant, but they deny that this warrant requires the ascription of metalinguistic (semantic) knowledge to speakers; it is instead secured by virtue of there being a RELIABLE connection between heard utterances and beliefs about what is said. Because the cognitive capacity for language comprehension, we assume, reliably produces the correct internal states on the basis of what is heard, such states are justified. Massimo is justified in believing that Maria said that it is snowing when he believes he hears her utter 'Sta nevicando' because Massimo's faculty for understanding Italian is such that it reliably produces true beliefs about what is said when he is confronted with linguistic sounds and shapes from Italian.

Someone's belief being justified and his having another belief which justifies his belief are not the same thing. For example, many of our perceptual beliefs are justified directly by the experiences on which they are based, and in principle a belief can be justified simply by being the result of a reliable belief forming mechanism. One's belief, for example, that one is currently in pain is clearly not justified on the basis of any other beliefs one has. The only explanatory story we are in a position to give at all is one which invokes a mechanism that connects reliably one's being in pain with one's believing that one is. Or, we don't expect that someone who sees that it's raining; or that the table is round; or that something is red must have reasons for what he sees. Fodor and Schiffer, I take it, feel the same way about linguistic comprehension.

What's on offer here is reliabilism [Dretske 1981; Goldman 1986; Nozick 1981]. Beliefs about what's said count as justified (known) just in case the processes that give rise to them tend, in the 'relevant' set of counterfactuals, to be truth inducing. There is indeed a lawlike correlation between an Italian speaker's mental states (beliefs about what is said) and the phenomena (heard utterances) that give rise to them.

Also, as expected from reliabilism, no 'KK principle' is invoked; your knowing (or being justified) that p does not entail your knowing (or being justified) that you know (or are justified) that p. This reliabilist feature serves Fodor and Schiffer well. If someone's belief fixation processes may be reliable and constitute knowledge (or justification) even though he doesn't realize that they do, then Fodor and Schiffer can deny that speakers have any special metalinguistic knowledge about the connection between what's uttered and what's said AND at the same time secure the justification essential to language comprehension.

Much has been written, pro and con, about reliabilism, but in this context whether it is a correct account of knowledge (or justification) is simply irrelevant. We want to know what Massimo's REASON is for believing that Maria said that it snowed when he hears her utter 'Sta nevicando'. That he has a certain faculty that, *cateris paribus*, takes him from heard utterances of Italian to true beliefs about what is said doesn't reveal HIS reason for believing that Maria said that it snowed when he heard her utter 'Sta nevicando'.

If Massimo KNEW that he was constituted in such a way, by virtue of having learned Italian, that he reliably comes to have true beliefs about what's said when he hears utterances of Italian asserted, then he would have a reason for believing Maria said it's snowing when he hears her utter 'Sta nevicando'. But obviously drawing on such knowledge here is illegitimate. It undercuts reliabilism's appeal by resurrecting the KK principle.

So, does MASSIMO have a reason for believing that Maria said that it snowed when he hears her utter 'Sta nevicando' EVEN IF he lacks second order beliefs about Italian? One might be inclined to answer yes because, after all, what better JUSTIFICATION can there be for the belief that Maria said that it snowed than that it is produced by a reliable mechanism? But even if the belief is JUSTIFIED, it doesn't follow that Massimo has a REASON for believing it. Indeed, it's easy enough to imagine a scenario where Massimo lacks a reason for beliefs so acquired.

Suppose Massimo were constituted in such a way that he indirectly quoted perfectly, and therefore, invariably CORRECTLY came to believe that someone said that p when he hears another utter some sentence S in Italian. But suppose further that he is unceasingly reinforced to believe, by a community of deceivers, that the indirect quotations he in fact attributes are false. So, when Maria utters 'Sta nevicando' and Massimo correctly comes to believe that Maria said that it's snowing; he's reinforced to believe, nevertheless, that that's not at all what she said. It's easy to imagine in such circumstances that Massimo will quickly come to believe that he doesn't understand Italian. Wouldn't in these circumstances we say, in whatever sense of warrant reliabilism underwrites, Massimo himself lacks warrant? My ears tell me yes.

We needn't be so perverse. Simply imagine, as is consistent with Fodor's and Schiffer's accounts, that when asked why he came to believe (correctly, let's suppose) that p when he heard uttered some S from Italian, Massimo invariably hasn't a clue. Would you want to infer that Massimo understands Italian perfectly well, but he just doesn't know or realize it?

Lest I be charged with a heavy dose of ordinary language philosophy, I simply ask you whether you wouldn't find poor Massimo's condition mildly pathological? Imagine him, poor dupe, running around the world telling all he meets that Richard Nixon said that he is absolutely not a crook, and Lord Acton said that absolute power corrupts absolutely, and Hegel said that the absolute absolutes, but when asked to defend his attributions, when asked his reason for attributing such astonishing declarations to such notable figures Massimo is clueless. This is not unlike the poor soul who goes around the world perpetuating terrible deeds, brought about and perhaps even rationalized by his beliefs and attitudes. But, he has no idea why he persists in these ghastly actions. And no degree of prodding or assistance can bring him to reconstruct his rationales, his reasons. Just as I'm inclined to think that we'd withhold agency from this unwitting wretch, I'm equally inclined to withhold linguistic comprehension from our clueless Massimo.

Fodor and Schiffer might reply that knowing doesn't entail that Massimo know that he knows or is justified in believing that he is justified in his beliefs. But what I'm urging is that we would not even attribute to Massimo the justified belief that Maria said that it's snowing, even though he correctly forms the belief that he did on the basis of a reliable belief producing mechanism.

Diagnoses: Even if reliabilism underwrites some notion of justification, it won't underwrite the one relevant to secure linguistic comprehension. When Massimo comes to believe that Maria said that it's snowing when he hears her utter 'Sta nevicando' I expect him to have some beliefs ABOUT Maria's utterance. But if such justification is integral to language understanding, it is difficult to see where it could spring from if not from knowledge or belief or other propositional attitudes about the sounds and shapes of the language itself.[10] To echo Davidson, 'nothing can count as a REASON for holding a belief except another belief' ('A coherence theory of truth and knowledge', my emphasis, p.123). I know no argument that defends this Davidsonian position *tout court*, but it seems right in the case of language comprehension. What is it about understanding a language that provides reason for a belief (for example, the belief that it snowed) when this understanding combines with another belief (for example, the belief that Maria uttered to Massimo 'Sta nevicando')? It would seem that we SHOULD seek reason through additional beliefs or knowledge the speaker has and the non-speaker lacks.[11] And it is with this EPISTEMIC feature of understanding that I rest my case.

In short, if Fodor's or Schiffer's cognitivism, contrary to, say, Skinner's behaviourism, is right, then it must make sense to ask about another's reason for what he believes on the basis of the linguistic shapes and sounds (he believes) he perceives. But then NOTHING LESS THAN APPEAL to other mental states about what he perceives will do the job in providing reason for the acquired belief.

There is an important feature of my argument that I have not flagged. Not all that long ago, Chomsky seemed to spend all his time defending the epistemic status of the grammatical theories postulated to account for language comprehension. My argument against Fodor and Schiffer completely circumvents these hairy issues. It's completely insignificant for the purposes of this debate what exactly is the epistemic relationship between a speaker and the metalinguistic information I am arguing is essential for understanding. If my argument is sound, then there MUST be some epistemic relationship. Whether it amounts to tacit or implicit or explicit knowledge; or whether the relationship is not knowing but 'cognizing'; or whether it is some completely different doxastic relationship is irrelevant to this debate. What's essential (and I think this amounts to some progress) is that if I'm right, there must be some such epistemic/psychological/doxastic relationship. We can leave open what its nature is. However, for convenience, I will continue to refer to this relationship as knowledge.

Section 6: Why Semantic Knowledge?

Suppose Fodor and Schiffer are wrong in stating that we don't need metalinguistic knowledge in order to explicate linguistic comprehension; still, it doesn't follow that we must invoke truth, reference or meaning to account for the transitions from heard utterances to beliefs about what's said. That language comprehension requires metalinguistic propositional knowledge does not imply that this knowledge must be semantic. Why can't Fodor or Schiffer simply retort, 'Ok, take my account and kick it up to the level of knowledge and be done with it.' So, take Schiffer's story. Why isn't it sufficient to say:

> ... for Harvey the only finitely statable theory needed [in order to interpret another's words] is a TRANSLATION MANUAL from [that language] into Harvey's public language; as no compositional semantics is needed to explain Harvey's understanding of his own public language, no compositional semantics, no 'meaning theory' is needed for [that other language] [Schiffer 1987, emphasis in the original, p. 204].

It's easy to get snowed both by Schiffer's formalism (in his book) and by what appear to be merely heuristic devices, for example, his appeals to Mentalese, to the belief-box, to talk about translating public language sentences into Mentalese. We want to know Massimo's reason for believing that Maria said that it's snowing when he believes Maria utters to him 'Sta nevicando'. According to Schiffer, it suffices to understand Maria's utterance that Massimo is CAUSED to believe (put in his belief-box) that Maria said that it's snowing (a sentence of Mentalese which expresses what 'Maria said that it's snowing' does) when he hears Maria utter 'Sta nevicando'. If I'm right that some epistemic relationship is required, why not say that it suffices for Massimo to understand Maria's locution that he knows there is a correct mapping from the Mentalese counterpart of 'Maria uttered "Sta nevicando"' (which is in Massimo's belief-box) to a Mentalese counterpart of 'Maria said that it's snowing' (which is to be put into Massimo's belief-box)?[12]

It won't work; and seeing why it won't work shows us why we need to posit knowledge about the connections between language mentioned and language used, i.e., SEMANTIC knowledge.

There are two choices: either Schiffer's function takes us from structural descriptions of linguistic expressions in Italian into STRUCTURAL DESCRIPTIONS of linguistic expressions in Mentalese, that is, it really is a translation manual, in which case Davidson's translation argument kicks in. Or, it takes us from structural descriptions of linguistic expressions in Italian, that is, language mentioned, e.g., Maria uttered 'Sta nevicando', into language USED, that is, that Maria said that it's snowing. Everything hangs on how we are to understand the locution that a certain SENTENCE is put into Massimo's belief-box. In short, there is a difference between a theory that says 's' says that p and a theory that says that 's' says what 'p' says.

Massimo hears Maria utter a certain sentence; he knows that what she uttered gets translated into a certain sentence of Mentalese; whatever corresponds in his *lingua mentis* to 'Maria said that' gets prefaced to this translation and the entire product goes into his belief-box, That's all he need know in order to understand Maria's language. What I'm doubting is that we can specify this knowledge in such a way that both avoids the standard translation argument and doesn't itself invoke semantic information, i.e., truth and satisfaction conditions.

The standard Fodorian reply that for Mentalese questions about understanding don't arise won't work here. It may be true, and I'll grant it for the purposes of discussion, that there is something illegitimate about asking IN VIRTUE OF KNOWING WHAT DOES ONE UNDERSTAND ONE'S MENTALESE [see Lycan 1984, p.237f]? But THIS isn't our question. We're asking, IN VIRTUE OF KNOWING WHAT DOES ONE UNDERSTAND ONE'S PUBLIC LANGUAGE? The suggestion that it is in virtue of knowing a translation manual from, say, Italian, into Mentalese won't work if the mapping is from structural descriptions into structural descriptions. But suppose it maps structural descriptions into, say, propositions or states of affairs. I want to conclude that a 'translation manual' in this sense either is (or determines) a truth theory.

Suppose there is a function F that in effect maps a set S of structural descriptions of sentences of language L into (not a set of structural descriptions of language L′) but rather a set P of sentences of L′ such that F(s) (in S) = p (in P) iff if a speaker X of L assertively utters s in L, then X says that p. I want to argue that F either is, or determines, a truth theory for L.

T is a truth theory for some object language L in some metalanguage L′ iff for all structural descriptions s of sentences of L, T implies a true sentence of L′ such that:

s is true in L iff p

where p is replaced by a sentence of L′, where each s translates (says the same thing as) what replaces p. Why does F determine a truth theory for L in L′?

Since F determines an adequate truth theory T for L in L′ iff for any structural descriptions s_1 and s_2 of sentences of L, $F(s_1) = F(s_2)$ only if T implies both (7) and (8):

7. s_1 is true in L iff p
8. s_2 is true in L iff p

for some sentences p of L′. But if $F(s_1) = F(s_2)$, then there must be some sentence of L′, p, such that both s_1 and s_2 'translate' (say that) p. But this establishes that there is a truth theory that implies both (7) and (8).

If F were merely a translation manual this result, of course, would not follow. From the fact that 'Sta nevicando' translates 'It's snowing' one cannot infer that 'Sta nevicando' is true iff it's snowing. The general disquotation principle behind this inference is NOT innocent. It assumes that 'It's snowing' is true iff it's snowing. And in this context (knowledge of) this assumption is question begging since it's exactly the assumption we are trying to argue for.

In 'Truth and Meaning', Davidson wrote:

> [A] theory [meaning] will have done its work if it provides, for every sentence s in the language under study, a matching sentence (to replace 'p') that, in some way yet to be made clear, 'gives the meaning of' s. One obvious candidate for matching sentence is just s itself, if the object language is contained in the metalanguage; otherwise, a translation of s into the metalanguage [1967, p.23].

As Davidson recognized, this is just what a truth theory does: it correlates [s is true] with s's disquotation. Moreover, the truth theory is recursive. But this is exactly what F does; and so, I conclude, there is at least prima facie reason to think that F either is or determines a truth theory.

Conclusion

We wanted to know in virtue of what does one understand a language? Fodor and Schiffer answer that it is in virtue of there being certain reliable nomological correlations between what one hears uttered and one's beliefs about what's said that one understands a language. Language comprehension, on this account, is constituted by such correlations. This account is deficient since, even if disposed to make the right causal correlations, the hearer's beliefs about what's said on the basis of what he hears uttered may lack warrant or entitlement. This objection is sound only if understanding a language requires justifications or entitlements for such correlations.

A quick reply we considered is that such justifications and entitlements exist and, in fact, the very correlations that constitute linguistic comprehension guarantee that they exist. If language comprehension is constituted by reliable causal correlations between heard utterances and beliefs about what's said, then, by virtue of there being such reliable correlations, such beliefs are warranted. Our counter-reply was that reliable connections between heard utterances and beliefs about what's said guarantee that there is SOME reason for (coming to) such beliefs, but it won't reveal the speaker's warrant of any particular belief. Instead, I'm recommending that what's needed is not just metalinguistic knowledge about the sentences of one's language, but semantic knowledge of the sort provided by an adequate truth theory for one's language.

I want to end by rejecting quickly what I take to be the most common reason for resisting the idea that speakers have such semantic knowledge. Why are so many philosophers afraid of positing semantic (theoretical) knowledge to speakers? A commonly voiced concern is that such knowledge is too complicated or sophisticated. But nothing I've recommended necessitates that Massimo have EXPLICIT representations or that he can himself consciously reconstruct pieces of practical reasoning from perceived sounds to extra-linguistic belief [Lepore 1982; Higginbotham 1983; 1987; George 1989]. He may be unequipped, incapable, or unskilled. But if he IS justified, then it makes sense for US to articulate his reasons. I don't need to take a stand on whether knowledge is justified true belief since I'm not claiming that speakers must have knowledge—explicit, implicit, tacit or any other kind. I've tried to avoid such discussions. They make me light-headed. My argument, if it's any good, simply says that there must be some sort of epistemic relationship toward metalinguistic states or information about one's language in order for one to understand this language. I don't have a clue what the psychological make-up of this relationship must be like.

A useful analogy would be mathematical knowledge. No one claims that when someone multiplies two numbers he goes through the processes suggested by an axiomatization of elementary arithmetic. It is important to separate the psychology of mathematical reasoning from its epistemology. And it is only with this epistemic mark that I rest my case.

A not unreasonable worry is whether this paper, if correct, isn't a setback for philosophy of mind/philosophy of language. After all, it may have looked, at least from Ockam's, or even a 'scientific', perspective that eliminating semantics from the study of linguistic comprehension was a step in the right direction. If I'm right, however attractive that option may have seemed, it's not open to us. No one said it was going to be easy.

Bibliography

Chierchia, G., And McConnell-Ginet, S., *Meaning and Grammar*, Cambridge, MIT Press, 1990.

Chomsky, Noam, *Knowledge of Language*, Praeger, 1986.

Cresswell, M.J., '*Semantic Competence*', in M. Guenthner Ruetter and F. Guenthner (eds.), *Meaning and Translation*, Duckworth, London, 1978.

Davidson, D., '*Truth and Meaning*', Synthese 17, 1967, pp. 304-23. Reprinted in Davidson (1984); page references are to the latter.

Davidson, D., 'Mental Events', Experience and Theory, eds. L. Foster and J.W. Swanson, University of Massachusetts Press, Amherst, 1970. Reprinted in Davidson (1980).

Davidson, D., '*Reply to Foster*', in Evans and McDowell, 1976. Reprinted in Davidson (1984); page references are to the latter.

Davidson, D., '*Radical Interpretation*', Dialetica, 27, 1973a. Reprinted in Davidson (1984); page references are to the latter.

Davidson, D., *Essays on Actions and Events*, Oxford : Oxford University Press, 1980.

Davidson, *Inquiries into Truth & Interpretation*, Oxford: Oxford University Press, 1984.

Davidson, D., '*A Nice Derangement of Epitaphs*', in Truth and Interpretation.

Davidson, D., '*A Coherence Theory of Truth and Knowledge*', in Truth and Interpretation, pp. 141-54.

Davidson, D., '*The Structure and Content of Truth*', Journal of Philosophy, 87, 1990, pp. 279-328.

Davidson, D., '*Three Varieties of Knowledge*', 1992, pp. 153-66.

Devitt, M., *Designation*, Columbia University Press, New York, 1981.

Dretske, F., *Knowledge and the Flow of Information*, Cambridge: MIT Press, 1981.

Dummett, Michael, '*What is a Theory of Meaning (I)?,' in Mind AND Language*, ed., S. Guttenplan, Clarendon Press, Oxford, 1975: 97-138.

Dummett, Michael, '*What Do I Know when I Know a Language*?' (1978), reprinted in *The Seas of Language*, 199X

Evans, G., '*Semantic Theory and Tacit Knowledge*,' in S.H. Holtzman and C.M. Leich, eds., Wittgenstein: *To Follow a Rule*, Routlege and Kegan Paul, London, 1981.

Fodor, J. A., *The Language of Thought*, New York: Crowell, 1975.

The Modularity of Mind, Cambridge, MIT Press, 1984. Psychosemantics, Cambridge, MIT Press, 1987.

Fodor, J. A., '*Why Must the Mind be Modular*', in *Reflections on Chomsky*, ed. A. George, Oxford, Basil Blackwell, 1989.

Fodor, J. A., '*Review of Stephen Schiffer's Remnants of Meaning*' in *A Theory of content and other essays*, Cambridge, MIT Press, 1990.

Fodor, J.A., '*Reply to Schiffer*', in *Meaning in Mind*,

eds. B.Loewer and G. Rey, Oxford, Basil Blackwell, 1991.

Fodor, J.A. and E. Lepore, Holism : *A Shopper's Guide*,

Basil Blackwell, Oxford, 1992.

Goldman, A., *Epistemology and Cognition*, Cambridge:

Harvard University Press, 1986.

Hacking, Ian, *Why does Language matter to Philosophy*?, 1975.

Harman, G., '*Language, Thought, and Communication*', in *Minnesota Studies in the Philosophy of Science, vol.* 7, ed. K. Gunderson, University of Minnesota Press, Minneapolis, 1975.

Higginbotham, J.,'*Is Grammar Psychological*?' in L. Cauman, et al (eds). *How Many Questions? Essays in Honor of Sidney Morgenbesser*, Hackett Publishing: Cambridge, MA., 1983.

Higginbotham, J., '*The Autonomy of Syntax and Semantics*', in J. Garfield, ed.

Modularity in Knowledge Representation and Natural Language Understanding, MIT Press, Cambridge, MA., 1987.

Haugland, J., *Mind Design*, Cambridge, MIT Press; 1981.

Hornstein, N., *Logic as Grammar*, Cambridge, MIT Press, 1984.

Katz, J. & J. Fodor, '*The Structure of a Semantic Theory*', *Language*, 39, 1963, pp. 170-210.

Larson, R., and G. Segal, *Knowledge of Meaning*, MIT Press, forthcoming.

Lepore, E., '*What Model Theoretic Semantics Cannot Do*', *Synthese*, 54, 1983, pp.167-87.

Lepore, E., '*In Defense of Davidson*', *Linguistics and Philosophy, 5*, 1982: 277-94.

Lepore, E., ed., *Truth and Interpretation: Perspectives on the Philosophy of Donald Davidson*, Oxford: Basil Blackwell Press, 1986.

Lepore, E., and B. Loewer, '*Translational Semantics*', *Synthese*, 48, 1981, pp.121-33.

Lewis, David, '*General Semantics*', *Synthese*, 22, 1970, pp. 18-67.

Lycan, W.G., *Logical Form in Natural Language*, Cambridge, MIT Press, 1984.

Nozick, R., *Philosophical Explanations*, Cambridge: Harvard University Press, 1981.

Partee, B., '*Montague Grammar and Transformational Grammar*', in *Linguistic Inquiry*, 6, 1975, pp. 203-300.

Partee, B., '*Semantics: Mathematics or Psychology*?' in Baurle, R., and E. Egli, eds., *Semantics from Different Points of View*, 1979.

Quine, W.V.O., 1970, '*Methodological Reflections on Linguistic Theory*', *Synthese*, 1970.

Richard, Mark, '*Semantic Competence and Disquotational Knowledge*', *Philosophical Studies*, 65, 1992, pp. 37-52.

Schiffer, Stephen, *Remnants of Meaning*, Cambridge: MIT Press, 1987.

Stich, S., *From Folk Psychology to Cognitive science*, Cambridge, MIT Press, 1983.

Thomason, R. (ed.), 1974, *Formal Philosophy* : selected papers of Richard Montague, Yale University Press, New Haven, Conn.

Wright, Crispin, '*Realism, Meaning and Truth*', Oxford, Basil Blackwell Press, 1987.

Notes and References

1. 'Nice Derangements of Epitaphs', p. 437.

2. [In Dummett 1976] Dummett says that understanding a language is a practical ability and does not involve having propositional knowledge. However, [in Dummett 1978] he argues that linguistic competence is somewhere between a practical skill (bicycling, swimming) and theoretical knowledge. Dummett even offers a test for distinguishing between purely practical abilities and mixed cases: When you ask someone, 'Can you F?', and he can sensibly answer, 'I don't know; I have never tried', then F-ing is a purely practical ability. If this answer is senseless, then theoretical knowledge is needed for knowing how to F. Can you cycle? Can you swim? Can you speak Spanish? Can you play chess? Only in the first two cases can you answer that you have never tried. Obviously, this does constitute a change in Dummett's views, but it won't upset anything I have to say in this paper.

3. Though I'm pretty confident that Davidson won't agree, I agree with Fodor, Schiffer, and Loewer and Rey that the supposition that there is a language of thought, Mentalese, 'is best viewed as simply the claim that the brain has logically structured, causally efficacious states' [Loewer, and Rey, 1991, p. xxxiii]. 'The empirical hypothesis that we are information processors and thus think, i.e., process, in a neural machine language is consistent with any philosophical position that is itself consistent with the thesis that our thoughts have physical realizations' [Schiffer 1987, p. 185].

4. I don't want to address here what has become a rather large rift between Fodor and Schiffer, namely, whether there must be a compositional semantic theory for Mentalese itself. Fodor argues that thought is productive and systematic because Mentalese is productive and systematic and this is best accounted for by assuming that there is an internalized compositional semantic-theory for Mentalese [Fodor 1987, 1991]. Schiffer, on the contrary, argues first that any language rich enough to express propositional attitudes lacks a compositional semantic-theory and so Mentalese lacks a compositional semantic-theory and secondly that he can show how productivity and systematicity could be otherwise explained [Schiffer 1987, 1991]. These issues are not unimportant but irrelevant to the topic of this paper, I hope.

5. This is not exactly right. We might succeed in communicating knowledge sufficient for understanding language but not in a way that a listener can utilize. We might succeed in identifying the correct temperature but one unfamiliar with the scale we employ cannot exploit the information we present. He may not yet know, for example, whether he should wear his heavy jacket or not !

6. Lou Goble asks me why couldn't there be a people who speak a language which lacks a truth predicate or any other semantic predicate; and which lacks anything that plays the role of quotation? These speakers are not only unable to ascribe truth and meaning to sentences of their language, they don't even have the resources for making metalinguistic statements about their language (or any other) within their language.

Goble wants to know (and I'm certain he's not alone) would it follow on the account that I'm pushing that these people don't (can't!) really understand their language? Not at all. Where's the argument that no linguistic expression implies no concept; or if 'concept' is too loaded, no linguistic expression, no subdoxastic or intentional states about truth or (something like) quotation? I'm not keen on ad homini, but if Goble's concern were a life one, most cognitive scientists would be out of work. Marr's calculations or Chomsky's representations would have an *a priori* refutation. That strikes me as a bit quick, though I am aware that many philosophers are prepared to rush in. (Of course, none of this affects Davidson's concerns, only those who dare to claim that semantic knowledge is necessary for understanding.)

7. This isn't entirely accurate. Fodor doesn't think that the 'metaphysical' issues are the only 'interesting' ones. As I noted, in note 3, he thinks MENTALESE must have a combinatorial truth theory (or another combinatorial semantics) on pain of the productivity of THOUGHT being inexplicable. Of course, he doesn't think one has to KNOW the truth theory for MENTALESE to be able to think.

8. This section has particularly benefited from discussion with Jerry Fodor and Kirk Ludwig.

9. —not that the latter belief provides good reason for the former.

10. Take our earlier tribe (footnote 5) of speakers who lack expressions for meaning, truth and quotation (or anything like it). Am I claiming that just because they are unable to CONSCIOUSLY construct a metalinguistic warrant of their direct/indirect quotation transitions it follows that they don't understand their language? No.

Poor Massimo, in our imagined scenario, really is clueless. He has no idea why he believes that Maria said that it's snowing when he hears her utter 'Sta nevicando'. This means that when he makes the transition but has no reason—CONSCIOUS, UNCONSCIOUS, TACIT, EXPLICIT, IMPLICIT, or any other sort. So, yes, I'm claiming that if our tribe understands a language they must have reasons for their direct/ indirect quotation transitions.

11. This is not meant to exclude other facts. For example, that the right causal connections obtain.

12. Complications created by the fact that we are using Italian are eliminable but I will ignore them here. Nothing would be gained by addressing these complications here.

Confucian Knowledge : Commensurability and Alterity

JOHN MAKEHAM

Prof John Makeham, Senior Lecturer in Chinese at the University of Adelaide, South Australia. Currently President of the Australiasian Society for Asian and Comparative Philosophy. His research interests are within the history of Chinese thought. His recent publication, *Name and Actuality in Early Chinese Thought* (SUNY, 1994) is a study of early Chinese theories of naming. He is currently engaged in a long-term project on the Chinese commentary tradition on the Analects of Confucius.

Western scholars of traditional Chinese philosophy have, in recent years, become more sensitive to the problem of incommensurability between the conceptual schemes inherent in our languages and the conceptual schemes inherent in the classical Chinese language. This sensitivity has been born in the context of a reaction to the professional marginalization of Chinese philosophy by the modern inheritors of the Western tradition in their insistence that Chinese philosophy is not really philosophy at all. This marginalization can, in part, be attributed to translators who all too often have rendered Chinese concepts in such a way as to make them intelligible in our own Western terms at the price of effacing these concepts of their full and/or appropriate range of significance. The price we pay for this reductionism is confirmation of the Western philosopher's culturally imperialistic prejudice that indeed Chinese philosophy is trivial, failing as it does to engage competently with the conceptual clusters that the Western philosopher has roped-off as being the proper concern of philosophy.

One reaction to this situation has been to subject to critical scrutiny received interpretations and translations of key terms in Chinese philosophy. This is a laudable and healthy development. There are, however, a number of dangers involved in the process of conceptual reconstruction, one of which is a tendency to find answers to the shortcomings of our philosophical tradition in the 'otherness' of ancient Chinese philosophy by selectively appropriating only those elements which can be reconstructed in such a way that they can be unproblematically co-opted to serve our own contemporary needs. Now while creative appropriation may be legitimate if it offers us new ways of looking at our own problems, whether or not one has reconstructed the Chinese vision in this process is quite a different matter.

With these considerations in mind, I want to consider the problem of translation and interpretation presented by the term *zhi* as it occurs in the Confucian *Analects*. The *Analects* is the main source for the teachings of Confucius and has traditionally been regarded as the earliest sustained record of philosophical discussion in classical China. It is also a text which has attracted the attention of a number of prominent comparative philosophers in recent years, with some even using it as the cornerstone for a radical reinterpretation of the early Chinese world view.

Discussion of the term *zhi* has informed part of this re-interpretation. The standard English rendering of *zhi* is 'to know' or 'knowledge'. Now while this is not an exact equivalent, some would argue that this is not a problem because like the commonly agreed equivalents of 'heaven' for *tian* and 'nature' for *xing*, 'they are satisfactory because if used consistently they enable a reader of a translation in which they recur to develop a sense of how they are diverging from the same words in an English context, an insight which is no more than assisted by the explanations in the introduction or notes of the book.'[1]

Others, however, see a danger in this approach because of the difficulty of avoiding the attribution of Western philosophical assumptions to Chinese thinkers.[2] Thus with respect to translating *zhi* as to know or knowledge, Chad Hansen, for example, argues that *zhi* in the *Analects* 'works only like English *know-how, know-to, or know-about*—but not *know-that*'.[3] Yet this latter claim is not sustainable as is evidenced by the following two examples:

> Ziyou said, 'Being fond of learning may be said to consist in daily coming to know that (*zhi qi*) which one had not known before and monthly keeping fresh in one's mind that which one has achieved'. (19.5)[4] Someone said, 'Although Yong is

humane he is not a clever talker'. Confucius replied, 'Of what use is clever talk? Manipulating others with one's verbal prowess often only makes them detest one. As to whether Yong is humane or not I do not know that (*zhi qi*), but what is the use of clever talk?' (5.5)[5]

Both of these are examples of what Christoph Harbsmeier has termed 'discursive knowledge' : knowing that something is the case. In the first example, this is stated positively, and in the second, negatively.[6] Of the other categories of knowing that Hansen recognizes, most examples in the *Analects* tend to fall under the category of 'knowing about' and would include such matters as knowing about ritual (3.15, 3.22), people (4.7, 9.6, 14.39), life and death (11.12), personal qualities (15.14). Given this, then if we were to modify Hansen's claim so as to allow for the inclusion of discursive knowledge we might feel safe to proceed with the standard rendering of *zhi* as 'to know' or 'knowledge'. Matters are not, however, as simple as this for there are still other objections to address.

Two influential American comparative philosophers, Roger Ames and David Hall, have developed the most sustained criticisms of the standard interpretation and translation of *zhi* as it occurs in the *Analects,* first in their *Thinking Through Confucius*[7] and more recently in Ames' paper, 'Meaning as Imaging : Prolegomena to a Confucian Epistemology'.[8] Their Critique is premised on the claim that early Chinese philosophy operated without a notion of transcendence that generated the familiar dualisms of the Western tradition: 'reality and appearance, knowledge and opinion, theory and praxis, God and the world, form and matter, mind and body, reason and experience, cognition and affection'[9] and so on. In place of 'to know', they propose that a more felicitous translation is 'to realize' in the sense of 'making real'. This, they argue, more faithfully renders the performative quality of *zhi*, which they understand to be 'a propensity for forecasting or predicting the outcome of a coherent set of circumstances of which the forecaster himself is a constituent and participatory factor'. And it also 'entails a casting of the form of the future in such a fashion and with such persuasive authority as to invite sympathy and participation'.[10]

Of the passages they cite in support of their interpretation, they generally make a persuasive case for translating *zhi* as 'to realize'. The strength of this interpretation is twofold. First it is consistent with the performative dimension evidenced elsewhere in Confucius' thought, and second, it highlights those instances where *zhi* is socially and communally determined. Consider, for example, 12.22 (which follows Ames' translation):

Fan Zhi asked about being humane. The Master said, 'Love others'. He then asked about *zhi*. The Master said, 'Realize (*zhi*) others'.

Fan Zhi still did not understand so the Master said, 'If you promote the upright and place them above the crooked then this can make the crooked become upright.'

Zhi here refers to the capacity of a ruler or a senior official to recognize men of worth and then on the basis of the recognition, promote them to office[11] whereby their worth may be properly realized in a broader social context. This action is both a creative performance on the part of the ruler and one where the very significance of what it is to be a worthy person is socially defined.

While acknowledging that in this and a number of other passages 'to realize' is a better translation than 'to know', I believe that it is only one of several meanings in which *zhi* is employed in the *Analects* and to recognize it exclusively at the expense of others, masks an impoverishing reductionism and essentialism. In his paper, Ames states that his purpose is 'to give an account of how the conventional translation of *chih* (*zhi*), 'to know', 'knowledge', while foregrounding our philosophical importances, pays the unacceptable penalty of concealing precisely those meanings which are most essential to an appreciation of its differences. This penalty is unacceptable because it is surely the possibility of identifying and appropriating what is not already ours that motivates the project of translatability.'[12] Pace Grahan I would argue with Ames that in the case of *zhi,* at least, its consistent translation as 'to know', 'knowledge' while foregrounding our own philosophical distinctions would be to do so at the expense of the differences inherent in Confucius' employment of the concept. What concerns me, rather, is what Ames in turn excludes in his own project of appropriation. This is not to claim that the range of characteristics that Ames has identified is mistaken; my claim, rather, is that it is incomplete in that it fails to acknowledge that there are many passages in the *Analects* where *zhi* does not have a sociological basis. Consider 16.9:

> Confucius said, 'Those born (*sheng*) knowing things are the highest. Next are those who know things through learning. After this are those who learn things through encountering them as obstacles. The common people, in so far as they make no effort to learn things even when encountering them as obstacles, are the lowest.'[13] The Master said, 'I am not one who was born knowing things, but as one who is fond of antiquity I am quick to seek things out.'
>
> The Master said, 'Although there are probably some people who innovate because they do not know, that is not a fault I have. Listening widely, I select what is best and follow it; looking widely, I note things and retain them. This is the second grade of knowledge.'

Instead of the translating *sheng* as 'to be born', Ames maintains that it is a term defined by a cluster of meanings and that, accordingly, the first line should be translated as 'those who are born, grow and live a life with *chih* (*zhi*).' Yet even if we accept this translation of *sheng*, a more accurate translation of the original would be 'those who are born, grow and live a life knowing things (*zhi zhi*) are the highest.' In other words, people who, from the moment of their birth and throughout the whole course of their lives, have an innate capacity to know things, without recourse to learning, are the highest. Learned knowledge, knowledge not acquired by this innate capacity, is secondary to this.

According to Ames, however, *zhi* or 'wisdom' is intuited 'from the ethos or character of the culture' in which a person lives. His grounds for insisting on the 'sociological basis' of *zhi* is that he finds no evidence of a nature/nurture distinction in early Confucian writings to support a contrary interpretation.[14] Yet there is good evidence that such a distinction was, in fact, made in 17.2 :[15]

> The Master said, 'By virtue of their nature (*xing*) men are close to one another but through habituation they diverge.' The Master said, 'Only the most wise and the most stupid do not change.'

While humans are close to one another by nature, importantly, they are not identical. Thus while humans share a common spontaneous tendency throughout the course of their lives (*xing*), nevertheless individual differences in how this tendency is realized vary from person to person as a consequence of the unique contingencies each of us encounter. Further, in extreme cases, certain innate qualities will consistently be apparent despite the vagaries encountered in individual lives. In short, even though socialization will significantly influence how and what a person knows, certain extreme grades of innate intelligence are fixed at birth and will consistently be manifest throughout the course of an individual's life. Confucius singles out two of these: superior wisdom and extreme stupidity.[16] Ames would presumably argue that the extent to which *sheng* is concerned with birth it is concerned with the environing conditions which a person is born *into* rather than the innate quality of birth. Yet if birth merely provides the possibility for social access to *zhi*, how is it that the most wise do not change, as they would have to, if *zhi* were socially based?

Lest it be thought that the interpretation I have developed for the above two passages would have been alien to early Chinese thinkers, it is worth pointing out that at least as early as the Han dynasty there were those who maintained that certain individuals, by virtue of their nature, are endowed with an innate ability to know things that others can only come to know through learning. Thus, citing 16.9, a nameless interlocutor with Wang Chong (27-c. 97) relates the (apocryphal) story of one Xiang Tuo, who at the age of seven (six by Western reckoning) was already teaching Confucius. He comments, 'At seven he had still not begun elementary schooling and yet he taught Confucius. This was because, by virtue of his nature, he innately knew things.'[17]

Wang Chong's own theory of human nature also reveals a more general belief that other qualities were also fixed from the moment that a person's nature was first constituted. The gist of this theory is that at the moment of conception, the quality of the *qi* that the embryo receives from its parents (and which, in turn, could be effected by the mother's state of mind at the moment of conception) determined such qualities as whether one be a person of moral worth (*xian*), a reprobate (*bu xiao*) or an idiot (*yu*), as well as one's physical appearance and life expectancy.[18] The quality of this *qi* also determines the quality of the five incipient virtues (*wu chang*, 'five constants', or *wa xing*, 'five forms of conduct', which include *zhi*) with which one was endowed.[19] These views on the role of *qi* highlight the view that certain conditions of human nature were given rather than spontaneously developed throughout the course of an individual's life. In citing them my purpose is to establish that it was not at all alien for these inheritors of pre-Qin thought to allow that human nature was not purely culturally and socially constituted.

The basis for this thinking is, in fact, already implicit not only in Xun Zi's but also in Mencius' conception of human nature. Now while Mencius gives greater emphasis to human nature as a process of growth throughout the course of a person's life, importantly, he also allows that it begins with certain innate, pre-cultural, tendencies. Included among the conditions that define human nature at birth are the four 'stirrings' of the heart which are the 'sprouts' (*duan*) of humaneness, rightness, propriety and wisdom (*zhi*). 'Men have these four sprouts just as they have four limbs' (2A.6). 'Humaneness, rightness, propriety and wisdom are not fused into us from outside; we have had them from the outset' (6A.6). Furthermore, as Angus Graham notes, even though 'Mencius does not question that education and self-discipline are preconditions of moral development in most people...(nevertheless) he thinks that there were a couple of sages who "had it by nature" (*xing zhi*)'.[20]

Conclusion

In making the move that *zhi* 'denotes a cluster of meanings that are not at all coincident with any in our tradition,'[21] Ames presents *zhi* as an unequivocal 'Other'. Yet he is only able to do this by insisting on the radical, incommensurable alterity of *zhi* vis-a-vis 'to know'. His grounds for denying the coincidence of this cluster of meanings with any in our own tradition is his characterization of *zhi* as 'performative, productive, social, affective, and, above all, fundamentally aesthetic as well as cognitive.'[22] Now while, bar the very last (which, it will be noted already contradicts Ames' previous claim about absolute non-coincidence), this cluster of meanings does make it incommensurable with *traditional* Western conceptions of 'to know' nevertheless in identifying this cluster of meanings he and Hall alternatively propose a degree of commensurability with a range of philosophical concepts that has been developed in the postmodern West in the wake of critiques of Cartesian and Enlightenment rationality. Thus they find commensurability between the aesthetic character of *zhi* and Whitehead's concept of harmony, between the performative character of *zhi* and Ryle's concept of the performative, and between the social and affective character of *zhi* and communitarianism. As it transpires, Hall and Ames are keen to appropriate the conceptual resources of early Confucian thought to supplement their vision of the postmodern project. Witness, for example, David Hall's confidence in the general commensurability of classical Chinese thought with the postmodern enterprise which allows him to maintain that classical Confucianism and philosophical Daoism 'share something like the problematic of postmodernism insofar as it is shaped by the desire to find a means for thinking difference.' Thus rather than allowing that Confucius might have proposed certain grades of fixed, innate intelligence—thereby admitting a serious counter-example to the claim that the early Chinese thinkers found it 'easier to think difference, change and becoming' and not 'in terms of identity, being and permanence'[23]—they opt for the more radical surgery of outright denial.

Nor do I believe that in making the above criticism I have unwittingly vindicated their interpretation by falling victim to the Fallacy of the Counter Example. The 'innate knowledge' interpretation that I have argued for is championed by many influential commentators, from at least the Han times on, in their discussions of the 'three grades' (*san pin*) theory of human nature (i.e. *shang, zhong, xia* -grades determined by the quality of *qi* one is innately endowed with), a theory that not only informed philosophical discussions about human nature but also influenced the rankings of persons in the official histories, character assessments in the Han, Wei and Jin, and through this, the recommendation system. Thus even if one were to allow that Hall and Ames' 'sociological' interpretation of Confucius' concept of *zhi* to be *the* correct interpretation, this does not mean that the 'innatist' interpretation is simply a misinformed modern, Western reading.

Discussion of 16.9 and 17.2 aside, there further remains a number of passages in which *zhi* is more appropriately rendered 'to know' rather than 'to realize'.[24] This is overwhelmingly the case in those passages where *zhi* is preceded by the negative *bu* and means 'do not know'.[25] In still other passages, *zhi* is variously also employed both positively and negatively, in the senses of 'to be aware that', and 'to understand'.[26] Indeed, even Hall and Ames are not able consistently to employ their chosen rendering, reverting on occasion to 'to know', despite their insistence on its inappropriateness.[27] The most striking example of this infidelity is Ames' translation of the passage in which Confucius defines *zhi*: 'To know that you know something when you do, and to know that you do not when you do not—this then is knowing.'[28]

I believe they pay an unacceptably high price in silencing those aspects of *zhi* which are incompatible with their postmodern vision, for in this reductive move, the very difference, singularity and alterity of Confucius' thought that Hall and Ames have otherwise been so successful in identifying in other contexts, is, in this instance, effaced. Ironically, it is this kind of reductionism that they find objectionable in rendering *zhi* as 'to know' in the first place..

Notes and References

1. A. C. Graham, 'Conceptual Schemes and Linguistic Relativism in Relation to Chinese', in *Unreason Within Reason: Essays on the Outskirts of Rationality,* Open Court, LaSalle, 1992, 66.

2. Somewhat contradictorily, in the preface to his *Later Mohist Logic, Ethics and Science,* The Chinese University Press, Hong Kong, 1978, xiv, Graham writes, 'As a general rule I have avoided English works with too precise a technical sense in philosophy, since they will carry with them their whole context in Western thought.'

3. Chand Hansen, *A Daoist theory of Chinese thought : A Philosophical Interpretation,* OUP, New York, 1992,8. His further claim (p.44) that this is so because 'there is no equivalent *belief* verb or a concept of *truth,*' has been convincingly discredited by Christoph Harbsmeier, 'Marginalia Sino-logica', in Robert E. Allinson (ed.) *Understanding the Chinese Mind,* OUP, New York, 1989.

4. References to *Analects* passages follow the Harvard-Yenching Institute Sinological Index Series 'book and section' divisions.

5. See also 5.8 for another three occurrences of this use.

6. Christoph Harbsmeier, 'Conceptions of Knowledge in Ancient China', in *Epistemological Issues in Classical Chinese Philosophy,* Hans Lenk and Gregor Paul (eds.), SUNY Press, Albany, 1993, 14-16.

7. SUNY Press, Albany, 1987.

8. In *Culture and Modernity: East-West Philosophic Perspectives,* Eliot Deutsch (ed.), University of Hawaii Press, Honolulu, 1991.

9. Ames, 'Meaning as Imaging', 227-8.

10. *Thinking Through Confucius,* 51, 55.

11. See also 13.2, 15.4, 4.14, 1.1, 1.16, and 11.24.

12. Ames, 'Meaning as Imaging', 227.

13. Cf. also the related passages, 7.20 and 7.28.

14. Ames, 'Meaning as Imaging', 237.

15. Following the *zhang,* 'section', divisions of the *Lun yu ji jie* test rather than *Lune yu ji zhu.*

16. Hall and Ames, *Thinking Through Confucius,* 54, provide no justification for their identification of superior wisdom with sagehood. It would seem, rather, that while superior wisdom may be a necessary condition for sagehood it is not a sufficient condition.

17. Wang Chong, *Lun heng,* Huang Hui, *Lun Heng jiaoshi* edition, 2 vols., Taiwan shangwu yinshuguan, Taipei, 1983, 2:1070.

18. *Lun Heng jiaoshi,* 1:50-51, 75, 2:781.

19. ibid., 1:75, 135.

20. 'The Background to the Mencian Theory of Human nature', *Studies in Chinese Philosophy & Philosophical Literature,* Singapore, Institute of East Asian Philosophies, 1986, 28. The passages he cites are 7A.30 and 7B.33.

21. Ames, 'Meaning as Imaging', 241.

22. Ibid., 241-2.

23. Hall, 'Modern China and the Postmodern West', in *Culture and Modernity: East-West Philosophic Perspectives*, 59.

24. Some of the more obvious being 4.21, 2.23, 3.11 and 9.23.

25. 2.22, 3.11, 4.21, 5.5, 5.8.

26. 9.28, 14.17, 5.9, 11.12, 13.3, 20.3, 7.14, 7.19, 7.28, 8.16, 14.17.

27. See, for example, their translations of 9.6 (*Thinking Through Confucius*, p. 191), 2.11 (p.48). Elsewhere they use terms synonymous with 'to know' rather than terms synonymous with 'realize' in the sense of 'making real' : 7.14 (p. 279; 'to have no idea'), 8.16, 13.3 (pp.60-1, 269; 'do not understand'), 5.9, 11.12, 20.3 (pp. 339, 197, 94: 'to understand')

28. *Analects*, 2.17, Ames, 'Reflections on the Confucian Self', in *Rituals and Responsibility*: Essays Dedicated to Herbert Fingarette, Mary I. Bockover (ed). Open Court, La Salle, 1991.

Knowledge and Ignorance

J. N. MOHANTY

Prof. J. N. Mohanty, Professor of Philosophy, Temple University, Philadelphia, Pennsylvania, USA. He has been a Visiting Fellow at All Souls College, Oxford, and is a Past President of the Indian Philosophical Congress. The author of many books, including *Transcendental Phenomenology An Analytic Account,* and *Reason and Tradition in Indian Thought.* Has contributed many articles to journals and anthologies. Guest professor and lecturer at a number of universities in various countries, but primarily in Germany, where he received his Ph.D at the University of Göttinghen. Regarded as the leading authority on Phenomenology.

One striking feature of Indian philosophers' concern with knowledge—especially in Advaita Vedanta—is the way a theory of ignorance is made to play a central role in the theory of knowledge (analogously to the role a theory of error plays in the theory of truth). In this paper I will focus on this dialectic of knowledge and ignorance (as I shall call it), and will draw attention to some interesting consequences of this way of looking at things.

I

For all Indian philosophers : (1) *knowledge manifests its object.* (Nothing like the Kantian Copernican revolution is to be found here.) This is almost an axiomatic truth. Better still, it is a fundamental descriptive determination of what knowledge is. It can be either knowledge of what is already known, or knowledge of what was previously unknown. The former presupposes the latter: at some point, the object (of knowledge) must have first emerged from the darkness of ignorance to the light of knowledge. (2) There is an undeniable phenomenon which may be called 'progress of knowledge'. *As knowledge progresses, what was hitherto unknown comes to be known.* This may be the same object which in one respect was known, and in others unknown, so that with the progress of knowledge, aspects hitherto undiscovered come to light. No matter if it is a new object or only a new aspect of an old familiar object, the phenomenon under consideration would be the same.

To these two phenomena, I will add a third: (3) If an object (or an aspect of an object) is known (i.e. manifested), there is an awareness of what lies beyond it in its generic features, even before the latter is manifested in its specificity. To be aware of the limits of one's knowledge (i.e., that one knows so far, not beyond) is to be aware of what lies beyond, on the other side of that limit. It is this awareness which makes progress of knowledge possible. What was beyond the horizon now comes to the focus. One explores what was vaguely anticipated. All this requires *some awareness of what is not yet manifested.*

(4) This leads to a fourth, and for the Advaita Vedanta, a most important phenomenon: In knowing I am not only aware of knowing what I know, but also aware of my ignorance of what I do not know. *Awareness of knowledge and awareness of ignorance go together* inasmuch as there is an awareness of the limit of what I know. Using the metaphors of light and darkness for knowledge and ignorance respectively, we can say : We find ourselves, in the empirical cognitive situation, in a state, as it were, of light and darkness mingled together. More and more light dispels more and more darkness. Just as there is awareness of light manifesting whatever is manifested, so there is awareness of darkness concealing whatever is concealed.

(5) If all things are divided into those that are known (by any subject) and those that are unknown (by the same subject), then we can say—can't we? —that *all things are objects of awareness, either as known or as unknown.*

II

In the above phenomenology, I have used three different terms: *awareness, knowledge* and *ignorance.* It is important that we clearly determine the differences between awareness and knowledge as I use those words. The closest Sanskrit words for these two are *cit* and *jñāna* respectively. However, the latter two words are not always used as though they stood for different things. As a matter of fact, sometimes they are taken to mean the same. For my present purpose, 'knowledge' means manifestation of an object to a subject; this manifestation occurs through a cognitive state which has that object as its object. As and when the subject has that cognitive state, and so *knows* the object, she is also *aware* of having that cognitive state. Thus, while knowledge is *of* an object, awareness is *of* the knowledge. What I am aware of—according to this usage—is not the tree over there, but my seeing it (likewise, not the snake I see, but my seeing it, also my being afraid of it, to consider non-cognitive states as well). In this sense I am also aware of my pleasure and pain, hopes and desires (and of their objects only secondarily inasmuch as their objects intentionally 'inexist' in them). I am also aware of not knowing what the prime number between 1000 and 2000 is, or of not knowing *who* the murderer of Mr. Smith is. If I am aware of knowing an object, one can elliptically express the same situation by saying that I am aware of that object qua known. Likewise in the case of ignorance.

The idea of 'ignorance' is not also free from equivocation. I will distinguish between two cases : first, the case where I can say 'I am ignorant of Q. M.'; and second, the case where I am not even in a position to say of an X that I am ignorant of it. Of Quantum Mechanics, I know that it is a part of modern physics, I know that it was founded by Bohr and Heisenberg, I know in general about Heisenberg's Principle of Indeterminacy, but I do not know the details of the theory, the mathematics of it, or the experimental part of it. So I can very well say, I do not know Q. M. Here some knowledge and mostly ignorance are together; so that I can say, *on my own*, that I am ignorant of Q. M., I do not know it as a physicist would. It is as though I see a thing in a dimly lit place, where I see *that* thing, but do not quite see what it is. But there are things of which I am ignorant, but it would seem that I cannot even say *what* those things are I am ignorant of. *I* cannot say, on my own, that I do not know it, that is to say, *unless* some one else asked me 'Do you know that ....?', in which case of course I would say 'no'. Of things at the bottom of the ocean, or of things deep inside the earth—to take examples from Berkeley—I can say I do not know what they are. For if I gave, or am given, some description of a thing, I can say whether I know it or do not know it. But of things of which I have no description save and except that they are unknown to me, I cannot say I do not know them for I cannot say what 'them' stands for. So it would seem that while in some cases of things of which I am ignorant I can say I am ignorant of them (in such cases some identifying description is at my disposal, even a demonstrative 'that thing over there'), in others I cannot *say* I am ignorant of them (for I cannot say whom I mean by 'them'), no identifying description other than that I am ignorant of them is available to me. Can I say in the latter case that the object is an object of awareness qua an object of ignorance? [To appreciate the logic of how the latter sort of case is possible, note that from the fact that I know that things belonging to a set W are unknown to me, it does not follow that of every w belonging to W, I know that it is unknown to me (for I may not know of a particular w, say w_n that it belongs to W)]

This case calls into question the Vedanta thesis that since a thing is either known or unknown to me, any object whatsoever is an object of my awareness either as known or as unknown. The putative w_n is not an object of my awareness qua unknown, even if it is unknown.

Before I return to this objection, let me go back to the phenomenology outlined in section I, and elaborate some of its rationale.

III

The Vedanta epistemologists had to face two questions which were directed against both their epistemological and their metaphysical theses. The metaphysical thesis concerned the locus, *āśraya*, of the original ignorance responsible for the appearance of world and finite individuals when there is only one undifferentiated reality. An obvious objection against this thesis was: *Whose* ignorance is it? Ignorance can belong only to a being who is capable of knowing. There are only two such: the finite individual and the infinite Brahman. To say that ignorance belongs to the former is to be involved in a circularity inasmuch as the finite individual, on the theory, is a product of that ignorance. The Vivaraṇa school, therefore, regards Brahman as the locus of ignorance. But such a position appears to be inconsistent, since Brahman is, on the theory under consideration, all-knowing, indeed of the nature of knowledge, *jñānasvarūpa*. How can such a being harbour ignorance?

The solution lies in distinguishing between two senses of 'knowledge', in one of which knowledge is opposed to (in the sense of destroying) ignorance, while in the other knowledge is not so opposed. In the latter sense, knowledge is the same as awareness (=consciousness, *cit*), in the former sense knowledge is a cognitive state. If a subject S is ignorant of an object O, that ignorance is removed by a valid cognitive state (in S) which has O as its object, a cognitive state which has O as its content or *ākāra*. (Those who know should be able to identify that I mean by 'cognitive state' what Vedantic authors mean by *vṛttijñāna*, and by 'awareness' what they mean by *sākṣicaitanya*.) What then opposes ignorance is knowledge as a valid cognitive state, when both have the same subject and the same object, whereas awareness (and *in the long run* Ātman =Brahman, the Self) is not opposed to anything (including ignorance) and so manifests all things including both knowledge in the first sense as well as ignorance. In the technical language of Advaita, awareness becomes a valid, cognitive state or *pramā* when it is reflected in an appropriately *form*-ed mental state. The light of the sun does not burn, but nourishes all things, the same sunrays burn a blade of grass if focused on it through a powerful lens. What destroys ignorance then, is knowledge, and what manifests ignorance is awareness.

My awareness of ignorance is expressed in the judgement, 'I am ignorant of O.' What kind of judgement is it? In the Advaita Vedanta theory, ignorance of O is not mere absence of knowledge of O, but something positive which, like darkness, conceals a thing. (It is to be expected that Advaita Vedanta would push this analogy through by arguing that darkness is not the mere absence of light but a positive entity.) One of the arguments given in favour of the view that ignorance is a positive entity, and not mere absence of knowledge is that if it were mere absence of knowledge it would be impossible to account for our knowledge of ignorance. For, then, my knowledge of my ignorance of O would be the same as my knowledge of the absence of knowledge of O in me, and since knowledge of an absence presupposes familiarity with that which is absent (I cannot know that elephants are absent here unless I know what elephants are); in order to know the absence of knowledge of O (in me) I must already have knowledge of O, in which case I would be knowing O and so not be ignorant of O. On the Vedanta theory, however, I can know of O as concealed by my ignorance, just as seeing something in a dark room I would say 'I do not know', i.e. 'am ignorant of, what *that* thing is.' But again, to be able to say 'I am ignorant of what *that* thing is,' I must also know *that* thing, even if merely qua that thing.

This argument leads to the conclusion *that nothing is unknown to me in all respects,* that with regard to any thing whatsoever there must be some respect in which it is known. To put it perspicuously,

(For all X) [there is a Ø such that X is Ø → X is known to be Ø]

Earlier I had formulated the Vedanta thesis, following the Vivaraṇa thus: All things are objects of awareness, either as known or as unknown.

(*Sarvaṁ vastu jñātatayā ajñātatayā vā sākṣicaitanyasya viṣaya eva*)

Now, I will slightly modify it: instead of 'either-or' in the above formulation, I will write 'and' (instead of '*vā*', write '*ca*'). Then we have:

All things are objects of awareness, as known *and* as unknown.

(Note, and I repeat, that an object *per se* is never an object of awareness, its knowledge and its ignorance are objects of awareness—which is the same as saying that the object qua object of knowledge and qua object of ignorance is an object of awareness.)

Now the position I have arrived at is no doubt a departure from the traditional Advaita thesis. Let us now focus on that and see what it amounts to.

The original thesis amounts to dividing up, at any time, and for any subject, all things into those that are known and those that are unknown, and then saying that both groups of things are presented to awareness—the former as known, the latter as unknown.

The revised thesis does not so divide up all things, but holds, with regard to each thing, at any time and for any subject, that it is both known and unknown—known with regard to some aspects and unknown with regard to others, generally speaking known with regard to generalities, *sāmānyataḥ*, and unknown with respect to specific aspects, *viśeṣataḥ*. Progress of Knowledge is not movement from complete ignorance to full knowledge, but from less adequate knowledge to more adequate. The revised thesis is quite compatible with the Nyāya thesis that no cognition is erroneous in all respects, and that no perceptual cognition can be erroneous with regard to the demonstrative element functioning as its subject term (*idantvena*).

IV

Uptil now, I have said that both knowledge and ignorance may have the same object O, in which case the former will destroy the latter. I have also said that when I see that thing over there in darkness, I say 'I do not know what that is', I may say 'I am ignorant of what that is,'—in which case one is tempted to say that ignorance (belonging to me) conceals that object over there. The locus or *āśraya* of the ignorance is my self (for ignorance must belong to the sort of entity which is also capable of knowledge), while the object or *viṣaya* of ignorance is that object over there. Now that is *not* quite the thesis of Advaita Vedanta. Even without the help of Vedanta, one can describe the situation by saying that that object over there is concealed by darkness (in the example given) and not by ignorance. The Advaita position therefore requires that despite the analogy pressed between darkness and ignorance, what conceals the object when I do not know it is ignorance, and not darkness (even if darkness is a contributing factor to my ignorance). But again as just said, this too is not the Advaita position.

The Advaita view is based on the right insight that the proper object of ignorance can only be that which, without such concealment, can show itself. A material object, or for that matter, an object in the strict sense, is not self-manifesting. For ignorance to conceal it therefore would be entirely pointless, for what is the need for concealing what in any case cannot show itself? What is needed then is to conceal that which manifests itself and also manifests all other things. (Pressing the analogy already hinted at, if you wish to conceal a thing from view, it would not do to cover it up with a cloth, what you should do is to cover the source of light which reveals it.) Since the only thing which is self-manifesting is Consciousness, that is the only proper object of concealment by ignorance. But obviously when I am ignorant of O_1, but know O_2, what is concealed is not consciousness as such, but consciousness as limited by O_1 (for otherwise if all consciousness were concealed, I would not know anything). The object of ignorance when I say 'I do not know O_1' then, is *consciousness as limited by* O_1 (not simply O_1).

Not only, as stated earlier, is it redundant for ignorance to conceal O_1, there is a further consideration why O_1 is not the proper object of ignorance. For if it were so, then my ignorance itself would not be known. Ignorance is revealed, manifested, established precisely by that very consciousness which it conceals. The author of *Vivaraṇa* illustrates the situation with the example of *Rāhu*—the demon whose existence is manifested only as it conceals the moon.

So the thesis is that ignorance of O_1 conceals consciousness as limited by O_1. But what is the locus, the *āśràya*, of that ignorance? In my previous and provisional account, the locus is 'I' (as expressed in 'I am ignorant'.) But if 'I' stands for the inner sense, the *antaḥkaraṇa* which in the theory is something *jaḍa* or *a-cit*, it cannot function either as the locus of ignorance or as the locus of knowledge. The locus then has to be consciousness but only as limited by the 'I'. What this entails is that the *locus* and the *object* of ignorance are the same—namely, consciousness. Ignorance, so it is said, has the audacity to seek to conceal precisely that on which it rests (just as the bottom of a lamp remains in the dark!).

Note that this is a description not alone of the ignorance of Brahman, but also of the ignorance of the shell in front of me which I mistake for silver. In the latter case, the locus of ignorance is consciousness as limited by I, while the object of ignorance (namely, that which is concealed) is consciousness as limited by the yonder shell.

Let me, at this point, briefly clarify how I construe the locution 'consciousness as limited by the shell'. There are two pictures it calls to mind. The one is that of a vast infinite space-like, all-pervasive substance which is then seemingly cut up into parts, but only seemingly, by the regions occupied by different objects (this tree, that mountain, and so on). The other one, more correctly, understands consciousness, not as a thing, not as an entity, not as what Heidegger would regard as something *vorhanden*, but as a function of manifestation, as just manifesting itself and others, as an aura of illuminating illumination, showing up, to the subject, each sundry object. The further locution of 'ignorance, concealing the consciousness as limited by the shell' fits the second picture better: what this covering up does is to let that aura, that light, be seemingly extinguished thus leaving the object in 'darkness' as it were, as unknown—but not in utter anonymity, but certainly manifested to awareness as unknown, which only testifies to the fact that ignorance does not totally extinguish the manifesting consciousness, for if it did so then the whole world would have been in darkness (*jagadāndhyaprasaṅga*). I prefer the second of the two pictures. Only one more remark is needed to correct it for my present story.

My story suggests that the light of consciousness was manifesting an object when it was suddenly extinguished, though seemingly so, by ignorance. However, this part of the picture is misleading, as far as the Advaita position is concerned. Knowledge in this view, is not cancelled by ignorance, manifestation by non-manifestation. Ignorance, being beginningless, is already there to begin with; it is destroyed by ignorance. From 'I am ignorant of O' (which articulates the awareness that the object is not being manifested to me by any of the *pramāṇas*), I pass on to 'I know O'. Ignorance *was* there to begin with, and points to the *future* possibility of knowledge. Likewise, knowledge of an object points to the *past* ignorance (of that object) which has been destroyed. With these last remarks, I am drawing close to the last phase of my account.

V

A DIALECTICAL REVERSAL. OMNISCIENCE, TEMPORALITY

There are many other aspects of the idea of ignorance which are rather fascinating. But I want to draw attention to only some of them.

1. The first puzzling aspect is that both consciousness and ignorance being beginningless (with the difference that ignorance alone of the two has an end), the relation between the two is also beginningless. This thesis

was for me, hard to understand for a long time. But I think I now understand why ignorance has to be beginningless. A very simple move shows that: It makes no sense to ask, 'when did you begin to be ignorant of such and such object?' You can only ask, 'When did you cease to be ignorant of it?' (Consciousness is held to be beginningless, for the absence of consciousness must itself be 'established' by consciousness. I will not here argue for this last thesis, however.) Now the thesis that consciousness and ignorance are related to each other from beginningless time has interesting implications. Pure consciousness, consciousness (*cit*), which constitutes the essence of Brahman, is not opposed to ignorance. Let us remember that in the Advaita theory, pure Consciousness is not opposed to anything, for it manifests all things including ignorance. The relation between consciousness and ignorance is *not due to* ignorance. Now this beginningless juxtaposition of the two—consciousness and ignorance—is a nice ontological reversal: What on a superficial understanding seems to be a contradiction, is not really so. The opposition is only seemingly so. Ignorance goes with consciousness, consciousness 'tolerates' ignorance and, as a matter of fact, has no 'partiality' towards knowledge: it manifests both—knowledge and ignorance—equally well with equal immediacy, i.e., without the mediation of a cognitive state. In the very heart and texture of consciousness, there is the interplay of knowledge and ignorance. If one is light and the other is darkness, the two are opposed, but in what sense? They indeed have *sahāvasthāna-sāmarthya*, they do coexist as in an ill-lit room. The coexistence of opposites is the very ontological nature of our experience. They both, in their interplay are evident, there is no unknown existence of either of them.

2. Add to this, my earlier version of the *Vivaraṇa* thesis, and the prospect of omniscience vanishes: If all things are manifested, i.e., become objects of awareness, *both* as known and as unknown, you cannot simply know a thing in all its aspects. This position is closer to the Husserlian perspectivism than to the Heideggerean, for the reason that according to Heidegger every unconcealment brings with it some concealment which would imply that some knowing would bring with it some unknowing—whereas in the Advaita view there is no passing on to ignorance, there is only movement in the other direction—from

ignorance to knowledge. True omniscience is not knowing *all* things including mountains on the moon or blackholes, but knowing the fundamental ontological principles, not the *ontic* sundry entities.

3. There is an irremediably temporal feature of the interplay of knowledge and ignorance. Very briefly, this can be shown in the following manner. A *pramā* is manifested by awareness *as* destroying the *past* ignorance (of the object of that *pramā*); likewise, awareness of ignorance also manifests the *future*, yet-to-be, *pramā* (of the same object). As is said in the *Advaitasiddhi, ajñānaviśeṣaṇatayā tu anutpannamapi jñānaṁ sākṣivedyamiti*. This temporality of the interplay between knowledge and ignorance, the reference to what has been and to what is not yet, is ingrained in the texture of our awareness.

All along I am using 'awareness' for *sākṣicaitanya*, whose ontological nature is not thematized in this paper.

Truth vs. Workability Rehashed

KARL POTTER

Karl H. Potter, Professor of Philosophy and South Asian Studies at the University of Washington, Seattle, Washington, U.S.A. The General Editor of the Encyclopedia of Indian Philosophy, and Editor of several of the volumes in that series. He is also the author of *Presuppositions of India's Philosophies,* and of over 50 other books and articles. Has visited India many times and taught for a period in 1982 at Jadavpur University, Calcutta, where he presented the paper to which his article in the present volume provides a sequel and support.

It is with a strong sense of *deja vu* that I find myself speaking to you in Calcutta on perception in the winter of 1995. Only about a mile from here, only twelve years ago now, I addressed some of you on the same topic, on the occasion of a memorable meeting that took place at Jadavpur University and was attended by a luminary body that included, besides numerous eminent Indian philosophers and others from India, the likes of Willard van Orman Quine and Donald Davidson from across the seas in my country. On that occasion I delivered a paper which was eventually (but only ten years later) published under the title 'Does *Prāmāṇya* Mean Truth?'[1], in which I made the claim that *prāmāṇya*, regularly rendered as 'truth' in translations of Sanskrit philosophical texts, doesn't mean that in general, but rather means something like 'workability' or 'practical efficacy'.

Actually, the Calcutta paper wasn't my first attempt to defend this view. In a seminar held, as I best recall, sometime prior to 1982 and dealing with much the same topic as we are gathered to consider today, I argued more or less the same thesis about truth vs. workability in a critique of J.N. Mohanty's excellent book *Gaṅgeśa's Theory of Truth* (Santiniketan 1966).[2]

All of this recent history is retold to set the stage for the present paper. In the second edition of Mohanty's book (Delhi 1989) he kindly included my paper from the seminar together with his reply. In the present paper I wish to comment on some of the points he raises in that helpful reply of his, in order to achieve some further clarity about what my position was and is.

For clarity's sake I must begin by recapitulating what my contention in those earlier papers was. What is a *pramā* in Sanskrit terminology? I argued that it must at least be a *niścayajñāna*, an awareness involving convictions (as opposed to doubt). But a false judgement, an *apramā*, must also be such an awareness. So what is the further property that differentiates a *pramā* from a *niścayajñāna* that is not a *pramā*?

A pramā is an awareness (*jñāna*) which has the property of *prāmāṇya*. It is standard practice to translate this latter term as 'truth', and thus to accept, through that standard practice, the result that if an awareness is a *pramā* it cannot, on pain of contradiction, be untrue, that is to say, it can't be anything other than true. Thus if an awareness is a *pramā* it must be true, and if it turns out to be not true, it can't be a *pramā*.

All very well, but just what is it that counts as a true awareness in Indian philosophy? As is well known by now, there is apparently no single answer to this question, any more than there is in Western philosophy. Just as in the West we have various theories about what makes a judgement true, theories such as correspondence, coherence, pragmatist, etc, so, one is forced to conclude, it is in India. In the 1984 paper I spent some time reviewing various theories, suggesting that what Buddhists mean by '*prāmāṇya*' in such a context is that acting on it works out in practice, leads to satisfaction of one's purpose, while what Naiyāyikas mean by the same term is that the thing spoken of possesses the very feature(s) that the awareness attributes to that thing, and the Advaitin, who can hardly espouse a correspondence account such as the Nyāya's, seems to hold some version of an idealist or 'coherence' theory. In this I was following the lead of Mohanty himself, who had pioneered this line of analysis in his book.

But if 'true' and 'false' or '*pramā*' and '*apramā*', mean such different things in different systems, doesn't this suggest that when these theories (and their Western cousins too) argue about what is true and what false they are not confronting each other directly? If I mean one thing by 'true', say that my theory is true because it corresponds to an independent reality, and you mean another, say that your theory is the only logically coherent account of things possible, can we enter into a useful debate, since what you and I mean by 'true', 'false', 'knowledge' and 'error' differ systematically and fundamentally, so that when I say something is true and you deny it we aren't disagreeing at all? If so, Indian accounts, perhaps all philosophical accounts, are subject to a rather basic doubt, namely, the doubt whether they are talking to each other at all. This is the worry about incommensurability, a worry I was quite concerned about when I wrote my critique of Mohanty's book.

To counter this worry I suggested that there is an assumption that is common to all the parties above—to Buddhists, Naiyāyikas and Advaitins alike—and that that fact saves Indian debates about epistemic matters from the incommensurability worry. Whatever else each of these theories has to say about 'truth', etc., they at least all agree, so I suggested, that at least a *pramā* has the following characteristic, that acting on the basis of it and others of its sort leads to satisfaction of one's purposes, or as I put it then, following Stephen Pepper, 'quiesces the purposive drive'. I suggested this as a common denominator, so to speak, among all the systems, not as an alternative theory, a preference for the pragmatist rather than the correspondence or coherence accounts. I am afraid, though that was my intent, I did not state the point as clearly and consistently as I should have.

Taking drive-satisfaction as the common denominator of all theories in this way enables one to consider theories of truth as theories about how the world must be in order that drive-satisfaction occur. Not only Western theories, but Indian ones as well, can be compared in this light. The advantage gained by thus discovering a common understanding underlying various warring epistemic theories is that we have, or can hope to have, a common, univocal set of terms in which to carry on the debate.

Note that I am not suggesting that, in order that this account hold sway, we need to find some Indian pragmatist system. The contention rather is that in the relevant sense **all** of the *darśanas* are to this extent pragmatists, but that the sense is not the sense in which we identify the theory held by a system, but rather in the sense that all the systems assume this much, though some a lot more. Let me explore this a bit. All the systems will allow that, at a certain level of analysis, one can distinguish a 'true' account from a 'false' one, even though a given system may have assumptions which make that distinction untenable from some higher standpoint. Indeed, this is just the kind of account we find notoriously in Indian systems such as Madhyamaka and Advaita Vedanta. That a system does, or does not, identify that distinction—the distinction between what I called 'workable' and 'unworkable' hypotheses—with the distinction between what is ultimately real and what is ultimately illusory is beside the point. Thus it leaves open the question, for example, whether there are actually any realists among Indian philosophers, since nothing said so far tells for or against the identification of the level of workability with that of reality. It also leaves open the question, e.g., of whether Madhyamaka Buddhists have a positive (or even a negative) theory or not. I think when philosophers have talked about pragmatist theories they have used this term to pick out theories which say that there is no truth beyond workability. This is not the 'pragmatism' being proposed here, and so it is just not true that I am saying that all Indian philosophers hold a pragmatist theory of truth. My hypothesis is ontically neutral, and despite Mohanty's concerns I do not think it favours any one theory of truth over others.

By the way, this is perhaps the point at which it is pertinent to face the question whether what I am saying has the disturbing result that Indian philosophers are not interested in truth, or in *the truth*. Suppose one thinks that the world is at rock-bottom ordered in some fashion or other, and that one's favoured philosophy is able, perhaps the only theory so able, to set forth the actual order that the world is based on. I should suppose that, among other things, such a theorist will automatically assume that basing one's practical activities on knowledge of the world order given by understanding of his favoured philosophy will lead to successful activity, in contrast to basing activity on any assumption inconsistent with that. So the view I propose is compatible with those who believe there is an 'external' reality which has a structure and that we are able to discern that structure. Again, if one believes that there is no structured world independent of our thinking, that the order of our thoughts is necessarily the order of all the world there is, that will also fit the basic assumption I propose.

However, suppose one takes the position I have sometimes dubbed that of the 'superskeptic' whose opinion is that there is, so far as we can tell, no world at all, either external or internal (whatever these terms might mean), that can provide the basis for discrimination between true beliefs and false ones. I rather think this position is in fact taken by Madhyamaka Buddhists, for example, and perhaps not only by them but by at least some Advaita Vedantins as well. Does this kind of nontheory defy our classifications? Not at all, since the very fact that those who say this are communicating their claims for this conclusion to us in language suggests that there must be, at some no doubt lower level, an understanding of 'truth' which renders their claim intelligible and, according to them, true. That level of understanding must, whatever else, constitute something 'workable', since if it were otherwise we would not be inclined to pay the appropriate kind of attention to what these philosophers are claiming.

I hope that this explanation of my position has set to rest some of the misunderstandings it seems to have engendered. But, as I said before, I should like now briefly to attend to one specific set of remarks, those offered by Mohanty in his response to my 'Gaṅgeśa's Theory of Truth' paper, in order to test whether my now-further-explained account of the 'workability' thesis can withstand his criticisms.

The Sanskrit word *artha* is variously rendered as 'purpose', 'object', 'linguistic meaning'. One of my claims was that '*prāmāṇya*', correctly understood as 'workability', is a correct exegesis of '*yāthārthya*' in an epistemic context. Mohanty asks me to consider whether this equation will stand up to scrutiny if we consider, for example, Vātsāyana's statement '*pramāṇato'rthapratipattau pravṛttisāmarthyāt arthavat pramāṇam*' where the word '*artha*' appears twice. Mohanty asks whether both of these occurrences of that item in this sentence can be understood as meaning the same thing. I do not see a great problem here. Here is a proposed translation of the statement : An instrument of 'knowledge' possesses a workable object when the instrument grasps an object's workability. The term '*pravṛttisāmarthya*' suggests precisely 'capacity for successful action'.

A second quotation that Mohanty suggests I consider as a test case for my theory is Vidyāraṇya's '*jñānasya arthaparicchedasāmarthyam*' (from the Vivaraṇa) which he takes to be a definition of *pramā*. He writes: 'If Vivaraṇa's definition were read, favouring Potter's suggestion, as "picking out the purpose", we would want to know: does a cognition show, pick out what its goal is, or does it "pick out" the goal in the sense of "satisfying it"? Only in the latter case, would *prāmaṇya* =workability; only in the former case, could *prāmāṇya* be *svataḥ*, as *Vivaraṇa* must be able to hold.' I guess my question here is, why can't the passage be read as meaning both picking out the goal and satisfying it? If a goal is satisfied it seems it must be picked out—otherwise it isn't a goal at all.

Mohanty's third remark charges me with favouring one theory, pragmatism, when I was expressly claiming to be theory-neutral. I plead guilty to having spoken in a way that might give that impression; I hope that my way of putting things earlier in the present paper shows that one can take the position I do without committing oneself to pragmatism as a philosophical theory.

Finally, Mohanty complains that 'On his (i.e., my) account, according to the *svataḥ* theory, to know an awareness is to know it as a *potential* purpose-satisfier, whereas on the *parataḥ* theory, an awareness can be called a purpose-satisfier only after actual satisfaction. So at a new point, i.e., with regard to the problem of *prāmāṇyagraha,* we have an incommensurability.' To explain this I need to tell you what my account of the *svatas/paratas* debate is.

What I wrote was this: 'The *svataḥ* theorist holds that, whatever causes us to be aware of J (for *jñāna*) causes us to be aware that J can satisfy its purpose, i.e., can lead to successful activity of the relevant sort. The *parataḥ* theorist denies this, holding that in order to become aware that J can satisfy its purpose we need a further awareness, presumably inferential, which is over and beyond the awareness which causes us to be aware of J itself.' Now when Mohanty says that 'an awareness can be called a purpose-satisfier only after actual satisfaction'

I take it he is reporting the very feature of the *paratas* theory I was alluding to in my remark just quoted. But we don't have to do it anew each time a question arises about whether J can satisfy its purpose. The 'further awareness, presumably inferential' of my account is what is needed in principle; if one has by previous testing concluded that a judgement leads to successful activity under circumstance C he may (though he may not!) be right in claiming it to do so on subsequent occurrence of those circumstances. We engage in lots of activity on a daily basis which we do not subject to verification anew each time that kind of activity arises; we expect that it will yield satisfaction, and we are right, at least a lot of the time. So the relation between awareness of J's purpose-satisfaction and its truth is a potential relation for both theories; the difference between the two theories concerns how many and which judgements are needed to yield knowledge that a J is a purpose-satisfier.

One obvious conclusion that might be drawn from my thesis is that if what I claim is correct we should stop translating '*pramā*' as 'knowledge' and '*prāmāṇya*' as truth. I have suggested '*workability*' for the latter term. What about '*pramā*'? If it is wrong to translate it as knowledge, how should it be translated? Consistently, one may suggest 'workable assessment' or something like that. And as is well known, '*pramāṇa*', which sometimes means the result of and sometimes the instrument of *pramā*, will mean sometimes a workable assessment and sometimes an 'instrument', a particular way of proceeding which helps to provide us with a workable assessment.

Note that this disposes nicely of a standard problem about these words which troubles every beginning student of this subject. I am referring to the point that the standard *pramāṇas* such as perception, inference and verbal testimony, seem so obviously to be kinds of things which may provide us with knowledge but may not. There are perceptual errors, fallacious inferences, and misspoken or misinterpreted language. It is obviously stupid to say that these three 'instruments' always provide knowledge; yet it seems uninteresting to say that they may—so may almost anything, one might retort—be wild guesses, Tarot cards, you name it. So why do philosophers spend such a quantity of effort worrying which are the *pramāṇas*, and why should we care what they say? The answer, I suggest, in keeping with my proposed translations of the relevant terms, is that what '*pramāṇa*' means is not 'instrument of knowledge' but rather 'instrument of workability', that is, the kind of reason which is frequently found to provide us with hypotheses about things which are likely to work out in practice. That a given awareness of a relevant sort, a perception, an inference or a statement, doesn't pan out in practice won't then, if '*pramāṇa*' is interpreted this way, lead us to question the entire epistemic category. What we were aware of was, no doubt, something of the relevant sort—a perception, an inference, a statement—but though it had the look (*ābhāsa*) of something which would lead to successful activity it turns out, on closer inspection, etc., not to. Thus it is a *pratyakṣābhāsa* or *hetvābhasa*, not a proper perception or inference even though it has the superficial features of a perception or an inference. This particular perception, or inference, we can then say, turned out not to provide us with a workable hypothesis, but still perceptions and inferences are the kinds of things we depend on to pick out workable hypotheses. Wild guesses and Tarot cards, on the other hand, even though they might pan out once in a while, are thin reeds to depend on when striving for practical success.

'So', you complain, 'you're saying there is no truth in Indian theories, that they provide no knowledge whatsoever. Why do you remain interested in the subject at all? If Indian thought is not interested in truth, in achieving knowledge, what is it good for?' In the paper published in 1992 I tried to suggest the answer to this: briefly, that Indian *darśanas* are concerned to arrive at a view which will allow for the satisfaction without residue, of all drives, of arriving at an ordering of and understanding of values which provide a means of achieving the highest value in the hierarchy of purposes, liberation from purposive activity itself. Whether this involves finding the 'truth about things' in terms of correspondence or coherence is a matter of a particular system's understanding of whether there is anything to correspond to, whether consistency is enough, etc. That is a matter of each school's theory or lack of theory. Thus it is not surprising that while some theories, e.g. Nyāya, require the actuality of objects referred to in a *pramā*, others, such as Advaita and Madhyamaka, use pramāṇas as whipping boys to illustrate counterproductive ways of thought rather than as bases for arriving at knowledge and truth. Their theories find in the *pramāṇas* sources of the bondage to be avoided, not insights as to how drives can be entirely satisfied without remainder.

Let me conclude this paper by making some remarks on what appears to be the basic contrast between Indian and Western epistemology, and why I feel that an appreciation of it provides a deepened respect for the Indian position. Alfred North Whitehead once remarked that all of Western philosophy is a set of comments on Plato. One aspect of Plato's thought that he probably had in mind was the contrast between knowledge and belief as is illustrated in the allegory of the cave, where knowledge provides certainty and belief mere opinion. I think Whitehead provides an important insight into a recurrent feature of Western epistemology, which is ever involved in what has been termed the 'quest for certainty'. Western philosophers have regularly sought for, not just beliefs that work, but those that are certainly true, that provide us with, as it were, a royal flush in life's game of poker. Plato found the model for such a perfect poker hand in mathematical truth, which he generalizes on in his resulting theory of forms. Western philosophers have been guided in their thinking by this model: the very subject matter and aim of epistemology—truth and knowledge—is predicated on this assumption that knowledge, to be knowledge, must not only not be erroneous but must not even brook the possibility of error. As a result philosophy in modern Western thought has been more and more dominated by the models of logic and mathematics.

Indian thought did not take this turn. Indian philosophers never, so far as I can see, assumed that they could achieve certainty about the universe from logic and mathematics, nor even from empirical science. Thus in contrast to the history of Western thought, which I find to be a series of attempts to either locate or escape from the quest for certainty, Indian philosophical theories are (or were) oriented toward another goal, a practical goal of achieving liberation. Indian philosophers never supposed they were going to be able to deduce the nature of things from self-evident truths, not that they would be able to derive necessary truths about matters of fact from mathematical or logical postulates. Perhaps it never occurred to them to try; at any rate, they did not try. And it seems to me this is a healthy thing, for the quest for certainty, at least viewed as the hope for an account of things deducible from necessarily true premises, is turning out to be an impossible dream.

In saying this I do not altogether despair of achieving the millennium of which Charles Sanders Peirce speaks. It is at least thinkable that we may one day be able to formulate a set of scientific generalizations such that we are able to predict, perhaps within some limits of cosmic probability, what will happen next and after that and so on. But it seems likely that such predictions will be based on empirical generalizations that are always open to error, so that although our continued success in prediction, while it gives us reason to predicate our actions on that success, nevertheless does not give us certainty in the sense that we couldn't possibly be wrong. And I doubt we'd really want it any other way, since if we should actually come to be able to lay out, whether by deduction or induction or abduction or all of them together, a foolproof account of how the world is and will always be, we'd have to be at its mercy.

In the acquisition of mathematical-like certainty about matters of fact lies the destruction of all human aspiration. 'Abandon hope, ye who enter here' must be the epitaph of those who achieve what classical Western philosophical assumptions hanker for. One may well have qualms about envisaging any ultimate aim which involves such certainty. Fortunately, classical Indian assumptions do not. Not that the assumptions of the classical systems about the ultimate goal have any final claim on us either. Indeed, it appears that assumptions about karma and liberation have been receding in Indian minds for at least several centuries, replaced by new goals which seem to accept the human situation for what it is and propose devotional acceptance of it as high-minded a standard as is appropriate to the circumstances.

But I suspect that the certainty of mathematics is not attainable anywhere except in the imagination. The ultimate goals of both 'Western' and 'Indian' philosophies, as they were classically understood—certainty about the facts, and liberation—are, I suspect, both impossible dreams. But dreams are not to be sneezed at. What has to be recognized is that, as dreams, comparative assessment of their worth does not turn on what is the case, or even what is possibly the case. It rather turns on what espousing a dream can lead to in those who dream thus. For that, we need some dreamers, lots of dreamers, and we need a careful, imaginative, sympathetic assessment of the likely outcome should we follow their dreams. That assessment cannot be derived from truth; it must be derived from what is held to be ultimately satisfying.

Notes and References

1. Karl H. Potter, 'Does *prāmāṇya* mean truth?', Asiatische Studien/ Etudes Asiatiques 46.1, 1992, 352-366.
2. The entire seminar was published in the Journal of Indian Philosophy, 12 December 1984, 307-356.

Knowledge, Truth and Scepticism

PRANAB KUMAR SEN

Prof. Pranab Kumar Sen, Professor of Philosophy, Jadavpur University, Calcutta. Author of *Logic, Induction and Ontology,* and *Reference and Truth;* editor of *Logical Form, Predication and Ontology* and *Foundations of Language;* co-editor of *The Philosophy of P. F. Strawson.* Has published articles and reviews in many journals and books.

A Commonwealth Academic Staff Fellow at Oxford in 1972-73, and Guest Professor or Fellow at Helsinki University, University of California, All Souls College and Magdalen College, Oxford, University of Poona, and the Indian Institute of Advanced Study, Shimla. A member of the University Grants Commission, India, 1992-1995, and at present a member of the Indian Council of Philosophical Research.

According to what may be termed 'the classical account' of knowledge, knowledge has been defined by laying down three conditions. Objections have been raised against this account; I want to add a few more objections to the ones which have now become well known. It may be said that there is one particular objection which is truly central to my critique of the classical account of knowledge. This objection concerns the condition laid down in the classical account of the proposition known by *true*, usually called 'the truth condition'. I want to show that an acceptance of this as a necessary condition of knowledge or knowing, not only leads to absurdities and contradictions but also relinquishes the case to the sceptic by sealing the fate of all knowledge claims for good.

I

One of the main preoccupations of epistemologists in recent years has been working out a correct definition of knowledge. This the epistemologists have usually tried to do by laying down a number of conditions each one of which is necessary for knowing, and which taken together are sufficient for it. The epistemologists' efforts begin, almost inevitably, with laying down three conditions. The conditions are standardly laid down in the following way:

S knows that *p if and only if*
i) *S* believes that *p*;
ii) S is justified in believing that *p*; and
iii) It is true that *p*.

To take a particular example, Galileo knows that the earth is round *if and only if*

i) Galileo believes that the earth is round;
ii) Galileo is justified in believing that the earth is round; and
iii) It is true that the earth is round.

That the three conditions just mentioned are individually *necessary* is something that has seldom been questioned. (It is not the case, however, that this has never been questioned. John Cook-Wilson and his followers have maintained that knowledge and belief are two *exclusive* mental states, besides maintaining that knowledge cannot be defined at all. If knowledge and belief are exclusive of each other, belief cannot certainly be a condition of knowledge.) What has been questioned in recent years is that these conditions are jointly *sufficient* for knowledge. After the publication of Edmund L. Gettier's classic paper 'Is Justified True Belief Knowledge?' in 1963, very few epistemologists have continued to hold that these three conditions, taken together, are sufficient for knowledge. They have either tried to add a fourth condition, or strengthen the second condition, to make the set sufficient. In his classic paper, Gettier has produced two counter-examples to show that it is possible for one to have justified true belief without having knowledge. But the examples are not designed to throw any doubt on the assumption that each of the three conditions is individually necessary for knowing. And discussions too have proceeded on this assumption. But it is this assumption itself that I want to question. I want to question in particular the assumption that the truth of the proposition that *p* is a necessary condition of knowing that *p*. I want to do this in spite of the fact that it is this assumption which looks the most innocuous: Can we really say that *S* knows that *p* if it is not true that *p*?

II

I want first to call attention to the idea that *all* the three conditions laid down above are considered necessary for knowing in the classical account of knowledge. What exactly is the significance of the claim that all these conditions are necessary? Let us be quite clear about this. Now, if we say about a number of conditions that they are all necessary for what they are conditions of, we certainly mean that *each one of them is indispensable*, that we cannot have the thing they are conditions of without each one of them being fulfilled. But that has the following implications:

(a) The conditions are *independent* of one another. (Obviously, the conditions cannot be incompatible with one another; and, if the fulfilment of any of the conditions entailed the fulfilment of any other, not both of them could be said to be necessary : it is only the entailing one which would be necessary, the one which is entailed would not be, i.e. it would not be necessary to lay it down as a condition the fulfilment of which too is necessary for the thing in question.)

(b) If the conditions are all *equally* necessary they are also *on a par* with one another.

If what is said about the claim that a number of conditions are all necessary for a thing to be true then we shall have to say about the three conditions laid down in the classical account of knowledge that these three conditions are all independent of one another and that they are on a par with one another as well. But can we say that?

Let us consider first a rather minor point, a point about the relationship of the first and the second conditions (calling them, respectively, the 'belief condition' and the 'justification condition', as usual). As these two conditions are formulated, they are *not* independent conditions at all. The justification condition, as it is formulated above, cannot be fulfilled unless the belief condition is.

Obviously *S* cannot be justified in believing that *p* if *S* does not believe that *p*. Because of this reason, it would be sufficient to lay down the second, i.e. the justification, condition as necessary. We need not lay down the belief condition as an additional condition.

One could, however, say that since it is possible for a subject to have evidence enough fully to justify believing that *p* and still not actually to believe that *p*, it is necessary to have both the belief and the justification conditions in the list of the conditions necessary for knowing. (The subject must actually believe that *p* to be credited with knowing that *p*. His merely having adequate evidence is not sufficient.) But, then, the condition in question must at least be rephrased. The following is a possible rephrasement:

ii) *S* would be justified in believing that *p*.

So rephrased, it would no longer be redundant.

III

The really important question relates to the third of the three conditions laid down in the classical account, the condition usually called 'the truth condition' : For *S* to know that *p*, it must be true that *p*. Is it really a necessary condition? I have pointed out that the condition would be necessary *only if* it was (a) independent of the two other conditions, and (b) on a par with them. But is it any of these? It seems that it is extremely difficult to answer the question in the affirmative.

Let us first note a difference between the truth condition and the two other conditions. The two other conditions are clearly conditions which the subject, the knower, *S* has to satisfy: *S* has to have a belief, and *S* has to be justified believing that *p*. (That is, *S* has to have enough evidence to be justified in believing that *p*.) But the third condition, i.e. the *truth* condition, can hardly be said to be a condition which the *subject* *S* has to satisfy. Does it make any sense at all to say that to know that *p*, *S* has to satisfy the condition that it is true that *p* ? To take our example, does it make any sense at all to say that to know that the earth is round *Galileo* has to satisfy the condition that it is true that the earth is round?

How can that be a condition for Galileo to satisfy? The truth condition, i. e. the condition of being true, is a condition for the proposition *that the earth is round* to satisfy. Or, since that the earth is round is true is equivalent with *that the earth is round* (in accordance with Tarski's famous equivalence), it is a condition for *the earth* to satisfy. (The condition, in the second case, is the condition of being round.)

So it seems that for *S* to know that *p*, there are two conditions which *S* has to satisfy, while there is one condition that the proposition *p*, or the object this proposition concerns, has to satisfy. (In our example, two conditions for Galileo, and one condition for the proposition that the earth is round, or for the earth itself, to satisfy.) Thus the third condition relating to truth must at least be very different from the two other conditions.

We can now come to the real question about the truth condition: Is it really necessary in the sense in which the two other conditions are? There are very good reasons to doubt that it is.

IV

I have already pointed out that, to be a necessary condition like the other two, the truth condition should be *independent*. (This should be the case in at least the usual sense of the word '*necessary*'.) It is extremely difficult to maintain that the truth condition is independent of both the belief and the justification conditions. The reasons why it is so difficult are the following:

There is something which can be said meaningfully and without contradiction about the belief and the justification conditions but cannot be about the truth condition.

About the belief condition it can be said—meaningfully and without contradiction—that

it is possible for S to know that p when S believes that p even if S does not know that he or she believes that p.

And about the justification condition it can be said—meaningfully and without contradiction—that

it is possible for S to know that p when S is justified in believing that p even if S does not know that he or she is so justified.

The possibility of saying the first really means that it is only the *presence* of the belief which is a necessary condition of knowing, it is *not the knowledge of the presence* of the belief which is. The possibility of saying the second really means that it is only being *actually justified* in believing which is necessary, it is *not the knowledge of being so justified which is.*

Now, with regard to the truth condition we cannot say anything like the above. We cannot say that

> it is possible for *S* to know that *p* when it is true that *p* even if *S* does not know that it is true that *p*.

We cannot say this for it would really involve a contradiction. According to the Tarski equivalence *that it is true that p* is equivalent with *that p*. Therefore, to say the above would be tantamount to saying that

it is possible for S to know that p when it is true that p, even if S does not know that p.

This fundamental difference between the truth condition on the one hand and the belief and justification conditions on the other really brings out the inherent mistake in the view that the truth condition is as much a necessary condition of knowing as the two other conditions are. Had the truth of the proposition believed been an independent necessary condition of knowing, on a par with the belief and the justification conditions, the above contradiction would not have followed.

V

The difference just pointed out has some devastating consequences for the necessity thesis, the thesis that the truth condition is as necessary a condition of knowing as the two others. I should like to trace some of these consequences now.

A. Ascription of knowledge to *others* becomes dubious. In order to be able ascribe knowledge to someone else we have to ascertain that he or she fulfils all the conditions necessary for knowledge. (To obviate the absurdity involved in saying that the truth condition is a condition which the *subject* has to satisfy we can put the requirement in a slightly modified form : We have to ascertain that all the conditions, including the truth condition, are satisfied in the case in question.) Now, since according to the classical account of knowledge under examination now all the three conditions are independently necessary we shall have to ascertain with regard to each of the conditions independently of the two others whether or not it is satisfied in the case. So, we shall have to ascertain, with regard to the truth condition, whether or not *it* is satisfied *independently* of ascertaining whether or not the two other conditions are satisfied. This is all right so far as the belief conditions, taken in isolation from the justification condition, is concerned. But there is a big question mark on the possibility of ascertaining the fulfilment or otherwise of the truth condition independently of that of the justification condition.

Consider briefly the truth condition vis-a-vis the belief condition. Certainly we can decide whether or not a proposition is true independently of deciding whether or not somebody believes it; likewise, we can decide whether or not somebody believes a proposition without deciding whether or not the proposition is true. The matter is not really that simple with the truth condition vis-a-vis the justification condition. Recall here that in order to keep the justification condition independent of the belief condition we formulated the belief condition in the following way: *S would be* justified in believing that *p*. But what exactly is the difference between ascertaining that somebody *would* be justified in believing that *p* and ascertaining that it is true that *p*? The *truth* of a proposition, maybe, I think, *is* independent of somebody's being justified in believing it; but can *ascertaining* the truth of a proposition be independent of ascertaining whether or not somebody would be justified in believing that *p* ? I doubt that it can be. I admit, however, that it is possible to argue to the contrary. One may say, as Gettier did say, that a subject may be justified, even fully justified in believing that *p* even though it is not true that *p*. Consequently, one may argue, it is possible to ascertain the truth of the proposition without ascertaining whether or not somebody is justified in believing it, and *conversely*. (It is the converse which is the more important.) So I am not going to press this point any further here. I would rather proceed to the next.

B. Ascription of knowledge to oneself, i.e. *knowledge of knowledge,* in other words, becomes, to all appearance, impossible altogether. Let us see how it comes about. In order to ascribe knowledge to myself I shall have to ascertain whether all the three conditions of knowing are fulfilled in my case, and I shall have to ascertain this for each of the conditions independently of the two others. Thus among other things, I shall have to ascertain whether or not I am justified in believing that a certain proposition is true independently of ascertaining whether or not I am, or would be, justified in believing the proposition; and that seems impossible. Even if it be possible in the case of others to keep apart ascertaining that they are justified in believing that *p* from ascertaining that it is true that *p,* it does not seem possible to keep these two things apart in the case of oneself. What is ascertaining the truth of a proposition that *p* but ascertaining that I would be justified in believing that *p* ? A different way of putting the problem I feel here is that *if* the necessity thesis is true of the truth condition *then* ascription of knowledge to oneself would be impossible, for it would lead either to *infinite regress* or to a *vicious circle.*

C. But the above two are not the only problems faced by the necessity thesis. There is another which is perhaps even more disturbing. If we say that there are three different and independent necessary conditions of knowledge then, in order to have knowledge that *p,* a subject will have to ensure that all these conditions are fulfilled with respect to *p.* This means that the subject will have to ensure not only that he or she believe that *p* and be justified in believing that *p, but also that it be true that p.* But how can the subject *ensure* that the proposition be true? It seems that the only way in which the subject can do this, if at all, is by ensuring that his or her belief be fully justified, i.e. be such that the proposition believed cannot but be true (or, at least, that it would be extremely unlikely that it would be false). But this is not enough according to the necessity thesis with regard to the truth condition, for this thesis demands that *this* condition be fulfilled independently of the fulfilment of the two other conditions. So, according to the necessity thesis, the subject will have to ensure the fulfilment of the truth condition *independently* of the fulfilment of the two other conditions, of the justification condition in particular. But how can the subject do this, and what exactly does doing this amount to? It seems that the subject will have to *make the proposition true,* besides having a justified belief with respect to it. But certainly the subject cannot make the proposition true.. How can Galileo make the proposition that the earth is round true? Unless we take a grossly idealistic view of things we cannot envisage the possibility of Galileo's making the proposition that the earth is round true. *For to make the proposition that the earth is round true is the same as making the earth round.* ('The earth is round' is true if and only if the earth is round.) How can Galileo make the earth round? Are we to demand, then, that to know that the earth is round Galileo has to make the earth round?

VI

The above critique of the account of knowledge that lays down the truth of a proposition as a necessary and independent condition of knowing the proposition, I want to show now, brings us to the heart of scepticism with regard to knowledge, to the view that knowledge as such is impossible. It does so because the laying down of this (truth) condition paves the way for the sceptical conclusion. In fact, it makes the sceptical conclusion inevitable : Since it is not possible for the subject to *make* the proposition true, but it is necessary for the subject to do this if the subject is to have a knowledge of the proposition, it is impossible for the subject to have any knowledge at all. I suspect that the greatest obstacle to refuting scepticism is the adherence to the truth condition. My hypothesis is that it is this adherence which perpetuates scepticism by giving it an invincible appearance: Whatever else the subject may do, he would never be able to make the proposition true. That is not something which is in his or her power. He or she can *believe* it, can marshal all the evidence that he or she needs to make the belief fully justified, but he can never make the proposition true, because that does not depend upon him. The truth of the proposition depends upon the nature and character of the things the proposition concerns, and all that is independent of whatever a subject (especially, a human subject) does. So it seems that there is no escape from a sceptical conclusion. Thus I conclude that if we want to refute scepticism, we shall have to abandon the truth condition. Scepticism may still survive, for there may be other routes to scepticism; but it would be worthwhile to block this route. Abandon the truth condition!

One may think that this proposal is dogmatic, that it is prompted by a combination of sheer lack of good sense and a blind prejudice against the sceptical position. Are we to suppose in compliance with my proposal that the truth of the proposition claimed to be known has nothing to do with knowing it? Are we to suppose, in other words, that we can be said to know that *p* even if it is false that *p*? I am not really saying any of these things when I am proposing an abandonment of the condition of truth as a necessary condition of knowing. There is a better way of understanding the necessity of the truth of the proposition than laying it down as a condition on a par with the two others. The truth of a proposition is necessary only in the sense that the object of knowledge, that which is known, is always a true proposition. This means only that there must be a true proposition *to begin with* or else we cannot have any knowledge. In other words, for knowledge to occur there must be something to be known, and what is to be known in any case is a true proposition. So the truth of a proposition, more accurately, the existence of a proposition which is true, is a *presupposition* of knowing, and a necessary condition only in that sense. (In a Strawsonian spirit we can say that it is also a presupposition of a failure to know !) I can try to make my point clearer by help of an analogy; in fact by help of an epistemological next of kin. I cannot see (in one sense of the word 'see') a snake unless there is a snake to see. But that does not mean that the existence of the snake is one of the conditions which the perceiving subject has to satisfy in order to be able to see. If we insist that it has to be, then we are very quickly led to the conclusion that nobody can ever see a snake, or anything else for that matter, for nobody can bring the object of vision into existence. Seeing is not creating. (Although I have heard of such a view held by some Indian philosophers.)

Epistemically, there is no difference between a true belief and a *justified* belief; and, therefore, there cannot be any difference between ascertaining that a belief is true and that it is justified. Addition of the truth of a belief as a separate independent condition is fundamentally wrong because of just this reason.

Knowledge : Some Contemporary Problems and their Solutions from the Nyāya Perspective

J. L. SHAW

Prof. J. L. Shaw, Senior Lecturer in the Department of Philosophy at Victoria University of Wellington, New Zealand, graduated with a B.A. (Honours), and an M.A. from Calcutta University. After having taught for a few years at Jadavpur University, he completed his Ph.D.at Rice University, Houston. He then worked at the University of Alabama and as an Associate Professor at the University of Hawaii.

In 1985, he jointly edited a book entitled *Analytical Philosophy in Comparative Perspective* (D Reidel Publishing Co., Holland). In 1998, his *Cognition of Cognition: A Commentary on Pandit Visvabandhu* was published. He has also published nearly 50 papers on topics such as meaning, subject and predicate, negation, cognition, higher order cognition, number, and existence, in international journals such as *Logique et Analyse, Notre Dame Journal of Formal Logic*, and others.

He has presented approximately 60 papers on Comparative Philosophy at different conferences in New Zealand, Australia, India, Japan, England, Sweden, Belgium, Holland, and the United States.

The aim of this paper is to discuss (1) Gettier's counterexamples to the analysis of knowledge as justified true belief, (2) post-Gettier counterexamples to the standard analysis of knowledge,

(3) the causal no-relevant alternatives approach of Goldman, and

(4) the Nyāya solutions to some of the problems of knowledge raised by contemporary philosophers.

In 1963, Gettier[1] argued that the analysis of knowledge as justified true belief is incorrect. He put forward two counterexamples to this analysis of knowledge, which has its origin in Plato. The counterexamples are as follows:

(1) Both Smith and Jones have applied for a job. Suppose the director of the company told Smith that Jones would get the job. Smith found ten coins in the pocket of Jones. On the basis of the following two premisses

(a) Jones is the person who will get the job;

(b) Jones has ten coins in his pocket, Smith infers,

(c) The person who will get the job has ten coins in his pocket.

Now suppose Smith got the job and he also had ten coins in his pocket. Since Smith has justified true belief in (c), the standard definition of knowledge applies to (c), but he does not know (c).

(2) Suppose Smith has always seen Jones driving a Ford, and just now he gave him a ride in a Ford. From these evidences Smith believes that Jones owns a Ford. On the basis of the premiss

(a) Jones owns a Ford, Smith validly infers :

(b) Jones owns a Ford or Brown is in Barcelona.

Now suppose Jones does not own a Ford, and Brown happens to be in Barcelona. That Brown is in Barcelona is just a lucky guess of Smith. Hence (b) turns out to be true. Moreover, it satisfies the other two criteria of knowledge. But Smith does not know (b).

Subsequently many other counterexamples were put forward, and they are called 'Gettier-type counterexamples'. These examples have the following features in common if we take the form '*S* knows that *p*'[2]:

(a) The truth-condition holds regarding *p*;

(b) The belief-condition holds regarding *p*;

(c) The justification or evidence-condition holds regarding *p*;

(d) Some proposition, *q*, is false;

(e) *S* is justified in believing *q*;

(f) *S* does not know that *p*.

The first attempt to avoid the Gettier-type counterexamples was suggested by adding a fourth condition which may be stated in the following way:

S's justification for *p* does not include any false beliefs.[3]

But subsequently other types of counterexamples were put forward by philosophers such as Goldman, Lehrer, and Feldman. In their counterexamples the believer does not infer *p* from any false beliefs. These are called 'post-Gettier counterexamples'. The following examples are of this type:

(3) Suppose John is driving through the countryside, and sees something which he takes to be barns. These things look like barns and

some of them are barns. The appropriate conditions for visual perception are also present. Hence John believes that they are barns, and his belief is also true by virtue of there being barns. Since all the appropriate conditions for visual perception are present, his belief is justified as well.

Now suppose people around that countryside have constructed several barn facades which cannot be easily distinguished from real barns. There are more barn facades than real barns. Since John has seen both real barns and barn facades, he cannot claim *to know* that what he has seen is a barn, although he has justified true belief.[4]

(4) Suppose a ball looks red to you and on this basis you judge it to be red, and it is really red. But the ball is illuminated by red lights, and you do not know that it is illuminated by red lights. Since it is illuminated by red lights, it would look red to you even if it were not red. Hence you do not know that the ball is red, although your belief has been justified and it is true.[5]

(5) Suppose Smith knows the following proposition:

p: Jones, who is an extremely reliable person and who works in his office, has told Smith that he, Jones, owns a Ford. Suppose that Jones told Smith that he, Jones, owns a Ford only because of hypnosis, and Jones has won a Ford in a lottery after entering the state of hypnosis. But this fact remained unknown to both Jones and Smith. Suppose further that Smith deduces the following proposition from *p*:

q: Someone, who is extremely reliable and works in his office, has told Smith that he owns a Ford. Now Smith deduces the following proposition from *q*:

r: Someone who works in his office owns a Ford. It is claimed that Smith has justified true belief in *r* and knows his evidence for *r*, but does not know that *r*.[6]

Counterexamples of this type have led to a number of defeasibility analyses of knowledge. A defeasibility analysis requires that there be no true defeaters. Following Klein and Pollock the defeasibility condition may be formulated in the following way:

There is no true proposition *t* such that if *t* were added to *S*'s beliefs then *S* would no longer be justified in believing *p*.

By applying the defeasibility condition it is claimed that the above examples do not represent cases of knowledge. In our last example, if Smith had known the true proposition that Jones had entered the state of hypnosis, then he would not have believed that Jones owned a Ford. Hence Smith would no longer be justified in believing that someone who works in his office owns a Ford.

But Lehrer and Paxson have put forward the following counterexample to the above defeasibility analysis of knowledge. To quote:

(6) 'Suppose I see a man walk into the library and remove a book from the library by concealing it beneath his coat. Since I am sure the man is Tom Grabit, whom I have often seen before when he attended my classes, I report that I know that Tom Grabit has removed the book. However, suppose further that Mrs Grabit, the mother of Tom, has averred that on the day in question Tom was not in the library, indeed, was thousands of miles away, and that Tom's identical twin brother, John Grabit, was in the library. Imagine, moreover, that I am entirely ignorant of the fact that Mrs Grabit has said these things. The statement that she has said these things would defeat any justification I have for believing that Tom Grabit removed the book, according to our present definition of defeasibility ....

'The preceding might seem acceptable until we finish the story by adding that Mrs Grabit is a compulsive and pathological liar, that John Grabit is a fiction of her demented mind, and that Tom Grabit took the book as I believed. Once this is added, it should be apparent that I did know that Tom Grabit removed the book.'[7]

Since this example involves a true defeater defeater, the above formulation of defeasible analysis cannot handle such cases. In order to deal with this type of example Moser[8] has suggested a more complex form of defeasibility analysis. According to him, if *S* knows that *p* on the justifying evidence *e* then *e* must be truth-sustained. In other words, for every true proposition *t,* when *t* joined with *e* undermines *S*'s justification for *p* on *e,* then there is a true proposition, *t*', such that when it is conjoined with *e* and *t,* it restores the justification of *p* for *S*.

Against this formulation it may be said that we can never be sure that we know the proposition in question, because it is not always possible to know a true proposition which will restore the previous belief. Moreover, this type of defeater defeater regress may occur again. It is also claimed that by adding a true proposition which will restore the previous belief we may be adding new reasons for believing the previous proposition. Hence we may not be restoring the old reasons.[9]

Some philosophers are also sceptical about the fourth condition of knowledge, which can handle both the Gettier and the post-Gettier type of counterexamples. Pollock[10] claims that no proposal of this sort has been worked out in the literature.

Similarly, Moser claims that there is no consensus among philosophers with respect to the fourth condition of knowledge. To quote Moser[11]: 'The history of the attempted solutions to the Gettier problem is complex and open-ended; it has not produced consensus on any solution.'

It may also be claimed that the proposals put forward to handle the Gettier-type of counterexamples are *ad hoc*. This is due to the fact that the belief-condition, the truth-condition and the justification-condition have been taken separately or in isolation. For this reason even if all the conditions are satisfied we fail to establish that it is a case of justified true belief, where *justification* is a qualifier of true belief. From the Nyāya standpoint justification is a qualifier of a true belief if knowledge is analysed as justified true belief. Before discussing the above six counterexamples from the Nyāya point of view let us mention the reliable process theory of Goldman which he hopes will solve some of the problems of Gettier-type counterexamples.

Goldman[12] considers the causal factor of knowledge, but not *any* type of causal factor. Let us consider his example. Tom wakes up in a foul mood one morning and says, 'Today is going to be a miserable day.' Let us suppose his day was miserable, and hence his belief was true. This type of causal justification is not adequate for knowledge. But the same belief will have the status of knowledge if it is based on an authority. Suppose, Tom gets a phone call from his colleague who reports on excellent authority that half of the staff will be laid off and Tom is one of them. Here also Tom believes that today is going to be a miserable day. But in this case Tom's belief will assume the status of knowledge. Since a belief based on feelings or moods can easily go wrong, these processes are not reliable. But if a true belief is based on a reliable causal process such as authority, then it will have the status of knowledge. For this reason Goldman's theory is called 'causal reliability approach', which is different from 'reliable-indicator' approach proposed by Armstrong[13]. Ramsey, for the first time, introduced the reliable process approach. He says, 'I have always said that a belief was knowledge if it was (i) true, (ii) certain, (iii) obtained by a reliable process.'[14]

Now we have several types of the reliable-process approach. The following three pairs would give rise to several types of reliable-process theories: (a) *global* reliability and *local* reliability, (b) *actual* reliability and *counterfactual* reliability, (c) *pure subjunctive* reliability and *relevant alternatives* reliability. The last pair is the division of counterfactual reliability. The following diagram may represent different types of reliability theories:

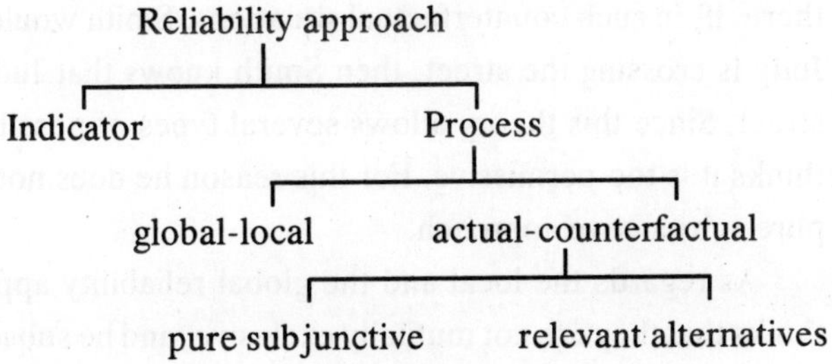

If we combine the members of one pair with the members of another, then several other types of reliability approach can be generated.

The distinction between the global and the local reliability is drawn in terms of the ranges of uses of the process. Global reliability is applicable to all uses of the process, but local reliability deals with the reliability of process in a particular case. The *actual-counterfactual* distinction deals with the reliability of a process in actual or counterfactual situations. The counterfactual approach is divided into *pure subjunctive* and *relevant alternatives*. The *pure subjunctive* approach considers the situations in which the proposition in question were false. The *relevant alternatives* approach considers the situations which are relevant alternatives to the truth of the proposition in question. According to the relevant alternatives approach a true belief, say *p*, fails to acquire the status of knowledge if there are any relevant alternative situations in which the proposition *p* would be false, but the process would cause the agent to believe in *p*. If there are relevant alternatives, then the process cannot discriminate the truth of *p* from other alternatives. Goldman claims that the relevant alternatives approach is better than the pure subjunctive approach. The following example might substantiate this claim.

Suppose Smith sees Judy crossing the street and correctly believes that Judy is crossing the street. If it were Trudy, Judy's twin sister, Smith could mistake her for Judy. If Smith could make this type of mistake, he does not know that Judy is crossing the street. The relevant alternatives approach considers only those alternatives which are relevant in that situation. Hence it considers the situation in which Judy's twin sister is crossing the street. But the pure subjunctive account considers the situations in which Judy were not crossing the street or Judy were not there. If, in such counterfactual situations, Smith would not believe that Judy is crossing the street, then Smith knows that Judy is crossing the street. Since this theory allows several types of possibilities, Goldman thinks it is too permissive. For this reason he does not subscribe to the pure subjunctive approach.

As regards the local and the global reliability approach, Goldman thinks that they are not mutually exclusive, and he subscribes to a theory which requires both of them. If a theory requires both, then a true belief assumes the status of knowledge if it results from a generally reliable process and not just reliable in that case. Moreover, Goldman follows the relevant alternatives approach. Hence knowledge of a proposition *p* involves discriminating the truth of *p* from relevant alternatives which are counterfactuals. If the word 'reliable' is interpreted in this way, then Goldman's definition of 'knowledge' may be expressed as follows:

S knows that *p Df S*'s belief in *p* results from a reliable belief-forming process.

As regards the nature of reliable belief-forming processes, Goldman says: 'For a belief to count as knowledge, I am arguing, it must be caused by a generally reliable process. Exactly *how* reliable I have not said.

Nor do I think this can be answered with precision. The knowledge concept is vague on this dimension,...'[15]

With respect to the question whether the belief-forming processes include or involve external factors, Goldman says: 'One thing we do not want to do is invoke factors external to the cognizer's psychology. The sorts of processes we're discussing are purely internal processes.'[16]

Now let us see whether the reliable relevant alternatives approach of Goldman can solve the Gettier problem.

As regards the example (2), Goldman claims that Smith does not know that Jones owns a Ford or Brown is in Barcelona, although it is true. This true belief is defeated by the following relevant counterfactual alternative.

Jones does not own a Ford and Brown is not in Barcelona.

In other words, Smith will hold the same belief even if Jones does not own a Ford and Brown is not in Barcelona. Hence Smith fails to discriminate this counterfactual situation from the actual state of affairs. Similar is the case with respect to our example (6). In this case I fail to discriminate Tom Grabit from John Grabit. Hence I cannot discriminate Tom Grabit's stealing the book from the library from John Grabit's stealing the book from the library. Here John Grabit's stealing the book is considered as a relevant alternative. Goldman also claims that when I come to know that John was a fiction of Mrs Grabit's demented mind, this alternative ceases to be a relevant alternative and I can be credited with knowledge.[17]

It seems to me that Goldman's proposal is a move in the right direction so far as the causal account is concerned, but it is still in the form of a programme rather than a full-fledged thesis. His theory requires a comprehensive account of counterfactual situations and hence a logic of counterfactuals. He needs to spell out in detail the concept of relevant alternative. Since the relevant alternative varies from one context to another, it is doubtful whether a precise definition can be formulated. He has also admitted that he does not have a theory of relevance. As he says:

'I do not, however, have a detailed theory of relevance.'[18]

Secondly, his solution to the Gettier problem does not seem to be satisfactory. With respect to our example (6) he claims my belief in Tom

Grabit's stealing the book ceases to be a case of knowledge as I fail to discriminate Tom Grabit's stealing the book from John Grabit's stealing the book. But when I came to know that John Grabit is a figment of imagination, then I am credited with knowledge. Since it is not a genuine alternative, the question is whether my initial belief is a case of knowledge. If it is, then I had knowledge prior to discrimination, and I do not have knowledge when I fail to discriminate, and again I am credited with knowledge when I come to know that John is a figment of imagination. It is doubtful whether the original justification has been restored or a new justification has been smuggled into the original one. Moreover, if an imaginary or non-existent entity is introduced in the relevant alternatives, then again I will cease to have knowledge if another relevant alternative is constructed. Hence it might be difficult to establish the very possibility of knowledge in view of relevant alternatives. For this reason Goldman's theory cannot solve the Gettier problem.

Now I would like to discuss how the Nyāya would handle the Gettier and the post-Gettier counterexamples.

With respect to example (1), the Nyāya philosophers such as Udayana would claim that the conclusion of this inference is false. Hence it is not a case of knowledge. The belief or the cognition expressed by the sentence 'The person who will get the job has ten coins in his pocket' can be expressed in the following way:

The person who will get the job presented under the mode of being identical with Jones has ten coins in his pocket. This is due to the fact that the conclusion is derived from the belief that Jones is the person who will get the job, and Jones has ten coins in his pocket. Since Smith got the job and has ten coins in his pocket, the belief of Smith is false.

As regards example (3), the Nyāya claims that a physical object is not inferred from its look. Our sense-organs are related to the physical object and the physical object is one of the causal conditions of perceptual cognition or belief. Since there are both real barns and barn facades, our sense-organs are related to both. If we know the mode under which a real barn is presented and the mode under which a barn facade is presented, then we can discriminate a real barn from a barn facade as we discriminate a cat from a dog. But if we cannot discriminate a barn from a barn facade, then we have not cognized their limitors, i.e. modes under which they are presented. According to the Nyāya the limitor determines the referents of a term, and the meaning of a term includes both its referents and the limitor. Hence the meaning of the term 'barn' will include both its referents and its limitor, i.e. barnness. If we know the meaning of 'barn', then we can discriminate a real barn from a barn facade as we discriminate a real horse from a wooden horse. In the case of perceptual cognition, our sense-organs are related to the object and some of its properties. The object is cognized under some mode of presentation. In this example John has cognized both a real barn and a barn facade. Since he cannot discriminate a real barn from a barn facade, he has not cognized the mode under which a real barn is presented and the mode under which a barn facade is presented. In this case he has cognized something which is common to both—a real barn and a barn facade. Hence a barn is not presented under the mode barnness. It is presented under a mode which is common to a real barn and a barn facade. This type of mode of presentation would determine both a real barn and a barn facade, not simply a real barn. Since John believes that these are barns and the mode of presentation which is common to both a real barn and a barn facade has been cognized as the mode of presentation of a real barn, the belief that these are barns is false.

With respect to example (4), the Nyāya would claim that our sense-organs are related to both the ball and its red colour. Moreover, both the objects and the relations between the objects and sense-organs are causal conditions for perceptual cognition. If the red colour of the ball is presented under the mode of redness which is its limitor, then it would be a case of knowledge. If a person knows redness which determines red colours only, not the reflection of a red colour, then he can discriminate a real red colour from a red colour which is due to illumination of red lights. Now it may be claimed the ball would look the same even if it were not red, but illuminated by red lights. On this point the Nyāya would claim that if a person cannot discriminate between these two types of red colours, then the mode of presentation is not redness which inheres in real red colours only. Hence with respect to the red ball illuminated by red lights the Nyāya would claim that it is a case of true belief and it would assume the status of knowledge if its colour is presented under the mode redness and thereby the perceiver can discriminate. If the perceiver cannot discriminate, then the truth of the belief (cognition) that the ball is red lacks justification.

As regards example (5), the Nyāya would claim that Jones does not satisfy the criteria for being *āpta* (authority or trustworthy person). A person is an *āpta* iff (a) he has a true cognition of what he says, (b) he selects the appropriate expressions to convey his true cognition, (c) he is not lying, and (d) his sense-organs which are causal conditions for his utterance or inscription are not defective.

In this example, since Jones does not know that he has won a car in a lottery, he ceases to be an *āpta* or a trustworthy person. Hence his utterance cannot be considered as a source of valid cognition, although the sentence he has uttered is true and the sentence would generate a true cognition in the hearer. If Jones were an *āpta* (a trustworthy person), then the true cognition of Smith generated by his utterance would have been justified. Since Jones is not an *āpta,* his utterances would generate both true and false cognitions. For this reason the Nyāya discusses the causal conditions of a cognition, the causal conditions of a true cognition, the causal conditions of a false cognition, and the causal conditions which would generate true cognitions only. Hence justification is given in terms of the conditions which will guarantee the truth of a cognition.

With respect to example (2), it seems to me that it is a case of belief, truth and justification in some sense of the word 'justification', but not a case of justified true belief, where justification is a qualifier of a true belief. The cognition (or belief) expressed by the sentence 'Jones owns a Ford or Brown is in Barcelona' is true by virtue of the fact that Brown happens to be in Barcelona. Since it is deduced from 'Jones owns a Ford', it is in accordance with the rules of logic. If 'justification' means 'being in accordance with the rules of logic' or 'being derived from premiss(es) by applying the rules of logic', then it has justification. Hence justification comes from the fact that it is derived from 'Jones owns a Ford'. Since Jones does not own a Ford, the truth of it does not come from the premiss 'Jones owns a Ford'. Its truth comes from the truth of the sentence 'Brown is in Barcelona'. In other words, the truth comes from the fact that Brown is in Barcelona and justification comes from the fact that it is derived from 'Jones owns a Ford'. Hence justification has nothing to do with its truth. Therefore, justification is not a qualifier of its truth. If the truth of 'Jones owns a Ford or Brown is in Barcelona' were derived from the truth of 'Brown is in Barcelona', then it would have been a case of justified true belief. Hence this counterexample of Gettier lacks justified true belief, although it is true and has justification in the colloquial sense.

From the above discussion it follows that the Nyāya theory of sources of valid cognitions (*pramāṇas*) can handle both the Gettier and the post-Gettier type of counterexamples. Moreover, the Nyāya theory can answer some of the questions raised by contemporary philosophers such as Goldman.

According to our positive thesis which is based on the intuitions of the Nyāya system, knowledge is a justified true belief if justification is taken as a qualifier of true belief. Hence justification is not a property of belief independent of truth. The word 'justification', in this context, means 'some sort of guarantee for the truth of a belief'. Since a true belief is a result of a process, it is justified in terms of certain features of the process which guarantee its truth. In other words, it is justified in terms of certain causal conditions which are not identical with the conditions of its truth.

Moreover, if there is justification for the truth of a belief, then the believer can identify or discriminate the fact which corresponds to this belief. The process which guarantees the truth of a belief is repeatable and objective. It can be used to generate a similar belief in others. Hence if I know that *p*, then you can also know that *p*. Since the process guarantees the truth of a belief, if I know that *p*, then I *cannot* be wrong.

Furthermore, there are different types of knowledge depending on the sources such as perceptual, inferential, or verbal. So there are different types of processes and different types of justification depending on the sources. Even if the sources are different, the content of a perceptual, inferential, and a verbal cognition may be identical.

The Nyāya philosophers have discussed the conditions or causal conditions of a cognition, conditions of a true cognition, conditions of a false cognition, and conditions which justify the truth of a cognition. The causal conditions involved in the process are not exclusively internal. Some conditions are external. In the case of an ordinary perceptual cognition sense-organs are special instrumental causes (*karaṇas*), and the sense-object contact is the operation (*vyāpāra*). The technical terms '*karaṇa*' and '*vyāpāra*' may be defined in the following way:

(i) *x* is a *vyāpāra* (operation) of the effect *E* iff (*Ey*) (*y* is a cause of *E* and *x* is a cause of *E*, but *x* is due to *y*).

(ii) *x* is a *karaṇa* (special instrumental cause) of the effect *E* iff *x* is a causal condition, *x* is related to the locus of *E* through an operation, and it is considered as a cause due to this relation only.[19]

Let us consider the following example of the Nyāya philosophers: The floor has a pot. In this case our visual sense-organ is the special instrumental cause and the contact between the visual sense-organ and the floor is the operation. As our sense-organ is related to the floor, it is also related to the pot which is on the floor. Since the cognition that the floor has a pot is due to the sense-organ, it is considered as perceptual. In this case the objects of cognition such as the floor, the pot and the relation of conjunction are related to the cognition. Hence the cognition is also related to them. The cognition will be related to these items even if it is false; in terms of the relation between these items and the cognition alone we cannot draw the distinction between a true and a false cognition. When a perceptual cognition is true there are two types of causal conditions. One type of causal condition is positive, while the other type is negative. For example, in the case of a visual perception, the visual sense-organ, the sense-object contact, light, etc. are positive causal conditions. But the absence of distance is a negative causal condition. Moreover, our sense-organ is related to the qualified object in the case of a true perceptual cognition. In our above example, our visual sense-organ is not only related to the floor, but also to the floor which is qualified by a pot on it.

Hence the cognition generated by this process will be related to the qualified object or the fact. The relation of the cognition to the fact is called '*viśiṣṭa viṣayatā*' which is a relational property of the object of cognition. The cognition is characterized by the converse of this relational property which is called '*viśiṣṭa viṣayitā*'. Thus a true perceptual cognition presupposes certain additional conditions.

A false perceptual cognition could be due to a defect (*doṣa*) or an inappropriate causal condition (*kāraṇavaiguṇya*). A defect (*doṣa*) is the negatum of a negative causal condition of a true perceptual cognition, but an inappropriate causal condition (*kāraṇavaiguṇya*) is the weakness of a positive causal condition of a true perceptual cognition. So a visual perception could be false due to distance (*dūratva*) which is the negatum of a negative causal condition of a true cognition. Similarly, it could be false due to weakness of the visual sense-organ. Hence a perceptual cognition could be false due to either of these two types of causal conditions.

In our above example, if the cognition is true, then it is related to the floor, the pot, the relation of conjunction, and the qualified object, i.e., the floor qualified by a pot on it. The causal conditions of this perceptual cognition would include the relation of the visual sense-organ to these items. But, in addition to these relations of the cognition to its objects, the Nyāya philosophers have accepted the relation of the cognition to the universal floorness and the relation of the cognition to the universal potness. Now the question is, what is the need for these additional relations?

In this context it is to be noted that some contemporary epistemologists claim that identification and discrimination are necessary for knowledge. On Goldman's theory, if *S* knows that *p*, then *S* can discriminate the truth of *p* from relevant alternatives. In his system these alternatives are counterfactual. But his theory cannot explain why a person, say Smith, is able to discriminate the truth of *p* from relevant alternatives, but another person, say Jones, is not able to discriminate the truth of *p* from relevant alternatives. The Nyāya can explain this phenomenon in terms of the relation of Smith's cognition to the universal floorness and the universal potness which are limitors of a floor and a pot respectively.

Since Smith's sense-organ is related not only to the floor and the pot, but also to their limitors, his cognition is related to these limitors as well. Since the cognition of limitors can explain our ability to discriminate, there is a need for these limitors in epistemic contexts.

Similarly, in the case of an inference[20], the Nyāya philosophers have discussed the causal conditions of an inferential cognition (*anumiti*), the causal conditions of its truth or falsehood, and the causal conditions which justify the truth of an inferential cognition or the ability to discriminate.

An inferential cognition, according to the Nyāya, has certain instrumental causal conditions (*nimitta-kāraṇas*) such as *parāmarśa* (operation), *vyāpti jñāna* (cognition of invariable concomitance between the probans and the probandum), and *pakṣatā* (a special relational property of the locus).

An inferential cognition (*anumiti*) is usually defined in terms of *parāmarśa* (operation). *Parāmarśa* (operation) is the cognition of the property of being the pervaded which appears as the qualifier of the probans which is present in the locus (*vyāpti-prakāraka-pakṣadharmatā-jñāna*). In other words, an inferential cognition of the form '*a* is *G*' is derivable from the cognition of the form '*a* is *F* which is pervaded by *G*', where *a* is the locus, *F* is the probans, and *G* is the probandum. The latter is a causal condition of the former. But the truth of the inferential cognition does not depend on this causal condition. Hence the truth of the cognition *a* is *G* does not depend on the cognition of *a* is *F* which is pervaded by *G*. The truth depends on the fact that the locus which is cognised in the operation is characterized by the probandum.

Now the question is whether a true inferential cognition would assume the status of knowledge. In this context it is to be noted that a false operation such as 'the mountain has fog which is pervaded by fire' might lead to the true inferential cognition 'the mountain has fire'. Since the occurrence of a false cognition can be prevented by a true one, the occurrence of the above false operation can be prevented by the true cognition that fog is not pervaded by fire. If the occurrence of the operation is prevented, then the occurrence of the inferential cognition which is due to this operation would also be prevented. In other words, if a person knows that fog is not pervaded by fire, then he would not use this operation to infer that the mountain has fire. For this reason the Nyāya would claim that the above true inferential cognition does not have the status of knowledge. In other words, if the inferential process which leads to a true cognition contains a false cognition, then the true inferential cognition does not have the status of knowledge.

The next question is whether the inferential cognition of the following inference has the status of knowledge:

(a) Wherever there is blue smoke, there is fire.

(b) The mountain has blue smoke.

(c) Therefore, the mountain has fire.

In this inference the conclusion follows from the premisses, and both the conclusion and the premisses are true. Now the Nyāya raises the question whether the cognition expressed by the sentence 'wherever there is blue smoke, there is fire' is such that the property of being the pervaded residing in blue smoke is limited by blue smokeness or by smokeness only. In other words, the question is whether the property of being the pervaded is presented under the mode of blue smokeness (i.e. blueness and smokeness) or under the mode of smokeness. If it is presented under the mode of blue smokeness, then the person, who has inferred the mountain has fire from the above two premisses, would not be able to infer the same conclusion from the cognition that the mountain has black smoke. On the contrary, if he would have inferred 'the mountain has fire' from 'wherever there is smoke, there is fire, and the mountain has smoke', then he would be able to infer 'the mountain has fire' from the observation of black smoke as well. This is due to the fact that the mode of presentation of the property of being the pervaded is smokeness, not blue smokeness. Since the property of being the pervaded residing in any smoke, blue or black, is limited by smokeness, the cognitions expressed by sentences such as 'wherever there is blue smoke, there is fire', and 'wherever there is black smoke, there is fire' would be true. In other words, if the property of being the pervaded is cognized under the mode of smokeness, then it reveals an ontological property of smoke, blue or black; the cognition of smoke as qualified by smokeness, not as qualified by blue smokeness, gives us a guarantee for making similar inferences. Therefore, a person is able to infer fire from any smoke, blue or black, if he has cognized the property of being the pervaded under the mode of smokeness.

Hence the Nyāya not only emphasizes our ability to discriminate in the case of inference, but also explains this ability in terms of the cognition of certain properties.

With respect to a verbal cognition also, the Nyāya philosophers have discussed the causal conditions of it, the causal conditions of its truth or falsehood, and the causal conditions which justify the truth of it.

The chief instrumental cause (*karaṇa*) of the cognition of the meaning of a sentence is the cognition of the words contained in it, and the operation of this cognition is the memory-cognition of the referents of the words. According to the Nyāya, the cognition of the meaning of a sentence, as distinct from the cognition of the meanings of its parts, lies in cognizing the relation between the referents of its parts which are sets of expressions. Hence the cognition of the meaning of the sentence 'A flower is red' lies in cognizing the relation of a red colour to a flower. If the sentence is true, then it would generate a true cognition, and the cognizer would apprehend the relation which holds between a red colour and a flower. If the sentence is false, then it would generate a false cognition, and the cognizer would apprehend a relation which does not hold between a red colour and a flower, but which holds between some other objects such as between a red colour and a table. Now the question is whether a true cognition generated by a true sentence has the status of knowledge. On this point the Nyāya claims that it would be a case of knowledge if the true sentence is uttered or inscribed by an *āpta* (a trustworthy person). So the true cognition generated by the utterance of an *āpta* has justification, and the status of knowledge.

From our above discussion it follows that knowledge is justified true cognition or belief, provided justification is a qualifier of true cognition or belief. A true cognition is justified by certain perceptual causal conditions, or by certain inferential causal conditions, or by certain verbal causal conditions. Hence the Nyāya technique for justifying a true cognition may be used for interpreting or explicating the meaning of the word 'knowledge'.

Notes and References

1. Edmund L Gettier, 'Is Justified True Belief Knowledge?', *Analysis* 23, 1963.

2. Robert K Shope, *The Analysis of Knowing*, Princeton University Press, New Jersey, 1983, p.4.

3. John L Pollock, *Contemporary Theories of Knowledge*, Rowman & Littlefield Publishers, New Jersey, 1986, p.181.

4. Ibid., p.181.

5. Ibid.

6. Paul K Moser, 'Gettier Problem', *A Companion to Epistemology*, edited by Jonathan Dancy and Ernest Sosa, Blackwell, Oxford, 1992, p.158.

7. Quoted in John L Pollock, p.182.

8. Paul K Moser, p.158.

9. John L Pollock, p.182.

10. Ibid.

11. Paul K Moser, p.158.

12. Alvin I Goldman, *Epistemology and Cognition*, Chapter 3, Harvard University Press, Mass, 1986.

13. D M Armstrong, *Belief, Truth and Knowledge*, Cambridge University Press, Cambridge, 1973.

14. F P Ramsey, *The Foundations of Mathematics*, Littlefield, Adams & Co., New Jersey, 1960, p.258.

15. Alvin I Goldman, p.51.

16. Ibid., p.50.

17. Ibid., p.55.

18. Ibid.

19. For a comprehensive discussion on causality in the Nyāya system, see author's article on 'Cognition of Cognition', *Journal of Indian Philosophy*, 24, 1996, pp. 178-82.

20. For a detailed discussion, see author's 'Cognition of Cognition', *op.cit.*

Madhyamaka on Naturalized Epistemology

MARK SIDERITS

Prof. Mark Siderits, Professor of Philosophy, Illinois State University, Normal, Illinois, U.S.A.; Ph. D., Yale, 1976. Dissertation: *The Formlessness of the Good: Toward a Buddhist Theory of Value.* Areas of Specialization: Buddhist Philosophy, Indian Philosophy, Metaphysics. Publications: Book, *Indian Philosophy of Language: Studies in Selected Issues*, 1991, The Netherlands. A number of articles on Buddhist and Indian Philosophy in professional journals, including *Philosophy East and West, Journal of Indian Philosophy, Synthese* 69, *American Philosophical Quarterly* 24, *Analysis* 48. Has also contributed articles to books, including *Analytical Philosophy in Comparative Perspective, Rationality in Question: On Eastern and Western Views of Rationality*, and *Relativity, Suffering and Beyond: Essays in Memory of Bimal Krishna Matilal.* Has read papers and given public presentations at many conferences and universities, in America, India, and England. Serves on a number of University Service Committees.

Contemporary analytic epistemology has seen growing interest in the project of 'naturalizing' epistemology, i.e., reconstruing the epistemological project as one that is continuous with the natural sciences. Such an approach should prove welcome to the classical Indian epistemologist or *pramāṇavādin*, whose own conception of the epistemological enterprise has never exhibited the sort of non-naturalism characteristic of the Cartesian tradition in modern European philosophy. But while the *pramāṇavādin* should be prepared to welcome the analytic partisan of naturalized epistemology back to the fold, the latter might yet exhibit undesirable tendencies stemming from the long dalliance with Cartesian projects. What I shall suggest is that the Madhyamaka critique of classical Nyāya *pramāṇavāda* is useful in helping us uncover certain problematic elements in contemporary naturalized epistemology. For the Mādhyamikas, while agreeing that the theory of the *pramāṇas* must employ just those epistemic strategies that we use to theorize the natural world, also proved particularly astute at detecting subtle foundationalist and metaphysical realist tendencies on the part of Nyāya. Similar tendencies may, I shall claim, be found in certain conceptions of the naturalized epistemology project. The Mādhyamika would, I believe, have interesting things to say about the contemporary theory of knowledge.

The project of naturalizing epistemology[1] is a reaction to the perceived failure of a program in the modern theory of knowledge that can be traced back to Descartes. According to that program, it is the special task of epistemology to securely ground all other forms of knowledge. Specifically, it is claimed that since the subject lacks direct access to the external world, it is the task of epistemology to explain how knowledge of the external world may be attained; and such an explanation will necessarily provide criteria of knowledge that are internally accessible to the knowing subject herself. Moreover, reality and truth are conceived along metaphysical realist lines: there is one true theory about the ultimate nature of reality, with reality understood as mind-independent and truth understood as correspondence.

Proponents of naturalized epistemology decry this Cartesian program as necessarily leading to an unanswerable form of radical skepticism. They reject its internalist conception of knowledge—its adherence to the KK principle, that in order to be said to know, one must know that one knows. Such a conception is to be replaced with a form of externalism: the epistemic states of the subject are to be accounted for through the methods of science. This means, of course, that epistemology cannot, on pain of circularity, be called upon to ground the natural sciences. But then it is also claimed that such foundational enterprises are in any event doomed to failure, since they require that certain beliefs have a privileged epistemic status which is incompatible with the program's official internalist criteria. In addition, certain critics of the Cartesian project also attack its metaphysical realist presuppositions. But insofar as such criticisms tend to call into question the fact/value distinction, they are eschewed by other advocates of naturalized epistemology. These prefer to assimilate epistemology into science not by introducing normative elements into science, but rather by stripping epistemology of its normative components. Epistemology is to be naturalized, in their view, by making it purely descriptive and value-neutral. We shall return below to this conception of the project.

That classical Indian *pramāṇavāda* never embarked on a Cartesian project should be clear. The very idea of epistemology as *pramāṇavāda*—determining the number and nature of the *pramāṇas* or reliable means of belief formation—suggests a non-foundationalist and externalist project. Non-foundationalist because the project presupposes the existence of knowledge, instead of seeking to prove its very possibility. And externalist because it seeks to distinguish between veridical and non-veridical states of the subject in terms of causal factors, and not in terms of states that are necessarily accessible to the subject.

There are, though, those modern scholars of classical Indian philosophy who claim to find elements of the Cartesian project within at least certain segments of the tradition.[2] Indeed some interpret Nāgārjuna's attack on Nyāya epistemology in *Vigrahavyāvartanī* in just this light. Before examining the debate between Madhyamaka and Nyāya over the possibility of *pramāṇavāda*, however, I should like to briefly address the more general historical question of whether the externalist approach of Nyāya was favoured as well by those other schools that also engaged in the *pramāṇavāda project.* What I shall seek to show is that no party to the dispute over the number and nature of the *pramāṇas* held the internalist KK thesis. If this is correct, this diminishes the plausibility of the claim that Nāgārjuna employed the KK thesis in his attack on Nyāya's *pramāṇavāda*. This result will prove useful in arriving at a proper estimation of the importance of his criticism of Nyāya.

If internalism was held by anyone in the Indian epistemological tradition, the debate over whether knowledge-hood (*prāmāṇya*) is intrinsic or extrinsic (*svataḥ/parataḥ*) is just the context in which we would expect it to be visible and prominent. So its absence here would strongly suggest its absence from the tradition as a whole. Let us look more closely at the views of those who hold that knowledge-hood is intrinsic to those cognitions that are instances of knowledge. For it is they[4] who are often suspected of internalist tendencies. What I shall seek to show is that the appearance of internalism here results from their opponents' misrepresentation of their view, and that in fact both sides in this dispute held straightforwardly reliabilist positions.

Those who hold that knowledge-hood is intrinsic make three claims about veridical cognitions: (1) those factors that serve as the cause of the cognition also serve as the cause of the inherence of knowledge-hood in that cognition (i.e., it was not some additional, extrinsic factor that brought about the knowledge-hood of this cognition); (2) a cognition is self-manifesting or self-illuminating, in the sense that it reveals itself in revealing its object (so that my ability to report that I am aware of the object is not the result of an inference or act of introspection occurring subsequent to the awareness of the object); (3) the knowledge-hood of such a cognition is intrinsic to that very cognition itself, i.e., it is not established only by some subsequent confirmatory cognition. Now thesis (3) certainly looks, to the eyes of one versed in Cartesian epistemology, like an affirmation of the KK thesis, in that when taken in conjunction with (2) it appears to claim that whenever I have knowledge I must be aware of the knowledge-hood of that item of knowledge. But the fact that those who held (3) also held thesis (1) makes this interpretation seem somewhat less straightforward. For it would be odd for an internalist to conjoin an affirmation of the KK thesis with any claims about the causal genesis of the veridicality of cognitions. Those are the sorts of claims that one expects the externalist to make.

In fact, the thesis of intrinsic knowledge-hood (or intrinsicalism) involves two claims that, while not always clearly separated by those who discussed the issue, still should be kept distinct if we are to understand the view in question.[5] First there is the claim that the veridicality of a given veridical cognition is intrinsic to it in the sense that those factors that are responsible for the production of this cognition *qua* cognition also serve as the cause of its veridicality. In making this claim, the intrinsicalist opposes those who hold that there must be some special virtue, in addition to the factors that caused the cognition, to account for the cognition's distinctive property of veridicality. Both sides agree that in the case of a non-veridical cognition, in addition to the factors that brought about the cognition *qua* cognition, there must be some extra factor in the form of a defect that explains the cognition's non-veridicality. But, argues the intrinsicalist, an additional factor in the form of a virtue could be posited to explain the production of veridical cognitions only if there were yet a third sort of cognition, namely one that was neither veridical nor non-veridical. For if the production of both veridical and non-veridical cognitions required additional factors, then it should be possible for the causes of cognition to occur in the absence of either special virtue or special defect. But every cognition is either veridical or non-veridical. Thus the knowledge-hood of a veridical cognition must be intrinsic in the sense that this cognition could not have come into existence lacking the property of veridicality. (Compare: because being wooden is essential to the material cause responsible for the production of this desk, the desk having been made from wood lumber, being wooden is an essential property of the desk, a property it could not have lacked.)

The second intrinsicalist claim concerns not the nature of the cognition but the epistemic attitude of the cognizer toward the cognition. It is the claim that upon the occurrence of a veridical cognition, the cognizer accepts it as an item of veridical cognition without awaiting confirmatory evidence via subsequent cognitions. In this they reject the view of the extrinsicalists, who maintain that the cognizer only establishes the veridicality of a given cognition Cl, and thus comes to accept it, through some subsequent cognition C2, namely either a cognition showing the efficacy of accepting C1 (my thirst is satisfied upon drinking what appears to me to be water), or else a cognition establishing the existence of the requisite 'special virtue' among the causes of C1 (my eyes are capable of accurate colour-discrimination under current lighting conditions). Here the intrinsicalist argues that there is an essential asymmetry between the attitudes of acceptance and rejection, such that it could not be the case that both occur immediately upon the occurrence of cognitions, or that both can occur only after subsequent reflection on the credentials of cognitions. The extrinsicalist claims that both acceptance and rejection occur only after subsequent confirmation and falsification respectively. The intrinsicalist agrees that a cognizer would reject a given cognition as non-veridical only after a distinct falsifying cognition. But they argue that the attitude of acceptance could not then likewise await subsequent confirmation. For in that case one would have no reason to seek out either confirmation or falsification of any cognition. In fact, the most common source of subsequent falsifying cognitions is failure of the test of efficacy. And a given cognition is not subjected to the test of efficacy unless we are inclined to accept it. (I don't seek to wash myself with water that I take to be just a mirage.) Thus the acceptance of a cognition as veridical is the 'default' attitude of cognizers; rejection as non-veridical occurs only in the presence of special additional factors that are extrinsic to the cognition itself. In addition, it is argued that an infinite regress would result were there not this asymmetry: if we were not disposed to accept a given cognition in the absence of countervailing evidence, then we would not accept C2 as either confirming or falsifying C1 in the absence of some distinct cognition C3 confirming C2, etc., etc.

Now given everything else that the intrinsicalist holds, this second claim concerning the intrinsic acceptance of veridical cognitions entails that whenever I have a veridical cognition, there is a sense in which I may be said to know directly that this cognition is veridical, and thus to be justified in accepting it without undertaking any subsequent scrutiny. And this is just the result that the intrinsicalist sought, since this claim in turn is used to establish the intrinsic authority of the Vedas. For it is asserted that cognitions caused by linguistic utterances can be falsified only by defects in their authors, but that the Vedas are authorless. Thus any cognition caused by hearing the Vedas is intrinsically veridical, and therefore one is always justified in accepting such cognitions without further inquiry.

There is clearly much about this alleged proof of the authority of the Vedas that can be questioned. But the extrinsicalist specifically attacked the first premiss (that one is justified in accepting a veridical cognition without subsequent scrutiny), taking it to mean that one ascertains the veridicality of a veridical cognition immediately upon its occurrence. Since this seems to attribute to us a sort of omniscience that we clearly lack, intrinsicalism thus comes to seem implausible. And it is this reading that also seems to have led some modern scholars to see a kind of internalism in intrinsicalism. For it is difficult to see what else could lead to so strong a claim concerning our awareness of our own epistemic states, save this notion that we do not know that p unless we can show that we are justified in accepting p. But this interpretation of the intrinsicalist premiss is mistaken. To say that one is justified in accepting a veridical cognition without further scrutiny is not to say that one ascertains the veridicality of a veridical cognition immediately upon its occurrence. One may, after all, be justified without being able to give one's justification.

It is true that if the cognitive state that I am in is intrinsically one of knowledge, and it is also self-illuminating, then I have justification that is in some sense accessible to me 'internally'. The difficulty here is to be clear on the sense of accessibility involved. I claim that it is not the sense involved in giving justification, but only of that involved in being justified. When I see water I may be said to perceive H_2O even if I do not know the chemical composition of water and am thus unable to say that what I see is H_2O; for being H_2O is intrinsic to water. By the same token, in having a veridical cognition I may be said to cognize its intrinsic nature of knowledge-hood, even though that feature be opaque to me. Justification for the claim that I know lies within me, since the cognitive state is mine, it is self-illuminating, and it is by its nature the product of reliable causes. When I accept it as veridical, I am justified. Yet I may still be unable to explain to others, on the basis of this cognitive state alone, why I am justified in accepting the content of this cognition.

The intrinsicalist claims that the cognizer of a veridical cognition is aware of the knowledge-hood of that cognition at the time of its occurrence. That it must be this opaque sense of 'aware', and not the sense involved in giving justifications, is clear from the fact that those who hold theses (1)-(3) also hold: (4) when a non-veridical cognition occurs, one may be aware of its non-knowledge-hood (*aprāmāṇya*) only by means of a distinct cognition. That this claim is required to make the overall view coherent is clear from the fact that otherwise the view would amount to the implausible position that upon the occurrence of a cognition we always know, immediately and non-inferentially, whether or not it constitutes knowledge. What they claim instead is that while our immediate attitude toward a cognition is always to accept it as veridical, a subsequent falsifying cognition may show the initial cognition to have been non-veridical and our acceptance to have been misplaced. That I accept a given cognition as veridical is no guarantee of its accuracy. Since non-veridicality is always extrinsic to a cognition in which it occurs, subsequent cognition is required to establish its non-veridicality. What a subsequent cognition cannot do is bring it about that I come to know a prior veridical cognition about which I was until now in a state of suspended judgment. So-called confirming cognitions might be necessary if I am to amass the evidence needed to convince others that my initial cognition was veridical. But they are not needed in order for me to be said to know. For that, all that is necessary is the occurrence of a reliably caused cognition.

I claim, then, that the KK thesis plays no role in Indian *pramāṇavāda*. For those who engaged in this project, to attribute knowledge to a subject is to remark on the causal history of that subject's cognition; it is not to attribute to that subject the ability to grasp whatever evidence would be required to rule out skeptical hypotheses. From the fact that, for all I now know, I might be dreaming, it does not follow that I am not justified in believing that there is a desk before me. But if internalism is otherwise unknown in the history of Indian epistemology, it would then seem implausible that the KK thesis should figure in Nāgārjuna's critique of Nyāya epistemology, as some have alleged. It seems far more likely that that critique shares the externalist conception of knowledge common to all *pramāṇavādins*. Let us turn now to the critique itself.

Nāgārjuna's discussion of Nyāya epistemology comes in the form of an extended reply to a Nyāya objection[6]. The Naiyāyika objects to the Madhyamaka claim that all things are empty (*śūnya*), i.e., devoid of essential nature (*svabhāva*) and thus not ultimately real. If all things were indeed empty, then all means of knowledge (*pramāṇa*) would likewise be empty, in which case there would be no available instruments for ascertaining that all things are empty. It then follows that we could have no reason to believe that all things are empty. To the extent that Nāgārjuna provides us with reasons to believe this claim, it must be false.

Nāgārjuna begins his reply by agreeing that it would be inconsistent for him either to assert or to deny any thesis, i.e., seek to establish some claim (positive or negative) about the ultimate nature of reality through the use of some valid means of knowledge. But, he claims, he does not have any thesis. He then turns immediately to a critical investigation of the project of determining the number and nature of the *pramāṇas*. Nāgārjuna uses what may be called a trilemma against the claim that a particular procedure counts as a valid means of knowledge: such a claim (1) is merely dogmatically asserted, or else (2) its defense results in an infinite regress, or (3) its defense is vitiated by circularity. (1) To claim that a certain cognitive process may be known to be a *pramāṇa* without employing any *pramāṇa* whatever would be dogmatic, since it is presumably only through the use of some *pramāṇa* or other that anything can come to be known. But if it were instead claimed (2) that some distinct *pramāṇa* is employed in establishing the *pramāṇa*-hood of this cognitive process, there would arise the difficulty of explaining how the second *pramāṇa* is itself known to be a valid means of knowledge. And the regress thus begun has no clear terminus. Finally (3), suppose it were claimed that a given cognitive process can be known to be a reliable means of belief formation through its producing veridical cognitions of its object, the *prameya*. In this case we must ask how we know these cognitions to be veridical. And the answer, if we are to avoid the previous faults of dogmatism and infinite regress, must be that we know this because we have reliable knowledge of the *prameya*—obtained through the use of the very *pramāṇa* whose credentials we are investigating. That is, we know that this procedure is a *pramāṇa* because we know the nature of its *prameya*, and we know the nature of the *prameya* because we know that this procedure is a *pramāṇa*. Here the circularity is obvious.

It might be thought that Nāgārjuna has too hastily dismissed the third possible strategy for establishing the *pramāṇas*. When that strategy is taken to involve just one *pramāṇa* and one *prameya*, it is rightly criticized as viciously circular. But given a sufficiently large number of instances of a variety of distinctive cognitive processes, employed on a wide array of different objects under a diversity of conditions, the strategy of using *pramāṇas* to establish *prameyas* and *prameyas* to establish *pramāṇas* would seem to hold some promise. Indeed this seems to be just the sort of strategy recommended by the proponent of naturalized epistemology. For what the latter proposes is just that in our investigation of the nature of knowledge we make free use of the established results of the natural sciences; yet the object of this investigation is precisely those instruments that we employ in attaining these results. Thus when Nāgārjuna objects to such a strategy, this gives rise to the suspicion that he sees epistemology as necessarily foundational. This may then be the source of the view that Nāgārjuna subscribes to an internalist conception of knowledge.

In order to see that Nāgārjuna is not presupposing foundationalism and internalism, we need to return to the objection to which he is responding. The Naiyāyika claims that the Mādhyamika's thesis of emptiness is incompatible with the use of any *pramāṇa* to support that thesis. This is because the doctrine of emptiness entails the denial that means of knowledge and object of knowledge are ultimately real. The *Naiyāyika* must then be assuming that in order for a cognitive process to result in veridical cognition, it and its object must both have a certain ontological status, viz., the status of being ultimately real, i.e., being entities that bear their own essential natures. When the Naiyāyika objects that there could be no knowledge of the emptiness of existents unless the object of knowledge possessed its own determinate nature, he is articulating the notion that true beliefs must correctly represent the nature of a mind-independent reality. His objection reveals the assumption that there could be no knowledge were there not already a determinate way that the world is. Likewise, the objection that there must be determinate means of knowledge if we are to ascertain that all things are empty, clearly presupposes that there is some fact of the matter, specifiable independently of human institutions and practices, concerning the conditions under which the world delivers the truth up to us. The picture at work here is just that of truth as correspondence to mind-independent reality: if we can have knowledge only when our beliefs are the result of antecedently specifiable causal conditions, this can only be because obtaining truth requires that we allow the world to shape our beliefs in accordance with its nature.

The general strategy of Nāgārjuna's reply to the objection is to seek to undermine the Naiyāyika's metaphysical realist presuppositions. His specific response to the proposal that *pramāṇas* and *prameyas* are reciprocally established, is to point out that such a strategy is incompatible with Nyāya metaphysical realism. For if *pramāṇas* and *prameyas* are reciprocally established, then it is in principle impossible to distinguish, in our final theory of the world, between those elements contributed by the nature of our cognitive apparatus, and those contributed by the nature of the world. And in that case, metaphysical realism—the notion that there is one true theory of mind-independent reality, with truth understood as correspondence—cannot coherently be stated. The reciprocity strategy might well be an effective procedure for discovering the nature of the valid means of knowledge. But there is no inconsistency in the Mādhyamika then using the *pramāṇas* thus discovered in defence of the doctrine of emptiness. It would be inconsistent only if the Mādhyamika intended his doctrine of emptiness to be ultimately true, to correspond to the nature of ultimate reality. And Nāgārjuna explicitly denies this when he says that emptiness is itself empty. The ultimate truth is just that there is no ultimate truth.

The Madhyamaka dialectic seeks to demonstrate that no empirically adequate theory of the world is possible on the assumption that there are ultimately real entities with fixed essences or determinate natures of their own. It is this result that Nyāya seeks to challenge. This is surely understandable. Asking the metaphysical realist to give up fixed essences is a bit like asking people to give up the gold standard. How can mere paper be worth anything if there isn't something solid to back it up? How can there be truth if there isn't some one way that things intrinsically are? Would not the currency of philosophers, truth, lose its value and become mere empty words?

Of course we know that paper money continues to have value after the gold standard has been abandoned. And we also know, at least roughly, why that is: given the institutions of buying and selling, the practice of employing a medium of exchange has a use. The value of a paper currency is just that use, against the background of those institutions. Indeed we can now see that a similar story must be told to explain how the gold standard might itself have anchored a currency. Gold could lend value to a paper currency only because many people had a use for it; gold has no intrinsic value. (Therein lies the moral of many a miser's tale.) While it has been a relatively stable fact of most human cultures that many people prize gold's aesthetic properties, this is a contingent fact all the same. Gold came to be a medium of exchange, and then later the anchor of the medium of exchange, only because some people who controlled surplus resources had a use for it.

To abandon metaphysical realism is, I suggest, to go off the Gold

Standard of Truth. Veridical cognitions continue to have value, as they still have a use. Indeed we can, as always, speak of a cognition's being veridical by virtue of its relation to how things are. But 'how things are' can no longer be read in terms of metaphysical Truth, i.e., as a function of the fixed essences of things. That things are one way and not another is in part a function of certain human institutions and practices. That clay is the material cause of pots is in part a function of such human practices as the firing of pots. That we can say neither that clay and pot are ultimately identical nor that they are ultimately distinct should tell us that the causal relation we recognize here obtains only by virtue of certain material practices that we happen to engage in. The dream of metaphysical realism is the dream of a way that things are independently of all human institutions and practices. We awaken from that dream when we realize that clay has a certain essence only against the background of purposes that we contingently share. There can be no question of clay's being ultimately identical with or ultimately distinct from pot; for the force of the 'ultimately' here is to make this a question of what clay would be were it not clay—the stuff that we use to make pots.

I attribute to the Mādhyamikas the claim, 'The ultimate truth is that there is no ultimate truth.' If, as the Madhyamaka arguments make out, things do not have fixed essences, then metaphysical realism is false and there can be no ultimate truth as other Buddhists conceived it. But why not simply put this as, 'There is no ultimate truth'? Why add the seemingly superfluous 'The ultimate truth is that ...'? As a way of suggesting a novel alternative: that there is only conventional truth. Now conventional truth in the earlier Buddhists' sense cannot stand alone. For theirs was a conception of truth as generated by conventions designed to facilitate communication by glossing over the fine details. On this picture, the notion of an ultimate truth must be retained in order to account for the fact that acceptance of merely conventionally true statements results in successful practice. But the Mādhyamikas seem to hold that we can preserve something of the original notion of conventional truth while stripping away the metaphysical realist elements implicated in the idea of ultimate truth. If things may be said to have determinate natures only against the background of certain human institutions and practices, we may still speak of 'the nature of things' within the context of those institutions and practices. And so we may still speak of a belief being true to the nature of things—against the background of those institutions and practices. But this is only an *ersatz* correspondence, not the correspondence of metaphysical realism. For what makes a given belief true can only be its functional role within a set of conventional human practices, not its relation to the ultimate nature of reality. It is because of our practice of making pots, and the whole host of related institutions, that we would be well advised to believe that pots are made of clay. There is no ultimate truth about the relation between pot and clay. The very notion of ultimate truth makes no sense. It is true that pots are made of clay. There is only conventional truth.

Metaphysical truth must then be replaced by a truth with significant epistemic content: since we cannot coherently articulate a sense of mind-independent reality, we must suppose that truth always involves epistemic practices of an idealized community of knowers. (While we must in practice take our own community to be ideal, we also know that no actual community is perfectly rational.) Facts thus come to have significant normative content. And this result is directly contrary to what many take to be the spirit of naturalized epistemology. On their reading of this project, to naturalize epistemology is to jettison its prescriptive pretensions and include it among the purely descriptive enterprises of the natural sciences. Proponents of naturalized epistemology have sometimes been accused of seeking to derive 'ought' from 'is'. Some naturalized epistemologists respond to this criticism by denying that epistemology may legitimately confer epistemic 'oughts' at all. That is, the objection wrongly assumes that epistemology has a normative role to play with respect to science. The bankruptcy of the Cartesian foundationalist project, together with the success of science, tells us that there are no distinctive epistemic 'oughts' to be discovered by a discrete meta-discipline of epistemology, that there are only the facts uncovered through scientific method—including the facts concerning how human cognizers come to have veridical beliefs. From this perspective, the Madhyamaka tendency to introduce epistemic content into truth will appear to illegitimately breach the fact/value gap.

The Madhyamaka response would, I think, be to question the fact/value distinction that is the basis of this objection. The naturalized epistemologist is right to reject a foundationalist conception of the theory of knowledge according to which epistemology prescribes how science is to describe. But it does not follow that a naturalized epistemology will be purely descriptive and value-neutral. The continuities between epistemology and science must be understood to proceed in both directions: not only is epistemology to be construed naturalistically, but the scientific investigation of cognition is also to be understood as inherently normative in nature. To suppose otherwise is to imagine that we can separate out in our scientific theories those elements contributed by our own epistemic constraints, and those elements contributed by the facts about a world independent of our epistemic constraints. But such a distinction could only be made sense of from the perspective of completed science. Only if we possessed the one true theory about the ultimate nature of reality could we discern those aspects of our theorizing that reflected facts about human cognitive practices. And, the Mādhyamika reminds us, the very notion of completed science, of the one true theory, is incoherent. Scientific practice does require that we posit an idealized community of knowers. And what such a community would presumably know is just all the facts. But here the ideal is purely regulative: it merely represents how we have arranged to continue the ongoing dialectic between scientific fact-finding and self-conscious criticism. Scientific investigation of the means of knowledge leads to better scientific practices, leading in turn to renewed scientific investigation of the means of knowledge. Because there is only conventional truth, because we cannot imagine an end to this process, 'is' and epistemic 'ought' must always be inextricably intertwined.

Here I am, of course, only speculating about how the Mādhyamika would respond to a dispute in current analytic epistemology. The reply I imagine them making does, though, closely parallel that which they made to the Nyāya objection concerning Nāgārjuna's use of *pramāṇas.* And just as that reply left Nyāya *pramāṇavāda* intact while stripping away metaphysical realist accretions, so this reply leaves unscathed the project of investigating the means of knowledge scientifically, requiring only that we abandon that other metaphysical realist legacy, an absolute fact/value distinction.

Notes and References

1. Two useful surveys of the project are: Maffle, James (1990). 'Recent Work on Naturalized Epistemology', *American Philosophical Quarterly* 27, pp.281-93; and Kitcher, Philip (1992), 'The Naturalists Return', *The Philosophical Review* 101, pp. 53-114.

2. See, e.g., J.N. Mohanty (1992), *Reason and Tradition in Indian Thought* (Oxford: Oxford University Press), pp.140-41.

3. See, e.g., B.K. Matilal (1986), *Perception: An Essay in Classical Indian Theories of Knowledge* (Oxford: Oxford University Press), pp. 51-65.

4. Namely the Mīmāṁsakas. It is sometimes claimed that the Sāṅkhyans held the view that both knowledgehood (*prāmāṇya*) and non-knowledgehood (*aprāmāṇya*) are intrinsic to the cognitions in which they occur—a view I shall later claim is implausible in the extreme. But this attribution seems based on a misreading of the actual Sāṅkhya position. In any event, the later Sāṅkhyan commentators consistently deny that their school holds this view.

5. Useful discussions of the intrinsicalist view may be found in *Ślokavārtika* of Kumārila Bhaṭṭa, 1.47-87;

Nyāyamañjarī of Jayanta Bhaṭṭa, III.91-4; *Tattvasaṅgraha* of Śāntarakṣita, vv. 2811-3122.

6. These occur in *Vigrahavyāvartanī*, the text of which is to be found in Vaidya, P. L. (1960), editor, *Madhyamakaśāstra of Nāgārjuna (Mūlamadhyamakakārikas) with the Commentary: Praśannapāda by Candrakīrti* (Darbhanga: Mithila Institute). The Nyāya objection is given at vv.5-6, Nāgārjuna's reply at vv.30-51.

What Limits to Thought, Inquiry, and Philosophy ?

RICHARD SYLVAN

Prof. Richard Sylvan, was a professor at the Research School of Social Sciences, Australian National University. Formal education at Princeton University. He taught at the Universities of Sydney and New England and was the author of 29 books and booklets and numerous articles on wide ranging subjects. Prof. Sylvan passed away in 1996.

Philosophers have been astonishingly eager to find credible limitations, particularly to their own activities. Often they have operated with such implicit objectives as: removing difficult issues thought to be beyond reach and locking away very censoriously unpalatable material or their own harder problems. Indeed it sometimes seems that modern philosophy has become a trifle obsessed with limits to its own activity, limits it soon projects elsewhere. So it is that the resounding idea of severe limits blasts through, in brain-storming strength, from two of its greatest idols, Kant and Wittgenstein, and is reinforced by powerful input from other idealist and empiricist, Germanic and British, sources.

Consider what has variously been put beyond reach, off limits, out of philosophical bounds, and life: metaphysics, especially transcendental forms, pretensions of reason, notably speculative reason, ultimate philosophical questions (conspicuously those about ultimate existence, life, purpose, meaning, and so forth), foundational and deep questions in ethics and elsewhere, issues of universal methods, and so on. More recently there has been a virtual deluge of limit claims: limits to logic, to analytic philosophy, to metaphysics, to ethics, to science, to technology (near enough, you name some reach of philosophy, there are limits acclaimed to it). Nor have philosophers been on their own in announcing limits; scientists of most sorts are no less enthusiastic in proclaiming limits, as will soon emerge. Previously development in mathematics, especially in calculus and analysis, encouraged limitation findings elsewhere (e.g. Malthusian limits to population appealed to divergence of geometric from arithmetic progressions). More recently, limitation 'findings' have been boosted by breakthroughs in logic, achieved through controlled use of semantical and intensional paradoxes (no doubt technically splendid recycling of dangerous fuel). Certainly limits to thought and philosophy were proclaimed by German-speaking philosophers, most conspicuously Kant, Bolzano and Wittgenstein, before Finsler and Gödel announced their remarkable results, clever applications of intensional paradoxes. Naturally however the technical results have been used to bolster the philosophers' claims, especially as the philosophers' own arguments were often found to be wanting. (By contrast, the logicians' assumptions were, once the logical power structure closed ranks, seldom questioned. Similarly for other paradoxes, such as those from social choice theory.)

Not only are many philosophers fascinated by limits; many fail to resist the temptation to throw the term *limit* or one of its combinations or variations into the titles of some of their works. A key-word search based on phrases containing 'limit', 'bound' and the like would produce an exceedingly large haul. Most of these works are, there is reason to suspect, pretending to disclose some sorts of limits—without, a limited sampling suggests, much at all in the way of substantial evidence. Some of these works never get around to detailing properly the types of limits (to science, to sense, to analysis, to ethics) that their titles proclaim; others advance no argument that admits straightforward extraction and assessment. While not proposing any reversion to traditional intolerance, such as commital of these works to the flames, a message from flawed competition theory might well be proffered: those philosophers should lift their game.

All is far from well with many of these limit claims. For many of the claims are ill-explained, still less well justified. Yet enthusiasm for limits has become overzealous, and (exponential-like) has surged out of control; it is due for damping down. While there *are* limits of various sorts, the extent and, character, unconditionality and problematicality of these limits has been grossly exaggerated.

An issue immediately raised, of critical importance for subsequent investigations, is: what exactly are these limits? And what are limits? How is 'limit' characterized?

1. Clarifying limits and limitations

The noun *limit* descends, through French, from the Latin *limen*, signifying: cross-path (between fields), boundary-line, boundary-wall. While it did acquire in English the broad sense of *boundary* or *frontier*—ripe for topological explication—it is now only used, according to the *Oxford English Dictionary* (OED) in a narrow sense: [1] 'a boundary ... considered as confining or restricting', [2] 'a bound which may not be passed, or beyond which something ceases to be possible or allowable'. Call these the *prime* uses. Observe that the term *limitation*, sometimes used by way of variation on these prime uses, means, in the relevant sense: *limit* (see OED; otherwise it means *limiting item*, e.g. limiting action, circumstance, condition, rule, period, including disability or inability). Mathematical and technical uses of *limit*, typically in the form L *is a limit of S,* characteristically *relative* limits (relative to S), are regarded by dictionaries as special elaborations of the second sense [2].[1] The uses of present relevance (e.g. for philosophy and thought need not depend upon or concern these *technical* notions, and accordingly *are not* transferred or metaphorical uses answering to them. Rather they go back to the more basic nontechnical senses [1] and [2]. But unnecessary confusion has arisen through conflation of these uses, an important example of which concerns limits to thought themselves. For, whereas on the prime use it may well be said that there are no limits to thought, on the technical use it could be contended that while there are (technical) limits these can be surpassed. We could no doubt have it both ways by conceding that, though there are no limits (prime use), there are technical limits (which however are not limiting).

Though we can bypass the technical notions, elaboration of the *boundary* notion, perhaps of a technical kind, will prove pertinent. Limits are limits *of* or *to something.* That is, for boundary 1, 1 is a limit of N, where N is a notion or set, the bounded notion. In pictorial representation:

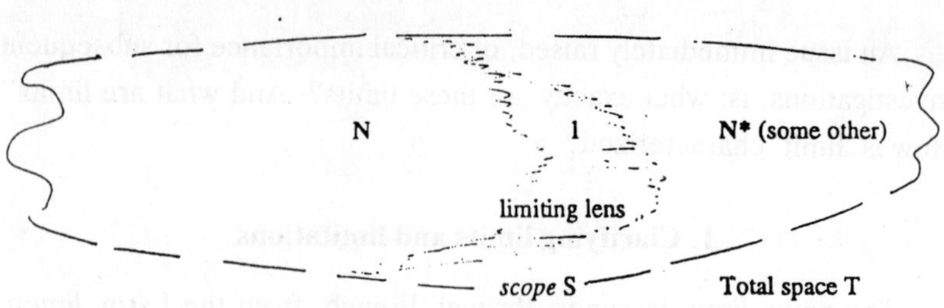

It is not just tempting, but important, to fill out an *initial* representation comprising just N and 1 through a *fuller* representation, which also includes N and a scope S within the total space T (but maybe one or both of N* (some contrasting other) and T can often be left out of consideration).

Scope functions like a significance range, to exclude items or matters that would not even enter in assessing limits. because for instance they make no sense for the topic concerned, they are outside the scope of that logic or whatever. Thus, to take relevant examples, it is not even a putative limit to philosophy that it does not enable a practitioner to tie shoelaces or put bread on the table, to play polo or make a fortune, to fly at the speed of light or square the circle. For these form no part of the scope of philosophy, of what it is properly or sensibly engaged in, or its practitioners properly practice. In a wide sense (a covered absurdity sense), there are many things philosophy *cannot* (cannot significantly) do, or enable its practitioners to do, such as those listed above. But these 'impossibilities', concerning matters *outside* its scope, do not represent limitations upon it. In short, there is no admissible inference from **'y**, e.g. philosophy (similarly thought, ...), cannot do *x'* (because *x* is outside the scope of ***y)*** to '*x* is a limit to **y'**. However there are many matters within the scope of philosophy, which it may lack any possible prospect of performing (such as providing a justification of ethical principles, to take William's presumptive example of limits to ethics), and which may constitute putative limits.

For related reasons, impossibility themes do not invariably yield limitation themes, as the *conditions* for limits are not established. There is not something, some information or similar, within the scope of what is limited which is beyond a barrier and inaccessible.[2]

Where 1 is a boundary of N, 1 is just outside N (or N without 1).

This and other features of boundaries strongly suggest that a *nearness* relation is required to define a boundary. For example, the boundary layer of a surface in fluid dynamics is that position *near* to the given surface but distinguished from it (e.g. because in motion relative to it). A first stab at defining *l is a boundary of N* topologically might run: each element of L is near to some element of N and every element of N that is near to 1 but not in 1 is interior to N.

More difficult to define (certainly beyond usual topological resources) is (what is aptly called) the *constraint feature* or *limit character of* 1's boundary of N within S. The two senses [1] and [2] supply three sorts of constraining features: 1 is restricting of N (roughly explicated: N would be grander but for 1); 1 is impassable from N; and outside N beyond l lie deontic infringements, the forbidden. Some, perhaps all, of these features strongly suggest that there is *more* than N and l that N*, the other, is not nothing. Roughly, the constraining feature comes to the following prohibitions: *l stops N including what it would,* what is part of its scope. Interestingly, the logical formulation of this prohibition appears to use logical resources which include deontics and conditionals, distinctly intensional topology. That is, limit assertions involve a significant level of intensionality.[3]

In sum, a limit is a boundary conforming to the constraining feature. 1 is a limit of N iff 1 is a constraining boundary of N.

2. Limits elsewhere, outside inquiry and philosophy : framework limitations

Outside philosophy there are, naturally, limits, limits of many significant sorts: Limits to growth, limits to speed, limits to technological capacity, to types of machines, to measurement, and so on. Many of these are practical limits, induced by a presupposed setting. The limits to economic growth, for example, presuppose an on-going terrestrial setting and also that humans are not able or clever enough to devise low-cost low-pollution high-energy sources, such as clean fusion (one successor to perpetual motion) once promised to be. The limits of human ground speed, so that 'the one minute mile' is beyond the aspirations of even the most dedicated or conceited atheletes, presupposes present human physiology. If human sports people were to evolve in the direction of the large cats (for example, with the help of some quiet gene transplantation biotechnology), then such new ground speeds would become realistic ambitions (whether Joe the Jaguar is a human still is another question).

Naturally too, there are more comprehensive limits, which have a more absolute look. The speed of light is an upper limit on (real not virtual) velocities—*given* however the theory of relativity. That limit does not obtain under a Newtonian synthesis. How 'solid' is the limit? Solid enough, but nonetheless pretty contingent. According to present best scientific information, less positively according to the prevailing scientific paradigm, this universe is relativistic, not Newtonian, indeed all physically possible universes are relativistic. While that sort of generalization may make relativistic claims look rather more absolute, it does not make them absolute. Outside relativistic frameworks in consistently modellable Newtonian universes (as in asymptotic relativistic settings where the velocity of light tends to infinity), there are no such limits. The limits may be solid enough for universe-bound life-forms, for all actual experience, but for all that they are quite contingent, and readily thought beyond. So it is similarly for thermodynamic limits, quantum limits, economic limits and so on. These depend upon contingent absence of large free sources of energy, on the contingent breakdown of ideal classical measurements at microphysical levels, and so on. Not only outside quantum frameworks, in embedding classical theory, but even within quantum frameworks under different conceivable theories or should different circumstances in fact obtain, quantum limitations upon measurement and so forth lapse.

The direction of travel already begins to appear in outline. *What limits there are depend upon a presumed background settings, a framework* (which may be quite extensive, as with this-worldliness); and these limits are *removed* as background and settings are moved back. Is this an endless game, with backgrounds always movable further back and limits removed, or does it terminate?

Prevailing wisdom is that the process does terminate—in logic. It does not terminate in tougher transphysical limitations, such as the unavailability of perpetual motion machines. For all the exclusion of such handy devices across the field of likely physics (by virtue of constraints from core mechanics and thermodynamics), the machines are still possible in other universes (and indeed persist in backward zones like economics). Nor does it terminate in mathematical limitations, such as the impossibility of trisecting the angle or the squaring the circle. For these are contingent upon the restriction of *methods,* for instance to ruler and compass, and vanish with lifting of that background (it is elementary to trisect an angle given quantitative protractor methodology).

For those aspiring to unconditional limitations, logical regions beckon, notably those of formalizability, expressibility, decidability, definability, computability, and so on. There are apparently many limits which may appear to the more naive, informed by popular science, to defeat my assertions: limitative theorems, in the form of what cannot be established in more formal settings, such as the Gödel-Rosser theorem, i.e. limits to proof; limits to reasoning; limits to knowledge; and so on. But, naturally, there are no such proofs or arguments as these claims depend upon, without an assumed setting, a consistent framework of some presumed sort. Namely, as regards these limitations, the recent classical logic tradition or paradigm is a major part of the backdrop. In suitable alternative settings, such as those of dialethic logic, these classical limitations too appear to be surmountable.

Many of the most-heralded limitations are restricted or *conditional* limitations where the conditions or background structure have been quietly suppressed. Nowhere is this practice more widespread than as regards restrictions as to *consistency* (the same condition is implicit in such things as standard interpretations, models, and the like, all of which are supposed consistency bounded). Results are proved, claims argued, for *consistent* so-and-sos. Then the restriction to consistency is quietly omitted.[4] Or else it is absorbed into what purports to be a completely general notion, but is not; thus for instance classical notions like *model, interpretation* and the like.

The reasons for suppressing conditions and assumptions are not difficult to find. They may, for one thing, simply not have been noticed.

So it has been with many axioms and assumptions in mathematics, particularly before the advent of formalization, but not *ending* with it. Also important, what is presented as conditional, rather than absolute, may not look so remarkable. Indeed it may look far from devastating when intellectual development at last proceeds into previous out-of-bounds regions. So it is, especially, when the ancient barriers of consistency and existence are breached, and inconsistent and nonexistent items seriously investigated.

3. Beyond technical and conditional limitations to pure reason, and to main theses

Even if these limits concerning formalism, effectiveness, frameworks and the like *should* obtain in some noncompromised form, they would not impact heavily on thought and philosophy. For thought and philosophy are not seriously limited by these sorts of features (except on unduly restrictive and implausible accounts of philosophy, such as nominalisms and constructivisms). Neither thought nor philosophy is limited by considerations of available symbolism, effectiveness, cost, economics or the like.[5] Both thought and philosophy are *propositional* and *objectual* in character, unlimited by considerations of effectiveness, mechanization, cost, and similar, ultra-economic business. That is one reason why highly acclaimed results concerning the features and limitations of formalism, constructivity, automation, and so on, are much less philosophically relevant and interesting than is often imagined (for all that this material is pushed by technically addicted certified philosophers).

Admittedly there is abroad the proposition that thought, and also intelligence, are algorithmic in character. Such a thesis appears prominent in reductive AI doctrine and associated theory of mind.[6] Were the proposition correct, then thought would be confined, computationally confined. But the proposition is without sound basis. Thought processes can and do operate in ways that are classically nonalgorithmic. One argument runs as follows: Thought is more comprehensive than reasoning, since it includes reflection, meditation, and such nonalgorithmic processes. But reasoning itself is not algorithmic, because it can include jumps, diagonal steps (surpassing all assembled algorithms), analogue procedures, plausible procedures, ineffective moves, and so on. Therefore, thought is nonalgorithmic in general character.

Such an argument takes for granted information which dictionaries supply, that thought is a process, such as reasoning, inferring, reflecting, considering and similar, as well as what such a process may yield, a content product, that which is thought, a conclusion, a concern, a conception, judgement or proposition. That superficial level of analysis appears too about as far as it is necessary to proceed towards a philosophical account of thought, for present purposes. For the main case to be argued can, fortunately, rest upon ordinary conceptions of thought.[7]

The preceding development may have appeared to presume that philosophy is systematic, and that philosophy can be represented through propositional-objectual systems, which so to say encapsulate its (partial) results. But this does not offer an altogether adequate representation; processes cannot be fully represented through (sequences of) products. What it tends to leave out are process features, namely, firstly genetic historical features, and secondly discursive features, dialectical activity. Similar points apply, to a lesser extent, to thought, which is also a discursive process yielding a product, and to a greater extent to inquiry, which is normally a process, perhaps not yielding a single product at all. Even so, practical and business controls do not apply; for example, there is no time limit on how long philosophical discourse may continue, or cost limit on its conduct. As a process or activity, philosophy is an *ideal* pursuit not effectively constrained or bounded by such factors.

Because of these features of thought and philosophy, and other relevant features, such as their generality and abstractness, *they* should be able to evade limitations, if anything can (the unlimited, inaccessibles, unthinkables, and other remote items are all within their compass). Although the predominant position in Anglo-American influenced philosophy continues the historical *status quo,* that thought and philosophy do not escape significant limitations, that position is now under challenge. Alternative theses, here preferred and pressed, run as follows:

RT. There are no absolute limitations to thought; all limitations are broadly conditional, relative to background conditions, constraints, assumptions, or the like, and are displaced with these.

Similarly thesis ***RP***, for philosophy, ***RI***, for inquiry: *there are no absolute limitations, only conditional ones.* Therewith too, proper room is again made for grand philosophy, which analytically concerns grand issues, and which aims to assess grand themes, of which ***RT*** is an example.

While there are alternative ways of stating the no-limitations claims here advanced—notably that there are (technical) limits but they can always be surpassed—this form of presentation (perhaps encouraged through the mathematical usage, where relative limits can regularly be surpassed[8]) is less satisfactory, for two connected reasons. First, it tends to ignore the prime use of *limit*, where limits instituted cannot be surpassed; and second it concedes too much to conventional philosophical wisdom, that there was a great deal to what it has pompously pronounced, and that it is only by some very funny business (such as paraconsistency) that its strictures are avoided.

It is one thing to propose such theses as ***RT*** and ***RP***; quite another to establish them. Perhaps as satisfactory an achievement as can be reasonably hoped for in this regard is that an attractive case be made for them. Such a case will consist, like standard legal and debating cases, of a combination of negative and positive components. Here the negative side consists in disarming, so far as feasible, oppositional (typically mainstream) arguments and considerations operating in favour of limitations. This extensive side, though important, can hardly be decisive, because of the real possibility of missing some crucial consideration. For that sort of procedure, very common in philosophy, does not aspire (or when honest, pretend) to be exhaustive; it is typically quasi-empirical, in terms of a selection of texts, but without (and without prospect of) adequate sampling. Even so, let us begin—after brief reflection on contrasting motivation for imposition of limits—with the negative side, a side which is highly instructive, before attempting positive arguments for the theses, components that are again less than conclusive (though for different reasons, because they make claims and adopt procedures exceeding what is considered admissible in mainstream philosophy).

Negative arguments divide roughly into two groups: those relying upon some sweeping philosophy or ideology, such as rationalism, and those concerning particular arguments of philosophers, such as Russell's. Treatment tends, in both, inevitably towards the piecemeal.

As a preliminary, it is appropriate to remark upon, and fun to play off, the *main*, but curiously diverse motivational bases for philosophic limits, and clashing *motivations* for limitation theses and like restrictions. Limits were intended : A. to *exclude* religion, and more generally to exclude transcendental, high spiritual or unscientific endeavours. Thus notably Hume, and a succession of hard-line empiricist philosophers, engaged in the fight against religion, anti-scientific activity, and spiritual slosh. A*. to *include* religion, to make room for faith, and so on. Thus conspicuously Kant, also differently James, and many others are trying to evade parts of the atheistic scientific Enlightenment steamroller.

It is worth expanding a little on each different sort of motivation in turn, beginning with exclusions. Often, a prime objective is to *stop* various intellectual enterprises, including, most sweepingly, *philosophy* as a whole or in very substantial part. The proposal to close down philosophy as a whole, popular enough with censorious forces from outside philosophy, has also been put from within from time to time, for instance by Wittgenstein. More bothersome is a concerted attempt to exclude *unscientific* philosophy made by empiricists and positivists (of most kinds). These philosophers were concerned to remove not only religion and such unscientific rubbish, but also grand philosophy such as transcendental metaphysical and difficult ultimate questions. In these objectives they were not always coherent, both because the philosophy in terms of which they operated did not conform to requirements for scientificness (e.g. it was unverifiable, or unempirical) and because some of their own themes looked themselves like grand philosophy (e.g. naturalism, materialism). Less sweepingly, an objective is to stop particular projects; for instance, formalization of this or that, intensional theories, deeper environmental thinking etc. etc. Obviously there is only a gradation between more sweeping and less sweeping empiricist destruction; for instance, a more comprehensive formalism may be restricted through targetting of crucial special cases.

More remarkable among motivations is that designed to make *room* for items that would otherwise appear to be excluded, items such as God and freedom, immortality and reincarnation. Of course to effect this sort of stoppage, of which Kant's enterprise is the supreme example, *other* enterprises have to be stopped, for instance rationalistic and dialethic philosophies which proceed far beyond the received bounds of experience. In significant ways, such an approach is likewise misguided. For it is premissed on the adequacy of what is narrowly seen as the opposition to effect exclusions. But philosophy, empiricist philosophy in particular, cannot effect the exclusions supposed. Arguments for scientific determinism, for instance, might have looked sound, but were not.

4. Deflating empiricist, rationalist, and like limitations

Both of the main ideologies in modern philosophy, empiricism and rationalism, try to impose limitations, often severe. It is again curious that they try to impose them at different places, already suggesting (correctly) that these limitations are not absolute, but at least *ideology dependent.* Such an initial objection is avoided in logical empiricism, which rationally distributes the limitations, in a way that will become plain (if it is not already).

With empiricism it is *experience,* or *possible* experience, that is the operative factor in effecting limitations; in rationalism it is *consistency,* characteristically intertwined with logic and *reasoning.* It is evident, given the meanings of 'empiricism' and 'rationalism', that the operative factors are intimately tied into the ideologies; so much so that in critically dismissing the limitations they claim to find, we shall be well advanced in critical dismissal of the ideologies themselves.

Under empiricism, experience provides the outer bound on knowledge, speculation, intelligible conjecture, and so on, indeed on all *epistemic* operations. Also under pure empiricism, as opposed to logical empiricism, logical operations such as reasoning, are similarly bounded. Thus emerges

EL. The empiricist limitation theme. There is no admissible knowledge, criticism, speculation, and the like, beyond the bounds of experience, about 'what' lies beyond (possible) experience. Similarly on the pure theory (of Mill, Mackie and many other go-getters), there is no sound reasoning or admissible rational operations (along with epistemic ones) beyond these experiential bounds.

There are familiar large corollaries: The grand issues of philosophy are inadmissible, inasmuch as they exceed legitimate bounds: *meaningless,* if that is how inadmissibility is cashed out (or inaccessible, or mystical, or ineffable: we have seen them all from tall empiricist poppies). Thus too, transcendental metaphysics is impossible. Sound philosophy is confined to austere empiricist territories. Naturally there are ways of trying to recover some of the lost territories (some of them well lost, because badly contaminated). Widening 'experience' is one way; catholic clerics talk confidently these days of religious experience, hoping for access to regions most empiricists were most concerned to put right out of bounds. Naturally, genuine experience, empirical experience, can be, and should be, more tightly circumscribed.

Arguments for bounds at (possible) experience derive directly from empiricism; and the case is correspondingly defeated by arguments against empiricism. Theoretically there is little need to reiterate those familiar arguments; in practice, of course, they need to be rehearsed often to counter the repeated refloating of the dreary themes of empiricism. Much information is accessible by means and through channels not empirically sanctioned, especially information concerning objects.[9] Conversely, arguments (themselves normally exceeding pure empiricist resources) to limit information accessible outside empirically approved confines all break down; either they are defective, even under revised logical theory (e.g. rather manifestly Kant's deployment of antinomies, designed to show that illegal extraempirical activity leads to contradiction), or else they involve contestable, if entrenched, narrow logical theory (e.g. attempts to outlaw modal information through modal paradoxes).

The severe weakness of pure empiricism in accommodating logic, assumption and postulation, inference and reasoning and surrounds, is overcome, notably in logical empiricism, by mixing in rationalist elements. A pure rationalism, despite its appeal back in the 17th century, is no longer plausible. With the formal development of logic and mathematics, it has become apparent how many assumptions, empirical assumptions especially, the 'pure' arguments of rationalism, rational mechanics, and so on, infiltrated. What logic and reasoning can; and cannot, accomplish has become much better appreciated. [10] Above all, they leave too many alternatives (too many logics, geometries, arithmetics, etc.), and they are (accordingly) too weak to establish much on their own. Logical argument only becomes powerful when a good deal, mostly at issue in fundamental areas, is already nailed down firmly. But while pure rationalism is aged and feeble, indeed presently comatose[11], the mix of rationalism and empiricism is more powerful. Empiricism provides an informational base (albeit still an excessively restrictive one) on which rational argument can go to work and build.

Parallelling the empiricist limitation theme stands an analogous theme limiting standard rationalism, namely

RL. The rationalist limitation theme. There is no admissible reasoning, conception, thought, knowledge and so on, beyond the bounds of consistency.

Consistency becomes the absolute constraint, in place of experience. Rationalism is commonly bolstered by re-presentation of logic as a theory of consistency, with logic simply read off consistency requirements (thus Von Wright). Similarly probability is re-presented as a theory of consistent betting (thus De Finetti). Mathematics is re-characterized in terms of consistent methods and systems (thus Hilbert). And so on. But *why,* as Wittgenstein and others finally asked[12], this enormous emphasis on consistency, which we can now plainly proceed beyond without losing control or losing our way? The case against ***RL*** too parallels that against ***EL.*** Rationalism too can be divided into types: conceptual rationalism, long ago heavily criticized by Reid, and judgemental rationalism, substantially demolished with the advent of paraconsistent logical theory.[13]

To illustrate how consistency bounds can be stepped beyond, consider an instructive argument that van Fraassen has advanced, purportedly for anti-realism, but more transparently for limits to language: to the effect that there can be no complete correct description of the world, no such adequate representation, or put differently, no adequate linguistic theory corresponding to the world.

> Suppose for a moment that there exists, or comes into being in the historical fulness of time, a language **L** so rich that every proposition is expressed by some sentence of **L**. Now draw a rectangle, and consider the proposition—call it *Pandora*—that no sentence of **L** ever written in the rectangle expresses a true proposition. Choose the sentence of **L** which expresses Pandora, and write it in the rectangle. Clearly it expresses a true proposition if and only if it does not. This thought experiment is one which, if you begin to execute it, leads you to the conclusion that you cannot execute it. It is certain that either the proposition Pandora, or the language **L**, does not exist. But if **L** existed, there would be nothing wrong with the described proposition. So the language **L** cannot exist. And therefore our natural language cannot be, and cannot become, like **L** (p.214).

Now, in defiance of van Fraassen, let us execute the experiment:

THE RECTANGLE

NO SENTENCE OF L (EVER) WRITTEN IN THE RECTANGLE EXPRESSES A TRUE PROPOSITION

The intended outcome is supposed to be:

Pandora is true iff *Pandora* is not true,

whence *Pandora* is true and *Pandora* is not true (given further rule Reductio and Simplification). Thus execution, which is entirely feasible, produces *none* of van Fraassen's certainties. Rather what it shows is firstly that *Pandora* is an inconsistent but true proposition, and hence no doubt both unusual and anathema to mainstream logic; and further that L is a language capable of representing such unusual propositions. But so are natural languages, the resources of which we have not really exceeded. In short, then, in a dialethic setting van Fraassen's contentions and further argument fall to the ground.

Without consistency imposed, there are no such limits to language. Rather similarly, an otherwise impressive array of restrictive and limitative results', generated by clever contradiction-avoiding variations of self-referential paradox, is neutralized.[14]

Such dialethism does not eliminate all resistance, and make things all too easy to access or establish. To the contrary, proofs (within relevant theory) often become much harder, severe restraints remain. However that does not imply that there are places that are rationally inaccessible, that reason cannot travel or illuminate. Compare exploring underground or through underwater caverns. While it may be difficult to reach some places, there may be none (in a given system) that cannot be reached. Difficult of access does not imply inaccessible, nor does offering much resistance; conversely, accessible does not mean offering no resistance to access.

Even if expanded, by relaxing consistency demands (to an ahistoric 'paraconsistent rationalism'), rationalism would remain unsatisfactory. For inquiry is not constrained by a *single* methodology, such as rational methods. Rational methods on their own are inadequate as a route to main philosophical desiderata, such as truth, knowledge and understanding. To attain these, more than a much wider class of structures is needed; access to further methods, including generous empirical methods at least, is essential. More generally, there is no single universal method, such as rationalism and empiricism variously sought (such as Descartes and others expected and extolled). Rather there are various methods, some providing input of information, and others affording processing and revision of information.[15]

To so dispose of rationalism (in the fashion gestured at) is not to dispute the importance of reasoning in intellectual activities, nor even to contest the paramount place of logic, argument and reason in thought and philosophy, but only to contest rationalist restrictions. Reasoning is one major method not bounded by consistency, one among others. Such a qualified commitment to rational methods imposes of itself, furthermore, no limitations.

Joint forces of empiricism and rationalism were marshalled under logical empiricism, a powerful movement in the first half of the 20th century, which, coupled with a succession of striking theories (such as logical atomism, picture theory, verificationism, and so on) managed to impose severe limits upon philosophical inquiry. Or so it seemed, until one by one the striking supporting theories duly became unstuck, whereupon severe limits evaporated.

Limits correlate with restriction of methods and constraints imposed. With methods expanded (beyond narrower empiricist and rationalist confines) and with associated constructing theories decoupled, limits tend to disappear. As positive arguments below will help to demonstrate.

Several of the further limitations ascribed to philosophy result from assumption of certain ideological frameworks as absolute when they are not. An elementary example concerns the supposed limitations of philosophy arising from evident limits in its presumed methods.[16] For example, it is presumed that philosophy is confined to analytic methods, and, by contrast correctly, that analytic methods do not afford an adequate technique for treating some philosophical issues. However while analysis may have its limits, philosophy is not just analysis. Similarly for other noncomprehensive classes of methods (such as phenomenological methods).

More plausible is the widespread framework assumption of some sort of realism, which delivers objectivity and certain absolutes. In *Ethics and the Limits of Philosophy* Williams tells us that 'philosophy should not try to produce ethical theory' (p. 17), because ethical theory does not have the authority to 'give some compelling reason to accept one intuition rather than another' (p.99). Many, like Williams, have presumed that a successful ethical theory would conform to realism, delivering a unique, uniquely warranted objective ethical theory.[17] Without such a presumption, which collapses under a proper pluralism, imagined ethical limits dissolve (and therewith acclaimed, but minimally argued, 'limits to philosophy'). But while a unique justification may be lacking, justifications are not; some considerations and intuitions are better than others (as assessed from here and elsewhere), and so on.

5. Further negative arguments of the philosophers, and their typical ideological character

Wittgenstein can function as a bridge from logical empiricism, the prime recent source of limitations, to particular philosophical impositions. For the very severe limits that Wittgenstein arrived at in his *Tractatus* depend upon a drastic version of logical empiricism, where empirical and logico-mathematical statements are given very different treatment. Any other statement than these types, any statement which fails either to picture a fact or to express a tautology, is nonsense. Most statements of philosophy, those of ethics and metaphysics (including those of the *Tractatus),* fall into this extensive nonsense chasm. As is well known, Wittgenstein subsequently, for good reason, abandoned this rather bizarre sort of position, therewith collapsing celebrated limitations. It is less well appreciated that he endeavoured to extricate philosophy from standard. rationalist restrictions altogether. But he did not really succeed.

According to Wittgenstein, 'philosophy both must and cannot be conducted transcendentally' (so reports Lear p.383). From this incorrect and unfounded dialethic result, Wittgenstein tends to leap to many conclusions: for instance, in the *Tractatus* to the futility of (such) philosophy; he also regularly misrepresents inconsistency, obtained as reaching beyond the bounds of (consistent) language, with nonsense. Then he leaps from inconsistency to its dual, incompleteness: 'the philosopher' must 'curb the impulse to say something metaphysical', 'one cannot succeed in saying what one wishes to say' (L, p.383). By wrongly inverting inconsistency to incompleteness, limits are secured.

Most important, the whole progressive transference from inconsistency to nonsense to silence is an intricate muddle, one confusion after another. There are several sources for such confusions. One is that 'an "illogical" world is not, for us, a world at all', 'we would not *say* what an illogical world would look like' (L. p.384). But now, of course, with the advent of paraconsistent logics, we can describe and model such worlds.

Those limits later gave way to limits upon philosophy. Consider the supposed roots of Wittgenstein's later *doctrine of noninterference*

Philosophy may in no way interfere, either with the actual use of language, or with the world. That leaves everything as it is.[18] There is vagueness and ambiguity in the doctrine: ambiguity between a normative form, stating that philosophy should not interfere or is not permitted to interfere, and a more factual form, that it does not interfere and indeed cannot by virtue of its character. The normative form generates the picture of the nonrevisionary Wittgenstein as a reactionary; the more factual form induces the more sympathetic picture of Wittgenstein caught, like someone determined, in a difficult or impossible place by the hard facts of the matter. The supposed roots of the noninterference doctrine support a more factual construal: Philosophy is transcendental, transcending the empirical world, which is accordingly left as it is. The transcendental conception arises from seeing philosophy as predominantly metaphysical (which it is not). Wittgenstein's pessimism about the possibility of doing philosophy, and theme as to the futility of doing it, are again both premissed on this transcendental conception. Philosophy must be conducted transcendentally, yet it cannot be. But, firstly, much of philosophy is not transcendental in this way: much of ethics and political theory for example. And secondly, transcendental philosophy itself is not excluded; philosophy is not so limited.[19]

Many of the limits that philosophers have claimed to detect derive from prominent ideologies, and they simply disappear into these ideologies, or altogether with their demise. For example, in Russell the limits of knowledge vanish (explicitly, by the last chapter of *Human Knowledge: Its Scope and Limits)* into the limits of empiricism. Similarly the limits hinted at in Chwistek's *The Limits of Science* disappear into limits of classical logical empiricism. But the limitations of a limited ideology (if nonetheless one with ambitious pretensions) demonstrate nothing as to limitations of what is wider—thought, information, science, knowledge, and so on.

Elsewhere, in logical empiricists such as Russell, we find other, apparently very different, limits to what philosophy can do, and to philosophical knowledge advanced. Philosophy cannot provide 'knowledge concerning the universe as a whole'; it is vain to expect from philosophy 'reason to believe' such things as the fundamental dogmas of religion, the essential rationality of the universe, the illusoriness of matter, the unreality of all evil, and so on *(Problems* p.82). What philosophy cannot thus accomplish, according to Russell, is not so utterly remote from what Kant had sought to argue—only no room at all is left for faith or other methods to operate. Logical empiricists had surveyed methods·exhaustively, so they imagined (mostly they had just inherited a set of prejudices), and had duly excluded all but their approved methods. Accordingly, logical empiricists were particularly inclined to pronounce that philosophy could not address many of the so-called grand questions of philosophy, and indeed that many of them were meaningless (for instance, applying a verification principle, because no admitted methods could apply).

However the whole enterprise was seriously flawed, as a jubilant opposition (that has now unfortunately faded from professional philosophical view) quickly emphasized. For the general principles applied concerning methods fell outside the scope of admissible methods (as the verification method exceeds its own scope, for example). It seemed too that empiricists were somehow able to survey the universe as whole and gain information therefrom, for instance as to all methods, and on philosophical claims, especially of a religious cast. They had confirmed, or most of them had, that matter existed, and that *nothing* else does, no gods or other spirits, and so on. They had vastly exceeded their own admissible methods. Thus too there *were,* or *appeared* to be, other less restrictive methods.

The slightly more detailed argument that Russell himself advances for 'the limits of philosophical knowledge' in *The Problems of Philosophy* is patently unsatisfactory for different reasons. The central argument consists, firstly, in faulting Hegel's argument purporting to prove 'that the universe as a whole forms a single harmonious system' (p.84). Let us concede, for the present, that Russell has succeeded in this, that the particular holistic construction of a particular philosophy fails irreparably. But Russell proceeds at once to generalize:

> And if we cannot prove this, we also cannot prove the unreality of space and

> time and matter and evil, for this is deduced by Hegel from the fragmentary and relational character of these things. Thus we are left to the piecemeal investigation of the world .... (p.84)

This last inference is plainly a nonsequitur: Russell has leapt to his own favoured conclusion—which he thereupon pronounces as a general result, and proceeds to back up on the basis of scientific philosophy. However the most that the failure of Hegel's argument shows is the failure of *Hegel's* way of trying to establish grand themes, not the general failure of such attempts, which might proceed by quite different methods and routes.

Many of the historic arguments *for* no boundaries, no limits, to this or that, are also defective. While they may look as if they aid the present cause, they are not endorsed; they would prove too much, and induce trouble elsewhere. Such are the arguments that cosmos is unbounded, the universe is boundless, which are characteristically based on ontologically flawed arguments for no boundaries. These arguments take the following sort of elementary form: A boundary has items on both sides of it. Thus, if the universe had a boundary, there would have to be something on the far side of it. But, since the universe is comprehensive (of what exists), this is impossible.[20] Such arguments fall with rejection of Ontological Assumptions. For without such assumptions items on the far side of the boundary need not exist (for sense or truth to prevail). Accordingly the universe comprising what exists can stop at a boundary, which has nothing existent on the far side of it.

Arguments concerning the character of items bordering a boundary or limit have naturally figured large in arguments both for and against theoretical boundaries. Many of these arguments are however, like that just considered, vitiated through importing restrictive assumptions about what kinds of items can figure. Apart from existence, favoured restrictions are of a broadly consistency cast, including consistency itself, imaginability, conceivability, sense and sensibility. Such features have been heavily exploited, particularly by idealists and empiricists. But the arguments thereby projected fail, for similar reasons to those already considered. While that completes the present piecemeal negative case, it does also point towards a way of obtaining some greater generality:

namely exhausting considerations of a piece with those of existence and consistency.[21]

6. Advancing the positive cause

To arrive at positive-looking arguments for the no-limitation themes advanced, it helps to separate supposed *objectual* limitations (for instance, to what objects are available for thought) from *statemental* limitations. Such a division corresponds roughly to a distinction between first-order and zero-order logic, and better to the traditional distinction between concept empiricism and judgement empiricism (both forms of which are refuted in JB). Of course, in item-theory, the division lacks the sharpness that it is usually accredited, because statements are sorts of objects, if rather unindividualistic rather abstract ones.

Now a first argument builds on the theme that there are no items whatsoever beyond the reach of item-theory. That theory is subject to *no* limitations in what items it can investigate, by contrast with empiricism which is limited to those 'constructed' from experiential elements, and with rationalism which traditionally is bounded by rationality and consistency constraints. No matter how strange or remote an item, it will have some features (those of strangeness, remoteness, ineffability or whatever, as consequential among others), through which can be investigated, and thought about. It will follow that there are no limits to thought. For thought is about items and their composition, more items, to which there are no limits.

Even so there may appear to be some items that stand outside thought's comprehensions, and so defeat this item-theoretic argument, namely absurd items such as green numbers, virtuous shapes, and so on. Absurdity does not supply a bound. Pythagoras could think that virtue is triangular, and we can reflect on his assertion and his thought.[22]

Similarly for other absurdities. But strictly there are two feasible approaches: a lesser vehicle, according to which such material is not propositional, and so is ruled out as a proper object for thought; and a grander vehicle, taken here, according to which such material is accessible to thought and does exhibit sufficiently many propositional features (such as entailments, equivalent classes of sentences etc.) to be assigned residual content, open to intentional investigation.

An associated argument *from freedom of assumption* (due to Meinong) runs as follows: One is free to assume anything one likes, however ridiculous. Put differently, there are no limits upon assumption. Not consistency (as some ancients knew), not absurdity. Anything propositional or assertoric can be assumed. But what can be assumed can be reflected upon, thought about. In short, any limits to thought would be transmitted to limits to assumption. But there are no such limits; so there are no limits to thought either. Presumably the critical transmission principle, from assumption to thought, can be defended through (what has been side-stepped) some further analysis of thought, which includes making assumptions and mulling and ruminating upon them.

A major argument to no limitations of statemental form takes this form: Limitation statements normally transform to conditional impossibility assertions. Then it is enough to emphasize the conditions. In the remaining exceptional cases the isolated contradictions revealed can simply be assimilated, under dialethism. To begin upon detailed elaboration: types of limits partially correlate with types of impossibility, logical limits with logical impossibility, physical limits with physical impossibility, practical with practical, and so on. Of course, as explained, not all impossibility yields something worth dignifying by the grander title of limitation; but certain important sorts do. It has become fashionable to highlight conspicious physical impossibilities in terms of limitations, statements concerning which can be converted back to impossibilities. The advent of famous limits in contemporary physics—the limiting velocity of light for genuine transport and communications, and of limit to simultaneous measurements in quantum theory—has encouraged the presentation of other parts of physics in terms of limitation results, of what were closely connected impossibility claims as limitation results. All these results can be transformed into physical impossibility claims. For example, the limited velocity result becomes the physical impossibility of non-virtual velocities in excess of the speed of light. But such physical impossibility amounts, in effect, to a conditional impossibility, namely, *in* relativity physics and its situations, it is impossible that non-virtual velocities exceed that of light. Hardly necessary to add, such relative or conditional impossibilities constitute no limits to thought or to philosophy. It is easy to think nonrelativistically, classically, or in terms of grander velocities. The point can be generalized, drawing on the primary sense of limit. A limit is a 'bound that may not or cannot be passed'; a physical limit is one that cannot physically be exceeded (the 'may not' is to accommodate deontic-type cases). So a physical limit is a bound that, relative to physical theory, cannot be exceeded. To pass it intellectually it is enough to change theory, or to access a different world.

Practical limits go the way of physical limits. The linkage of such limitations with impossibility is of course familiar. Certain general statements of impossibility as to what agents can achieve are taken to present limitations. Conversely, a practical limitation characteristically states a practical impossibility, a general inability, something agents cannot do, normally presentable in terms of some sort of bound that cannot be passed. The same moves already applied in the case of physical limits, apply also with practical limits. None of these limits need impede or block thought or philosophy.

A tougher case again invokes logic. Many of the harder limits are logical limits, or limits arising out of matters intimately tied with logic, such as reasoning, reasoning ability, computability, formalism.... Related limitations concern omnipotence, omniscience, and so on; these touch even the gods. As regards all these matters, there are many impossibility results, which once again may naturally issue in limitation propositions. While the extent and severity of such propositions have been much exaggerated, many such propositions, of major importance, there no doubt are.[23]

Thus, it is not claimed that everything is possible.[24] What is contended, instead, is that it is possible to think past, inquire past, and philosophize past what is possible, to what is impossible. After all, the principal themes concern not no limitations whatsoever, but no limitations to specific abstract investigations and processes: namely, regarding thought, inquiry, philosophy.

The groundwork has already been done, and basic theory supplied, for belief and conception, assumption and thought.[25] Nothing excludes conceiving or believing, reasoning and thinking about, what is impossible or paradoxical. There are no objects of any sort, propositional, attributive, or whatever, beyond the reach of thought.

The bounds and barriers that have been proposed are accordingly no bounds. Consider expression and expressibility. No doubt there are limits to what can be expressed, due to physical constraints. But these do not constrain thought. While not all propositions can be expressed, all can be thought about, conclusions derived about all (as now: all can be thought about), and so on. For similar reasons, effability is no bound upon thought, which does not need to be uttered or expressed. What is ineffable, though perhaps excluded from further investigation by terrestrial authorities, can in principle be thought about, its features, as far as they are revealed, can be probed, analysed, and so on.

Apparently too, trickier issues like that of comprehension can be bypassed. For what is thought about may include topics that are not fully comprehended. A theme of no limits upon thought is compatible with pockets of topics beyond comprehension. For all we know, though there is little impressive evidence in this direction, there may be some restrictions upon what terrestrially evolved creatures can comprehend. This would happen because the level of complexity of a topic exceeds the complexity such creatures are capable of processing. But what that shows, far from limits, is that to process such complexity more complex creatures are required. Bounds to intellectual reach do not loom—without further different considerations, such as further exploitation of philosophical paradoxes.

Intertwined with limits are inaccessible topics and objects, which are somehow beyond human, creature or even intellectual reach. Among putative examples are the Absolute, the Alle, the Unthinkable, God on some accounts, Infinity formerly, inaccessible numbers, noumena.... Many of those objects are inaccessible by say-so only, often the say-so of high authorities or exalted personages, so notice is taken, but inaccessibility is not ensured (some however, like so-called inaccessible numbers or sets are 'inaccessible' only by virtue of misleading choice of terminology).

More important, with the development of dialethic object theory, and penetration into features and idiosyncracies of radically inconsistent and incomplete items, mysteries surrounding such 'inaccessible' objects will dissipate, as those concerning Infinity did with the advent of theories of transfinite sets.[26] The Unthinkable, for example, is a radically vague object (as virtually no features are anywhere specified), which is inconsistent if the object is, as it presents itself, unthinkable. For we are already theorizing and thinking about it, so it is in fact thinkable, for all that it presents itself as not.

More generally, it would seem, nothing is unthinkable. For suppose that something were. Then it has been thought of (insofar as supposed). Then apply *reductio,* to yield that the arbitrary something is thinkable after all. The neat argument is reminiscent of Berkeley's 'master argument' (presumed to tell against realism) that nothing is inconceivable. That argument, which mixes up both conceiving and thinking of, and conceiving and conceivability, fails in its intended idealist purpose.[27] But suppose that (some) arguments of this genre succeeded: Would they reveal some limit to thought? The very contrary looks to be the fact of the matter; it *removes* an alleged 'boundary between thought and the [equivocal] thought-independent world', a boundary taken to 'provide one of the limits of thought'.

The neat argument closely resembles an argument extracted from Hegel, that there are no limits to thought.[28] Suppose there were a limit to thought. Then there is a barrier and another side, of which there is some conception. So, in a sense, what is beyond the barrier can be thought of; it is accessible by thought. Therefore, by *reductio*, there is no limit. Naturally however, there is further ado concerning this neat argument. Firstly there is an issue (here footnoted) as to the adequacy of the *reductio* argument.[29] Secondly, there is the substantive question whether such limited conceptions of what lies beyond 'the barrier', perhaps unthinkables and the like, amount to requisite thought. But further reflection, like that outlined above, suggests that here is little restriction (object-theoretic-wise) at all upon information so accessed, and no genuine barrier to access.

As the pithy tale of the Unthinkable suggests, best prospects for absolute limits perhaps lie with, what have long fascinated human thinkers, intensional paradoxes. In the first place, analogues of familiar paradoxes concerning proof, knowledge, and similar, do not appear to intricate thought (even if they were to, it might not matter, as dialethic considerations reveal). Simplest versions of these puzzles, for some functor Y, consider some statement p that asserts of itself that it is not Y, not known, not true, etc. That is,~YP.

For puzzles to emerge further conditions are however required, typically a certain authenticity (what is known, proved, etc., is thereby true or right) and invariably consistency. *Thought does not conform to such requirements.*[30] That is what makes it so promising for no-limitation purposes. But, in the second place, there are self-referential thoughts inducing paradoxical situations. Often these operate indirectly, perhaps contingently, through a chain of circumstances, and in combination with other notions. Simpler cases consider situations like that of the person in fact in room 27, who is thinking only that nothing [nothing true, on a Liar paradoxical up-grade] is being thought in room 27.[31] That is merely another situation in which a person has, so it turns out in fact, inconsistent thoughts (namely, that thinking is not happening in room 27, when in fact thinking, just that, is happening in room 27)—a quite commonplace occurrence. Insofar as *any* among these sorts of occurrence impose any restraints that it would be worth signifying by the title of 'limitation', they yield limitations *on consistent thought,* not on thought.

7. Beyond thought, to inquiry and philosophy

What holds for thought also holds, in a similar way, for intellectual inquiry in general, and for philosophy within that. The detailed arguments proceed along somewhat similar lines to those for thought. But short-cut arguments, appealing to the critical role of thought within inquiry, can take advantage of the results attained for thought. Whence again, there are no limits.

Nonetheless the short arguments are too short. Fuller argument for inquiry looks to features of inquiry, in general, and more specifically to its logical and structural features. Broadly, inquiry takes the logical form of generalized dialogue, what has elsewhere been called polylogue.[32] At any given stage, an on-going inquiry can, like a Socratic dialogue, be seen as an opening branching tree at nodes of which thoughts or contents cluster, with some of these under consideration or up for question.[33] Now there are limits neither upon how the branches branch, at least in the absence of censorial pruning, nor, by the previous inquiry, upon what thought or content is considered. In terms of a different (more causal and less easily technically up-graded) image, there are bounds neither upon where inquiry roams nor upon what, in its roaming, it focusses upon or considers. Conversely, if there were limits they would become manifest either in what could enter or be considered or where discussions wandered; but, by preceding investigations, no limitations need be expected in either case.

As regards philosophy, it is smart to avoid being bogged down in trying to give an account of what it, conceived very broadly, comprises; to skirt around that messy and controversial matter. Philosophy can be seen as free-ranging inquiry unrestricted to features of specific disciples. Accordingly it inherits features of inquiry, including its unlimited character. For ask where there would be limits to philosophical investigation: they would, as with inquiry, concern either what routes, trains of inquiry, could be pursued, or else what thought or propositions could be assembled at any stage. But as before there are no limitations upon either, upon branches or upon propositions at nodes.

Given that the main themes can be sustained, there are entertaining corollaries. Among them are interesting failures in all those varieties of philosophy which claim to ascertain limits. These include not only empiricism and its stock contrasts, but such newer Continental varieties as critical theory, in the very idea of which limits to thought are presumed.[34]

References

L. Chwistek, *The Limits of Science,* Kegan Paul, London, 1948.

L. Goddard and R. Routley, *The Logic of Significance and Context,* Scottish Academic Press, Edinburgh, 1973.

J. Lear, 'Leaving the world alone', *Journal of Philosophy* xxx (1982), 382-403, referred to as L.

C. Mortensen, 'Anything is Possible', *Erkenntnis* 30(1989) 319-337. Prior, 'On a family of paradoxes', *Notre Dame Journal of Formal Logic* 2 (1960), 16-32.

R. Penrose, *The Emperor's New Mind,* Cambridge University Press, Cambridge, 1991.

G. Priest, *in Contradiction,* Nihoff, Holland, 1987.

G. Priest and others (eds.), *Paraconsistent Logic,* Philosophia Verlag, Munich, 1987; referred to as PL.

G. Priest, 'The limits of thought-and beyond', *Mind 100* (1991), 361-370.

T. Regan, *All that Dwell Therein,* University of California Press, Berkeley, 1982.

S. Rosen, *Limits of analysis,* Basic Books, New York, 1980.

R. and V. Routley, 'The role of inconsistent and incomplete theories in the logic of belief', *Communication and Cognition* 8(1975), 185-235.

R. Routley, 'Necessary limits to knowledge: unknowable truths', in *Essays in Scientific Philosophy* (ed. E. Morscher and others), Comes-Verlag, Munich; referred to as NL.

R. Routley, *Exploring Meinong's Jungle and Beyond,* RSSS, Australian National University, 1980; referred to as JB.

B. Russell, *The Problems of Philosophy,* Oxford University Press, Oxford, 1967.

B. Russell, *Human Knowledge: Its scope and limits,* G. Allen & Unwin, 1961.

R. Sylvan, 'Introducing polylogue theory', *Philosophica* 33(1985), 53-69.

R. Sylvan, 'Towards an improved cosmological synthesis', *Grazer Philosophische Studien* 25/6 (2986), 135-178.

R. Sylvan, 'Wide-ranging applications of relevant logic', typescript, Canberra, 1990; referred to as WR.

R. Sylvan, 'Grim tales retold', typescript, Canberra, 1992.

R. Sylvan, *Deep Pluralism,* University of Edinburgh Press, Edinburgh, 1994; referred to as DP.

B. van Fraassen, 'The world we speak of, and the language we live in', *Philosophy and Culture,* Proceedings of the XVIIth World Congress of Philosophy, Montreal, 1986, 213-221.

K. Wilber, *Eye to Eye,* Anchor Books, New York, 1983.

B. Williams, *Ethics and the Limits of Philosophy,* Fontana, London, 1985.

L. Wittgenstein, *Tractatus Logico-Philosophicus,* Routledge and Kegan Paul, London, 1933.

L. Wittgenstein, *Philosophical Investigations,* Blackwell, Oxford, 1953, referred to as PI.

L. Wittgenstein, *Remarks on the Foundations of Mathematics,* MacMillan, New York, 1964.

Notes

1. There are two basic cases of *l is limit of* S according as S is a sequence or given by a function; l may or may not belong to S. In the first, limit l is an element towards which members of S tend; in the second, with function f(x) the limit is the value f(x) approaches as x tends to a particular value. Both are nowadays given stock explications—of *tending* to or *approaching*—through E-D methods (though there are alternative explications through infinitesimals). For example, in English, the limit of a set is an item such that no matter how small a distance from it is chosen there is a member of the set closer to it.

2. This gives a reason too why God's omnipotence need not be compromised by impossible tasks (such as making a stone 'he' can't lift).

3. Since it is now appreciated that intensionality can be substantially accounted for model theoretically through relations between situations or worlds, with main relations those of accessibility, and since the constraining feature looks like one of *inaccessibility,* prospects are promising for a modelling of this constraint. At a first stab, N is constrained by l if there is some c in N* that is inaccessible (l-inaccessible) from N (or from arbitrary a in N). Not much has been done so far in intensional logic to exploit barriers and inaccessibility; there is evidently a fruitful field there.

4. For several examples, see WR a large sustained example, see Penrose, e.g. pp. 117, 417.

5. Unremarkably such different matters as quantity of philosophy produced, number of philosophers, and similar, may be significantly affected.

6. The idea gets its force from the presumption that the brain or central nervous system is some sort of carbon-based computing system and so basically computational in character. But the mind is (at most) some sort of function of this nervous system, and thought is part of the mind's activity. So thought too must be essentially computational. Something at least is rotten in these considerations; no doubt several things are. A large part of Penfold's quixotic quest is organized around these considerations. He starts by considering the (mistaken) theme that thought is algorithmic in chapter 1, but some hundreds of pages later scrambles to the view that conscious thought characteristically involves nonalgorithmic components (e.g., p. 413).

7. Fortunately, not merely because the case would become vexed if it had to

appeal to other than ordinary conceptions, but because satisfactory philosophical accounts are extraordinarily difficult to locate. Among philosophers thought is often conflated with consciousness (e.g. Descartes, Price). But a useful starting point for an account, which includes proper combinatorial components, is offered by Kant, who maintained that thought is cognition by means of concepts.

8. Finite limits can always be surpassed obviously, and transfinite limits can typically be surpassed with higher infinities. Priest, who prefers the surpassing-limits form to the no-limits discourse, appears to be working with the technical usage of limit.

9. See JB p.740 ff., on the failure of both concept empiricism and judgement empiricism.

10. That these important means are, like ruler and compass procedures, limited in what they can deliver, tells but little as to limitations to thought or to mathematics. Too much still hangs on what *other* means are available.

11. One might imagine it is dead, but such philosophical theories almost never die. Even today pure rationalism lives on, hangs on, in ethics; see e.g. work of Regan and the Carolina School (of which Regan is a leading member).

12. Others before Wittgenstein had asked this question but they were successfully rubbished or silenced (or conveniently died and were forgotten).

13. On the first and Reid see JB, on the second see PL.

14. See, e.g., PL and Sylvan 92.

15. A helpful model for this is afforded by the theory of change. For a detailed case against envisaged universal methods, see NL.

16. For substantial elaboration of this example, see Rosen.

17. Thus e.g. Commentators on Williams such as Gáte, and also a growing band of antirelativist ethical theorists.

18. PI 1.124.

19. For a working example, and detailed argument, see DP, chapter 11.

20. Although such arguments, dating from antiquity, having become very fashionable in the early modern period (see Priest 91 p.361), waned in popularity thereafter, variants of them persist in cosmology. For although smart non-Euclidean geometry was applied to defeat spatial boundaries, strong ontological and verificational assumptions are still invoked as regards time: to exclude, as meaningless, items before the initial Big Bang event. Without the assumptions there is nothing the matter with times before the Big Bang when nothing at all existed : see Sylvan 86.

21. Arguments like those to the boundlessness of the Universe have also been used to show that the Absolute has nothing outside it. The claim is that 'if there were anything outside the Absolute, that would immediately impose a limitation on It' (Wilber, pp. 294, 296).

Some greater generality, for there are still arguments coming from unexpected directions to field, such as the following with these premisses: Everything (every item) has a nature; but natures are always limited. The second premiss should be rejected, because of ultimate items such as greatest cardinal and greatest ordinal, God, etc.

22. For more on this topic and how absurd items and assertions can be accommodated within significance theory, see Goddard and Routley.

23. On the exaggeration, see again PL and Sylvan 92.

24. Contrary to Mortensen, whose arguments do not withstand detailed examination, except insofar as Mortensen has inadmissibly shifted the impossibility goal posts. But of course, were Mortensen right, no-limitation results would be easily obtainable, since what is possible is not rationally inaccessible.

25. For details see JB, PL and, esp. as regards belief, R. and V. Routley.

26. The general point is elaborated at the end of PL; also in Priest 87.

27. It fails because of the mix-up and because *reductio* does not succeed in the given setting. An argument like this is examined in some detail in Priest 91, from whom the following quotes are drawn; as to how the argument breaks down, see p.369 therein. Priest appears to be asserting, on p.362, that the argument *does* indicate limits to thought; but what it 'limits' is not thought but rather certain exaggerated independence claims of realism. For here two conflations play significant roles (pp.361-62), one between things and things which exist, and one between what is conceived and what is conceivable (in addition to the conflation of thought with conception). Roughly, it is enough for the 'conceptual realist' that there are things which exist which are not conceived (and are independent of thought in that respect), a theme which is untouched by 'conceptual idealism', according to which there are no items that are not conceivable.

There appear, furthermore, to be some interesting features of the argument that have escaped Priestâs formalization. One is an illicit each-all inference (without which the criticism of realism does not succeed). It may be, for instance, that each proposition can be selected, examined, etc.; it does not follow that all can. While each element of that totality, and others, is accessible, the whole may not be so accessed.

28. Both the passage from Hegel and that it contains an argument were drawn to my attention by Priest who had already made good use of the passage in his 91 article.

Observe that the argument concerns thought, products of thinking, not thinking as a process (with thinking N* goes awry, as David Sapir observed).

29. The *reductio* takes the form: suppose A; then»A; therefore»A, and will succeed if the *suppose-then* connection can be cast into a genuine implication. (Otherwise rejectable assumptions may have been suppressed.)

30. For one detailed development, see NL.

31. An example Prior struggles with, erroneously concluding that there is no thought rather than simply no consistent thought.

32. See Sylvan 85. A logic of inquiry is roughly an amalgamation of erotetic logic with a logic of discourse, what can be absorbed in polylogue theory.

33. Contents comprise a broadening of propositions to include nonstatemental forms, and so include assumptions, queries and so on. No limitation themes hold of course for content.

34. Thanks to Graham Priest for comments and helpful suggestions on an earlier version. The current version has benefited from presentation and discussion at the University of Witwatersrand.

The Action of the Subject towards the Outer World in Indian Realism

TOSHIHIRO WADA

Prof. Toshihiro Wada, Associate Professor, Department of Indian Philosophy, University of Nagoya, Japan, and one of the editors of *Sambhāṣā*, a journal of Indian Culture and Buddhism, Ph.D., Sanskrit, University of Poona. Dissertation : *The Concept of Invariable Concomitance in Navya-Nyāya*. Publications: book, *Invariable Concomitance in Navya-Nyāya,* 1990; 9 articles in various journals on Navya-Nyāya, in English; and 7 articles in Japanese on Nyāya and Indian realism.

Introduction

We can assume two fundamental attitudes towards the relation between cognition and the outer world as its object: naive realism and idealism. Naive realism is the standpoint that the outer world exists independently of cognition. The existence of the outer world precedes the occurrence of cognition of it and when cognition grasps it, it is designated as the object of cognition. Idealism, on the other hand, is the standpoint that cognition is more fundamental and that the outer world as the object of cognition does not exist independently of cognition.

There are two other standpoints to be taken into consideration when we apply the terms 'naive realism' and 'idealism' to an analysis of Indian philosophies. They are 'realism' and 'nominalism'. Realism maintains that universals carry objective reality, and nominalism denies the reality of universals. Though realism and nominalism are not necessarily concerned with conceptual realism and idealism respectively, in India the schools of realism vindicate conceptual realism and the schools of nominalism warrant idealism.

Let us designate the theory of naive realism plus realism as Indian realism and the theory of idealism plus nominalism as Indian nominalism. Thus 'Indian realism' means that not only the outer world but also universals exist independently of cognition while 'Indian nominalism' means that the outer world does not carry objective reality and that universals are a mental fabrication.

We can place the Nyāya, Vaiśeṣika, Bhaṭṭa Mīmāṁsā schools, Sarvāstivāda Buddhism, and so on in the category of Indian realism, and Advaita Vedanta, Mādhyamika and Yogācāra Buddhism, and so on in the category of Indian nominalism. We may assume that there is an intermediate position between Indian realism and nominalism such as Sautrāntika Buddhism, Sāṁkhya, and Viśiṣṭādvaita Vedanta schools. Sautrāntika Buddhism reduces the number of the dharmas which are constituents of the world and correspond to the universals in Indian realism in a sense. Thus Buddhism does not negate the reality of the outer world, but it maintains that the outer world cannot be perceived directly. When Sautrāntika scholars grasp the presentation which comes into existence in the mind, they say that they perceive the outer world. As long as they have this mental presentation (*ākāra*), they can infer the cause of such presentation. To this extent, the reality of the outer world is guaranteed, but this reality depends considerably upon mental presentation. This view paved the path to Yogācāra Buddhism, which argues that the outer world exists as the reflection of mental presentations. The theory of Sautrāntika on the dharmas or universals appears to be similar to Indian realism, but its theory of the outer world places it nearer to Indian nominalism.

It may also be possible to classify Sāṁkhya as a philosophy that comes between Indian realism and nominalism. The twenty-five principles (*tattva*) are real, and hence the reality of the outer world cannot be negated. The first, consciousness *(puruṣa)*, is immaterial; the twenty-four other principles of which the phenomenal world consists can be reduced to materiality (*prakṛti)*. The outer world appears from materiality through some principles, and the cause-effect relationship functions between materiality and other principles. Sāṁkhya conceives that effect is one mode of cause, and that in this sense the reality of the principles as effect is weaker than the reality of the principles as cause. Sāṁkhya reductionism is a physical process and not a theoretical process. Thus in Sāṁkhya the reality of the outer world is not so firm as in Nyāya and Vaiśeṣika.

We can place Viśiṣṭādvaita Vedanta philosophy as standing in an intermediate position, as well. This philosophy argues for the reality of the outer world, but it does so as long as the reality of Brahman guarantees the reality of the outer world. Viśiṣṭādvaita Vedanta does not accept the reality of the outer world to such an extent that Indian realistic schools do.

The above-mentioned two axes of Indian realism and nominalism hold good to a great extent, when we look into the fundamental attitudes of Indian philosophies towards philosophical issues. We can find realistic views in both Hindu and Buddhist schools, and also nominalistic views in both. It was quite natural for Hindu realistic schools such as Nyāya and Vaiśeṣika to furiously dispute with Buddhist nominalism. We can place realism on the left end of the scale, and nominalism on its right end. As the distance between those two views on the same scale widens, the dispute between them becomes more furious. The difference between Hinduism and Buddhism is another cause for the fury of their disputes.

In this paper I would like to point out that what Indian realism such as Nyāya and Vaiśeṣika represents is not pure realism, and that it adopts a nominalistic theory in some aspect of ontology. Vaiśeṣika seems successful in applying a nominalistic theory to the origination of cognition-dependent qualities (*guṇa*) such as number (*saṁkhyā*), remoteness (*paratva*) and proximity *(aparatva)*. I am going to make clear how Vaiśeṣika integrates the nominalistic explanation of the origination of those qualities into its realism. However, I would like to point out that its integration is not complete without recognizing an essential function of cognition or the subject. This paper will also refer to the importance of such a function in order to explain how the existence of a self-linking relation *(svarūpa-sambandha)* is recognized, though this relation is not cognition-dependent according to Navya-nyāya.

Let me remind the readers again that whenever I hereafter employ the terms 'realism' and 'nominalism', I mean respectively Indian realism and Indian nominalism. The adjective forms of those terms similarly preserve the specific meaning I have offered.

2. The origination of number as quality *(guṇa)* in Vaiśeṣika

It is quite natural that when some man looks at plural objects, for instance two trees, he may count two; but another man may not count two but one plus one. In this way different numbers may be counted by different men even when the same number of objects are observed. If Vaiśeṣika adopts pure realism to explain the recognition of number in the above case, number two residing in those two trees through the relation of inherence *(samavāya)* must exist before that man counts two; then he perceives number two in those two trees. From this example, it can be deduced that one object always carries all numbers even when it is not counted by anyone. It is not easy to assume that one entity carries all numbers at any time, and it is no easy task to explain why we can choose a particular number such as two among all numbers residing in that one object.

To avoid these problems, one way may be to assume that number is originated by the subject. Then we need not assume that one entity always possesses all numbers objectively. Since the subject of a recognizer originates the number possessed by objects in question, this number is recognized only by him and not by others. Vaiśesika adopts this method of explanation for the recognition of number.

Let us take up the *Padārthadharmasaṁgraha* or *Praśasta-pādabhāṣya* in order to understand the Vaiśeṣika method of explanation. This text makes use of the visual perception of two objects to illustrate the method. The process of the origination and recognition of number two is accounted for as follows:

1) When a man recognizes two objects with his eyes, he has the cognition of oneness (*ekatvasāmānya* or *ekatvatva*) inhering in number *one* (*ekatva*) which inheres in each object. Here oneness is a universal *(sāmānya* or *jāti*) which exists in number *one* through the relation of inherence (*samavāya*). Number *one* is a quality in the Vaiśeṣika system and is regarded as an individual (*vyakti*) like a substance (*dravya*) and action *(karman)*. To give an example, number *one* residing in one person differs from number *one* residing in another person. In this sense it is possible to use a plural form of the expression of each number, for instance number *ones*, number *twos*, number *threes*, and so forth.

2) Due to three factors, i.e. oneness, the relation of oneness with

number one, and the cognition of oneness, a person generates the cognition of two number *ones* with regard to the two objects.

3) Depending upon this cognition, number *two* is generated by those two number *ones* residing in each object.

4) The recognizer grasps twoness *(dvitvasāmānya* or *dvitvatva)* inhering in number *two* which has been generated in the two objects. At the same time the cognition of number *two*, qualified by twoness is about to occur to the recognizer.

5) The recognizer possesses the cognition of number *two*, and at the same time the cognition of twoness is about to disappear. And due to three factors, i.e., number *two*, the relation of number *two* with the two objects, and the cognition of number *two*, the cognition that there are two objects is about to present itself.

6) The cognition that there are two objects is generated. At the same time the cognition of twoness disappears.

Vaiśeṣika realism maintains that the existence of the outer world as an object of cognition precedes the occurrence of its cognition, and in the above process the origination of number *two* certainly precedes the generation of the cognition of number *two*. Hence, that process seems to conform to Vaiśeṣika realism.

However, step 3 in the above process shows that the number *two* simultaneously existing in the two objects is produced by two number *ones* existing in each object, but that there is another factor that produces number *two*. The cognition of two number *ones* also plays a role of the cause of number *two*. Unless this cognition functions as a cause, we do not understand why two number ones are collected or grasped simultaneously and the loci of two number *ones* are counted two. One cannot answer this problem by saying that there are only two objects in front of the recognizer. As a matter of fact, we can count *one, two, three, four,* and so on even when there are one hundred objects. Therefore, it holds good to say that cognition plays an important role in grasping number or determining at what number the recognizer stops counting.

Unlike the *Padārthadharmasaṁgraha* we cannot argue for the simple importance of the cognition of plural ones in order to explain why counting becomes possible. Suppose a man sees a heap of one hundred coins. Looking at this heap of coins, he can count to one hundred. It is natural that he cannot reach the number of one hundred because he can count only the coins which he can perceive with his eyes. Even if he sees ten coins of the heap, he may stop counting at number *five*. In this case also, he perceives ten number *ones* which respectively exist in those ten coins. But he counts five not ten. If the cognition of plural number *ones* functions as a genuine cause, the above case must make him count only ten. Hence it does not seem that the cognition of number *ones* directly generates the cognition of a plural number.

In Vaiśeṣika, cognition has the passive function of accepting something in the outer world as its object. However, the action of counting cannot be explained only by such a kind of passive function. Vaiśeṣika sometimes compares cognition or knowledge to a mirror and holds that cognition has no mental presentation (*ākāra*). In the process of the occurrence and recognition of number *two*, the *Padārthadharma-saṁgraha* states that the cognition of two number *ones* and those two number *ones* generate number *two*. Thus this text acknowledges some active function to cognition, i.e., *apekṣā buddhi*, to illustrate the occurrence of number *two*. However, as long as Vaiśeṣika does not argue that the active function of determining grouping or choosing objects is ascribed to cognition, it does not fully succeed in explaining how the action of counting becomes possible.

Vaiśeṣika maintains realism in all its arguments on philosophical issues. But in the case of cognition-dependent qualities, it holds that cognition generates such qualities in the outer world. This is nothing but idealism. If Vaiśeṣika does not proceed to make further elucidation, its philosophical standpoint will contain contradiction. To reconcile the two opposite standpoints of realism and nominalism, Vaiśeṣika argues that another cognition grasps those qualities which have been generated by the previous cognition. This Vaiśeṣika attempt of reconciliation appears successful. However, as long as cognition has no active function in grouping or choosing objects, Vaiśeṣika fails to elucidate the process of recognizing number. If Vaiśeṣika contends that cognition has no such function, the subject or soul *(ātman)* must carry this function.

3. Self-linking Relation (*svarūpa-sambandha*) and Cognition-dependent Object in Navya-Nyāya

Cognition-dependent properties such as number, remoteness, proximity and so on are included only in the list of qualities (*guṇa*). It seems possible to mention more properties apart from those qualities in the later Nyāya Vaiśeṣika system, viz., Navya-nyāya. However, since Navya-nyāya scholars adhere to the realistic standpoint, they do not say that cognition generates properties in a nominalistic way. Here taking up the self-linking relation *(svarūpa-sambandha),* I would like to point out that this relation is also cognition-dependent, and that the same conclusion can be drawn as in the case of number.

To understand the concept of self-linking relation, let us first see that relation in Navya-nyāya. There are four kinds of relation: contact *(saṁyoga),* inherence (*samavāya*), self-linking (*svarūpa*) and identity (*tādātmya*). (1) The relation of contact is the physical connection between two substances which exist separately. For instance, when there is a pot on the ground, the pot exists on the ground through contact. (2) The relation of inherence lies between two entities which cannot exist separately. For instance, when there is a blue pot, blue colour exists in the pot through inherence. (3) Self-linking relation is that which is regarded as identical with one of its relata *(sambandhin).* To give an example, when there is a pot, this pot is considered to exist in time because the pot is retained for a certain period. Here Navya-nyāya regards the relation between the pot and time as time itself. (4) Identity regarded as relation is also difficult to understand, like self-linking relation, but scrutiny on this relation is beyond the scope of this paper.

Navya-nyāya does not accept relation as an independent category, and maintains that all relation can be reduced to elements each of which belongs to one of seven categories: substance (*dravya*), action (*karman*), quality (*guṇa*), universal *(sāmānya* or *jāti*), particular (*viśeṣa*), inherence (*samavāya*) and absence (*abhāva*). As mentioned above, a self-linking relation is nothing but one of two relata which are connected by that self-linking relation. In other words, there is not a third entity between those two relata, but either of them connects itself to the other. Though self-linking relation is designated as relation, it is in reality an entity or property.

In accordance with this, Navya-nyāya can consider any entity a relation. Suppose there are two pots, *A* and *B*, on the table. Strictly speaking, the relation between those two pots consists of three parts: (1) the contact between pot *A* and the table, (2) the table itself (a substance), and (3) the contact between the table and pot *B*. In this case also, Navya-nyāya scholars would simply say that the relation between *A* and *B* is the table. They even name something concrete *relation*, although we do not call such a thing *relation*. We think that relation is something abstract which connects more than one thing.

Navya-nyāya classifies substratumness or containerness (*ādhāratā*) and superstratumness or containedness (*ādheyatā*) as self-linking relations. This means that substratumness and superstratumness can be regarded as identical with either the substratum (*ādhāra*) or the superstratum (*ādheya*). On the other hand, substratumness is necessarily a property which exists in the substratum and not in the superstratum, and superstratumness is likewise a property which resides in the superstratum and not in the substratum. Hence, one can question if substratumness is identical with the substratum in an ontological sense, but not if substratumness is identical with the superstratum.

According to Jayarāma Nyāyapañcānana who flourished in the first half of the seventeenth century, substratumness cannot be reduced to the substratum nor to some particular relation such as contact or inherence. The former claim of Jayarāma presupposes the characteristic of self-linking relation: the ontological status of this relation can be reduced to either relatum of the relation. The latter claim may require more comment. Suppose there is a book on the table. The book is the superstratum *(ādheya)* of the table, and the table is the substratum (*ādhāra*) of the book. The table possesses not only the substratumness to the book but also the contact with the book. Some Navya-nyāya scholars equate the substratumness to the book with the 'contact with the book'. Jayarāma asserts that their equation of those two entities does not hold good, and finally that substratumness is an independent category. In a similar way, Navya-nyāya scholars give independence to many properties such as counterpositiveness *(pratiyogitā),* objectness (*viṣayatā*), and so on, so that their list of categories becomes long. This means that they cannot develop their ontology within the system of the fixed number, viz. seven, of categories, and that they cannot help discarding a 'closed' system and adopting an 'open' system. Since I do not aim to discuss the number of the categories in Navya-nyāya, I will proceed to the discussion of a specific characteristic of substratumness.

If in the case of the cognition of substratumness Navya-nyāya holds a realistic position, substratumness exists before its cognition is generated. Furthermore, if substratumness exists independently of cognition, all entities in the universe must carry this property. This is because at any time we can perceive that there is something *A* on another thing *B*, and there is *B* on *C*. To put it in another way, *B* has substratumness with reference to *A* and *C* has substratumness with reference to *B*. In these cases, the substratumness possessed by *B* demands the existence of *A*, and likewise the substratumness possessed by *C* demands the existence of *B*. Since substratumness cannot subsist by itself, it is difficult to assume that all entities in the universe always possess this property. Accordingly we cannot help conceiving that only when one perceives that there is *A* on *B*, substratumness occurs in *B*. From this it follows that substratumness depends upon cognition to subsist.

One may object that substratumness does not depend upon cognition. Suppose a man looks at a pot on the table. According to Navya-nyāya, he perceives the substratumness in the table and the superstratumness in the pot. Even if he closes his eyes, the above fact does not change. In other words, even if he does not watch the pot and the table, they do not exchange their positions with each other. From this example, one may conclude that substratumness is an objective property like universals such as potness, cowness, and so forth.

To argue that substratumness is dependent upon cognition, let us refer to the following example. Suppose a man stretches out his right hand with its palm facing upward, places his left hand on it with the palm facing downward, and slowly turns both hands counterclockwise. In the beginning stage of the turn of the hand the man certainly perceives that the left hand is put on the right hand. Then he will come to the stage in which he cannot clearly say that the left hand is on the right hand or that the right hand is on the left hand. After he passes this stage, he will again clearly say that the right hand is on the left hand.

If substratumness exists in all entities in the universe independently of cognition, the right hand which has come on the left hand must possess substratumness with reference to the left hand. But this is not true. If someone argues that substratumness had disappeared at the stage in which the man could not say which hand was on which hand, every perceiver of the turn of the hands must utter one and the same angle of the hands at which angle the perceiver had no answer to the question which hand is upper. We cannot expect such an answer of the same angle. No one can concern oneself with the occurrence of substratumness without taking some function of cognition into consideration.

To say that the origination of substratumness depends upon cognition demands acknowledgement of some active function of cognition. But cognition in Navya-nyāya like in Vaiśeṣika has no active function through which a new object of cognition is created in the outer world except in the case of number, remoteness, proximity, etc. To explain the origination of substratumness, Navya-nyāya must presuppose some active function in cognition. Otherwise soul as the subject must possess this function.

4. Concluding Remarks

Vaiśeṣika realism contends that the cognition of number must presuppose the origination of number as quality in objects. Furthermore, in Vaiśeṣika, number is generated by cognition. However Vaiśeṣika keeps silent about how cognition originates number, in other words, how cognition chooses and groups plural number *ones* residing in plural objects. Neither does it explain why cognition possesses this capability of choosing and grouping. As long as Vaiśeṣika adopts a realistic standpoint, these problems are left unsolved.

In the case of self-linking relation, Navya-nyāya realism also faces similar problems. We have seen that it is almost impossible to elucidate the occurrence of substratumness without assuming the function of cognition. In the modern terminology we can use subject in place of the term cognition. To accept the function of cognition or the subject means to take a nominalistic standpoint. This contradicts the fundamental attitude of Navya-nyāya towards the outer world. Presumably Navya-nyāya scholars will say the same thing that Vaiśeṣika says about the origination of number, and they adopt realism for the whole system of

Navya-nyāya and integrate a nominalistic view into their realistic system.

We have seen that Vaiśeṣika and Navya-nyāya, which are placed in the centre of realistic schools of Indian philosophy, maintain nominalistic views in some cases. Similarly, Buddhist schools, such as Yogācāra, which are placed in the centre of the nominalists' group will hold realistic views to a certain extent in order to explain the structure of the outer world and human action therein. In this sense, we cannot find a school of 'pure realism' or 'pure nominalism' in India.

To understand the philosophical characteristics of various schools in India, we must accept the axes of 'Indian realism' and 'Indian nominalism'. However, if we adhere to these two axes too rigidly, we will fall into a misapprehension that a realistic school completely excludes nominalistic views and a nominalistic school utterly rejects realistic views. This misapprehension would certainly prevent our proper understanding of Indian philosophy.

APPENDIX

A Translation of the *Ādhāratāvāda* Chapter of Jayarāma's *Padārthamālā*

Substratumness is not [an independent category] either, because [we have] no proof [for this]. One should not argue: the meaning of the locative case-ending is substratumness in the case of *'kuṇḍe badaram'* [there is a jujube fruit in the vessel] and so forth, for [substratumness] would occur [in the jujube fruit] in the cases of *'badare kuṇḍam'* [there is the vessel in the jujube fruit] and so forth in the condition of only contact being the meaning of that [case-ending].This is because substratumness in the form of each substratum is nothing but substratumness [in question]. The reason for this is as follows: [we can have] the cognition that the substratum of the jujube fruit is nothing but the vessel itself and that [the substratum] of the vessel is not the jujube fruit itself. That is why [we can have] no valid cognition that the qualified highest universal exists even in the possessor of inherence of the highest universal because the substratumness to the qualified universal is absent from a quality, etc. One should not argue: there would be no cognition that there exists the substratumness of the jujube fruit with reference to the vessel because substratumness which does not differ from the vessel itself is absent from the vessel, and otherwise there would also arise [the cognition] that there is the vessel in the [same] vessel. This is because even the vessel which is nothing but substratumness can occur in the vessel. The reason for this is that [we can have] the cognition that the vessel, exactly [as the opponent has stated] exists in the same vessel.

Or substratumness with reference to the jujube fruit etc. would be nothing but the contact etc. qualified by the state of possessing the vessel etc. as the counterrelatum [of the contact]. [Therefore, it is not true that substratumness exists] in a quality, etc., due to inherence qualified by the state of being described by the highest universal qualified by the differences from a quality, etc. Or substratumness with reference to that [substanceness] is nothing but inherence of substanceness, etc. This is because to postulate the manifoldness of that [inherence] is logically simpler than to postulate substratumness as an independent [category]. That is why clothness etc. cannot be perceived since [the object (clothness) of this perception would possess] inherence in a pot, etc, is connected with the eyes.

Navya-nyāya scholars, on the other hand, say the following. Because it is cumbersome to accept that [substratumness is identical with] the substratum itself and because [substratumness to the jujube fruit] does differ from the contact qualified [by the state of possessing the jujube fruit as the counterrelatum], substratumness is an independent category, but it differs according to the varieties of relation, etc. That is why one can have the cognition that there is no vessel in the jujube fruit even when [one possesses] the cognition whose epistemic qualifier with reference to the jujube fruit is the vessel due to only the contact whose counterrelatum is the vessel. This is because only cognition possessing the relation of the substratum [with the superstratum as its object] prevents [the generation of the cognition that there is the substratum (the vessel) in the superstratum (the jujube fruit)].*

---

* I wish to express my thanks to Professor Keiichi Miyamoto of Kokugakuin University, Tokyo, Professor Mark Siderits of Illinois State University and Professor Jayshankar Shaw of Victoria University of Wellington for their helpful critical comments on this paper.

Patañjali's Classical Yoga : An Epistemological Emphasis

IAN WHICHER

Dr Ian Whicher, currently Deputy Director of the Dharam Hinduja Institute of Indic Research in the Center for Advanced Religious and Theological Studies of the Faculty of Divinity at the University of Cambridge. Until recently, he was a Lecturer in Religious Studies at the University of Alberta in Edmonton, Canada, where he taught a wide range of courses in Hinduism and Buddhism and comparative and thematic courses in World Religions, such as Mysticism in East and West, and Identity and Selfhood. A specialist in Hinduism, his main area of expertise is in Yoga theory and practice. He has published papers on Yoga philosophy in various journals including the journal Asian Philosophy, published in U. K. His book, *A Study of Patañjali's Central Definition of Yoga : Disclosing the Integrity of the Yoga Darśana*, will soon be submitted for publication.

In this paper I challenge and attempt to correct conclusions about Classical Yoga philosophy drawn by traditional and modern interpretations of Patañjali's *Yoga-Sūtras*. My interpretation of Patañjali's Yoga—which focuses on the meaning of 'cessation' *(nirodha)* as given in Patañjali's central definition of Yoga *(YS* 1.2)—counters the radically dualistic and ontologically-oriented interpretations of Yoga presented by many scholars, and offers an open-ended, epistemologically-oriented hermeneutic which, I maintain, is more appropriate for arriving at a genuine assessment of Patañjali's system *(darśana)* of Yoga.

What is Yoga philosophy and how can it enrich our understanding of human nature? What is the relationship between knowledge, self-understanding, morality and spiritual emancipation in Yoga thought? As a response to these questions, my paper will explore, within the Hindu tradition, Patañjali's (ca third century C.E.) authoritative system *(darśana)* of Classical Yoga—a philosophical perspective which has, I submit, far too often been looked upon as excessively spiritual to the point of being a world-denying philosophy indifferent to moral endeavour, neglecting the world of nature and culture, and overlooking human reality, vitality and creativity.

Contrary to the arguments presented by many scholars, which associate Yoga exclusively with extreme asceticism, mortification, denial and the renunciation and extrication of material existence *(prakṛti)* in favour of disembodied liberation—an elevated and isolated spiritual state *(puruṣa)*—I will argue that Patañjali's Yoga can be seen as a responsible engagement, in various ways, of spirit *(puruṣa* = Self, pure consciousness) and matter *(prakṛti* = mind, body, nature) resulting in a highly developed, transformed and participatory human nature and identity, an integrated and embodied state of' liberated selfhood *(jīvanmukti)*. In support of the above thesis, textual evidence has been drawn from the two main authoritative sources of Classical Yoga: the *Yoga-Sūtras (YS)* of Patañjali and the *Vyāsa-Bhāṣya (VB)* of Vyāsa (ca 500-600 C.E.).[1]

Cessation (*Nirodha*) : Transformation or Negation of the Mind ?

In Patañjali's central definition of Yoga, Yoga is defined as 'the cessation of [the misidentification with] the modifications (*vṛtti*) of the mind *(citta)*' *(YS* 1.2, p. 4).[2] *Nirodha* ('cessation') is one of the most difficult terms employed in the *YS* and its meaning plays a crucial role for a proper comprehension of Patañjali's system of Yoga. The 'attainment' of liberation is based on the progressive purification of mind *(sattvaśuddhi)* and the increasing light of knowledge *(jñāna)* that takes place in the process of *nirodha*. Since, as I shall now argue, the misunderstanding of this process has been fundamental to the misapprehension of the meaning of Patañjali's Yoga, there is a need to clarify it.

The word '*nirodha*' is derived from *ni* : ('down, into') and *rudh:* 'to obstruct, arrest, stop, restrain, prevent' (Monier-Williams, 1899, p. 884). In some well-known translations of *YS 1.2, nirodha* has been rendered as 'suppression' (Aranya, 1963, p. 1; Dvivedi, 1930, p.2), 'inhibition' (Taimni, 1961, p. 6; Leggett, 1990, p.60), 'restriction' (Woods, 1914,

p. 8; Koelman, 1970, p. 237; Feuerstein, 1979, p. 26), 'cessation' (Larson, 1987, p. 28; Varenne, 1976, p. 87) and 'restraint' (Tola and Dragonetti, 1987, p. 5; Chapple, 1990, p. 33). These meanings, I submit, are highly problematic, erroneous or misleading if understood, as many scholars do, with a view which emphasizes *nirodha* as an ontological negation or dissolution of the mind and its functioning. I am suggesting that any attempt to interpret Patañjali's Yoga as a practice which seeks to annihilate or suppress the mind and its modifications for the purpose of gaining liberation grossly distorts the intended meaning of Yoga as defined by Patañjali. In regard to the process of *nirodha,* the wide range of methods in the *YS* indicates an emphasis on the ongoing application of yogic techniques, not a deadening of the mental faculties wherein the operations of consciousness, including our perceptual and ethical natures, are switched off. By defining *nirodha* as 'cessation,' I mean to imply the 'undoing' of the conjunction (*saṁyoga*) between *puruṣa,* the 'Seer' *(draṣṭṛ),* and *prakṛti,* the 'seeable' *(dṛśya),* the conjunction which Vyāsa explains as a mental superimposition *(adhyāropa, VB* 2.18, p. 84) resulting in the confusion of identity between *puruṣa* and the mental processes. Our intrinsic nature as *puruṣa* becomes *as if* misidentified with the mental processes *(vṛtti)* thereby creating, in the words of Vyāsa (*VB* 2.6, p. 96), 'a mental self out of delusion.' *Nirodha,* I am suggesting, refers to the cessation of the worldly, empirical effects of the *vṛttis* on the *yogin's* consciousness, not the complete cessation of *vṛttis* themselves. *Nirodha* means to cease the congenital, epistemological power of the *vṛttis* over the yogin, *i.e. nirodha* is the epistemological cessation of *vṛttis* in the form of the congenital ignorance *(avidyā, YS* 2.3-5) of our true spiritual identity and ultimate destiny.

One will naturally ask how practitioners who attempt to obey any teachings resulting in death to their minds would have the capacity to comprehend or carry out any further instructions. Perhaps, more importantly, how could one function practically as a human being without the faculties of thinking, memory, discrimination and reason, and an individual I-sense with which one can distinguish oneself from other people and the world? Surely such a person would have to be mad or unconscious. If all the great Yoga masters of the past had obliterated or so thoroughly suppressed their minds in order to become liberated, how did they speak, teach, reason, remember, empathize, or even use the word 'I'? The mind and the body are the only vehicles in which to attain liberation. It is the mind, as Yoga readily admits, that must be utilized to study and listen to the guru; it is the mind that is needed to follow a spiritual path to liberation; and it is equally the mind that is required by the aspirant in order to function as a human being in day-to-day life.

By advising or explaining that the mind and its various faculties are to be negated, suppressed or abolished, many scholars, teachers and writers on Yoga have, I maintain, missed the point of practising Yoga. For it is not the *mind,* but rather the exclusive identification with material existence as one's true Self which is the source of all human difficulties and dissatisfaction *(duḥkha);* it is a specific state of consciousness or cognitive error evidenced in the mind and not the mind *itself,* which is at issue. Misidentification refers to the process wherein our self-identity conforms *(svārūpya, YS* 1.4, p.7) to the changing nature of *vṛtti. Avidyā*—the root affliction *(kleśa)* in Yoga which gives rise to four other afflictions (*YS* 2.3-9, pp. 59-65): I-am-ness/egoity *(asmitā),* attachment (*rāga*), aversion *(dveṣa)* and the desire for continuity or fear of death *(abhiniveśa)*—is a positive misconstruction of reality which mistakes *puruṣa* for *prākṛtik* existence. It is the condition of misidentification—the *sāṁsārik* condition of self and world—and not the mind in total which must be eradicated in Yoga. Any advice to destroy the mind is, it seems to me, detrimental to a human being and to the practice of Yoga. How could progress on the path of Yoga be made with such an approach? What would the ethical ramifications be? The belief that mental annihilation leads to spiritual liberation has become a popular and unfortunate teaching of modern interpretations of Yoga. Despite the fact that it is neither truly yogic, practical, logical, nor appealing, and furthermore, may be destructive for aspirants, recent teachings and works on Yoga have often prescribed the negation or suppression of the mind, ego and thoughts as the primary means to self-emancipation.[3] This stance, I submit, is a gross misrepresentation of Yoga; a confused, misleading and, at best, naive attempt at conveying the depth and profundity of the practice termed by Patañjali—*nirodha.*

It is my contention that *nirodha* denotes an epistemological emphasis and refers to the transformation of self-understanding, not the ontological cessation of *prakṛti* (i.e. the mind and *vṛttis). Nirodha* thus is not, as some have explained, an inward movement that annihilates or suppresses *vṛttis* or thoughts, nor is it the non-existence or absence of *vṛtti;* rather, *nirodha* involves a progressive expansion of perception which eventually reveals our true identity as *puruṣa.* Elsewhere (Whicher, 1992) I have argued that *cittavṛtti* describes the very basis of all the empirical selves: under the influence of *avidyā* the unenlightened person's mental processes (*vṛtti*) both generate and are ineluctably driven by *(VB* 1.5, p. 10) deeply rooted impressions *(saṁskāras, YS*2.15, 4.9) and personality traits *(vāsanās, YS*4.8, 4.24) sustaining an afflicted I-sense *(asmitā)* Seen in the above context, *cittavṛtti* can be understood as a generic term standing for a misconceived knowledge *(viparyaya-jñāna, VB* 2.24, p. 95) or error which is structured in the network of our psychological makeup and veils our identity as *puruṣa.* The epistemic distortion or erroneous knowledge *(mithyā jñāna, YS* 1.8, p. 12) functioning as the *vṛtti* of *viparyaya* acts as the basis for all misidentification with *vṛttis* in the unenlightened mode *(vyutthāna, YS* 3.9) of perception and 'being.' In short, our afflicted identity rooted in spiritual ignorance functions through *viparyaya.* Oddly enough, this fundamental insight, which can be attributed to Vyāsa (*VB* 1.8, p. 13), has not been clearly noted by scholars. I have attempted to clarify Vyāsa's position and furthermore suggest that this insight into the nature of *viparyaya* has profound implications for our understanding of Patañjali's whole system.

Accordingly, *cittavṛtti* does not stand for all cognitions or emotive processes in the mind but is the very seed *(bīja)* mechanism of *Puruṣa's* misidentification with *prakṛti* and from which all other *vṛttis* or thoughts arise and are appropriated in the unenlightened state of mind. Spiritual ignorance gives rise to a malfunctioning of *vṛtti* which in Yoga can be corrected thereby allowing for the 'right' functioning of *vṛtti* (Whicher, 1992). *Cittavṛtti* is an analogical understanding of consciousness in that the consciousness which has become the mind is analogous to *puruṣa's* consciousness.[4] It is the *cittavṛtti* as our confused and mistaken identity of *puruṣa,* not our *vṛttis,* thoughts and experiences in total which must be brought to a state of definitive cessation.

Aloneness (*Kaivalya*) and Integration

I would now like to contend that in Yoga the state of liberation or 'aloneness' *(kaivalya)* in no way destroys or negates the personality of the *yogin.* Rather, *kaivalya* can be seen as a state in which all the obstacles preventing an immanent and purified relationship or engagement of person and spirit *(puruṣa)* have been removed. The mind, which previously functioned under the sway of ignorance, colouring and blocking our perception of authentic identity, has now become purified and no longer operates as a locus of misidentification and dissatisfaction *(duḥkha). Sattva,* the finest quality *(guṇa)* of the mind, has the capacity to be perfectly lucid/transparent, like a dust-free mirror in which the light of *puruṣa is* clearly reflected and the discriminative discernment *(vivekakhyāti, YS* 2.26) between *puruṣa* and the mind can take place *(YS* 3.49). The crucial point to be made here is that *prakṛti* ceases to perform an obstructing role in *kaivalya.* The mind has been transformed, liberated from the egocentric world of attachment, its former afflicted nature abolished; and *puruṣa,* left alone, is never again confused with all the relational acts, intentions and volitions of empirical existence. There being no power of misidentification remaining (i.e. in *nirbīja-samādhi, YS* 1.51*),* the mind can no longer operate within the context of the afflictions and their impressions, *karmas* and consequent cycles of *saṁsāra* implying a mistaken identity of selfhood subject to birth and death.

The *YS* has often been regarded as promoting the severance of *puruṣa* from *prakṛti;* concepts such as liberation, cessation, detachment, etc., have been interpreted in an explicitly negative light. Max Müller (1899, p. 309), citing Bhoja Rāja's commentary (eleventh century C.E.), refers to Yoga as 'separation' *(viyoga).* More recently, numerous other scholars, including: Eliade (1969), Koelman (1970), Feuerstein (1979) and Larson (1987), have endorsed this interpretation, i.e. the absolute separateness of *puruṣa* and *prakṛti.* In asserting the absolute separation of *puruṣa* and *prakṛti*, scholars and nonscholars alike have tended to disregard the possibility for other fresh hermeneutical options and this has surely proved detrimental to Patañjali's Yoga by continuing a tradition based on a misreading of the *Yoga-Sūtras* and Vyāsa's commentary. Accordingly, the absolute separation of *puruṣa* and *prakṛti* can only be interpreted as a disembodied state implying death to the physical body. Yet, interestingly, *YS* 2.9 states that even the wise possess the 'desire for continuity' in life. What is involved in Yoga is the death of the egoic identity which generates notions of one being a subject trapped in a particular body-mind.

Yoga is a practical way of life implying physical training, exertion of will power and acts of decision because Yoga deals with the complete human situation and provides real freedom, not just a theory of liberation. To this end, Patañjali outlined an 'eight-limbed' path *(aṣṭāṅga-yoga, YS* 2.29, p. 101) dealing with the physical, moral, psychological and spiritual dimensions of the yogin, an integral path which emphasizes organic continuity, balance and integration in contrast to the discontinuity, imbalance and disintegration inherent in *saṁyoga.* The idea of cosmic balance and of the mutual support and upholding of the various parts of nature and society is not foreign to Yoga thought. Vyāsa deals with the theory of 'nine causes' or types of causation according to tradition (*VB* 2.28, p. 98). The ninth type of cause is termed *dhṛti*, meaning 'support,' 'sustenance.' Based on Vyāsa's explanation of *dhṛti* we can see how mutuality and sustenance are understood as essential conditions for the maintenance of the natural and social world. There is an organic interdependence of all living entities wherein all (i.e., the elements, animals, humans and divine bodies) work together for the 'good' of the whole and for each other. At this point I would like to emphasize a much overlooked aspect of Yoga thought. Far from being exclusively a subjectively-oriented and introverted path of withdrawal from life, Classical Yoga acknowledges the intrinsic value of 'support' and 'sustenance' and the interdependence of all living entities, thus upholding organic continuity, balance and integration within the natural and social world. Having attained to that insight *(prajñā)* which is 'truth-bearing' *(ṛtaṁ-bharā, YS* 1.48) the yogin perceives the natural order of cosmic life, 'unites' with and embodies that order. To be ensconced in ignorance implies a disunion with the natural order of life and inextricably results in a failure to embody that order.

In contradistinction to the above interpretation of Yoga as 'separation,' I am suggesting that far from being incompatible principles, *puruṣa* and *prakṛti* can engage or participate in harmony having attained a balance or equilibrium together. The enstatic consciousness of *puruṣa* can co-exist with the mind and indeed all of *prakṛti (YS* 3.54-55). The yogin fully reconciles the eternally unchanging Seer with the eternally changing realm of relative states of consciousness only by allowing the mind, in the practice of *samādhi,* to dwell in its pure sāttvik nature in the 'image of *puruṣa*', and then to be engaged once again in the field of relative existence. The process of *nirodha* culminates in *asamprajñāta-samādhi (VB* 1.18), the supra-cognitive awareness where the Seer abides in its own form *(svarūpa, YS* 1.3*)*. According to Vyāsa, the repeated practice of the temporary 'experiences' of ecstasy gradually matures the yogin's consciousness into *kaivalya,* permanent liberation. The stability of the consciousness in *kaivalya* should not be misconstrued as being sheer inactivity, pacifism or lethargy; rather, stability in *samādhi* allows for a harmony in activity, in which the *guṇas* do not conflict with each other and are attuned to *puruṣa.* One is no longer in conflict with oneself and the world. We need not read Patañjali as saying that the culmination of all yogic endeavour, *kaivalya,* is a static finality or inactive, isolated, solipsistic state of being. In fact, *YS* 4.34 (p. 207) tells us that *kaivalya* has as its foundation the very heart of the unlimited dynamism or power of consciousness *(citiśakti)* that is *puruṣa.* In terms of our primary analogue of empirical life *(cittavṛtti), puruṣa is not seen to be active.* In terms of *puruṣa's* inexhaustibility, *purusa* is *supremely active.* To conclude that *puruṣa* is incapable of any activity whatsoever simply amounts to a tautological statement. In the liberated condition, it can be said that *prakṛti* is so integrated in the yogin's consciousness that it has become 'one' with the yogin. *Kaivalya* incorporates a perfectly integrated, psychological consciousness and the independence of pure consciousness, yet pure consciousness to which the realm of the *guṇas* is completely attuned and integrated. Through the consummate phase of supra-cognitive *samādhi,* in *dharma-megha* ('cloud of *dharma*'), a permanent identity shift—from the perspective of the human personality to *puruṣa*—takes place. No longer dependent on knowledge (*vṛtti*) and fully detached from the world of misidentification, the yogin yet retains the power of discernment, omniscience (*YS* 3.54) and activity (*YS* 4.7). The autotransparent knower, knowledge and action co-exist in a state of mutual attunement.

The culmination of the Yoga system is found when, following from *dharma-megha samādhi* (*YS* 4.29), the mind and action are freed from misidentification and affliction (*YS* 4.30) and one is no longer deluded regarding one's true identity. At this phase of practice one is disconnected from all patterns of egoically-motivated action. The *karma* of such an adept is said to be neither 'pure,' nor 'impure,' nor 'mixed' (*VB* 4.7, p. 180). Though transcending the normative conventions and obligations of *kārmik* behaviour, the yogin acts morally not as an extrinsic response and out of obedience to an external moral code of conduct, but as an intrinsic response and as a matter of natural, purified inclination. The stainless luminosity of *puruṣa* is revealed as one's fundamental nature; the yogin does not act *sāṁsarically* and is wholly detached from the egoistic fruits of action. The yogin does not, for example, indulge in the fruits of ritual action, in the merit (*puṇya*) and demerit (*apuṇya*) generated by good and bad observance of traditional ritualistic religion. By the practice of a detached ethic, the yogin must transcend this ritualistic, self-centred mentality. This does not imply that the yogin loses all orientation for action. Detachment, in its highest form (*para-vairāgya, YS* 1.16), is defined by Vyāsa (*VB* 1.16) as a 'clarity of knowledge' (*jñāna-prasāda*). Only attachment (and compulsive desire), not action itself, sets in motion the law of moral causation (*karma*) by which a person is implicated in *saṁsāra*. The yogin is said to be neither attached to virtue nor non-virtue, is no longer oriented within the egological patterns of thought as in the epistemically distorted condition of *saṁyoga*. This does not mean, as some scholars have misleadingly concluded, that the spiritual adept is free to commit immoral acts (Zachner, 1974, pp. 97-8) or that the yogin is motivated by selfish concerns (Scharfstein, 1974, pp. 131-32). Acts must not only be performed in the spirit of unselfishness (i.e.

sacrifice), or non-attachment, they must also be morally sound and justifiable. If action depended solely on one's frame of mind, it would be the best excuse for immoral behaviour. Moreover, the yogin's spiritual journey—far from being, as Feuerstein (1979, p. 81) describes it, an 'a-moral process'—is a highly moral process! The yogin's commitment to what can be termed as the 'sāttvification of consciousness,' including the cultivation of moral virtues such as compassion *(karuṇā YS* 1.33) and non-harming *(ahiṁsā YS* 2.35), is not an 'a-moral' enterprise, nor is it an expression of indifference, aloofness or an uncaring attitude to others. Moral disciplines are practised as a natural outgrowth of intelligent self-understanding and commitment to self-transcendence which takes consciousness out of (ec-stasis) its identification with the rigid structure of the monadic ego thereby reversing the inveterate tendency of this ego to inflate itself at the expense of its responsibility in relation to others.

Having defined the 'goal' of Yoga as 'aloneness' *(kaivalya),* the question must now be asked: What kind of 'aloneness' was Patañjali talking about? 'Aloneness,' I submit, is not the isolation of the Seer *(puruṣa)* separate from the seeable *(prakṛti),* as is unfortunately far too often maintained as the goal of Yoga, but refers to the aloneness of the power of 'seeing' *(YS* 2.25) in its innate purity and clarity without any epistemological distortion or moral defilement. The cultivation of *nirodha* uproots the compulsive tendency to reify the world and oneself (i.e. that pervading sense of separate ego irrevocably divided from the encompassing world) with an awareness which reveals the transcendent, yet immanent, Seer. *Puruṣa* is said to be 'alone' not because there is an opposition or a separation, but simply because there is no misconception of *puruṣa's* identity. Yoga is not, as Feuerstein (1980, p. 24) would have us think, a Cartesian-like dichotomy (of thinker and thing). Nor can Yoga be described as a metaphysical union of an individuated self with the objective world of nature or more subtle realms of *prakṛti.* More appropriately, Yoga can be seen to unfold states of epistemic oneness *(samādhi)*—the non-separation of knower, knowing and known *(YS* 1.41*)*—grounding our identity in a non-afflicted mode of action. As *puruṣa* is self-luminous, in *kaivalya* '*puruṣa* stands alone in its true nature as pure light' *(VB* 3.55, p. 175). *Puruṣa* no longer needs to know itself reflexively, is peaceful and immutable because it needs/lacks nothing. *Kaivalya* implies a power of 'seeing' in which the dualisms rooted in our egocentric patterns of attachment, aversion, etc., have been transformed into unselfish ways of being with others *(YS* 1.33). 'Seeing' is not only a cognitive term but implies purity of mind, i.e. it has moral content and value. *Kaivalya* does not destroy feeling or encourage neglect or indifference. On the contrary, the process of cessation *(nirodha)* steadies one for a life of compassion and discernment and is informed by a 'seeing' in touch with the needs of others.

Yoga goes beyond the position of Classical *Sāṁkhya* which seems to rest content with a discriminating knowledge *(viveka)* leading to an absolute separation between *puruṣa* and *prakṛti.* At the end of the day, *prakṛti's* alignment with the purpose of *puruṣa* appears to be all for nought. Yet, if *puruṣa* were completely free to start with, why would it get 'involved' with *prakṛti? Puruṣa's* 'entanglement' does intelligize *prakṛti (YS* 4.22) which on its own is devoid of consciousness. The end product of *puruṣa's* 'involvement' with *prakṛti,* the state of liberated omniscience, is enriching and allows for a verifying and enlivening of human nature/ consciousness. Classical *Sāṁkhya's* adherence to an absolute separation, implying a final unworkable duality between spirit and matter, amounts to an impoverishment of ideas. In Yoga, however, knowledge can be utilized in the integrity of action and being. Thus, Vyāsa states that 'the knower is liberated while yet living' (*VB* 4.30, p. 202). The *puruṣa* is 'alone' not because it is a windowless monad, but because it transcends the faulty mechanics of *saṁyoga,* i.e. 'selfhood' as it is 'whirled about' within the confinement of *cittavṛtti.* Free of all forms of obsession, and all ideas of 'acquiring' and 'possessing,' *puruṣa* is never a product of, nor is it affected by, the *guṇas* and *karma.*

Can *puruṣa's* existence embrace states of action and knowledge, person and personality? The tradition of Yoga answers in the affirmative. Vyāsa asserts that having attained a state of perfection beyond sorrow, 'the omniscient yogin whose afflictions and bondage have been destroyed disports himself [herself] as a master' (*VB* 3.49, p. 168). The enstatic consciousness and pure reflection of the *sattva* of the mind 'merge' in *kaivalya (YS* 3.55*)* resulting in a natural attunement of mind and body in relation to *puruṣa*. The *kārmik* power of *avidyā* functioning within *prakṛti* ceases to have a hold over the yogin, the *kārmik* ego having been exploded. The yogin's attention is no longer sucked into the vortex of the conflicting opposites *(dvandvas)* in *saṁsāra*, is no longer embroiled in the polarizing intentionalities of desire: the vectors of attraction and aversion. Free from the egoic intrusions of worldly existence, the yogin is said to be left 'alone.' The *puruṣa* can express itself in the time-space continuum in a particular body and with a particular personality. Yoga does not deny the existence of individuality; it allows for a trans-egoic development which is not the dissolution of the individual person and its personality but, rather, includes their extension into the recognition, moral integrity and celebration of the interconnectedness of all beings, all life. Enstasy *(kaivalya)* is lived simultaneously with the mind or 'consciousness-of.' The link between the enstatic consciousness and the world is the purified *sattva* of the mind.

We must question assertions to the effect that having attained liberation the psychical apparatus of the yogin is destroyed (Koelman, 1970, p. 249), or that the yogin's body lives on in a state of catalepsy until death (Feuerstein, 1979, p. 142). What disappears for the yogin is the 'failure to see' *(adarśana, VB* 2.23) or the world-view born of *avidyā*, not *prakṛti* itself. The purified mind and the evolutes of *prakṛti* (e.g. intellect, ego) can now be used as vehicles for an enlightened life of interaction and service, such as imparting knowledge to others: the purity and cognitive power impersonated in the *guru* is transformed from an end into an available means. When one accomplished in Yoga opens one's eyes to the world of experience, the knower *(puruṣa)* will be one's true centre of existence. The *guṇas (i.e. vṛttis)* will be subordinate to the knower *(YS* 4.18). Once the final stage of emancipation is reached, the lower levels of insight previously gained are incorporated, not destroyed. It can be argued (see Whicher, 1992, chapter 5 and 6) that through the necessary transformation of consciousness brought about in *samādhi*, an authentic and fruitful coherence of self-identity, perception and activity emerges out of the former fragmented consciousness in *saṁyoga*. Only *puruṣa's* misidentifications with phenomena are ended. When it is said that one has realized *puruṣa* through *nirodha*, it is meant that there is no further level to experience for one's liberation. *Nirodha* does not indicate the denial of formed reality or the negation of relative states of consciousness. Nor is it rooted in a conception of oneself which removes identity as a social, historical embodied being. *Nirodha* refers to the expansion of understanding necessary to perceive every dimension of reality from the direct perspective of pure, untainted consciousness.

If Patañjali had destroyed his perception of forms and differences, how could he have had such insight into Yoga and the intricacies of the unenlightened state? If through *nirodha,* the individual form and the whole world had been cancelled for Patañjali, he would more likely have spent the rest of his days in the inactivity and isolation of transcendent oblivion rather than presenting Yoga philosophy to others! Rather than being handicapped by the exclusion of thinking, perceiving or experiencing, one can say that the liberated yogin actualizes the potential to live a fully integrated life in the world. The yogin simultaneously lives as it were in two worlds: the dimension of unqualified (*nirguṇa*) existence and the relative dimension *(saguṇa),* yet the two worlds work together as one. I conclude here that there is no reason why the liberated yogin cannot be portrayed as a vital, creative, thinking, empathetic, balanced, happy and wise person. Having adopted an integrative orientation to life, the enlightened being can endeavour to transform, enrich and ennoble the world. I am therefore suggesting that there is a rich affective, moral and cognitive as well as spiritual potential inherent in the realization of *puruṣa,* the 'aloneness' of the 'power of consciousness'.

Concluding remarks

Although many valuable, contemporary, scholarly writings on Yoga have helped to present Patañjali's philosophy to a wider academic audience, it is my contention that Patañjali has far too often been misinterpreted/misrepresented due to the use of inappropriate methodology: partial and misleading definitions of Sanskrit yogic terms and reductionistic hermeneutics. Many scholars have repeatedly given ontological definitions and explanations for terms which, I maintain, are more appropriately understood with an epistemological emphasis. Consequently, the specialized sense inherent in Yoga soteriology is diminished. The soteriological intent of Yoga need not preclude the possibility for an integrated, embodied state of liberated selfhood. A bias is invariably created within the language encountered in the translations and interpretations of the *YS* resulting in an overemphasis on content, due consideration not having been given to form, structure and function. It is crucial to study the process of Yoga contextually, as it is lived and experienced by the yogin, and not simply impute a content-system to the whole process. The bias extends to the ontological priorities of *puruṣa* over *prakṛti* and by consequence the priority of axiology over epistemology. *Puruṣa* is generally explained as the enlightened and ultimately hegemonic principle of pure consciousness, our true identity which alone has intrinsic spiritual value. *Prakṛti,* we are often told, is the non-spiritual cosmogonic principle comprised of the three *guṇas (sattva, rajas* and *tamas),* has a deluding, binding yet paradoxically subservient nature, and eventually disappears from the yogin's purview thus having no real value in the liberated state. It is not clear that the language of the *YS* is explanatory. It could equally be descriptive in which case the axiological and ontological priorities would collapse thereby challenging the widely held scholarly view that the relationship between *puruṣa* and *prakṛti* is exclusively an asymmetrical one, i.e. *prakṛti* exists for the purpose of *puruṣa,* and her value is seen only in instrumental terms and within the context of a soteriological end state which excludes her.

In Patañjali's central definition of Yoga *(YS* 1.2*) nirodha* has far too often been understood as an ontological cessation, suppression or 'deadening' of the mind, and this misunderstanding has led, I submit, to some major interpretive errors. Firstly, one can witness a reductionistic application of positivistic presuppositions to a mystical system: scholars have often concluded that once the stage of liberation has been attained the yogin will no longer be capable of experiencing the world since the body-mind has ceased to function. Secondly, the oral/historical teaching tradition has either been ignored or else this important pedagogical context of Yoga has not been sufficiently taken into consideration. Our hermeneutics must include a way of reading the tradition of Yoga within the culture we are studying. Thirdly, by understanding *nirodha* to mean the ontological cessation or negation of *vṛttis,* many scholars have given a negative, one-sided and spurious definition of Yoga. The result is a volatile concept of *nirodha* that is world-denying and mind-and-body negating, wherein phenomenal reality is dissolved into nothingness or a meaningless existence for the liberated yogin. Consequently, Patañjali's philosophy as a whole becomes trivialized and can be viewed as impractical, unapproachable, unintelligible and unattractive.

Puruṣa indeed has precedence over *prakṛti* in Patañjali's system, for *puruṣa* is what is ordinarily 'missing' in human life and is ultimately the consciousness one must awaken to. According to this study, liberation as 'aloneness' *(kaivalya)* need not denote an ontological superiority of *puruṣa,* nor an exclusion of *prakṛti. Kaivalya,* I have argued, can be positively construed as an integration of both principles—an integration which, I maintain, is what is most important for Yoga. To break *puruṣa* and *prakṛti* apart, keep one and try to discard the other, is an enterprise which creates psychological and social conflict involving confused notions of 'self' which, I submit, are clearly inimical to Yoga. Such notions may have an aversion-orientation *(dveṣa, YS* 2.8), e.g. an exaggerated (and impoverished) sense of 'isolation' from the world as in the flight or escape of self with an impulse toward self-negation; or such notions may have an attachment-orientation *(rāga YS* 2.7), e.g. whereby we only succumb to the world and can easily become enmeshed in forms of narcissism and egocentrism by aggressively objectifying and exploiting the world. Both of these extremes: escape from the world and worldly entrapment, must be transcended in Yoga. I have proposed that the *YS* does not uphold a path of liberation which ultimately renders *puruṣa* and *prakṛti* incapable of 'co-operating' together. Rather, the *YS* seeks to 'unite' these two principles, to bring them 'together' in a state of balance, harmony and a fullness of knowledge in the integrity of being and action.

Thus, Patañjali's Yoga need not result in the extinction or the evaporation of our 'personhood' along with the material world; rather, it is more accurate to say, that Yoga culminates in the eradication of spiritual ignorance, the root cause of our misidentification with, and attachment to, worldly (or otherworldly!) existence. In this way, Yoga removes our selfishness and suffering *(duḥkha)* rooted in an afflicted and mistaken self-identity *(asmitā).* Liberated from the pain of self-limitation and all destructive personality traits, and having incorporated an expanded and enriched sense of personal identity embodying virtues such as non-violence, compassion and wisdom, the yogin can dwell in a state of balance and fulfilment serving others while feeling truly at home in the world. The yogin can function in relation to the world not being morally or epistemologically enslaved by worldly relationship. Morality and perception both are essential channels through which human consciousness, far from being negated or suppressed, is transformed and illuminated. Yoga combines discerning knowledge with an emotional, affective and moral sensibility. The enhanced perception gained through Yoga must be interwoven with Yoga's rich affective and moral dimensions to form a spirituality that does not become entangled in a web of antinomianism, but which retains the integrity and vitality to effectively transmute our lives. By upholding an integration of the moral and the mystical, Yoga supports a reconciliation of the prevalent tension within Hinduism between: spiritual engagement and self-identity within the world *(pravṛtti),* and spiritual disengagement from worldliness and self-identity which transcends the world *(nivṛtti).* Yoga teaches a balance between these two apparently conflicting orientations.

This paper has been an attempt to counter the radically dualistic and ontologically-oriented interpretations of Yoga given by many scholars—where the full potentialities of our human embodiment are constrained within the rigid metaphysical structure of Classical Sāṁkhya and offer instead an open-ended, morally and epistemologically-oriented hermeneutics which frees Classical Yoga of the long standing conception of spiritual isolation, disembodiment, self-denial and world-negation and thus from its pessimistic image. I have elsewhere suggested (Whicher, 1992) that Patañjali can be understood as having adopted a provisional, practical, dualistic metaphysics but that there is no proof his system ends in duality.

Patañjali's *YS* has to this day remained one of the most influential spiritual guides in Hinduism. In addition to a large number of people in India, hundreds of thousands of Westerners are actively practising some form of Yoga influenced by Patañjali's thought, clearly demonstrating Yoga's relevance for today as a discipline which can transcend cultural, religious and philosophical barriers. The universal and universalizing potential of Yoga makes it one of India's finest contributions to our modern/postmodern struggle for self-definition, moral integrity and spiritual renewal. The purpose of this present study has been to consider a fresh approach with which to re-examine and assess Classical Yoga philosophy. There is, I submit, nothing in what I have argued which can be proven to be incompatible with Patañjali's thought. Thus, it is my hope that some of the suggestions made in this paper can function as a catalyst for bringing Patañjali's Yoga into a more fruitful dialogue and encounter with other religious and philosophical traditions both within and outside of India.

References

ARANYA, SWAMI HARIHARANANDA : *Yoga Philosophy of Patañjali* (Calcutta, Calcutta University Press, 1963).

CHAPPLE, CHRISTOPHER KEY and YOGI ANANDA VIRAJ : *The Yoga Sūtras of Patañjali* (Delhi, Sri Satguru Publications, 1990).

DVIVEDI, M. N. : *The Yoga-Sūtras of Patañjali* (Adyar, Madras, Theosophical Publishing House, 1930).

ELIADE, MIRCEA : *Yoga: Immortality and Freedom* (Princeton, Princeton University Press, 2nd edn., 1969).

FEUERSTEIN, GEORG : *The Yoga-Sūtra of Patañjali: A New Translation and Commentary* (Folkstone, Kent, Wm. Dawson and Sons, 1979); *The Philosophy of Classical Yoga* (Manchester, Manchester University Press, 1980).

KASINATHA SASTRI AGAṢE ed. : *Pātañjala-Yogasūtrāṇī*, with the *Vyāsa-Bhāṣya* of Vyāsa, the *Tattva-Vaiśāradī* of Vācaspati Miśra and the *Rāja-Mārttaṇḍa* of Bhoja Rāja (Poona, Anandasrama Sanskrit Ser., 47, 1904).

KOELMAN, G. M. : *Pātañjala Yoga: From Related Ego to Absolute Self* (Poona, Papal Anthenaeum, 1970).

LARSON G. L. and BHATTACHARYA R. S. eds. : *Sāṁkhya: A Dualist Tradition in Indian Philosophy*, Vol. 4 of *The Encyclopedia of Indian Philosophies* (Princeton, Princeton University Press, 1987).

LEGGETT, TREVOR : *The Complete Commentary by Śaṅkara on the Yoga Sūtras* (London and New York, Kegan Paul, 1990).

MONIER-WILLIAMS, SIR M. : A *Sanskrit-English Dictionary* (Oxford, Oxford University Press, 1899).

MULLER, MAX : *The Six Systems of Indian Philosophy* (London, Longmans, Green and Co., 1899).

SCHARFSTEIN, B.-A. : *Mystical Experience* (Baltimore, Penguin Books, 1974).

TAIMNI, I. K. : *The Science of Yoga* (Wheaton, Ill., The Theosophical Publishing House, 1961).

TOLA, F. and DRAGONETTI, C. : *The Yogasūtras of Patañjali, On Concentration Of Mind* (Delhi, Motilal Banarsidass, 1987).

VARENNE, JEAN : *Yoga and the Hindu Tradition* (Chicago, The University of Chicago Press, 1976).

VIVEKANANDA, SWAMI : *The Complete Works of Swami Vivekananda*, 8 Vols. (Calcutta, Advaita Ashrama, 1977).

WHICHER, IAN R. : A *Study of Patañjali's Definition of Yoga: Uniting Theory and Practice in the Yoga-Sūtras* (Cambridge, Cambridge University Ph.D.Thesis, 1992).

WOODS, J. H. : *The Yoga System of Patañjali* (Cambridge, Harvard University Press, 1914).

ZAEHNER, R. C. : *Our Savage God* (London, Collins, 1974).

Notes

1. Due to obvious limitations of space, this paper can only present a summary of some of the main arguments given in an earlier, more thorough study (see Whicher 1992) which is presently being revised for publication, I have not offered a critical analysis of Vyāsa's commentary for the purpose of trying to determine in how far Vyāsa correctly explains the *YS.* Rather, the study draws upon the wealth of philosophical and experiential insight which the *VB* brings to aid our understanding of the *YS.* For the Sanskrit text of the *YS* and *VB* I have used *Pātañjala-Yogasūtrāṇī,* edited by K. S. Agase (1904). Unless otherwise specified, all translations are my own.

2. *YS* 1.2 states: *yogaścittavṛttinirodha.* The modifications or functions (*vṛtti*) of the mind are said to be fivefold, namely 'valid cognition' *(pramāṇa),* 'error' (*viparyaya*), 'conceptualization' *(vikalpa),* 'sleep' *(nidrā)* and 'memory' (*smṛti*) (*YS* 1.6), and are described as being 'afflicted' *(kliṣṭa)* or 'nonafflicted' (*akliṣṭa*) (*YS* 1.5). *Citta* is an umbrella term which incorporates 'intellect' (*buddhi*), 'sense of self' (*ahaṁkāra*) and 'lower mind' (*manas*), and can be viewed as the aggregate of the cognitive, conative and affective processes and functions (*vṛtti*) of phenomenal consciousness, i. e. it consists of a grasping, intentional and volitional consciousness.

3. See, for example, the works of Swami Vivekananda (1977, Vol. 2, pp. 255-56 and Vol. 8, p. 48). In an otherwise excellent book, Varenne (1976, p.114) appears to support a mind-negative approach to *Yoga* and qualifies a statement by adding '... the *chitta,* whose activity ... yoga makes it an aim to destroy....'

4. For a deeper analysis of this analogical understanding of consciousness see Whicher (1992, pp. 156-63).